D0202594

# The 100 Most Significant
# Events in American Business

**Bryant & Stratton Library**
**Hampton Location**
**5030 Kilgore Avenue**
**Hampton, VA 23666**
**(757) 896-6001**

# THE 100 MOST SIGNIFICANT EVENTS IN AMERICAN BUSINESS

*An Encyclopedia*

**Quentin R. Skrabec, Jr.**

GREENWOOD

AN IMPRINT OF ABC-CLIO, LLC
Santa Barbara, California • Denver, Colorado • Oxford, England

Copyright 2012 by ABC-CLIO, LLC

All rights reserved. No part of this publication may be reproduced, stored in a retrieval system, or transmitted, in any form or by any means, electronic, mechanical, photocopying, recording, or otherwise, except for the inclusion of brief quotations in a review, without prior permission in writing from the publisher.

**Library of Congress Cataloging-in-Publication Data**

Skrabec, Quentin R.
   The 100 most significant events in American business : an encyclopedia / Quentin R. Skrabec, Jr.
        p. cm.
   Includes bibliographical references and index.
      ISBN 978-0-313-39862-9 (hbk. : alk. paper) — ISBN 978-0-313-39863-6 (ebook)
1. United States—Commerce—History—Encyclopedias.   2. Industries—
United States—History—Encyclopedias.   3. Business—History—Encyclopedias.
I. Title.   II. Title: One hundred most significant events in American business.
   HF3021.S57   2012
   338.097303—dc23        2011050442

ISBN: 978-0-313-39862-9
EISBN: 978-0-313-39863-6

16   15   14   13   12      1   2   3   4   5

This book is also available on the World Wide Web as an eBook.
Visit www.abc-clio.com for details.

Greenwood
An Imprint of ABC-CLIO, LLC

ABC-CLIO, LLC
130 Cremona Drive, P.O. Box 1911
Santa Barbara, California 93116-1911

This book is printed on acid-free paper ∞

Manufactured in the United States of America

To the Star of the Seas, who guided Columbus to the American shores

B+T SP14 Reg. by AP C. Librarian from Richmond dist.

# CONTENTS

# PREFACE

This work embodies over 20 years of research in building a literary pantheon of American capitalists and business leaders. This project gave me a new look at business in America. I was often struck by the role that government played in the development of American capitalism. Events such as the National Road, the Erie Canal, overland mail, Republican protective tariffs, railroad expansion, the Panama Canal, Hoover Dam, and the space program clearly showed that infrastructure played a major role. These government projects were proactive, often combining government and private resources to accomplish major goals in the advance of American business.

Another theme that emerged was the reoccurring business models built around speed of product delivery by canal, clipper ships, Pony Express, railroads, or trucks, as well as the speed of communications using the mail, clipper ships, telegraph, telephone, radio, satellite communications, and 3G networks. Doing something faster was a major theme of America's most successful companies.

Another conclusion is that the moment an invention occurred often preceded its commercialization by years. Commercialization often required a new business model and a vision beyond that of the inventor. The most successful inventors, such as Thomas Edison, George Westinghouse, and Steve Jobs, were able to combine their inventions with commercial use.

Lastly, this research clearly showed the interconnections of business events. Business events tended to be evolutionary versus revolutionary. Commercial events were often the confluence of different streams of progress toward a market-driven need. Often it was the businessperson who put together many scientific advances to achieve commercialization.

# ACKNOWLEDGMENTS

I would like to thank my editor, Brian Romer. This work is his vision. I was blessed with four of the country's best archival staffs at the Library of Congress, the Smithsonian, Senator John Heinz History Center, and the Benson Research Center at The Henry Ford. At the Heinz Center, I had the expertise of Lisa Lazar, Lauren Paige Zabelsky, and Art Louderback as well as the entire staff. In addition, I would like to thank Terri Blanchette, Sandra Baker, and Rob Ridgeway of the Heinz History Center in Pittsburgh. At The Henry Ford Benson Research Center, I had the same outstanding assistance from Carol Whittaker and Kira Macyda and the whole staff at the center. I would like to thank the staff at the Carnegie Library of Pittsburgh as well. Reference librarians are often the forgotten people behind a successful book; thanks also to Rebecca Quintus.

I would like to especially thank Alesha Shumar, archivist at the University of Pittsburgh; Wendy Pfleg of the University of Pittsburgh; and Barry Ched and Gil Pietrzak of the Carnegie Library of Oakland. Thanks also to Julie Ludwig, associate archivist of the Frick Collection (New York), and Greg Langel of the Frick Center in Pittsburgh. I would like to give special thanks to Julie McMasters of the Toledo Museum of Art and Kimberly Brownie, Ann Bowers, and Barbara Floyd of the Ward M. Canaday Center at the University of Toledo. I would particularly like to credit the help and vast knowledge of Janet Metzger at the William McKinley Presidential Library and Museum. The staffs at both the Canton and Niles Presidential memorials are outstanding sources of information on 19th-century industrial America. The Clement Library of American History at the University of Michigan was another important reference library. Another important facet of the search was done at the Hayes Presidential Center archives. At the center, I would like to thank Nan Card, chief archivist, and Merv Nall.

# INTRODUCTION

This encyclopedia explores the history and impact of the 100 most significant events in American business, intended for students, researchers, business professionals, historians, writers, and general readers. The time period covered will be from 1700 to 2010. The encyclopedia is about major U.S. business issues, business models, and emerging trends that impacted the way America does business. The discussion of these key historical events will be linked to their impact on the nature of business today. The events covered are those that influenced the nature of business in the United States primarily, but in many cases, there was also an international effect. It covers key inventions from the point of their commercialization.

The encyclopedia is intended to enhance the basic business literacy of students and researchers, providing stand-alone, objective, informative, and factually driven entries on all the major themes and topics in business, compiled chronologically. The encyclopedia is a ready reference on key business events in American business history, exploring the commercialization of innovations, major economic events, and the implementation of new management systems. It is also a reference on the nature of labor and business laws in practice today. The chronology offers a reference for the evolution of many of today's trends, business theories, and business models. It is designed to go beyond mere history by revealing the foundations of business today. American history does, however, offer the reason behind differences in American business culture. For example, American unions are notably different from their counterparts in Europe. Events such as the Great Exhibition of 1851, the Haymarket Riot, the Pullman Strike, the Homestead Strike of 1892, and the National Labor Relations Act of 1935 help define those differences between America and Europe.

The selection of events was reviewed by practitioners and professors as to significant events that had the greatest impact on American business. The following guidelines and factors were used to pick events.

- *Commercialization.* For the business researcher, the first flight of the Wright Brothers' glider had no impact on business. However, a few years later, the *use* of the airplane to deliver federal mail as well as the first commercial flight *was* a significant event. Technology is often cataloged according to the date of the invention, but that may be far from the time and event that lead to the *commercialization* of the innovation.
- *Economic factors.* The encyclopedia will detail major economic events affecting business, such as the Panics of 1837, 1857, 1873, 1893, and 1907; the stock market crash in 1929; inflation and resulting wage and price controls in 1972; and the banking crisis and great recession in 2008.
- *New business models.* A new business model might include such things as modular design, used by Dell to market computers, or Federal Express's overnight delivery system.
- *Management systems development.* Management systems would include scientific management, commercialization of assembly, and new physiological approaches to motivation, such as those of Abraham Maslow.
- *Long-term impact.* The encyclopedia will look at links to future events.

The analysis of events includes the identification of central themes, such as bubbles behind economic recessions, the trade-offs between free trade and protectionism, and the reoccurrence of underlying factors in business models, like speed of delivery. Reading the full chronology will reveal some themes that show the historical roots of the nature of business in the United States.

—*Quentin R. Skrabec, Jr.*

*The 100 Most Significant*
*Events in American Business*

# Privatization of the Plymouth Colony (1623)

While short-lived, the Plymouth Plantation has a special place in American business history. The Plymouth colony of the Pilgrims started in November 1620. The Pilgrims were a group of Christian Separatists from the Anglican Church of England that first moved to Holland but found little freedom for their religious practices. The Pilgrims left Holland to obtain freedom of religion. They were financed by a group of wealthy venture capitalists who hoped to use them to achieve a profit in the New World. These venture capitalists had formed a joint stock known as the Virginia Company of London, having a royal charter issued in 1606. The Virginia Company had been behind the failed Jamestown Colony, which did not start paying any dividends until 1620. The Virginia Company hoped for a similar trade profit in New England with furs, fish, and crops. The company considered the Pilgrims as indentured servants, although the Pilgrims did negotiate a profit-sharing deal after seven years. The Pilgrims initially argued against communal ownership of property but were left with no choice. The Pilgrims, for their part, never viewed themselves as indentured servants but as paying taxes to the company. It was an unclear and disputed vision, but all property was under communal ownership. Even the houses they built were considered communal property and could be reassigned. This initial model of communal ownership has been called both exploitative capitalism and communism. Contrary to some claims, the communal pact was not based on their religious beliefs but was forced on the Pilgrims by the company. Privatization of property would prove to be evolutionary in the colonies.

The Pilgrims came to New England on the *Mayflower* and *Speedwell*. In total, there were 120 Pilgrims on the journey, along with a smaller group known as the "strangers." The "strangers" were hired as managers of the company, and they included Miles Standish as the colony's military leader and Christopher Martin as royal governor. The first year proved the most difficult, with the ships arriving in late fall with no growing season left. Nearly half the colonists died the first winter. It was only by the aid of the local Indians, which allowed for a solid planting of corn in the spring, that the colonists survived. They managed to construct a common house for living quarters. William Bradford kept a diary of the plantation (*Of Plymouth Plantation*), detailing social breakdown under the communal ownership system. Initially, the Pilgrims were forced to beg and steal from the Indians, but even the first planting and building of houses proved disastrous. Bradford described a culture of "free-riding." The elderly, sick, young, and women soon excluded themselves from communal labor. Others tended not to pull their weight under the communal economic model. Even the most able men were soon angered by having to support free-riding and reduced their effect. Bradford decried the communal system as the root of the problem. He noted in his diary: "For the young men, that were the most able and fit for labor and service, did repine that they should spend their time and strength to work for other's men's wives and children without any recompense. The strong, or man of parts, had no more division of victuals and clothes than that of the weak and not able to do a quarter the other could; this was thought an injustice."

The Pilgrims were surely aware of the limited success at Jamestown when the colonists there were given small plots of land to work as their own. By 1621, the Jamestown colony had limited private property, but the communal system still required a tax on private earnings and several months of communal work a year. Bradford and Plymouth faced a crisis point in the spring of 1623. The colony was down to four adult women and dependent on the Indians for daily survival. Bradford made the decision to fully convert to private property. Bradford reported the amazing success: "For it made all hands industrious. . . . The women now went willingly into the field, and took their little ones with them to set corn; which before would allege weakness and inability." The new system made the colony profitable and would be the new model for future settlements. The system also proved compatible with their religious beliefs as the colonists gave freely of their surplus to help the less fortunate. The model would augur the American system of capitalism and philanthropy. The taxation model of the colony would also be a model for the government role in communal needs. Home ownership strengthened and motivated house building in the colony. It would also augur the failure of collectivized agriculture in 20th-century communist nations. It served as a case study for Adam Smith's premise of individual needs and self-interest as an economic force.

*See also: Wealth of Nations*

### References

Bethell, Thomas. *The Noblest Triumph: Property and Prosperity through the Ages.* New York: St. Martin's, 2007.

Bradford, William. *Of Plymouth Plantation.* New York: Knopf, 2002.

DiLorenzo, Thomas J. *How Capitalism Saved America.* Boston: Three Rivers, 2004.

# Navigation Acts (1651)

The Navigation Acts were really a series of acts over decades to impose and maintain British mercantilism and to control trade to and from the colonies. The series included the Navigation Ordinance Act of 1651, the Molasses Act of 1733, the Iron Prohibition Act of 1750, the Sugar Act of 1764, the Stamp Act of 1765, and the Townsend Act of 1767. The acts would start a long list of complaints, abuses, and smuggling activities that would ultimately lead to the American Revolution. They would ultimately control American trade for 100 years and British trade for 200 years.

The Navigation Acts left a deep impression on the nature of American business. The first business activity in America had been based on trade for Europe. European stock companies that hoped to receive profits in return had financially backed settlers. The Spanish had been successful at finding gold in the south to enrich their nation, while the British looked to raw materials such as furs, glass, iron, tobacco, cotton, and timber. The Navigation Ordinance Act of 1651 required all of a British colony's imports to be either bought from England or resold by English (or Scottish) merchants in England, no matter what the price. It was aimed directly at knocking out the Dutch shipping and trading advantage.

The trade monopoly actually inspired British and Scottish investment in America by developing extensive trade networks and a wave of new immigrant traders. Scotland's Lowlanders had become world traders in the 1600s, controlling the New World tobacco market and the American fur trade. With the Act of Union in 1707, Scotland became a beneficiary of the Navigation Acts. They also had an active trade in American ginseng. This trading network and mercantile system would birth a type of economic democracy. Scotch-Irish and Scottish traders and settlers rushed to America to participate in this booming trade network. Glasgow, Scotland, rapidly became the world's warehouse and market for American furs, tobacco, and cotton. Scottish Lowlander Adam Smith would herald that new approach in his book *Wealth of Nations.* Along with these economic ideas, the Scottish Enlightenment would develop democratic concepts such as the "pursuit of happiness" that would be incorporated in the writings of Thomas Paine, Thomas Jefferson, and James Madison. The roots of the American Declaration of Independence and the Constitution are clearly traceable to the lowlands of Scotland. More than any other nation, Scotland integrated the ideas of economic freedom, democracy, and world trade.

The Navigation Acts created an influx of Scotch-Irish, who poured into America to become traders, pushing the American frontier even further west. The New England colonies prospered as trading ports for England. An extreme shortage of wood in England forced the development of a new shipbuilding industry in the colonies in the late 1600s. The wood shortage in England restricted wood to use in shipbuilding, forcing the shutdown of the British iron industry and making them dependent on Sweden for iron for cannons and manufacturing. The New England colonies and England in 1641 were both short on iron and, in particular, iron nails. England had lumbered out most of its hardwood, needed to fuel iron furnaces, and thus was open to colonial production. Colonial iron could now be made only for export to England. Without colonial iron, England itself would have been dependent on Sweden, a political enemy. The colonies were encouraged to produce raw pig iron to supply mother England. New England got some capital from England but opened the investment up for colonists as well. A number of Puritan ministers invested. Two ironworks were in operation by 1645 around the Boston area. Saugus Iron Works became very successful at producing iron products, but it struggled for capital throughout its existence. Saugus was America's first large industrial complex, having an iron furnace, rolling mill, and slitting mill. The Pilgrims also learned the technology and started operations by the late 1600s. The iron-making technology would spread quickly to the frontier where iron nails, cast iron stoves, and cast iron utensils were in demand.

Under the Navigation Acts, the Scotch-Irish developed frontier industries around their trade network such as iron making and whiskey production. They first developed these industries in the Cumberland Valley of Maryland and then moved to western Pennsylvania. They built large charcoal iron furnaces to manufacture a variety of frontier products. These smaller Scotch-Irish iron furnaces would compete with the larger iron plantations of central and eastern Pennsylvania. As the Scotch-Irish moved down the Monongahela River valley toward Ohio, they established America's whiskey industry. The need to deliver products to eastern ports fostered the growth of turnpikes for wagons. Wagon roads were lined with Scotch-Irish blacksmiths to repair wagons and shoe horses. These early rest stops also produced and sold rye whiskey. This "Monongahela rye" won international acclaim as it was shipped to Europe via the Scotch-Irish trade network. The Scotch-Irish's manufacturing and trade village became today's Pittsburgh. Even today the linguistic accent of Pittsburghers is the mark of the Scotch-Irish.

The very prosperity created by trade and the Navigation Acts would become the undoing of the acts in the mid-1700s. Prosperity brought internal demand for goods such as iron. It also created a consumer-oriented middle class. The first problems appeared with the Molasses Act of 1733. The Molasses Act levied duties on the trade of sugar from the French West Indies to the American colonies, forcing the colonists to buy high-priced sugar from the British West Indies. The act increased the cost of meals for American colonists. The Americans were no longer willing to be part of a great British plantation. The colonists resisted by creating smuggling networks. Smugglers included many of the founding fathers such as Samuel Adams and Paul Revere.

England's need for iron had helped bring prosperity to the colonial iron industry. The colonial industry had, however, expanded into finished iron products such as knives, nails, tools, and tinplate and a wide variety of tinplate products. England's industry was being hurt, and Parliament wanted to limit colonial production of iron implements. The next of the Navigation Acts came with the Iron Prohibition Act of 1750. This act was intended to force all raw pig iron produced in the colonies to be shipped to England to be made into iron implements that then would be shipped back to America. Colonial authorities were extremely lax in the enforcement of the act because many British colonial officials were themselves investors in the American iron industry. Many of the Scotch-Irish furnace operators preferred to move west to avoid colonial oversight over their iron making.

Eventually, the later Navigation Acts such as the Stamp Act, Tea Act, and Townsend Act would lead directly to the American Revolution, which was more about economics than religious freedom. These acts also levied taxes on products, which outraged the colonists. Amazingly, the Navigation Acts would not be fully repealed until 1849. The repeal heralded the acceptance of Adam Smith's economic theory of free trade over British mercantilism, but it would also mean the end of the British Empire and begin the slow decline of Britain as a manufacturing power.

*See also:* Jefferson Embargo; Tariff of Abominations; *Wealth of Nations*; Whiskey Rebellion

### References

Davidson, John. *Commercial Federation and Colonial Trade Policy.* Ithaca, NY: Cornell University Library, 2009.

Lee, Susan, and Peter Passell. *A New Economic View of American History.* New York: Norton, 1979.

Shepherd, James, and Gary Walton. *Shipping, Maritime Trade and the Economic Development of Colonial North America.* Cambridge: Cambridge University Press, 2010.

# *Wealth of Nations* (1776)

Two revolutions began in this famous year of 1776, and both would change the world. The *Wealth of Nations* was first published by Adam Smith in 1776; today it remains the cornerstone of free trade thinking and capitalism (although neither term was used at the time or in the book). This 900-page *War and Peace* of nonfiction is one of the world's most printed books. Smith's work was an extension of the Scottish Enlightenment, which had all aspects of freedom as a root. The *Wealth of Nations* reasons from the simple self-interest of the individual. The book was popular with founding fathers such as Thomas Jefferson. Smith tied self-interest to freedom with the following statement: "Every man, as long as he does not violate the laws of justice, is left perfectly free to pursue his own interest his own way, and bring both his industry and capital into competition with those of any other man or order of men." James Madison used it to oppose the implementation of a national bank. Alexander Hamilton and the Federalists, however, would argue against its government-free approach to economics. The chapter on labor in a pin factory laid out the ideas of labor specialization that would lead to mass-production techniques. It was used in England in the mid-19th century to justify the elimination of the Navigation Acts and promote the adoption of free trade.

Thomas Jefferson hailed the *Wealth of Nations* as a revolutionary book. It was considered a leap forward in the field of economics, similar to Sir Isaac Newton's *Principia Mathematica*. The core of Smith's thesis was the natural tendency of man toward self-interest. Both individuals and nations behave in terms of self-interest. Smith argued further that all should have complete freedom to act in their self-interest—in other words, free markets. Smith declared that a nation's wealth was in its manufacture, which opposed the mercantilism of the time, which said that wealth was measured by the nation's store of gold and silver. Mercantilism promoted a national strategy of selling goods to other countries while buying nothing from them. Mercantilism further promoted tariffs on incoming products to discourage the buying of imports. For England, this was a strategy of taking raw materials from the colonies and selling them back to the colonies as finished goods. Smith argued for letting the market decide the wealth of a nation. Smith laid out the major tenets of capitalism as self-interest, limited government, division of labor, free exchange, and social cooperation.

Smith's work was based on freedom, limiting the role of government to defense, universal education, punishment of crime, and the enforcement of legal rights, which were the basic principles of the Scottish Enlightenment. The American colonies quickly accepted Smith's concepts of freedom, but as a new nation, the United States soon adopted an opposing strategy of protecting home industries and placing tariffs on incoming products. In fact, until the 20th century the main source of income for the U.S. government was tariffs. Furthermore, in general, the United States had a policy of protectionism until the 1930s. The debate over free markets, protectionism, tariffs, and fair trade continues to this day.

The *Wealth of Nations* is often used incorrectly to support free trade, but some precautions are needed in general. Smith's world was one of agriculture. Other than crafts-produced items, manufacturing was nonexistent. The steam engine had not yet been commercially developed. Smith took some exceptions directly to free trade such as the nation's defense industries or core industries. Smith's world lacked currency markets on a metallic base (gold and silver). Smith argued for freedom of trade because he lived in a world of government-chartered monopolies. The application of tariffs during Smith's time was primarily on agricultural products. It would be more correct to see Smith as a fair trader in light of the economic forces of today—in other words, free markets without government currency manipulation, government-controlled monopolies, government printing of money, and government-controlled production and financing.

Adam Smith, 18th-century Scottish economist. (Jupiter images)

Another sometimes overlooked part of the book is its treatise on improving productivity through the division of labor. Smith studied the division of labor in a local British pin factory that had claimed a significant increase in productivity over its former crafts production. Smith argued that this improved productivity resulted from three causes. First, the laborer's dexterity improved with task specialization. Second, no time was lost in passing of the work between craftsmen. Finally, tools could be specialized to fit the specific individual task. Smith suggested a broader use of this division of labor in crafts production of the time. Smith even argued for task specialization in agriculture. Smith believed this specialized production could reduce costs and allow poorer nations to compete with rich nations. Smith did live to see some of these principles applied in the manufacture of guns. More than any other country, America embraced Smith's ideas on manufacturing. By the 20th century, task specialization was the cornerstone of mass production. Another contribution of the *Wealth of Nations* was in the measurement of wealth being the nation's output per capita, not its total output.

The book would have many unintentional and latent effects on the United States and the world economy. Smith's basic argument opposed the use of slavery and servants as making the owners lazy and preventing innovation to improve real productivity. Smith noted, "A man grows rich by employing a multitude of manufacturers; he grows poor maintaining a multitude of menial servants." Smith particularly argued against the servants of the landowning class as unproductive. Smith saw cheap labor or slavery as reducing productivity in the long run. For example, we might argue today that if cheap immigrant farm labor was not available, there would be investment and innovation in labor-saving equipment that would eventually increase productivity and lower overall costs. Smith extended this thought to nations and the economy as a whole. Clearly much of the book can be considered out-of-date or obsolete, such as Smith's 23-page rant on the Corn Laws, which restricted the exportation of corn. Still, it is amazing how much of the book remains pertinent after more than 220 years.

*See also:* Abraham Lincoln Establishes Protectionism; First Japanese Auto Sold in the United States; Jefferson Embargo; McKinley Tariff of 1890; Navigation Acts; "Report on Manufacturing"; Tariff of Abominations; Whig Party Evolves

### References

McCreadie, Karen. *Adam Smith's The Wealth of Nations: A Modern Day Interpretation of an Economic Classic*. New York: Infinite Ideas, 2009.

O'Rourke, P. J. *P.J. O'Rourke on the Wealth of Nations*. New York: Atlantic Monthly Press, 2007.

Smith, Adam. *An Inquiry into the Nature and Causes of the Wealth of Nations*. New York: Random House, 1937.

# Patent and Copyright Statutes (1790)

It is amazing that the young nation of the United States put such emphasis on the protection of copyrights and patents. However, this focus would lead to America's greatest period of creativity and invention. Without the protection of intellectual rights, it is impossible for capitalism to flourish. Two founding fathers, Thomas Jefferson and Benjamin Franklin, attributed the growth of the nation to the spread of the useful arts. In 1783, as the Continental Congress considered the Articles of Confederation, a number of American authors, including Noah Webster, petitioned the Congress "that nothing is more properly a man's own than the fruit of his study, and that the protection and security of literary property would greatly tend to encourage genius and to promote useful discoveries." Jefferson, an inventor himself, took particular interest in copyright and patent law.

The colonies had had copyright and patent laws in place since the 1600s. Early colonial law was based on English law, which allowed for royal monopolies when the Crown chartered protection for the inventor; however, much of the profits would go to the Crown. The view was that inventions were the property of society, to be managed by a monarch. In the colonies, colonial courts could offer protection. The first colonial patent was issued to Joseph Jencks for the production of scythes in 1646. The General Court of Massachusetts chartered Jencks's patent. In 1710, the Statute of Anne gave protection for a fixed period of usually 14 years. The Statute of Anne would become the basis for American patent and copyright law. Prior to 1790, the colonies and the states continued the practice of granting monopolies as a reward, but this actually reduced creativity. The state of New York, for example, gave John Fitch a steamboat monopoly in 1787 (but it would be repealed by federal law; see article 8 of the Constitution). Challenges to patents were possible but were debated among politicians as to their validity. Such a system favored the well-known and wealthy. Most colonial inventors chose to keep their improvements secret rather than applying for a weakly enforced colony law.

At the Constitutional Convention of 1787, James Madison championed the need for federal protection versus protection by individual states. Intellectual property ownership was considered a basic right from our beginning as a nation. Copyright and patent law was authorized by the U.S. Constitution in Article I, Section 8, Clause 8, which states: "The Congress shall have the Power . . . To promote the progress of science and useful arts, by securing for limited times to Authors and Inventors the exclusive right to their respective writings and discoveries." There was a debate between the Federalist James Madison, and Jefferson. Jefferson wanted to encourage invention but feared the monopolies that might result from patents. Madison preferred unlimited periods of protection until the death of the inventor, while Jefferson argued for a maximum of 14 years. This debate continues to this day.

In 1790, the Congress passed the Copyright Act and the Patent Act. The Patent Act was meant to encourage creativity in the useful arts. These acts were unique in the world, offering an inventor for the time an intrinsic right to profit from his invention under protection of the law. It went far beyond British law, which had focused on the rights of society versus those of the inventor. British inventors' rights were dependent on the prerogative of the monarch. American law now made the ownership of intellectual property an individual right. This was a break from English law that looked at invention as the property of society. It would inspire a wave of immigration by craftsmen and the European middle class to come to America as entrepreneurs. These American acts extended no protection to British copyrights, which allowed many machine and toolmakers to bring their processes to America.

The Patent Act of 1790 named Secretary of State Thomas Jefferson as patent examiner. He proved a tough enforcer. Once reviewed, a patent received the signatures of the attorney general and the president. The inventor was charged a fee of around four dollars (a fairly large sum at the time). The first U.S. patent was given to Samuel Hopkins of Vermont for the improvement in the manufacture of potash (a necessary ingredient in soap and gunpowder). The duties of patent examiner soon overwhelmed Jefferson. The Patent Act, like the Copyright Act, allowed for protection for 14 years, with renewal possible for another 14 years. Another concern of Jefferson was the possibility of frivolous lawsuits preventing the use of improvements. In fact, Jefferson would be sued over one of his gristmill improvements and was forced to pay American super-inventor Oliver Evans.

Jefferson was totally in charge of enforcing the new law. Jefferson demanded extensive proof that an invention was truly an improvement. He often demanded demonstrations and experiments as proof. He often requested the building of models to ensure the functioning of bigger projects. One example of his thoroughness was the application of Jacob Isaac's process for distilling freshwater from seawater. The idea was complex, and Jefferson appointed a board of scientists to review it. The board included famous American glassmaker Casper Wistar and astronomer David Rittenhouse. Finally, after extensive testing, the patent was denied. The rigorous evaluation of patents made the American approach very unique in the world. Jefferson continued to improve the patent process. In 1793, the act was revised at his recommendation to establish a State Department clerk to aid in patent review. A full office of clerks was established in 1802. More so than any other person, Jefferson is responsible for American patent law and enforcement, which tries to balance individual rights, monopoly abuse, and the good of society. It was a unique balance that set the stage for a 200-year boom in American creativity. By the 1820s, the United States had issued 535 patents, compared to 145 patents in England, which was the greatest industrial power on earth at the time.

*See also:* Automated Sewing Machine; CD-ROM; Centennial Exposition; First Steamboat to New Orleans; Great Exhibition of 1851; Western Union Telegraph Company

**References**

Khan, Zorina. *The Democratization of Invention: Patent and Copyrights in American Economic Development.* Cambridge: Cambridge University Press, 2009.

Pursell, Carroll. *Technology in America.* Cambridge, MA: MIT Press, 1990.

Skrabec, Quentin. *The Metallurgic Age.* Jefferson, NC: McFarland, 2006.

# "Report on Manufacturing" (1791)

The "Report on Manufacturing" (also called "A Treatise on Manufacturing") is considered the magnum opus of Alexander Hamilton, the first secretary of the Treasury. It was presented to Congress on December 5, 1791, and is considered the guiding document for the economic principles of the United States. The "Report on Manufacturing" was followed by specific reports on banking and credit. The "Report on Manufacturing" was analogous to an economic Declaration of Independence, to be followed by constitutional specifics. It was originally opposed by the then secretary of state, Thomas Jefferson. The disagreement between Hamilton and Jefferson derived from two different visions. Jefferson saw the United States as an agrarian nation where manufacture would be done on large plantations. Hamilton foresaw an urban nation of manufacturing cities. By Jefferson's death in 1825, he had come to accept Hamilton's vision of an industrial America.

The "Report on Manufacturing" was considered a blend of mercantilism as practiced in England and the practices of Jean-Baptiste Colbert of France. It would reject the recent ideas of Adam Smith's free trade and minimal government interference. It would be the foundation of the emerging Federalist Party. Ultimately, Hamilton's ideas would be incorporated in the "American System" of Henry Clay's Whig Party in the 1830s. The young Whig, Abraham Lincoln, would incorporate it into the newly formed Republican Party. Later, in the 1880s, William McKinley would make it the cornerstone of Republican Party platforms for decades to come. Much of Hamilton's vision for the United States has come to pass. In 1790, Hamilton faced a financial mess. The country lacked international and domestic credit. The currency was worthless, and soldiers paid in script were near rebellion. While free, the country was facing financial collapse.

Hamilton believed that America would fail if it did not excel in manufacturing. He reasoned this from his experience as a young military officer under George Washington in the Revolutionary War. The army had suffered from lack of arms, gunpowder, uniforms, iron implements, and ammunition, which nearly cost America the war. American manufacturing lacked capacity, and the success of the British blockade nearly crushed the struggling Centennial Army. In the report,

Hamilton noted, "The extreme embarrassment of the United States during the late war, from incapacity of supplying themselves, are still matter of keen recollection." After that experience, Hamilton believed that the United States needed to build a strong manufacturing sector if it wanted to remain free. Furthermore the country lacked a transportation system to supply the army. Hamilton stated, "Those hands, which may be deprived of business by the cessation of commerce, may be occupied in various kinds of manufactures and other internal improvements. If . . . manufactures should . . . take root among us, they will pave the way, still more, to the future grandeur and the glory of America." Hamilton argued that national industries should be supported through protective tariffs, direct subsidies, a national banking system, and a national transportation system. Hamilton refuted Adam Smith's work on the grounds that it was based on agricultural society.

The following is an important excerpt from the "Report on Manufacturing":

But though it were true, that the immediate and certain effect of regulations controlling the competition of foreign with domestic fabrics was an increase of price, it is universally true, that the contrary is the ultimate effect with every successful manufacture. When a domestic manufacture has attained to perfection, and has engaged in the prosecution of it a competent attend the importation of foreign commodities, it can be afforded, and accordingly seldom or never fails to be sold cheaper, in process of time, than was the foreign article for which it is a substitute. The internal competition, which takes place, soon does away everything like monopoly, and by degrees reduces the price of the article to the minimum of a reasonable profit on the capital employed. These accords with reason of the thing, and with experience. Whence it follows, that it is in the interest of a community, with a view to eventual and permanent economy, to encourage the growth of manufactures, in a national view, a temporary enhancement of price must always be well compensated by a permanent reduction of it.

Hamilton argued for protective tariffs not only to protect infant industries but also to provide a source of revenue for the government. A Congress in need of money to pay off war debts quickly adopted this part of the report. Most opponents were southerners such as Jefferson and James Madison, of the Democratic-Republican Party of the time. The South feared that tariffs on imports would cause retaliation affecting their exports of cotton and tobacco. The division would remain and would be the root cause of the Civil War. The Hamilton tariff was to be a moderate one that was of more use in raising money for the government than full protection would have been. The more hotly debated part of Hamilton's plan was direct government subsidies to manufacturers. Most argued for indirect subsidies such as the building of roads and canals. Even manufacturers preferred a high tariff for protection versus government subsidies, which might lead to political favoritism.

Hamilton was correct in that American industry was starved of cash needed for investment. Banks were almost nonexistent in America except for those serving large planters. England had been the source of capital for America, so banks had failed to fully develop. On Hamilton's recommendation, Congress chartered the First Bank of the United States on February 25, 1791. Hamilton modeled the bank after the Bank of England. It was opposed by the southern states. Hamilton used the "commerce clause" of the Constitution to justify this expansion of the federal government. The First Bank was a chartered private company with government backing. Stock of $10 million was sold, with the federal government buying $2 million, which was financed by an excise tax on domestically distilled whiskey. This would ultimately lead to the Whiskey Rebellion. The First Bank did establish order in the newly formed United States. Part of the "bank bill" established a National Mint to replace the more than 30 currencies in circulation. The First Bank allowed New England merchants to establish international credit to promote trade. Furthermore, the First Bank supplied badly needed capital to manufacturers in Pennsylvania, Connecticut, and New York. The bank also served a secondary role as a depository for government accounts. The debate over the bank would lead to the formation of two political parties—the pro-Federalists of Hamilton and the Democratic-Republicans of Jefferson.

The First Bank of the United States was chartered only until 1811, and it continued to be opposed by the southern states, which saw no benefit from it. The bank's charter was allowed to expire under President Madison, and Congress, by a narrow margin, did not re-charter it. Overall, Hamilton's Federalist approach to business would be called "supply-side economics" today. The Federal Reserve today functions similarly to Hamilton's original thinking. Hamilton would have agreed with many government actions to foster manufacturing. Hamilton, however, would not agree with the free trade practices of today.

*See also:* Abraham Lincoln Establishes Protectionism; Erie Canal; Jefferson Embargo; McKinley Tariff of 1890; National Road; Whig Party Evolves; Whiskey Rebellion

### References

Chernow, Ron. *Alexander Hamilton.* New York: Penguin, 2004.

Land, Michael. *Hamilton's Republic: Readings in the American Democratic Nationalist Tradition.* New York: Free Press, 2004.

Skrabec, Quentin. *Pig Iron Aristocracy.* Westminster, MD: Heritage Books, 2008.

# Whiskey Rebellion (1794)

The Whiskey Rebellion of the Scotch-Irish in western Pennsylvania in the 1790s would be the root of American domestic politics for centuries. The primary cause of the rebellion was a federal excise tax on whiskey. The Monongahela Valley was filled with the smoke of whiskey stills in the 1790s. Rye whiskey was a mainstay of the area's Scotch-Irish. Whiskey was a favorite manufacture of grain farmers, since grain was a high-volume, low-cost commodity not worth the cost of transporting long distances. Monongahela rye distilled in Pennsylvania was easy to transport down the Ohio-Mississippi River system, making its way via New Orleans and the Atlantic to the East Coast and to the taverns of Europe. When the region was a British colony, the whiskey production had been controlled and taxed, but the remoteness of the Monongahela Valley made it almost impossible for British tax collectors. The resistance to taxes had been part of the Revolution, and feelings ran deep on the government imposing taxes.

The Articles of Confederation had prevented the federal government from levying taxes, but as the national debt reached over $50 million, the need for a federal tax increased. President George Washington and Alexander Hamilton imposed an excise tax on whiskey in 1791, believing it to be one of the least offensive taxes possible. The tax would be used to pay off the national debt and to support road building and the national bank, all of which would benefit the area. Hamilton also preferred this excise tax to further increasing tariffs, which had become the federal government's major source of income. The whiskey tax was also considered a "sin tax," which would gain the support of the Christian base. While the Scotch-Irish of the frontier loved their whiskey, many in their Presbyterian Church were concerned about its impact on society. Hamilton clearly understated the role of whiskey on the frontier. Whiskey offered a large profit for farmers.

General Neville was chosen to collect the tax among the Scotch-Irish in western Pennsylvania even though he had initially opposed it. The tax schedule varied, but it was around 6¢ to 10¢ a gallon (a gallon of rye whiskey sold for a dollar). For months, the resistance was modeled after the colonists' resistance against British taxes. The resistance to the tax also had national support in the western counties of Maryland, Virginia, North Carolina, and South Carolina. Even within the Washington administration, there was division, with Thomas Jefferson opposing such a federal tax. The Pennsylvanian Scotch-Irish mustered a militia and burnt the estate of tax collector General Neville. It was the first test of the federal government. Jefferson became publicly sympathetic with the whiskey rebels. For months Scotch-Irish militia roamed the area. The predominantly Scotch-Irish frontier was split over the tax, with antitax followers in the Jeffersonian Republican Party and the supporters in the Federalist Party. The Whiskey Rebellion is the heart of a basic political split that exists to this day.

In August 1792, a convention was held in Pittsburgh to discuss options. The convention had few moderates with the exception of Albert Gallatin, a future secretary of the Treasury. Gallatin had served on the Pennsylvanian Constitution ratification committee, which voiced opposition to taxes yet supported a strong federal government. This position was more consistent with that of the majority of voters. Gallatin was elected to Congress in 1790 to represent Allegheny, Washington, and Fayette Counties. This congressional district included Pittsburgh and was the heart of pig iron production and use. He was elected to the U.S. Senate in 1793 when the convention failed to obtain a solution. By 1794, the crisis had reached a peak, with federal agents determined to collect back taxes. A rebel army of 600 men was mustered at Braddock's Field, eight miles from Pittsburgh. The rebel leader, Revolutionary War General James MacFarlane, was killed. The army swelled to 7,000 as they marched on the city of Pittsburgh.

Hamilton persuaded Washington to send 12,000 troops to western Pennsylvania to put down the rebellion. Before the militia had reached Pittsburgh, the uprising was diffused as the Presbyterian Church preached enforcement of the law. The Scotch-Irish, however, moved into Kentucky and Tennessee to produce their whiskey. Tennessee and Kentucky to this day remain the center of whiskey making. The new frontier was out of the reach of the federal tax collectors. These Pennsylvanian emigrants would form the Kentucky and Tennessee bourbon and whiskey families of today. One legacy of the Whiskey Rebellion would be a realignment of the political parties to better reflect a compromise between government and the free market. It would also demonstrate the continued sensitivity of Americans to taxes that had been part of the Revolutionary War.

Farmers in Pennsylvania protest the tax on whiskey in 1794. (Library of Congress)

More than anything, the Whiskey Rebellion caused a political divide among the Scotch-Irish along economic lines. The Whiskey Rebellion was really a reflection of the struggle of the new nation with federalism. The wealthy Scotch-Irish industrialists and the Presbyterian Church leaders had supported the federalist application of the law to enforce the whiskey tax. Their poorer cousins in the Pennsylvanian hills opposed a strong central government and taxes. The whiskey tax forced many frontier Scotch-Irish into Jefferson's "Republican" Party. Still, western Pennsylvania was prospering with the aid of the U.S. banking system and the related growth of industries. Like today, there was a search for the correct balance of government and the free market. The Whiskey Rebellion also showed an inherent dislike of taxes that had been part of the American Revolution. In 1800, the tax was repealed as Jefferson's Republican Party took power. In the 1820s, the "clapboard junta" of Pittsburgh (those who lived in clapboard houses) put together a strong opposition to the federalist manufacturers. It would take another 30 years for pro-manufacturing forces to take back politics in the area. The Jacksonian Democratic Party (known as the clapboard democracy) controlled the area in the 1820s, but Pittsburgh's congressmen were protectionists. The manufacturers ultimately wrestled the vote away from the Democrats as Andrew Jackson's policies turned anti-manufacturing.

Gallatin became a Jeffersonian Republican, like most of his Scotch-Irish neighbors after the Whiskey Rebellion, but he belonged to the segment of the party that believed in a strong federal government. Gallatin became secretary of the Treasury for President Jefferson. He had been a moderate in the Whiskey Rebellion but helped sign a compromise in the end. In Congress, he continued his battle against the whiskey tax, becoming a hated enemy of the Federalists. Still, Gallatin was the first to propose a national road in Congress in 1797. While a Jeffersonian Republican, he was of the unique pig iron branch of the party that supported Federalist national improvements and protectionism. The pig iron producers and manufacturers wanted government improvements such as canals and roads. Ultimately, decades later, this branch of the Jeffersonian Republicans and a similar branch in the old Federalist Party would lead to the Whig Party and then the Republican Party founded in Pittsburgh.

*See also:* Income Tax; Jefferson Embargo; McKinley Tariff of 1890; National Road; "Report on Manufacturing"; Tariff of Abominations; Whig Party Evolves

### References

Baldwin, Leland. *Whiskey Rebels: The Story of a Frontier Uprising.* Pittsburgh, PA: University of Pittsburgh Press, 1939.

Buck, Solon. *The Planting of Civilization in Western Pennsylvania.* Pittsburgh, PA: University of Pittsburgh Press, 1968.

Hogeland, William. *The Whiskey Rebellion: George Washington, Alexander Hamilton, and the Frontier Rebels Who Challenged America's Newfound Sovereignty.* New York: Scribner, 2006.

# Jefferson Embargo (1807)

The Embargo of 1807 remains a valuable learning tool for economists, politicians, and businesspersons. It offers a study of the effects of restrictions on trade, both positive and negative. Many consider it the first international commercial war. The embargo clearly demonstrates the interaction of politics, trade, and business. In many ways, it was an extension of the decades-long war between England and France. It would also lead to the War of 1812. While the embargo created an economic recession initially, it would launch new American production of textiles, iron, tools, tinplate, glass, hemp, hats, and nails.

In the years prior to the embargo, Europe was struggling with the Napoleonic Wars. France's advantage on land was checked by England's advantage on the seas. England used blockages and seizures to enforce its naval advantage. England now used force to expand its Navigation Acts on the free shipping of the United States. British ships blocked key foreign ports, forcing American ships to first go through British ports. In addition, the British Navy boarded American ships looking for deserters. This system of impressment of American sailors created a public outcry in the United States. President Thomas Jefferson was determined to avoid war and demonstrate economic alternatives to war. The United States was a major importer of British goods and an exporter of raw materials such as cotton, furs, pig iron, lumber, farm goods, and tobacco.

In December 1806, Congress passed the Nonimportation Act of 1806, which declared a "prohibition of the importation of certain goods and merchandise from the kingdom of Great Britain." America depended on England for the import bands to protect IT industries, which included iron nails, tinplate, tin, glass, hats, clothing, silk, paper, wool, hemp, and leather. Initially, Canadian and American smugglers found ways around this prohibition. In January 1807, a supplementary act was passed to close loopholes that had excluded whaling, fishing, and coastal boats, which were actively involved. The act was met with mixed opposition. Dependent on shipping, New England opposed any restriction of trade, as did the South, which exported farm goods to England. The initial economic impact was to move the country into a recession and increase unemployment. Treasury receipts dwindled, wiping out a surplus that had resulted from the earlier tariff policies of Alexander Hamilton and the Washington and Adams administrations. Over 30,000 seamen were out of work, creating a true depression on the New England seaboard. Jefferson stuck to the policy, believing it was a social experiment on how to avoid war. The Federalists rallied political opposition and revitalized their party. The middle states started to benefit as iron production expanded. Textile manufacturers started to expand in New England as well. Still, overall, the embargo had suppressed the economy.

Another problem was that Jefferson had no money for federal projects such as the canals and roads wanted by the Federalists. For these reasons, Jefferson's

Political cartoon lampoons the "cursed Ograbme" (embargo spelled backwards). (Benson J. Lossing. *The Pictorial Field-Book of the War of 1812*. New York: Harper & Bros., 1868)

secretary of state, Albert Gallatin, opposed the embargo as well. Jefferson, however, saw it as the only alternative to war. By March 1808, a new Embargo Act was passed to stop all ships leaving for foreign ports. From the standpoint of restricting trade, the act was successful. Exports fell from $108 million in 1807 to $22 million in 1808. This worsened economic conditions across the nation. Poor economic conditions replaced public anger over British impressments, and the presidential election of 1808 went to James Madison and the Federalists. The Democrat-Republican Party of Jefferson had been split by the embargo. The election was the first example of Americans voting for their pocketbooks over international affairs.

As Jefferson left office, the Embargo Act (not the embargo) was repealed. However, the embargo was lifted on all countries with the exception of England, France, and their possessions. It was replaced with the Non-Intercourse Act, which extended the embargo until it was safe from British interference of trade. The decision was left to President Madison as a discretionary authority. England was being hurt far more than America, since its manufacturing growth was based on imports to America.

One positive aspect of the embargo was the development of domestic manufacturing. Jefferson played on this success by dressing in homespun clothes for the Fourth of July celebration in 1808. The lack of iron, in particular, caused the startup of America's iron furnaces that had been dormant for decades. Saltpeter and gunpowder mills were restarted. American manufacturing was reborn as the foundries and forges of the Revolutionary War opened again. Americans would prove to be adaptive and creative. Textile mills opened in New England to process southern cotton, and a new industry was born. The application of new machinery would also give the domestic industry a new advantage in productivity. Francis Cabot Lowell copied the British water-powered loom and built factories. Lowell would also develop a whole new system of textile manufacture. The success of textile production created a machine industry as well. New England would ultimately emerge a more economically balanced region. In the middle states, the iron industry, which was still suffering from the colonial Navigation Acts, started to awake. The glass industry came alive in New England and New Jersey. The rise of domestic manufacture under the embargo became a model for the Whig Party of the 1820s to suggest tariffs to restrain imports.

At Pittsburgh, nail and tinplate mills were built to supply the growing needs of the West. Iron foundries also started to supply the needs of an industrial boom. As the war approached, the manufacturing Connecticut Valley became America's armory. Western Pennsylvania and eastern Ohio opened hundreds of iron smelting furnaces, rolling mills, nail factories, tinplate manufacturers, and forges. Pittsburgh Foundry would become the producer of cannons for the War of 1812. The seeds of America's iron and steel industry were planted. Rolling mills in Middle America started to apply steam power instead of waterpower. England realized too late that America was becoming a manufacturing nation out of necessity. In 1810, England wisely tried to end the problems, but it was too late, as the war was already beginning. After the war, England continued the commercial war, this time flooding America with cheap manufactured goods to once again put American manufacturing into hibernation.

*See also:* Abraham Lincoln Establishes Protectionism; Navigation Acts; "Report on Manufacturing"; Tariff of Abominations; *Wealth of Nations*

### References

Smelser, Marshall. *The Democratic Republic.* New York: Harper & Row, 1968.

Spivak, Burton. *Jefferson's English Crisis: Commerce, Embargo, and the Republican Revolution.* Charlottesville: University Press of Virginia, 1979.

Temin, Peter. *Iron and Steel in the Nineteenth Century.* Cambridge, MA: MIT Press, 1964.

# First Steamboat to New Orleans (1811)

The history of the steam engine is a long and well-documented one, but the commercial history is more specific. Thomas Slavery in England won a "catch-all" patent for a steam engine to pump water in 1698. The invention addressed a specific need in England to remove water from coal mines, so coal could be used as a fuel to address the shortage of wood in the nation. If water could not be removed, the deep mines needed for coal production were impossible. The Slavery machine was inefficient, however. Thomas Newcomer had a much better machine in 1712, but because of Slavery's patent, he was forced into a partnership with Slavery (see Patent and Copyright Statutes). In 1769, James Watt broke Slavery's monopoly and was awarded a new patent for a much-improved steam engine. He teamed up with manufacturer Matthew Boulton to produce these improved machines. Wood-rich America lacked the powerful economic stimulus to pump water out of coal mines, as it had cheap wood to fuel the nation. One American inventor, Oliver Evans, was starting to apply steam engines to grain mills, but transportation was the real need in the United States. So while steam engines were not needed for mining, America needed the power of the steam engine to improve transportation.

Robert Fulton had been visiting England and had taken an interest in the steam engine. He developed a model for a steam-driven warship, but it would be built only after his death. More important, he was able to get Boulton and Watt engines shipped to the United States for some reverse engineering of the low-pressure engine. Fulton started to experiment with steamboats on the Hudson River in 1807. American inventors gained knowledge and invented high-pressure steam engines. High-pressure engines were capable of supplying the steam needed to power boats. Evans went into the production of these newer machines and more powerful engines in Philadelphia. Fulton had found success in steam propulsion. He teamed up with Robert Livingston, who had been granted a state monopoly on steam navigation in New York until 1818 (it was being challenged in federal court under the Patent Act of 1790). The Fulton monopoly lasted until the famous Supreme Court case, known as *Gibbons v. Ogden,* found it invalid in 1824. Fulton progressed with successful trials with his boat *North River Steamboat* (also known as the *Clermont* after rebuilding) on the Hudson River. Similar boats were already running in Europe.

Fulton, however, was now able to use new American high-pressure engines in his ships. Fulton took the first step toward commercialization by offering passenger service between New York and Albany. Within a year, Fulton added a second steamboat to the service. The boat could move 60 to 90 passengers at five miles an hour on a 30-hour trip. The boat cost $20,000 but returned $1,000 in three months. Another businessman, Nicholas J. Roosevelt (brother to the grandfather of President Theodore Roosevelt), wanted to compete on the Hudson River, but the state monopoly prevented him from doing so. Roosevelt formed a loose partnership with Fulton to develop a steamboat service on the Ohio and Mississippi Rivers. River transportation offered a higher potential for profit. Downriver keelboat navigation from Pittsburgh to New Orleans was aided by currents, but upriver transportation was next to impossible. Roosevelt started his building in the shipyards of

Pittsburgh. Not only did Pittsburgh have an extensive keelboat-building industry, but Evans was also building steam engines at a new factory there. Still, most river men believed the enterprise would not be successful.

Roosevelt's boat was based on a different business model than that of utilitarian keelboat companies. Roosevelt's *New Orleans* would have bedrooms, a dining hall, a fireplace for cooking, and larger conference-style rooms. The boat was 116 feet long by 20 feet wide and cost $38,000. It was to stop at Cincinnati, Louisville, and Natchez to develop future docks and fueling stops. The steam engine used wood, although it did use some coal, which was actually dug on the riverbanks. Keelboats charged $160 for the trip from Pittsburgh to New Orleans, while it would be $30 when the *New Orleans* started fully commercial trips. The first voyage left Pittsburgh on October 25, 1811. Roosevelt had scouted the route on a honeymoon keelboat trip in 1809.

The first trip was accompanied with great fanfare, typical of commercial launches of the time. Roosevelt and his wife (the daughter of famous architect Benjamin Latrobe) would make the trip. The steamboat passed Indian canoes on its passage down the Ohio River. The boat had a banquet for visitors at Louisville. It was a marketing manager's dream, with the great Comet of 1811 at its height of visibility. As it approached the Mississippi River, the Great New Madrid earthquake hit, actually causing the flow of the Mississippi to reverse briefly. The riverbanks caved in and islands disappeared. Roosevelt's wife also gave birth during the trip. The boat reached New Orleans on January 12. The leisurely trip of 1,700 miles had taken 71 days versus the 80-day average for keelboats.

After the voyage, the *New Orleans* was put in service on the Mississippi between Natchez and New Orleans. The first steamers did eight miles an hour downstream and three miles an hour upstream. The cost had dropped to $15 by 1820. Steamboat travel and commercialization quickly accelerated. By 1817, steamboats had contracts to carry U.S. mail. Designs started to include two levels to increase the passenger trade. Early records suggest that while the cost of building steamboats ranged from $20,000 to $40,000, the time to receive a return on the investment was about one year. Passengers and cargo each contributed about 50 percent to the profit. Building of steamers boomed at Pittsburgh and Cincinnati. By 1834, Pittsburgh shipyards had built 221 steamers, and Cincinnati had built 103. In the 1820s, shipping companies used steamers to push barges of cargo such as coal, iron, and limestone, which greatly enhanced profits. Pittsburgh cast iron foundries, steam engine factories, and nail factories were created to support shipbuilding. The canal-building era of the 1820s also increased the demand for steamboats.

*See also:* Baltimore & Ohio Railroad; Patent and Copyright Statutes

## References

Kroll, Steven. *Robert Fulton: From Submarine to Steamboat.* New York: Holiday House, 1999.

Sale, Kirkpatrick. *The Fire of Genius: Robert Fulton and the American Dream.* New York: Free Press, 2002.

# National Road (1811)

At the dawn of the 19th century, the biggest barrier to the progress of the nation was the lack of a transportation system connecting the East Coast to the then western frontier. There was no water connection, as the Allegheny Mountains separated the Potomac and Ohio Rivers. Lack of transportation limited the growth of western industry and agriculture. Following an old Indian trail, George Washington had been one of the first settlers to make the portage between the Potomac and Ohio Rivers as a young surveyor in 1753. The path was known as Nemacolin's Trail after the Delaware Indian chief. The trail connected Maryland and Pennsylvania via the Cumberland Gap in the mountains. A few years later, Washington helped build a rough road along this trail for General Braddock's failed expedition to take the headwaters of the Ohio (present-day Pittsburgh) from the French. The trail, known as Braddock's Road (today's Route 40), and its competing trail, known as Boone's Trail, were the only paths west at the start of the 1800s. Forbes Road was a longer trip that went through Pennsylvania to Philadelphia.

One of America's first highways in the 1730s was known as "the Great Philadelphia Wagon Road." German and Swiss families set up a transportation network between Philadelphia and Lancaster to support the extensive trade. The road was built privately on the belief that it would foster trade and wealth. It was America's first toll road. This first turnpike allowed German farmers to become wealthy, supplying both Philadelphia and Lancaster. The rise of capitalism surrounding the turnpike rivaled that of the shipping ports of New England. At the western terminus of the road, German craftsmen developed the Conestoga wagon, also called the prairie schooner. These giant freight wagons were named after Conestoga Creek at Lancaster. They were watertight and used iron belts around the wooden wheels. Six- to eight-horse teams pulled these freight wagons. They moved in convoys of up to 100 wagons. By the 1740s, around 10,000 Conestoga wagons were in use. The Germans went into breeding "Conestoga" horses to further improve the overall transportation system. Lancaster not only moved farm products to Philadelphia but also gathered furs and whiskey from the western frontier for shipment to Philadelphia and on to Europe. The turnpike became a vital link in the Scotch-Irish trading network of furs, whiskey, tobacco, ginseng, and grain. Philadelphia became the nation's major port because of this turnpike. The word *turnpike* came from the use of wooden pikes to mark turns and direction. This turnpike played a key role in the development of whiskey production in western Pennsylvania. In the early 1800s, Federalists were calling for a national road.

In 1794, the federal army was sent on the old Braddock Road through the Cumberland Gap to put down the Whiskey Rebellion. Sinkholes, poor drainage, and old stumps slowed the army. Ironically, Albert Gallatin, a participant in the Whiskey Rebellion, became the National Road's biggest supporter as Thomas Jefferson's secretary of the Treasury. In 1806, a bill was introduced by Kentucky congressman Henry Clay to build a road through the Cumberland Gap to connect the Ohio River to the East. More than anybody, Clay was weary of the month long trip from Lexington, Kentucky, on the Ohio River to Washington. Virginia and Maryland favored a road that would choose their ports over those of New York and Philadelphia. While Jefferson signed the bill in 1806, political arguing as to the route continued. In 1811, Congress finally let contracts for the construction. Congress had also decided to bypass Pittsburgh, with the National Road going through Wheeling, a decision that was probably due in part to Pittsburgh's role in the Whiskey Rebellion.

Construction of the first leg of the road from Cumberland, Maryland, to Wheeling, West Virginia (130 miles), took six years. This first road had a 66-foot right-of-way with a 20-foot roadbed. It tapered from the centerline for drainage and at the center had 18 inches of crushed stone. Wages for road workers ranged from 12¢ to 80¢ a day. It was tough work through the Pennsylvania mountains, and many streams had to be crossed. Costs were as high as $13,000 per mile in this difficult stretch. The first economic benefit was the use of the road for federal mail to the frontier. The early road was a combination of leveled earth and stone. In areas of heavier traffic, wooden planks were often used (many of these areas retain the name "plank" even today). In the 1820s, the road was resurfaced using a layer of crushed stone. John Macadam invented the method, which became known as "macadamization."

The road progressed along the present Route 40 from Wheeling to Vandalia, Illinois. The Ohio portion from Wheeling followed "Zane's Trace," a federal horse path financed by the federal government back in the 1790s to increase trade. In 1834, Democratic President Andrew Jackson vetoed a bill from Clay, of the Whig Party, to extend the road again into his home state of Kentucky. In addition, Jackson turned most of the eastern part of the road over to the states. The states turned it into a toll road. Tollhouses were placed every 15 miles, and a toll of two to five cents was charged based on the type of cargo and estimated weight (a practice that still exists). In the 1830s, an express wagon could make 150 miles a day on the road. Average travel was slower, with nightly stops at major inns along the road.

The National Road advanced the fields of civil engineering, road building, and bridge building. Both the Federalists and the Democrats believed in the need for government involvement in building infrastructure but disagreed on who should pay for and maintain the roads. The main opposition to the road was based on regional politics because some sections of the country like the South had little benefit from it. New England opposed it because it strengthened more southerly ports such as Baltimore. In general, however, road building had strong support throughout America. The first accepted local taxes in America were for roads and schools. Tolls, however, proved less popular as travelers developed trails around tollgates known as "shunpikes." The success of the National Road to expand business made road building an important part of the emerging Whig Party, which was dedicated to the economic prosperity of America.

*See also:* Baltimore & Ohio Railroad; Clipper Ships; Erie Canal; Federal Aid Highway Act of 1956; Overland Travel and Mail Service; "Report on Manufacturing"; Whig Party Evolves; Whiskey Rebellion

### References

Raitz, Karl. *The National Road.* Baltimore, MD: Johns Hopkins University Press, 1996.

Schneider, Norris. *The National Road: Main Street of America.* Columbus: Ohio Historical Society, 1975.

# Erie Canal (1825)

The Erie Canal would become a major engineering and business feat for the new nation. The canal would connect the western markets to New York City and the world through the port of New York. When finished, it would be 363 miles long, 40 feet wide, and 4 feet deep. The canal was an amazing combination of locks (84 in total), bridges (about 300), and aqueducts (32 in total) to traverse the uphill path. The construction by engineer Canvass White led to the invention of hydraulic cement. It would be the motivation for the first major wave of immigrant labor, particularly Irish workers. When finished, the canal would reduce shipping costs from New York Harbor to Lake Erie by an amazing 94 percent. The canal dropped the cost of freight between Buffalo and New York from an average of $90 a ton to $4 a ton. A person traveled the canal at five cents a mile. The Midwest profited as much as New York. In 1820, less than 1,000 bushels of wheat had been shipped to New York; by 1841, that had increased to over a million bushels a year. The Erie Canal became a truly national project and an example to this day of how government can grow the economy without adding government debt. Such projects would become a model for the newly emerging Whig Party and other state corporations such as in Ohio and Pennsylvania.

The idea of a serious canal project to connect upper New York State with Lake Erie began in 1792. Private companies found the financing of it, at a cost of $5 to $7 million, too difficult. By the 1800s, there was growing political support for a canal. The Federalist Party and its opposition, the Democratic-Republican Party, both supported large government investment into projects that would grow commerce. In 1810, an effort by the state of New York to get federal funding failed because President Thomas Jefferson was looking for support for his own canal project on the Potomac River. In 1816, Congress approved federal funds for the canal, but President James Monroe vetoed it, believing the bill to be unconstitutional. New York did have some political visionaries who would make the state the driving force in canal building. It would be Governor DeWitt Clinton who got the canal approved through the state legislature in 1817. Banks bought bonds issued by the state of New York to raise the money. The canal was a toll canal, allowing the original cost to be paid back after 9 years, and all dividends paid were covered in less than 20 years. It was a very successful model that states and the federal government have used since to finance transportation infrastructure. Chief engineer Benjamin Wright would become recognized as the father of civil engineering.

The Erie Canal connected to the port of New York City by beginning at the Hudson River near Troy, New York. The Hudson River flows into New York Bay and past the west side of Manhattan. From Troy, the canal went to Rome, New York, and then through Syracuse and Rochester to Buffalo on Lake Erie. The path was uphill, but engineering was not the problem. There was a labor shortage for such a large project.

Work on the canal began on July 4, 1817. The workers had been enticed to leave Ireland and Wales for $12 a month, free lodging and meals, and even a whiskey allowance. The state was short on native-born laborers to supply the needed thousands

The opening of the Erie Canal in 1825. (Library of Congress)

and so advertised in Europe for laborers. Labor shortages forced wages up to $1 a day by 1825. In general, wages were at least three times higher than in Europe. The work was extremely hard, requiring digging by hand, hauling dirt, removing tree stumps, and cutting trees. Much of the path was marshy, and workers faced contracting malaria. Hundreds of skilled masons from Germany came to help line the canal with stone and clay. Progress slowed in the first year, and political opposition quickly arose. The project picked up the infamous name of "Clinton's Ditch." However, as sections opened, the commerce was amazing and tolls started flowing. Villages became towns, and towns grew into cities as economic growth continued. Laborers became permanent residents to work for the canal system and handling companies. General commerce and population growth for the state soon outpaced the gain from the trade. The economic growth model augured the future of American railroads.

The canal was formally opened on October 25, 1825, with a major celebration at Buffalo, New York. The first canal boats left for New York for another celebration on their arrival on November 2. The celebration was called the "Marriage of the Waters." To symbolize the international trade expected, water from the Ganges of India, the Seine in France, the Amazon in South America, and the Columbia of America's Northwest was poured into New York Harbor. Dignitaries included President John Quincy Adams and former presidents John Adams, Thomas Jefferson, James Madison, and James Monroe. Future president Andrew Jackson was also in the crowd.

The canal created commerce and a population boom; the system of 4,000 canal boats alone employed over 25,000 workers. A trip from New York City to Buffalo took about four days. Buffalo grew from a town of 800 in 1820 to a city of 15,000 in 1830. In 1832, the Ohio and Erie Canal branch connected the Great Lakes to the Mississippi River. The Erie Canal and the branch canals opened up the American breadbasket to European markets. The canal had a second boom when England repealed the Corn Laws in the 1850s, allowing grain to be imported into England. New York Harbor became one of the busiest in the world. It was an example of what the government could do for economic growth. The Whig Party incorporated canal and road building into its national and state platforms. States such as Ohio, Pennsylvania, Virginia, and Indiana expanded the national canal with amazing economic results until the railroads became major competitors in the 1850s.

*See also:* Baltimore & Ohio Railroad; Federal Aid Highway Act of 1956; National Road; Overland Travel and Mail Service; Transcontinental Railroad Completed; Whig Party Evolves

## References

Andrist, Ralph. *The Erie Canal.* New York: Harper & Row, 1964.

Goodrich, Carter. *Canals and American Economic Development.* New York: Columbia University Press, 1961.

Payne, Robert. *The Canal Builders.* New York: Macmillan, 1959.

# Tariff of Abominations (1828)

The Tariff of 1828 would highlight the basic arguments on free trade versus protectionism that continue to this day. The study of this tariff allows a basic understanding of the pragmatic side of both free trade and protectionism. The Tariff of 1828 had many related side effects: the roots of the Whig Party, the seeds of the economic reasons behind the Civil War, and the legal argument for states' rights. Tariffs have been a part of American economic policy since the first secretary of the Treasury, Alexander Hamilton, proposed them. Since the 1790s, the federal government had been funded mainly by tariffs and a small amount of unpopular excise taxes. Prior to 1816, tariffs were aimed at funding the federal government, not protecting domestic industries. The rates of the Tariff of 1789 were around 8 percent of the incoming value.

After the War of 1812 and the years during and prior to the Jefferson Embargo, English manufactured goods had been stockpiled in warehouses. In 1815, the English began to dump cheaply priced goods such as woolen goods and iron products onto the world markets. In addition, Britain had its Corn Laws, which eliminated American grain shipments to Britain. In 1816 and 1824, Congress passed tariffs with the leadership of Henry Clay to protect domestic industries. These tariff rates were about 20 percent of the value of the shipped product. The 1824 tariff took tariffs a step further to increase revenue to pay for federal aid to road and canal building. In 1824, the government was essentially funded by tariffs. However, the tariffs did also have a protective factor in them as well. The tariffs or duties helped protect the hemp, wheat, and liquor industries for the western farmers, the textiles and clothing goods manufacturers of New England, forged iron industries in Pennsylvania and Ohio, whiskey and liquor production in Kentucky and Tennessee, and the glass industries of New Jersey. The South, however, was hurt by the tariffs because it had to pay more for imported and domestic goods and received no benefit. The tariffs hurt Britain, and, in turn, it purchased less southern cotton and tobacco. The political sides were the pro-tariff National Republicans of John Quincy Adams and the anti-tariff Democratic Party of Andrew Jackson.

The 1828 bill was designed to truly be a protective tariff versus a revenue tariff. The rates were up to 45 percent of the product value. One of the strong arguments for a protective tariff centered on the iron industry, so critical to the defense of the nation. The British had, even prior to the Revolution, limited the production of iron in America. The War of 1812 showed how dependent the nation was on England for iron. Only the ingenuity of the Scotch-Irish iron makers of the middle states saved the country in the war. Adam Smith had even made this point and made an exception in *Wealth of Nations* for products needed for national defense.

The 1820s had been a time of recession, bringing demands for more protection of American industries. The middle states particularly wanted more protection on iron, which England continued to dump on the market to maintain their own home employment. The Tariff of 1828, or Tariff of Abominations, as it became known in the South, was a political maneuver gone badly. The congressional debate took place in a presidential election year with Adams running as the candidate of the National Republicans and Jackson representing the Democratic Party. Jackson's supporters in Congress proposed an elaborate scheme to prevent the passage of higher tariffs. The South was clearly against the increased tariffs; the middle states were clearly in favor. New England was also pushing for higher tariffs for its textile factories. The Jacksonians actually proposed a very high tariff rate on products coming into New England. It was so high that it would drive prices up for most New Englanders, while obviously protecting some of their key industries like textiles. The high tariff would even affect part of the textile manufacturers by increasing the price on imported wool. The hope was that more moderate New England representatives would oppose the bill and defeat it.

The Jacksonians and the Democratic Party had badly miscalculated the vote. The majority of the New England votes did go against the tariffs, but enough held with the middle states' votes to pass the high tariffs. Many of the predicted effects of the tariff were felt quickly. Prices on many goods rose as much as 50 percent, and some shortages were actually created. The poor design of the bill put the burden on the middle class, which in those days was the voting public. Costs of necessities such as food and clothing increased. Only the industrial sweet spot of eastern Ohio and western Pennsylvania gained substantially on balance. Another result was the defeat of Adams by Jackson in the presidential election, but the real political impact was just beginning. The anti-tariff forces had figured that, as a last resort, their new president would reduce the tariff, but Jackson did not act. Jackson hoped to play the protectionist in the North and the free trader in the South.

South Carolina was particularly upset with the Tariff of 1828. Jackson's vice-president, John Calhoun, was from South Carolina and the author of the tariff. Behind the scenes, Calhoun opposed the tariff. Jackson did sign a reduced tariff in 1832, but it was not enough to appease states like South Carolina. Calhoun resigned in December 1832. The party and its heads were divided on the importance of action by Jackson to reduce the tariffs. A radical movement started in South Carolina, culminating in 1832 with a state convention being called to act. The convention called for South Carolina to call for nullification of the tariff on the grounds it was unconstitutional and unenforceable. The convention further advocated preventing the federal government from imposing protectionist tariffs. This led to the Nullification Crisis, with Jackson sending naval ships to enforce the tariff. The nation had reached the edge of war when Clay and Calhoun came together in Congress to propose the Compromise Tariff of 1833. This bill gradually reduced tariffs over a 10-year period to the 1816 level of 20 percent, which was considered revenue producing rather than protective. This compromise averted a nullification crisis, but it would be a precursor to the states' rights argument of the Civil War. In addition, the high tariff levels were reinstated in 1842.

Tariffs did have some positive results. By 1835, the government had paid off its debts and ran a surplus, allowing it to invest in internal improvement projects. American industries such as glass, iron, textiles, hemp, tools, and forgings showed significant growth. The Tariff of 1828 and the history of tariffs offer a manual of the consequences (both negative and positive) for business and the economy.

*See also:* Abraham Lincoln Establishes Protectionism; Jefferson Embargo; McKinley Tariff of 1890; Navigation Acts; *Wealth of Nations*; Whig Party Evolves

### References

Dangerfield, George. *Awakening of American Nationalism.* New York: Wineland, 1994.

Remini, Robert. *Andrew Jackson.* San Francisco: Harper Perennial, 1999.

Walters, Raymond. *Albert Gallatin: Jeffersonian Financier and Diplomat.* New York: Macmillan, 1959.

# Baltimore & Ohio Railroad (1828)

The Baltimore & Ohio Railroad was America's first common carrier, but its history predates the steam locomotive. The motivation for the Baltimore & Ohio initially was an effort of the city of Baltimore to counter the Erie Canal, which favored the ports of New York and Philadelphia. A group of Baltimore businessmen first got together in 1827 to discuss ways to save the port of Baltimore. The founders of the railroad, Philip Thomas and George Brown (both officers of the Mechanics' Bank), had been in England two years prior studying the new technology of steam locomotion. Thomas and Brown had additional pressure in that a canal to Baltimore was also being proposed. Also, Pennsylvania had proposed a state canal from the port of Philadelphia to the Ohio River. While the railroads were new and canals were proven technology, the railroad offered speed and lower building and operating costs.

The initial idea was to go from the port of Baltimore to Wheeling, Virginia. The proposal required a charter from Maryland and Virginia (West Virginia did not exist until the Civil War), which they acquired in 1828. Land and right-of-ways were required for the project. The initial company was created with a stock capitalization of $5 million (more than $100 million in today's dollars). The federal and state governments initially showed no interest in funding the new technology, preferring the known technology of road and canal building. The stock offering was extremely successful, with most citizens of Baltimore buying a few shares. Over 20,000 shares were initially in circulation. The legal battles with the Chesapeake & Ohio Canal, which had some federal and state investments in it, continued. Construction began on July 4, 1828, with a ceremony featuring the last remaining signer of the Declaration of Independence—Charles Carroll. On the same day, President John Quincy Adams opened the construction of the Chesapeake & Ohio Canal. The Baltimore & Ohio Railroad was not yet firm on the technology and was experimenting with horse-drawn trains and even sails. Still, the investors seemed confident in the new technology of steam, even though the federal government was convinced it could never compete with a canal. By 1854, the railroad proved highly profitable, making a profit of $2.7 million. In the meantime, canals were past their peak, and most were unprofitable.

The amazing part of the project was that it progressed on the cutting edge of the technology of the day. The railroad was built along the banks of the Patapsco River to Mount Airy, where it encountered a major ridge. The builders were not sure if steam-powered engines could grip the rails enough for uphill traction, so a parallel inclined plane was built to possibly use horses to pull the engines uphill or use the steam-powered winches that had been used to move canal boats up inclines. The first trial runs in 1830 tried both wooden and cast iron rails. The first rails were laid on a base of cut granite and were built to be sturdy. The first steam engine to be tested was the *Tom Thumb*. It was built by Peter Cooper and was the first American-built locomotive. It would be unrecognizable today, since it was a vertical boiler. The *Tom Thumb* could make the upgrade 13-mile trip in 72 minutes, hauling a car of 42 passengers. The railroad actually offered a $4,000 prize for a better engine, which resulted in the horizontal locomotive engine. These types of competitive prizes were a common Victorian business technique to inspire innovation.

The opening of the first 13 miles of track in 1830 proved extremely successful for passenger service. In 1832, the Baltimore & Ohio proved the freight-hauling potential of the railroad. The locomotive *Atlantic* hauled 50 tons of freight 40 miles, using a ton of anthracite coal. The cost of the trip was $16, about half the cost of a horse-drawn equivalent. The cost of the *Atlantic* was $4,500. This trip showed the significantly lower cost of railroads over canals and roads. Stock prices rose as the technology proved out.

By 1852, the Baltimore & Ohio reached the Ohio River. It was an engineering marvel, including the construction of the Thomas Viaduct, the longest in the United States. In 1843, the Baltimore & Ohio approved the federal construction of the country's first telegraph lines on its right-of-ways. Congress provided $30,000 for the 38-mile telegraph line, and the Baltimore & Ohio would have free use of the line. The Baltimore & Ohio would face major competition in the 1850s as the Pennsylvania Railroad linked Philadelphia to Pittsburgh at the head of the Ohio

River. Still, at the start of the Civil War, the Baltimore & Ohio was America's largest railroad with 236 locomotives, 3,451 cars, and 513 miles of rails. The Baltimore & Ohio branched out in the 1860s to connect Pittsburgh, the country's largest inland port, with rivers throughout the nation. After the Civil War in 1871, a bridge was built over the Ohio River at Wheeling, West Virginia, and tracks moved westward.

The growth of railroads was the root of the American Industrial Revolution. The railroads stimulated the iron, steel, and coal industries while forming symbiotic relationships with them. From its start, the Baltimore & Ohio Railroad pioneered the use of iron in its bridges, creating more new industries. For example, the growth of the American steel industry was based on the spread of railroads. Most steel made between 1860 and 1890 was used in railroad rails. The Baltimore & Ohio Railroad would be one of America's first big corporations. Railroad stocks dominated the stock market and were the major component of insurance and bank stock portfolios. Railroads would be at the root of many other financial panics for years to come. The financial health of the railroads was the economic barometer of the United States. Another important development of the Baltimore & Ohio Railroad was its contribution to business organization. In 1847, Benjamin Latrobe reorganized the Baltimore & Ohio. The new organization would be formed according to functions such as road maintenance and repair shops. Along with Edgar Thomson at the Pennsylvania Railroad, Latrobe at the Baltimore & Ohio pioneered decentralized management control and improved information control and cost accounting. The massive expansion of an organization also changed the perspective of state regulatory rights to that of federal regulatory authority with the formation of the Interstate Commerce Commission (1878).

*See also:* Erie Canal; National Road; Panic of 1873; Transcontinental Railroad Completed; Western Union Telegraph Company

### References

Dilts, James. *The Great Road: The Building of Baltimore & Ohio, the Nation's First Railroad.* Stanford, CA: Stanford University Press, 1993.

Pangborn, J. G. *The Golden Age of the Steam Locomotive.* New York: Dover, 2003.

Stover, John. *The History of the Baltimore and Ohio Railroad.* West Lafayette, IN: Purdue University Press, 1987.

# Whig Party Evolves (1834)

The Whig Party was a political party dedicated to the economic development of the United States through modernization, infrastructure, self-sufficiency in manufacturing, and protectionism. Initially, the Whig Party was an economic movement free of any social issues. Its platform was designed by Kentucky congressman Henry Clay and was known as the "American System" in the 1820s. The Whig Party would have four presidents—William Harrison (1841), John Tyler (1841–1845), Zachary Taylor (1849–1850), and Millard Fillmore (1850–1853). The Whig Party's roots went back to Alexander Hamilton's "Report on Manufacturing" in 1794, believing in the need for manufacturing to be at the center of national economic policy. The Whig Party took in old Federalists who believed in federal funds for infrastructure such as canal and roads. The difference is that the Whigs saw tariffs as the way to finance such internal improvements. They argued that tariffs would not bring the resistance and outcry caused by taxes as seen in the Whiskey Rebellion. Of course, many farmers and southerners argued that tariffs were a tax on basic goods via a price increase on imported goods such as woolens, iron products, glass, and clothes. The Whigs countered that the use of domestic production would boost the overall economy. Clay was the founder and guiding light of the Whig Party. The basis of the Whig Party would be Clay's economic system, known as the American System. Some historians have called it "economic nationalism." Clay was able to tie economic nationalism to Manifest Destiny.

Clay was a lawyer from Virginia who moved to Kentucky to launch a career. In 1810, he was elected to the U.S. Congress. Clay was a nationalist, patriot, republican, founder of the Whig Party, and a Federalist. He had been a supporter and follower of Hamilton. In his junior years in the Senate, he advocated a strong national bank and a national road system. Often, Clay favored the good of the nation over that of his own constituents in Kentucky. His oratory, compromising skills, and patriotism brought him quickly to the position of Speaker of the House. Clay not only fashioned the position of Speaker but also formed the powerful standing committees such as the Ways and Means Committee, which would be the pedestal to launch the career of William McKinley years later and would lead to the Republican Party's reign of protectionism from 1860 to 1920. Clay also created a Committee on Manufactures to help stimulate American manufacturing as Hamilton had suggested years earlier. Clay appointed members for these powerful committees and thus centralized legislative power under the position of Speaker. Clay used the power to create a national infrastructure for early industrial America. Clay's vision of an industrial empire took him from Jeffersonian Republicanism to Federalism and then to conservatism and republicanism. Some Federalists, however, were New England-based free traders. Clay's arguments and the rise of American manufacturing won over many Federalists who believed in the destiny of the American republic as a world power. One of the most important New England converts was Daniel Webster. Clay and Webster had grown up in the economic debates between the Jeffersonians and the Federalists over the National Bank. The Whigs also supported the National Bank, which President Andrew Jackson opposed so forcibly.

Their support of the National Bank was rooted in the need for available credit for manufacturing.

Clay pulled together the anti-Jackson segment and built on the support of the textile workers of New England to unite with his middle-states support. Clay toured the textile industry several times in the 1830s to further promote his American System. One of the mills was named after Clay to honor his protective tariffs. Even Clay's enemy Jackson honored the textile industry with a personal tour. Clay was now able to address the hero of free trade and the Democrats' philosophical heart—Adam Smith. Smith's 1776 book, *Wealth of Nations,* had become the banner for free trade. Clay now argued that free trade could reduce prices in the short run but at the expense of capital investment, invention, and automation. Furthermore, Clay saw capitalism as a national philosophy, not an attribute of free trade and internationalism. Still, the farming majority saw it much differently, fearing international reprisals and higher prices for domestic goods if America put tariffs on incoming products.

The counterrevolution of Clay and Webster resulted in an alliance between labor and capital under protectionism, which would be embodied in the formation of the Whig Party and later the Republican Party. Clay believed the laborer to be part of American capitalism. This fundamental premise of an alliance of labor and capital and the strength of that alliance would define the success of the new Whig Party as well as the Republican Party for the next 60 years. Laborers and mill workers also realized their annual pay depended on eliminating long layoffs due to recessions and plant closings more than wage rates or strikes. To counter the 1820s folk hero Andrew Jackson, the Whigs elected their own Scotch-Irish hero, Davy Crockett of Tennessee, to Congress. The Whigs would also attract future leaders such as Abraham Lincoln, James Garfield, and the Scotch-Irish McKinley in the 1850s. This idea of an alliance between labor and capital did not assume two distinct classes but realized that America offered upward mobility not known in Europe; today's laborer could be tomorrow's capitalist.

Henry Clay was U.S. secretary of state under John Quincy Adams as well as a senator and presidential candidate. Clay formed the Whig Party with its platform of the "American System." (Library of Congress)

Upward mobility was the fuel of the capitalistic engine; without it, we would have a feudal system, socialism, and/or an aristocracy established by birth.

Clay's American System tariffs had funded thousands of miles of canals and roads. The American System had expanded the iron, glass, textile, forging, casting, lumber, and meat industries. Tariffs were, of course, central to the Whig Party but were opposed by the farmers in the Democratic Party as well as the union leadership. In the breakup of the Whig Party over slavery, the pro-slavery Whigs formed the Republican Party, running ex-Whig Lincoln as their presidential candidate. The ex-Whigs dominated the early Republican Party, reinforcing the use of protectionism. Since the Whig Party had been based on economic development, major social issues like slavery readily fractured it. The Protestant-based Whigs further promoted the return of profits to society through philanthropy, which became capitalism's response to the socialism of Europe. They expanded colleges and schools on the state level. They argued that a healthy American economy was the medicine for many of the nation's social ills.

To focus solely on the political ramifications of Clay's American System, however, would be to overlook the realization of Clay's (and ultimately McKinley's) dream of an industrial Eden. And it truly was a system where tariffs were focused to help infant industries, and the tariff revenues were used to build roads and canals. In the Northeast, textile mills were growing; in Pennsylvania and Ohio, iron furnaces were being built; and the American nation was moving from an underdeveloped country to an industrialized one in the first decade of the 1800s. The heart of the Whig Party was in the manufacturing districts of New England's textile industry, the iron industry of Ohio and Pennsylvania, and western mining districts in Illinois and Michigan. In Ohio and western Pennsylvania, the Whigs were known as the pig iron aristocracy because of the iron manufacturers' financial support of the party. Even industrial critics such as Charles Dickens were holding the American system of industrialization up as utopian. The manufacturing methods and automation of American industry were rapidly becoming the standard of efficiency for the world. Pioneering American industrialists such as Francis Cabot Lowell started to develop uniquely American textile factories. While the work was still physically demanding, the factories were clean and offered schooling and training. Even old Jeffersonians were proud of the rise of American manufacturing supremacy.

*See also:* Erie Canal; National Road; "Report on Manufacturing"; *Wealth of Nations*; Whiskey Rebellion

## References

Howe, Daniel Walker. *The Political Culture of the American Whigs.* Chicago: University of Chicago Press, 1979.

Poage, George. *Henry Clay and the Whig Party.* Chapel Hill: University of North Carolina Press, 1936.

Remini, Robert. *Henry Clay: Statesman for the Union.* New York: Norton, 1991.

# Panic of 1837

In the United States, recessions are an integral part of the business cycle of expansion and contraction. Their study brings unique perspectives to today's businesspersons. The Panic of 1837 was one of America's first depressions, resulting in high unemployment and extensive bank failures. It had a classic bubble at its start. The Panic of 1837 lasted about five years, although there was a brief upturn in 1839. The bank failures started in the financial center of New York; about 30 percent of America's 850 banks either failed or partially failed. Many construction projects across the nation were shut down because payrolls could not be met. There were food riots in New York, and, for the first time, major soup kitchens were opened in New York City. The causes of the Panic of 1837 are still being debated, but some classic business problems can be identified. In most recessions, the cause is often a confluence of factors, resulting in a perfect storm. In the Panic of 1837, these factors included a land speculation bubble created by the railroads and bank excesses in the printing of money. Other secondary factors included government mismanagement, large state debts for canal and railroad building, and crop failures. These are issues that are commonly seen in the business cycles in the United States.

Like most financial panics, the Panic of 1837 was preceded by a period of expansion and prosperity. Even the government found itself with a surplus of money for expansion. Internal improvement projects made American wages the best in the world. The first problem was the defunding of the National Bank by Andrew Jackson in 1833. Jackson opposed the bank as an aristocratic organization favoring the wealthy. The elimination of the National Bank forced smaller state banks into the financing of business and internal improvements. State banks fueled a boom of land speculation and lending by the overprinting of unsecured currency. These banks made loans without sufficient reserves of gold and silver. In addition, western states such as Michigan had no bank regulations, allowing anyone to open a bank. The term *panic* was related to bank runs due to uninsured depositors rushing to get their money. In the meantime, railroads and canals were creating a land speculation boom, driving prices up. In five years, land prices increased 50 to 75 percent, creating a boom and a bubble. Western farmers joined in the speculation, as land sales rose from 1830 to 1836. Inflation created the classical price increases in commodities. Canal building was also at its peak in Ohio and Pennsylvania. Canal construction went from 23 miles in 1830 to

1,273 miles in 1836. With excess cash, imports flooded in, and paper money went into the hands of foreign countries.

The speculation and inflation worried Jackson in 1836, and he issued *Specie Circular,* with gold and silver to be used to buy land. Jackson hoped this would stop the overexpansion of printed money. Jackson's actions quickly reduced land sales but also created a price decline that left many investors with high amounts of debt. Most banks had far overprinted their paper money, lacking the gold and silver needed. Foreign countries were the first to demand gold and silver for state paper money. Banks began the process of calling in loans, which resulted in a "panic." Bank depositors lost all, with no recourse to the government. State banks mismanaged the debt obligations, which led to a financial crash. Without any Federal Reserve, such panics were unstoppable and left to natural economic forces. President Van Buren refused to get involved. It would cost him the election of 1840 as the Whig William Henry Harrison became president. In addition, on the international scene, the Bank of England also tightened credit in 1837, so there was also an international contraction. At the same time, England took advantage of the lower tariffs of the 1833 compromise to dump iron products. Cheap pig iron and iron products came into the American market, hurting the newly emerging iron producers in Ohio and western Pennsylvania. The Whig Party in these areas was strengthened by the need to protect the infant iron industry.

The Panic of 1837 created five years of tough times, which would help forge the economic policies of the Whig Party. The federal government, dependent on tariffs, suffered from the major reduction of imports as countries refused credit. Imports of manufactured goods actually increased as the recession spread worldwide. This would lead to increased rates in the Tariff of 1842. In New York, warehouses and dry goods dealers were forced into bankruptcy. State governments operated in or near bankruptcy, unable to pay back wages on construction projects. Wages dropped from one dollar a day to a few cents a day. The frontier froze up, as settlers lived off the land. Farmers saw crop prices reach bottom. In the South, hundreds of plantations failed as cotton dropped from 20¢ a pound to 5¢ a pound in 1840.

Government was forced to take some limited action. The national government had little power, and most action lay in the hands of the states. States enacted stay laws and restrictions on forced foreclosures. These are the types of policies we still see today. State legislatures also enacted laws limiting state debt. States like Ohio even tried printing their own money. The Panic of 1837 started the debate nationwide on the gold standard and the use of paper money. During the crisis, former secretary of the Treasury Albert Gallatin brought the banks together at a convention in an effort to resolve the crisis. Gallatin did succeed at bringing the New York banks together in a loose confederation, which helped stabilize the currency. It also strengthened New York's position over Philadelphia as the nation's banking center. The market slowly adjusted money, loans, and mortgages and ended speculation. By 1842, the natural economic contraction ended and growth returned.

On the national level, the popularity of the Whig "American System" grew and would lead to increased tariffs in 1844. These tariffs started to focus on the protection of America's iron, glass, and textile industries, which had been crushed in the Panic of 1837. While limited, the Panic of 1837 highlighted international factors and the interconnectedness of the world economy.

*See also:* Baltimore & Ohio Railroad; Jefferson Embargo; Panic of 1857; Panic of 1873; Panic of 1893; Panic of 1907; Stock Market Crash/Great Depression; Tariff of Abominations; Whig Party Evolves

### References

Kaplan, Edward. *The Bank of the United States and the American Economy.* Westport, CT: Greenwood, 1999.

McGrane, Reginald. *The Panic of 1837: Some Financial Problems of the Jacksonian Era.* New York: Russell & Russell, 1965.

Sharp, James Roger. *The Jacksonians versus the Banks: Politics in the United States after the Panic of 1837.* New York: Columbia University Press, 1970.

Sobel, Robert. *Panic on Wall Street: A History of America's Financial Disasters.* New York: Macmillan, 1968.

# Automated Sewing Machine (1846)

Like most significant events in business, an invention, or series of inventions, acts only as the seed to full commercialization. The market decides the usefulness of an invention, and the workplace determines the speed of implementation. The advent of the automated sewing machine is the perfect example of the process of commercialization of an invention and the evolution of a manufacturing process. The more classless society of America in the 19th century brought on a curious distinction from that of Europe. The lower- and middle-income groups had a propensity to dress well, approaching the dress of the wealthy. Tailors and seamstresses came together to "manufacture" clothing in factories such as the Quincy Hall Clothing Manufactory in Boston and Opdyke Manufacturing in New Orleans. Still, prior to 1850, just as Alexander Hamilton had reported in his 1794 "Report on Manufacturing," about 70 to 80 percent of American clothing was handmade. There was, however, a huge potential market if the price could come down. The automated sewing machine would lead to a revolution in ready-made clothing.

Tailors were considered skilled craftsmen and formed guilds and unions. They were immigrants who were very sensitive to the automation of their crafts. The power loom had created major unemployment in the crafts in the early 1800s in Europe. In England, a group known as the Luddites had burned and destroyed power looms from 1811 to 1813. Similarly, in 1841, French tailors had destroyed a factory of 80 semi-automated sewing machines, fearing job loss. In America there was less pressure, but tailors still resisted automation. The market potential, however, could not hold back creativity in America. The French sewing machine and early American machines of the 1830s showed little promise, but creativity continued, driven by the market for clothing in the United States. One of the first machines was that of Walter Hunt, but he discontinued development fearing that low-wage seamstresses would lose their jobs. Not surprisingly, several inventors appeared on the scene simultaneously in the 1840s.

One of the first successful patents for automated sewing machines was that of Elias Howe in 1846. The Howe machine had many limitations such as a hand crank, limited seam length, and the need to readjust often, but it did serve as inspiration for further development. Isaac Singer was one of those inspired. Singer improved on the Howe machine but faced an army of lawyers defending the Howe patent. A foot pedal drove the Singer machine. Singer proved the better salesman, successfully selling his $2,000 machine to factories. Ultimately, Singer lost a patent infringement case to Howe; Singer had impacted the market and chose to pay royalties to Howe. A number of inventors entered the battle, which became known as the "Sewing Machine War" and would augur the legal battles over inventions in America. At least 10 inventors had received patents on machine improvements, particularly with thread-feeding systems and the type of stitch.

While the sewing machine was reducing clothing costs and allowing for more customization of clothing, the manufacturing companies were bogged down with the patent infringement cases. Various inventors had keys to full automation; for example, Benjamin Wilson's 1849 patent for automated thread feeding was as critical as Howe's and Singer's features. The manufacturers brokered a deal between the inventors known as the Sewing Machine Combination in 1856. The various patent owners pooled all their features for the sewing machine into a single fee. The patent owners would also have the franchising rights for manufacturers. Howe, whose machine had never been a commercial success, became the highest paid of the inventors, receiving $5 per machine sold. The other inventors shared a royalty of another $10 per machine. The combination agreement remained in effect until 1877. Years later, General Electric and Westinghouse Electric would use this patent-pooling business model to end the "war of the currents." Today, such arrangements would not meet the test of our antitrust laws.

The Singer sewing machine not only revolutionized the clothing industry but also automated the shoe industry by 1860. The Civil War and Abraham Lincoln's domestic manufacturing and tariff policies created the ready-made clothing market. The government submitted a type of standard sizes for uniform manufacturers.

The first functional lockstitch sewing machine, invented by Elias Howe. (Hulton Archive/Getty Images)

The manufacturers used this statistical normal distribution of human sizes to develop the science of sizing—that is, that certain measurements occurred with predictable repeatability. The combination of automation and market made clothing America's major business in 1870. The clothing market doubled from 1860 to 1870 and reached a billion dollars by 1890. Similarly, the shoe market grew. The sole-sewing machine in 1858 revolutionized shoe manufacture. Ready-made, standardized shoes took over the market by 1890. Now, a customer knowing his or her size could shop at the newly emerging department stores of the 1890s. Sewing machine sales from 1860 became an international market, which the United States dominated.

Singer proved the best marketer, and by 1865, he controlled 70 percent of the market. In 1877, Singer went on to add the continuous-stitch feature and formed the Singer Sewing Machine Company. Singer electrified his machine first in 1889 to further increase productivity. The time to make a simple dress dropped from 10 hours for handmade to under 1 hour with machines in 1890. The skill level dropped from that of a craftsman tailor to that of an immigrant laborer. Automated sewing led to labor specialization and subassembly operations. The automation further led to the "sweating" system (task system) where subcontractors opened small shops in the poor districts of New York and Chicago. These shops used cheap immigrant women workers. The manufacturers cut the cloth, marked the parts, and enclosed instructions for the subcontractors, allowing for a form of standardized mass production. Individual families even got into the bidding process, working out of their homes. The bidding among subcontractors drove costs and prices down. The system of subassembly and bidding is an early example of supply chain management. Abuses would lead to a general strike in 1910 of 40,000-plus immigrant garment workers. The strike led to the formation of the United Garment Workers and the Amalgamated Clothing Workers of America.

*See also:* Patent and Copyright Statutes; Revolution, Famine, and Immigration; War of the Currents; Westinghouse Air Brake

### References

Boorstin, Daniel. *The Americans: The Democratic Experience.* New York: Vintage Books, 1974.

Montgomery, David. *The Fall of the House of Labor.* Cambridge: Cambridge University Press, 1987.

Schlereth, Thomas. *Victorian America: Transformations in Everyday Life.* New York: Harper Perennial, 1991.

# Revolution, Famine, and Immigration (1848)

The peak immigration year 1848 is a major example of events outside the country having a lasting impact on American business. The year 1848 was key in the first wave of European immigration to America resulting from economic and political crises across Europe. The first great wave of immigration came in the period from 1840 to 1860. This period saw millions of immigrants come to America. The population went from 17 million in 1840 to 31 million in 1860. Immigrants arrived at the rate of 300,000 a year. Immigration was driven by crop failures and political turmoil throughout Europe. While the Irish and Germans dominated the period, many came from the world over. The Germans commonly came to the port of New York and moved west through the Erie Canal. Buffalo, in particular, developed a large German population as well as the Great Lakes region. The Irish poured into their base in Boston as well as in New York.

The 1848 immigrants were often known as "forty-eighters." This influx of Western Europeans was driven by revolution, famine, religious persecution, and the industrialization of Europe. Germany was at the heart of this first big wave of immigration. Germans lived in a collection of German states such as Bavaria, Württemberg, and the largest, Prussia. In addition, Austria had a large population of German-speaking people. Turmoil was almost a daily standard in these countries. The Catholic-Protestant divide became embroiled in politics, and revolutions spread across the European continent. Political struggle led to economic crisis. Industrialization in the German states slowed as Germany tried to stop the spread of automation and the decline of craft guilds. In 1847, Prussia had only 2,268 mechanical cotton looms and 116,832 handlooms, while England used predominantly mechanical looms. The industrialization of the British textile industry was bringing change throughout Europe. Cheaper automated cotton products from Britain further suppressed the German economy and accelerated the decline of craft guilds.

In addition, socialism was on the rise, and a more radical approach was evolving in Germany. Then, in the late 1840s, revolutionary ideas banned craft guilds. In the 1840s, many German craftsmen had gone to France to learn their trades, but France followed the German approach to free trade in the late 1840s, and German manufacturing all but disappeared. German craftsmen looked next to the United States. German locksmiths, tailors, shoemakers, cigar makers, brewers, bakers, brick makers, and others headed for America. This influx brought needed skills, but it also brought trade unionism and socialism.

The Germans brought new techniques for farm productivity as well. The Germans moved into heavily wooded areas in states like Wisconsin. They cleared the land of trees, stumps, and Ice Age rocks. It was common in New England not to remove the stumps, which reduced productivity and land usage. The immigrant Germans introduced the use of crop rotation and fertilizer. They created a more balanced type of small farming, adding dairy production and animal husbandry. They improved plowing methods, which would birth the farm equipment industry in the Midwest. They added wine making and beer making whenever possible. They stressed self-sufficiency of the small farmer. A German farm had crops of corn, wheat, oats, pumpkins, and potatoes. The Germans brought hearty winter strands of these crops that grew well in the Great Lakes region. There was always a special vegetable garden. Where possible, they added cotton to the mix for home use. The animal mix included chickens, cattle, sheep, hogs, and bees. German farmers talked of the homestead rather than the farm. They had a long-term outlook. It was a type of family "plantation" that required large families to get the work done.

The Germans improved and developed a highly productive agriculture in the Midwest that drew a new industry to towns like Chicago. A Scotch-Irish Virginian, Cyrus McCormick, moved his farm implement shop to Chicago in 1847. Eastern small farmers were slow to buy $100 reapers because tree stumps limited the use of such equipment. German farmers around Chicago embraced the new technology. McCormick's bigger problem with the thrifty German farmers was to persuade them to pay on credit, so that he could increase his sales. The Germans consistently resisted any type of bank borrowing. Even German capitalists avoided bank borrowing. In 1849, McCormick sold 1,500 reapers. His exhibit at the Great Exhibition of 1851 created a huge international market, and Chicago's railroad network allowed that to prosper. McCormick and others like John Deere turned their blacksmith shops into huge factories. German farmers created a huge demand for Deere's steel plows and new farm technology.

The countries of Scotland and Ireland lacked the automation of England, forcing more immigration of Scotch and Irish weavers to America. The crop failures of the 1840s across Europe created famine and disease. Tens of thousands of Europeans contracted typhus. There was a failed revolution that uprooted the Germans. The political upheaval, disease, lack of jobs, and religious oppression resulted in a wave of immigration to America. The turmoil would also give rise to the ideas of Karl Marx. The immigrant families of the 1840s included people like H. J. Heinz, George Westinghouse, Henry Ford, and Andrew Carnegie.

The 1840s were even worse for Ireland than continental Europe. The Catholic population of Ireland had endured the worst type of religious oppression. They were hardly better off than American slaves. No Catholic could own a gun, keep a sword, hold office, vote, or even join the army. They paid rent on their own land. The Catholics had also been stripped of their native language (Gaelic) just as American slaves had been. Their cherished rosary was outlawed in public, even for prisoners. Their diet of potatoes, a little buttermilk, and maybe a small piece of pork every couple of months was far below that of American slaves. The final blow came in 1845, when ironically, the potato rot emanated from America. Famine left most without the meager diet they had survived on for decades. Typhus and starvation spread quickly. America was the only choice left for many. In 1847, Irish roads were literally clogged with immigrants going to the sailing ports. The impact on American ports was just as dramatic. In Boston the Irish accounted for only 2 percent of the population in 1845, but 10 years later it was 25 percent. Some historians believe there were as many as 300 Irish disembarking every day from 1845 to 1851.

The ocean crossing for the 1840s Irish was much worse than the slave passages. Slave ships had self-economic reasons to transport slaves alive, while the Irish ships did not. The death rate was as high as 35 percent. Many times whole ships, often known as "coffin" ships, were lost to typhus or icebergs. Most came as "steerage" and were restricted to the ship's cargo bays. There were, of course, notable survivors such as Henry Ford's father and John F. Kennedy's great-grandfather. The size and problems of the Irish immigration led to "Passenger Acts" by both the American and British governments. America allowed only two people per five tons, while the British allowed three people per five tons on cargo ships. On passenger ships, America allowed 200 people while the British allowed 300.

These acts were not enforced, and ships commonly had loads close to those of American slave ships. America was badly in need of workers for canal, road, and railroad building. Many came at the bequest of American canal, railroad, and coal companies who paid for the passage of the entire family. To mute native opposition in the United States, tens of thousands went to the ports of Quebec first and later immigrated to the United States. French-speaking Quebec offered little to Irish immigrants. It is possible that most of Boston's Irish population actually came through Quebec.

Finally, a smaller but important group of immigrants of the late 1840s were the Chinese. While they numbered only 200,000, they supplied the necessary labor for the transcontinental railroad. The so-called forty-eighters were the core of America's industrial future, building the necessary infrastructure for it.

*See also:* Baltimore & Ohio Railroad; Clipper Ships; Great Exhibition of 1851; Tariff of Abominations; Transcontinental Railroad Completed; *Wealth of Nations*

### References

Boorstin, Daniel. *The Americans: The Democratic Experience.* New York: Vintage Books, 1973.

Freeman, Joanne. *Affairs of Honor: National Politics in the New Republic.* New Haven, CT: Yale University Press, 2001.

Kennedy, John F. *A Nation of Immigrants.* New York: Harper & Row, 1964.

Wittke, Carl. *We Who Built America.* New York: Prentice-Hall, 1945.

# Clipper Ships (1849)

The clipper ships represented a new way to segment the international transportation industry. The business model used is analogous to today's expedited trucking services as well as services such as Federal Express. Clipper ships specialized in smaller, highly profitable cargo for long distances at high speeds. Cargoes included tea from China, wool from Australia, ice from New England, and passengers wanting fast travel to California. The California gold rush stimulated the growth of the clippers with the need to move products and hopeful miners from the East Coast to California via Cape Horn. Tea was the initial cargo because it needed fast delivery to maintain its taste. The tea trade broke open with the repeal of the British Navigation Acts in 1849, allowing non-British ships to participate in the tea trade. The clippers were an American invention, capitalizing on the element of speed in delivery of cargo. American clippers quickly dominated the tea market after the British export and import restrictions were dropped. Americans had been forced to develop the early technology of fast ships to break the blockades of the 1770s and 1810s by the British.

An early form of these blockade breakers was known as the Baltimore clipper and became popular in the 1830s to run from naval vessels. These were the favorite of illegal traders, opium traders, privateers, and slavers. Still, these early clippers carried little cargo. New England shipyards started to improve on the design. They trimmed the hull to cut the waves and applied a three-mast system with square sails. These clippers had sleek, narrow hulls with long lines. They could achieve 250 to 400 miles a day versus the 150 miles of the traditional cargo ship of the period. They could average 16 to 18 nautical miles per hour. The ships were 150 to 250 feet long and displaced 800 to 2,500 tons. Later clippers increased displacements to as high as 5,000 tons. Building costs approached $300,000 for these larger displacements. A small clipper might cost $80,000. Crews averaged between 25 and 50 sailors. The ships were high maintenance but very profitable. Tea clippers, in particular, proved highly profitable.

New Englanders, with a long history of trade and shipbuilding, embraced the clipper ship design. Ship designer and New Englander Donald McKay built a number of high-tonnage and fast models. Trading firms like A. A. Low & Brothers found ways to optimize trade and shipments. The Low brothers teamed up with ice king Fredrick Tudor to ship ice to China and return with tea and exotic products. Tudor harvested ice from New England ponds, using cheap Irish labor. He used hay, rice, and bark to insulate the ice for shipment to China. In 1843, the first ice shipment reached Hong Kong after 111 days. The clipper returned with tea, spices, mocha, and gum arabic. The tea trade led to the formation of the Great Atlantic and Pacific Tea Company (A&P), which imported large amounts of tea and cut the retail price from $1.00 per pound to $0.30 a pound. The A&P Company added other clipper ship products of coffee and spices at low prices to its store in New York City. The notion of low-priced products through bulk purchases led to the chain store concept across the nation in the 1850s.

Similarly, the Gold Rush of the late 1840s created a demand for hopeful miners and supplies alike to go from the East Coast to San Francisco. The voyage would take 90 days around Cape Horn in a clipper ship, about half the time as for a normal vessel. A $5 barrel of flour from the East Coast could bring $50 in California. Profits were so high that the time to see a return on investment in building a clipper was less than one year. Brandy, whiskey, and other agricultural products then went to China from San Francisco. Spices, coffee, and tea were welcome products for the mining camps. Clippers also brought Chinese laborers from China to San Francisco. Clippers found a good business in moving British to Australia and New Zealand and returning with much-needed lumber and wool. Clippers also merged cultures, with Japanese and Chinese art pieces becoming very popular with Victorians. Exotic Chinese products included porcelains, fans, ornate ivory art pieces,

Currier and Ives print of the clipper ship *Great Republic.* (Library of Congress)

and lacquer ware. Clippers also enhanced international mail and communication. England, in particular, benefited from the improved speed of diplomatic packets with India, Hong Kong, and their other colonies.

Another group of clippers specialized in rich travelers to augment the tea and spice trade. Clippers were built with expensive lodgings and dinner rooms. Chickens were kept on the poop deck to supply fresh eggs for the passengers. Dances and special meals were arranged for these first-class passengers. Some owners started to advertise exotic voyages to the Orient. Other clippers specialized in the Australian wool trade as well as the jute and sugar trade of the Philippines. One-way travel for the 16,000-mile trip from the East Coast to San Francisco was not cheap at $300 (about $8,000 today).

The clipper ship trade created a boom during the 1850s for East Coast shipbuilding. In 1855, over 2,000 American ships were produced. The United States not only supplied national demand but became the world's supplier of clipper ships. In 1855, the market for exported ships was over $5 million. Being short on wood and not seeing the market, England was late getting into the clipper-building business, and England soon became dependent on North American shipbuilding. The wood requirements for an average clipper were over 1,000,000 board feet of pine and 25,000 cubic feet of oak. As much as 200 tons of iron was also needed. Shipbuilding itself created a boom in the copper-mining industry. Copper and its alloy brass were used extensively in the manufacture of ships. A typical American clipper required 50 to 60 tons of copper for its manufacture. Copper working and brass foundries became a major industry in New England. New England capital promoted the copper-mining industry of upper Michigan.

The American clipper ship era lasted from 1845 to 1860, but the British clipper ship era went into the 1870s. The opening of the Suez Canal in 1869 ended the era of tea clippers, which rounded the Cape of Good Hope. The Suez Canal allowed for larger cargo ships with an equivalent sailing time from China. The wool trade of Australia remained profitable for clippers into the 1880s, as the need for coal refueling limited steamers from reaching Australian ports. Finally, large steamships made clippers unprofitable.

*See also:* Navigation Acts; Revolution, Famine, and Immigration; Transcontinental Railroad Completed; *Wealth of Nations*; Western Union Telegraph Company

### References

Laing, Alexander. *The Clipper Ships and Their Makers.* New York: G. P. Putman's Sons, 1966.

Lubbock, Basil. *The China Clippers.* Glasgow, UK: Brown, Son & Ferguson, 1946.

Whipple, A. B. *The Clipper Ships.* Alexander, VA: Time-Life Books, 1980.

# Western Union Telegraph Company (1851)

The telegraph had been evolving since the 1830s. It was the confluence of many electromagnetic experiments and inventions. In England, William Cooke and Charles Wheatstone constructed a one-mile telegraph line in 1837. The first practical telegraph was demonstrated at the Great Exhibition of 1851 in London. Its earliest use was to carry news of events. About the same time Samuel Morse in America was developing an improved telegraph using the new electromagnets of Joseph Henry. Morse added battery relays to greatly increase the distance of the Cooke and Wheatstone system. Just as important was Morse's addition of a binary code using dots and dashes to spell out words. The dots and dashes were audio signals using a sound key to produce a "click." By 1840, Morse's system had a 10-mile range. Congress had originally funded the first telegraph line between Baltimore and Washington, D.C., in 1843 in hopes of combining it into the postal system. Congress appropriated $30,000 for the construction of a 38-mile line along the Baltimore & Ohio Railroad. Congress, however, refused to establish further funding for the telegraph postal service and purchase of the patent rights from Morse. This opened the technology to the private sector. Morse formed the Magnetic

Telegraph Company of 1845. Morse built a highly profitable line connecting Washington, D.C., and New York with the help of Ezra Cornell. Cornell (founder of Cornell University) was the inventor of the trench digger. The Magnetic Telegraph Company had started to use underground cable but soon switched to poles to save money and speed up construction. Even though underground cable failed, Cornell proved the better manager and took over the company.

Additional private companies extended lines to Pittsburgh, Cincinnati, and Louisville. The Morse patents licensed most of the small companies. The newspapers were the first to make the telegraph profitable and caused its rapid expansion. In 1847, the battles of the Mexican-American War were transmitted to waiting reporters across the nation. President James K. Polk's State of the Nation address was carried directly via telegraph in 1848. In Europe, Reuters News used carrier pigeons to carry financial messages between telegraph lines and expand across Europe. In America, the parent company of Western Union would be the New York & Mississippi Printing Telegraph Company, created in 1851. The name comes from the fact that the first telegraphs printed the Morse code on paper, but the audio system was quickly accepted. A good operator could send 8 to 10 words a minute. The company started to buy out and merge with smaller companies with a vision of creating a fully integrated national service.

The telegraph spread by competing companies setting up their own lines. Two major East Coast companies were the New York & Mississippi Printing Telegraph Company of Hiram Sibley and the New York & Western Union Telegraph Company of Cornell. Sibley decided that it was cheaper to buy up smaller companies than to build new lines. This type of business model would be repeated by railroads, telephone companies, and, more recently, cell phone companies. Sibley also decided to standardize all service on the use of the Morse code. The spread of the telegraph augured the business model of the telephone and cell phone markets. The larger companies soon realized the advantages of merging to build even larger markets and gain economies of scale and effort. To that end the East Coast competitors merged in 1855 to form the Western Union Telegraph Company. The next phase of innovation was, as for all inventions, cost reduction. The major cost of the telegraph was in the iron wire connections on miles of poles, which inspired cost-saving inventions. J. B. Stearns invented a relay sensing system that allowed two messages, one in each direction, over a single wire in 1858.

As railroads expanded, the use of the telegraph avoided railroad crashes and facilitated switching on the then one-way tracks. The railroad right-of-ways also provided land for the spread of the telegraph. Business created demand for the telegraph as well. Businessmen could now be connected to the markets in New York and their operations in other cities. Bankers were also early adopters of the telegraphs. Initially, telegraph stations were at rail stations in major cities. Once the operator decoded a message, boys then ran the messages to business offices. Many famous businessmen and inventors, such as Andrew Carnegie and Thomas Edison, started as telegraph operators and messengers. The Civil War created even more demand for the telegraph. President Abraham Lincoln used it to send his 1860 call for troops to governors. During the war, Lincoln was like a teenager with a cell phone, hanging out at the White House telegraph station for news of the war. Union generals quickly adopted the telegraph as a means of communication. During the Civil War, an estimated 6 million messages were sent using 1,500 telegraph operators. The first transcontinental telegraph system was established in 1861 by connecting smaller services across the West to a line through Alaska to Moscow. The transcontinental line was sponsored and funded by the U.S. Congress because no company had the necessary funds for such a large project. Western Union did win the bid to build it. By the end of the war, there were over 200,000 miles of telegraph in operation.

In 1866, Western Union completed the first stock ticker service, which proved to be a highly profitable business. The first successful transatlantic telegraph cable was completed on July 27, 1866. In 1871, Western Union continued its horizontal integration with new businesses with a money transfer service. Now banks could "wire" funds across the country rapidly. In 1884, Western Union became one of the 11 original American companies to be tracked in the Dow Jones stock average. Eventually, Western Union absorbed over 500 companies to become a major corporate giant by 1890. In the 1870s, Western Union tried to defend itself against the telephone by entering the business, hoping to utilize its wired infrastructure. Alexander Bell's patent challenges prevented Western Union from entering the telephone business, however. As the telephone took over, Western Union focused on their money transfer business. Western Union was considered one of the first industrialized monopolies and was able to merge into the telephone business, which was also dependent on electrical wires. In 1908, Western Union was briefly absorbed into the American Telephone and Telegraph Company (AT&T). The government would use antitrust laws to force the two to separate.

*See also:* Baltimore & Ohio Railroad; Clipper Ships; First Commercial Telephone; Overland Travel and Mail Service; Transatlantic Cable

## References

Kranzberg, Malven, and Carroll Pursell Jr. *Technology in Western Civilization.* New York: Oxford University Press, 1967.

Thompson, Robert Luther. *Technology and Society.* New York: Arno, 1972.

Winston, Brian. *The Telegraph in Media Technology and Society, A History: From the Telegraph to Internet.* London: Routledge, 1998.

# Great Exhibition of 1851

At the famous Great Exhibition of 1851 in London, America shocked the world with its machines, technology, and tools. America was now a manufacturing power on par with England. After the Great Exhibition, the "American manufacturing system" became hailed throughout the world. The husband of Queen Victoria, Prince Albert, had planned the Great Exhibition of 1851 as a world's fair for years. It was to be a celebration of England and its technology. The theme was "the great exhibition of all the works of industry of the world." It is also known as the "Crystal Exhibition." A glass-and-iron palace was to be the centerpiece of the fair as an example of what industry could do. This "Glass Palace" would be 772,784 square feet, or about six times the size of St. Paul's Cathedral. The palace used 3,500 tons of cast iron, 500 tons of wrought iron, and 900,000 square feet of glass.

The Great Exhibition was a true triumph of technology and science. The Great Exhibition was part future, part museum, part science fair, part Olympics, and part amusement park. Exhibits included submarines, the McCormick reaper, graphite yellow pencils, sulfur matches, Goodyear rubber balloons, the Colt revolver, the Singer sewing machine, Krupp crucible steel, Eli Whitney's demonstration of interchangeable parts, and the first reconstructed dinosaur. Just as important were the rows of machines and tools from all over the world. The surprise was the huge number of American contributors.

The Great Exhibition chronicled the dramatic rise of American technology. America took gold medals in virtually all the high-technology areas, the American surge that Europe had overlooked and ignored. Prince Albert was so shocked that he formed a committee to detail how America had surged ahead of industrial Britain. The committee traveled to America to observe firsthand the American manufacturing system. Their report is informative for today's managers as well. The committee outlined America's success as rooted in (1) the use of logic to exploit abundance, (2) a high literacy rate, (3) few barriers to organizing business, (4) American workers' lack of resistance to innovation, and (5) a highly competitive nature. Furthermore, the committee outlined the new approach of American manufacturing that centered on interchangeable parts and factory organization. These same attributes might be cited with regard to China's rise today.

These European observers were amazed to see that what had been labeled "backward" or "underdeveloped" was revolutionary. The American system of manufacturing had broken with the ideas of Europe. Americans had broken from the guild thinking of Europe, which grouped skills by crafts and trades. The American system was a general system that could be applied to making many different things. Its secret was in organization rather than specific skills. Work was broken into operations that the unskilled could perform. This idea, of course, had European roots in

Adam Smith's idea of job specialization in his *Wealth of Nations.* Americans were forced to make many things without the aid of guilds and craftsmen. Manufacturers had to be flexible as well as workers. New England farmers were jacks-of-all-trades. Farm youth often were skilled in carpentry, blacksmithing, masonry, mechanics, and woodworking. The manufacture of smaller interchangeable parts reduced the skill level even more. The power of the system was not in the processes but in the organization. Worker flexibility was greater in America because of a high literary rate and a lack of labor organizations such as guilds.

Standardized and interchangeable parts were also at the heart of the American manufacturing system. Whitney had used tempered steel patterns to make the same part over and over. The root of the idea was French, but guilds had prevented its full application. Whitney, however, honed the idea to make muskets with interchangeable parts. Prior to that, gunsmiths had made muskets individually. When a single part broke in the field, a gunsmith was required to fit a unique piece. With Whitney's system, not only could lower-skilled workers make parts, but standardized parts also made field repair easily. Whitney had demonstrated the procedure to Thomas Jefferson in 1812. By the 1820s, Whitney had perfected the steel pattern and gauge system, and in 1842, the U.S. standard-issue musket was being mass-produced. These standardized production methods quickly spread throughout the Connecticut Valley of New England. Other standardized-parts machines at the Great Exhibition included Singer's sewing machine, Samuel Colt's revolver, and Cyrus McCormick's reaper. Manufacturing fits were not always perfect due to process variation, but "fitting" departments used standardized inspection gauges to improve the fits further.

The American textile industry started to integrate operations in the 1830s around the American system of manufacturing. Departments were built around various operations such as spinning, weaving, finishing, and ending activities. Management was based on functional departments versus the master craftsman system of Europe. Managers were not technical experts but leaders and supervisors. The idea of a manager was uniquely American and represented a major break from crafts-apprentice system of manufacture. It allowed Americans to bring in women and children in labor-short areas.

The lack of guilds had also freed the American worker and manufacturer from resisting automation. In fact, Americans were often short on labor and so embraced labor-saving automation. Europe had met automation with violence and riots. Anti-automation groups that burnt factories formed, like the Luddites. Another issue was that the American machine industry was built by British mechanics who had left England for more opportunity in America. Prince Albert's committee suggested a radical change in British gun manufacture, which was limited by British crafts production. Not only were the British guns of lower quality, but the gunsmiths could not keep up with the demand using the crafts system. Prince Albert forced the American manufacturing system on England. Through military contracts, England encouraged the building of a Colt factory in 1853.

Another factor noted by Prince Albert was the invention and creativity of Americans. Americans had few barriers to inventing and reaping the financial rewards. Many of the American machinists had fled Europe to make their fortunes in America. American industry fed on its success. The shipbuilding industry created a copper industry; the textile industry created a machine industry; and the machine industry created a steel industry. Fortunes were made. Americans such as George Westinghouse and Thomas Edison dreamed of being inventors in generic terms. Invention was the way to fortunes.

While positive at the time, one finding of the committee would not be cherished today. Americans exploited abundance. They tended to be wasteful in their pursuit of production. They dealt with shortage only when the market forced them to, which was not often. Americans tended to do things in a bigger way for competitive reasons. They utilized all energy sources, often recklessly. The Great Exhibition of 1851 would inspire two American world's fairs in 1876 and 1893.

*See also:* Automated Sewing Machine; Centennial Exposition; Chicago World's Fair; First Steamboat to New Orleans; Patent and Copyright Statutes; *Wealth of Nations*

**References**

Boorstin, Daniel. *The Americans: The National Experience.* New York: Vintage, 1965.

Morris, Charles R. *The Tycoons: How Andrew Carnegie, John D. Rockefeller, Jay Gould, and J. P. Morgan Invented the American Super Economy.* New York: Henry Holt, 2005.

Skrabec, Quentin. *The Metallurgic Age.* Jefferson, NC: McFarland, 2006.

Wren, Daniel A. *The History of Management Thought.* New York: Wiley, 2005.

# Transatlantic Cable (1857)

The need for rapid transatlantic communications had been demonstrated vividly to Americans in 1815. The Battle of New Orleans, while decisive, was fought two weeks after the peace treaty had been signed. Messages from London to Washington took over three weeks. Businesspeople and bankers wanted faster communication as well. In the 1850s, both sides of the Atlantic had made tremendous progress in implementing the telegraph. The success of the telegraph commercially suggested that private funding could be found. This instantaneous electrical wire communication was opening new worlds to all, but transatlantic communication required a wire connection under the ocean, which required the best technology possible for the time. Samuel Morse had used submarine cables in New York Harbor in 1842.

In 1850, John Brett engineered a telegraph cable under the English Channel. The distance for a transatlantic cable would be 1,686 nautical miles, however.

Such a connection was a monumental engineering problem and no less a major business problem in 1857. The cable would require financing, international cooperation, new processes, industrial innovation, and new materials. But like the Internet today, it would lead to more growth of American business and industry. The first hurdle was to find financing for the vision. Both the United States and England supplied naval ships to make soundings on the course between Newfoundland and Ireland. Government, however, was hesitant to supply full funding. Private interest was great enough to allow for private financing. The joint international company would be one of the first with large investments on both sides of the Atlantic.

The vision would be that of Cyrus West Field. Field was a seasoned businessman, having made a fortune in the paper business. Field started to look for investors in both England and America. In America, Field proved a great salesman, forming the "cable cabinet" of wealthy New Yorkers who pledged $1 million. Field partnered with British businessman Charles Bright and cable engineer John Brett. They formed a company known as the Transatlantic Telegraph Company with capital of $1.4 million. Field alone owned a quarter of the company. He was a businessman, not an engineer; he therefore called in experts such as Samuel Morse for consultation. Bright was named chief engineer. Telegraph wire at the time was iron, but copper wire was suggested because of its better electrical conductivity. The cable consisted of seven copper wires insulated in the newly found material of gutta-percha (an early type of rubber) and then sheathed in a heavy iron wire casing. The cable weighed about 2,100 pounds per nautical mile. The American and English government supplied naval ships to lay the cable. Each government did supply some financial aid to the project as well.

Throughout 1857, the project struggled with cable breaks in the early laying of the cable. Finally, the British ship (*Agamemnon*) and the American ship (*Niagara*) succeeded in connecting the cables in 1858. The very first message of Queen Victoria to President James Buchanan, consisting of 99 words, took over 16 hours. The connection was short-lived as deterioration of the cable caused it to fail after a month of operation. The Transatlantic Telegraph Company failed shortly after that, and the Civil War disrupted progress in a new venture. Field, however, was able to raise capital to launch a new company in 1864. This time, most of the capital came from England with railroad baron Thomas Brassey and shipping magnate Daniel Gooch being major investors. The interest in England remained high because of the extensive British Empire separated by oceans. The new company was capitalized with over $2.5 million in funds. The focus was on an improved cable. Pure copper and added layers of insulation improved the cable, but the weight was 4,000 pounds per nautical mile. The world's largest ship, the *Great Eastern*, contracted to lay the new cable. The new project had several setbacks as well, but on

The American steamship *Niagara* lays cable in 1857. (Corbis)

July 27, 1866, the contact connecting the continents was made at Newfoundland. The transatlantic cable, using the telegraph system in place, allowed the mayor of Vancouver, Canada, to send a message to the mayor of London (8,000 miles) by the end of 1866.

The cable was hailed as a great success, but it had many limitations. It took about two minutes to transmit a single letter, or 0.1 words per minute. Still, this was 50 times faster than the first connection of 1858. Innovation quickly followed as the potential for financial reward could better be seen. The reception was extremely poor, but Lord Kelvin, a stockholder in the company, designed the optical galvanometer to allow better operation with weak currents. Reserve currents allowed for a dot and a dash of Morse code. Electrical improvements took the rate to 8 words a minute by 1859. The cost of a few lines in a letter (cablegram) was $100 (about $2,100 today) at a time when a laborer earned about $0.70 a day. The application of sending multiple messages at a time using the duplex (1872) and Edison's quadruplex message system (1874) brought the cost down to $46.80 per 10 words. The cable helped expand big business in the last 25 years of the 19th century. The major beneficiaries were big city newspapers, who were able to overpower their smaller competitors by having correspondents around the world. The cost could be high. Horace Greeley paid $5,000 for a report on the Franco-Prussian War in 1870. The high cost of the telegraph favored the larger papers, which could now supply full international news. The industrial titan Andrew Carnegie, a former telegraph operator and message boy, used the telegraph to manage Carnegie Steel while globetrotting. Carnegie was one of the first to use the telegraph for social networking. For banks, large sums of money could now be quickly transferred internationally. The interlocking of international banks helped stabilize some of the effects of financial panics, but the quick transfer of news also helped spread panic faster, as could be seen in the Panics of 1857 and 1873.

In 1871, India, China, and Australia were connected by cable. The cable proved profitable, and within 20 years, there were 107,000 miles of submarine cable around the world. The cable reached New Zealand in 1902, fully circumnavigating the world. By 1920, submarine cables were carrying 40,000 cablegrams a day. The cable remained the only method of carrying large amounts of communications until satellite communications challenged it in the early 1960s.

*See also:* Baltimore & Ohio Railroad; Overland Travel and Mail Service; Panic of 1873; Telstar Communications Satellites; Transcontinental Railroad Completed; Western Union Telegraph Company

### References

Bray, John. *The Communications Miracle—The Telecommunications Pioneers.* New York: Plenum, 1995.

Kaempffert, Waldemar. *Modern Wonder Workers.* New York: Blue Ribbon Books, 1924.

Standage, Tom. *The Victorian Internet.* New York: Walker, 1998.

# Panic of 1857

The study of panics reveals striking similarities that exist to this day. The Panic of 1857 is no different, having many characteristics of those of today. The Panic of 1857 was preceded by one of the great business expansions during the period of 1850 to 1857. Railroad track mileage went from 9,021 to 22,076 miles, gold production increased 30 percent, and cotton production also doubled. With the repeal of the Corn Laws and the Crimean War in Europe, western grain producers became a major supplier to Europe. Wheat prices reached $2.19 a bushel, leading the inflationary trend in commodities. The railroads were the biggest beneficiaries of the movement of grain to Europe. American ports also boomed with grain shipments. The railroads, however, overexpanded, fueled by an investment bubble in railroad stock prices. These basic economic trends created a boom market in mining, iron production, farm machinery, and transportation to the West. In 1857, President

James Buchanan noted in his inaugural address, "No nation has ever before been embarrassed from too large a surplus in the Treasury." The prosperity had brought inflation. Commodity markets reflected a bubble. In the booming stock market, a bubble was building in railroad stocks. There was also a great deal of social unrest with the large influx of immigrants.

One of the big problems was that speculation in railroad stocks and land had created a bubble. The rapid price increase was followed by more corruption and land schemes. Railroads used the stock and bond floats to raise excess money. The railroads had overexpanded and were overcapitalized and underutilized. The bubble of 1857 was essentially no different from those of today. Grain shipments to Europe in the early 1850s caused the railroads to further overexpand. Then, in 1856–1857, Europe experienced a good crop, and that hurt the western railroads that depended on grain shipments. In addition, the end of the Crimean War brought Russian grain back into the market. Wheat dropped to $0.80 a bushel, causing a major drop in shipments. The rapid fall in grain prices gave the name "Western Blizzard" to the panic. The drop in railroad revenue was rapid and deep. The word started to spread, putting pressure on inside investors to dump railroad stocks. The new telegraph contributed to the quick spread of the problem.

Speculation had created bogus landholding companies known as "paper railroads." These paper railroads were land schemes based on speculation over new railroad routes. Scandals involving stock fraud increased throughout the 1850s. In July 1857, stock prices started to fall. Finally, in August, a major grain wholesaler, N. H. Wolfe & Company, failed. The market's confidence was badly shaken. Rumors started about the potential failures in the grain-dependent railroads. Foreign investors became nervous and started to pull money out of American stocks. In mid-August, Ohio Life & Trust, which specialized in managing foreign funds for western investments, went into bankruptcy. The manager of Ohio Life would be charged with embezzlement. The Ohio Life failure started a true stock sell-off. A week later, the Michigan Central Railroad failed, causing a further sell-off on the market. Then there was a brief recovery, followed by the bad news of a large gold shipment lost in the sinking of the steamer *Central America*. A total of 15 tons of gold heading for eastern banks was lost. The nation's currency was at that time backed by gold. The loss of a large amount of gold created a rush to redeem paper backed by gold. The American Treasury tried to slow the panic by putting Treasury gold into circulation.

Problems continued into September with thinly capitalized railroads such as the Delaware, Lackawanna & Western Railroad failing. With Europe connected by the transatlantic cable, people got the news daily and started a panic in Europe. Not surprisingly, trading corruption also surfaced. Prime Minster Disraeli said, "All the bubbles, blunders, and dishonesties of five years' European exuberance and experimentation in credit were tested or revealed." Clearly, this has been repeated down to the bubbles and recessions of today. With foreign money being pulled out of railroad stocks, the bankruptcies of the Erie and Pittsburgh Railroad, the Fort Wayne & Chicago, and the Illinois Central created a bigger panic in October. Most of these railroad company stocks had been overinflated due to speculation. The government halted its gold transfers to banks, which created a run on the banks. While the stock market crisis bottomed in late October, the panic moved on to Main Street. Banks were forced to take bank holidays throughout the month to limit the runs.

Pig iron production dropped dramatically through 1858. Pittsburgh, Ohio, and Michigan were hit particularly hard. Bankruptcies of small businesses started to ripple throughout the West and Midwest. Banks closed throughout the United States. Insurance companies and small towns struggled as many had railroad bonds in their portfolios. Over 5,000 businesses failed within a year. Layoffs added to the social unrest and gang wars in New York. The Whig Party and newly emerging Republican Party called for a proactive response with tariff increases. The more immediate result was a lowering of tariffs as the Democrats gained seats due to the poor economic times. The Democrats were strong in the cotton-producing South and the grain-producing West, which favored low tariffs because of their exports. President Buchanan and Congress put together an alliance of private banks to function as a central bank to stop runs on gold. In New York and other large cities, local public works were planned to help the unemployed. Soup kitchens were organized due to fears that European-style unrest might spread to America. The Panic of 1857 created stress between regions. The South, which maintained its cotton-based economy, felt burdened by the "greedy" New York bankers and Wall Street. The public, in general, was upset with the scale of corruption unveiled by the panic. It would take the Civil War to fully pull America out of recession. Typically, in the days before the Federal Reserve and active government interventions, recessions would last 5 to 10 years.

*See also:* Abraham Lincoln Establishes Protectionism; Banking Crisis and Great Recession; Panic of 1837; Panic of 1893; Panic of 1907; Stock Market Crash/Great Depression; Transatlantic Cable; *Wealth of Nations*

### References

Calamiris, Charles, and Larry Schueikart. "The Panic of 1857: Origins, Transmission, and Containment." *Journal of Economic History,* 51, no. 4 (1991): 15–21.

Sobel, Robert. *The Panic of 57, Machines and Morality: The 1850s.* New York: Crowell, 1973.

Stamp, Kenneth. *America in 1857: A Nation on the Brink.* New York: Oxford University Press, 1990.

# Overland Travel and Mail Service (1859)

Stagecoaches became an integral part of American business in the 1840s; they are the origin of American Express Company and Wells Fargo. In the 1840s, Americans turned west for land and gold. Congress had surveyed both the Oregon Trail and the Santa Fe Trail, which moved people west, but early turnpike building in the East had taught the government to stay out of road building. The gold miners preferred the speed of clipper ships, but families tended to travel on bigger ships to Central America and cross Nicaragua via a road built by Cornelius Vanderbilt to promote his steamer lines. The Nicaragua road took 10 days, and then travelers again took ships to San Francisco. The gold rush created a true demand for transportation.

One of the first organizations to advertise was Pioneer Line, which offered a stagecoach from St. Louis to California. The cost of the 2,500-mile trip was $200. The trip took 70 days. If a family wanted to travel in a wagon train, the cost of a wagon was $500 to $1,000, and the horses cost around $150 each. The families would have to hire a wagon master for $150 a month. Mule trains were also available for $200 a person. Families faced Indians, drought, and blizzards. These operations grew in 1858 as the Congress built the "Oxbow" route, or Butterfield Overland Stage Route. This southern route went from St. Louis to El Paso, then from El Paso to San Antonio, and finally north to San Francisco (2,758 miles). The cost was about $500,000 initially, with $600,000 a year in maintenance. The government asked for bids to deliver mail twice weekly for its subsidy of $600,000 a year. John Butterfield and a group of associates including William Fargo won the bid. About eight employees were needed to maintain 200 way stations and relay points. The government involvement was based on Butterfield and associates providing mail service between Missouri and San Francisco. The first stage left on September 16, 1857, from St. Louis and arrived 23 days later in San Francisco. The cost for a person was $200 to San Francisco or 15¢ a mile for shorter distances. A coach carried six people. Mail cost 20¢ per ounce. Butterfield was required to deliver mail twice weekly.

Butterfield maintained a substantial business, with way stations supplying overnight lodging and food. Coaches were expanded to carry 10 persons. The stations provided blacksmiths, stables, and other services. Initially, a passenger was asked to ride beside the driver with a gun ("shotgun"). Butterfield expanded the operation to 250 Concord stagecoaches and over 1,800 horses. Branch routes were also established. Mule trains used Celerity wagons and tank wagons to carry goods and water. The discovery of silver and gold in Nevada created demand for new services.

Another private company, Wells Fargo and Company, entered the market to deliver silver shipments to eastern banks. Freight companies such as Central Overland California and Pikes Peak Express Company moved into the heavy freight market to the West. Freight companies used the more direct northern route (1,900 miles) following the old Oregon Trail. The Central Overland had a network of 4,000 employees, 3,500 wagons, and 50,000 oxen and mules. The immediate effect of the stagecoach routes was to stimulate further settlement and growth westward. Towns like Fort Smith, Arkansas; Gainesville, El Paso, and San Antonio, Texas; and Little Rock, Arkansas grew into major western population centers.

By the end of the 1850s, a great communications and transportation revolution was underway with the telegraph, clippers, steamers, and the railroad racing west. Speed was even then a marketable attribute for both communications and transportation. In 1850, the competitors Henry Wells, William Fargo, and John Butterfield combined their express operations on the East Coast to form American Express. In 1852, Fargo and Wells each formed express companies to supply banking services to California while remaining directors on American Express's board. They used clipper ships as well as steamers, and later Fargo invested in Butterfield's

Stagecoach in front of Wells, Fargo, & Co.'s Express Office in Virginia City, Nevada, 1866. (Library of Congress)

mail service. Alliances were formed with American Express to service the nation coast to coast, briefly maintaining an express monopoly through interlocking directors. Butterfield's mail service of 25 to 28 days remained too slow for some financial banks. Between 1859 and 1862, a niche service known as the Pony Express evolved.

The Pony Express was a mail delivery system of the Central Overland California and Pikes Peak Express Company. The Pony Express delivered mail in 10 days over a 2,000-mile route. The Pony Express used the northern route starting with the Oregon Trail. The route started at St. Joseph, Missouri, following modern-day U.S. Route 36 to Maryville, Kansas, then went on to Salt Lake City and across the Great Basin, and finally through the Sierra Nevada to Sacramento. A steamer took the mail from Sacramento to San Francisco. The cost for a half-ounce letter was $5, which the market forced down to $1 (about $85 today). To achieve this, special requirements such as young light riders were needed, which drove costs to unacceptable levels. The system required a stable of 500 horses and stations at 10- to 20-mile intervals. Each rider covered around 75 miles a day, changing horses every 15 miles. The service employed 120 riders at a high salary of $25 per year. The rider could carry only a 20-pound packet. The estimated actual cost to carry a letter was as high as $40, making the operation unprofitable throughout its short history.

The Pony Express had the market for a short period but lost out as the telegraph lines reached the West Coast. It suffered from a flawed business plan as the telegraph would reach the West Coast within two years. The Pony Express closed two days after the telegraph reached San Francisco. The Pony Express lost $200,000 over its short life (18 months). After the Civil War, Wells Fargo purchased the Butterfield Stage Company and the assets of the Pony Express for $1.5 million. Wells Fargo continued stagecoach operations until the transcontinental railroad in 1869. Wells Fargo created a new business model to utilize and augment both the railroad and telegraph in their finance, bank services, communications, and transportation business. Wells Fargo supplied the needed travel service and mail to local points from the railroad stations.

*See also:* Clipper Ships; Transcontinental Railroad Completed; Western Union Telegraph Company

### References

Bourne, Russell. *Americans on the Move: A History of Waterways, Railways, and Highways.* Golden, CO: Fulcrum, 1995.

Chapman, Arthur. *The Pony Express: The Record of a Romantic Adventure in Business.* New York: Cooper Square, 1971.

Merk, Fredrick. *History of the Westward Movement.* New York: Knopf, 1978.

Moody, Ralph. *Stage Coach West.* New York: Crowell, 1967.

# Abraham Lincoln Establishes Protectionism (1860)

Abraham Lincoln is most often remembered for freeing the slaves, but many consider his contributions to business as on par in importance. Lincoln, a former Whig, actually ran on a strong economic policy of American protectionism and the advance of technology. Lincoln was the first national candidate since Henry Clay to have the united support of labor and manufacturers. That alliance would include the manufacturing districts of Illinois, Pennsylvania, Ohio, Kentucky, and Virginia, which carried Lincoln into the presidency. It was no surprise that the Republican Party would be born at an 1856 convention in Pittsburgh at the heart of Whig country. Lincoln carried industrial Pittsburgh's Allegheny County by a record 10,000 votes. He called the concentration of votes in this manufacturing area "the State of Allegheny." Pittsburgh had finally overcome the divides of the 1794 Whiskey Rebellion and turned solidly to the new Republican Party, uniting segments of various parties under a banner of American growth. Lincoln's winning margins were similar in the iron districts of Ohio, where Iron Whigs and protectionist Democrats had found a new home in the Republican Party. In western Virginia, the pig iron aristocrats' (as the iron manufacturers were known) support of the protectionist Lincoln split the state and created West Virginia. These pig iron aristocrats had forged an alliance with iron labor as well. A strong pig iron industry was necessary for both management profits and labor employment. The German and Irish immigrants of the 1840s came for economic opportunity, and they united with wealthy Scotch-Irish to form a new Republican machine in the iron districts of the middle states. Industrial growth took priority over unionism and profits. These districts knew the recessions caused by free trade policies, believing the still-lingering Panic of 1857 was a result of the Democrats' passing of lower tariffs. As a result of war and protectionism, the pig iron industry would see great advances in technology. The pig iron aristocrats were rewarded for their votes with the 1862 Tariff Act, which had the highest-ever tariff on pig iron, at 32 percent. As the pig iron aristocrats responded with massive investments in industry, the Congress moved the rate to 47 percent in 1864. The pig iron industry grew an amazing 65 percent during the Civil War. By the end of the war, the pig iron aristocrats were a real national political force, with wealth and the ability to employ tens of thousands. The American pig iron industry was the world's greatest.

Besides technology, tariffs would drive pig iron production up, and there is no demand such as that of war. As much as 25 percent of the union's artillery was made in Pittsburgh (15 percent at Fort Pitt Foundry alone). At least 80 percent of the union's naval iron plate for ships was made in Ohio and rolled in Pittsburgh.

Most of the union's armor plate was rolled in Pittsburgh, and all of the artillery carriage axles and most railroad axles were forged there. Most of the raw pig iron, however, came from Ohio. In 1860, Cleveland, Ohio, had no iron foundries, but after the war, the city had over 50 foundries. The pig iron aristocrats were not only the ones who won the war but also the ones who profited the most. The Republican tariffs assured a boom in national production for years to come. The great iron triangle of Ohio, West Virginia, and Pennsylvania saw growth as never before. The war would also stimulate huge leaps in pig iron technology, railroads, and manufacturing. The huge profit margins in the pig iron–related businesses assured that the profit was poured back into these businesses because they offered the highest return on the dollar. Just as important, the pig iron end users such as the railroads experienced similar growth. The expansion of American industry during the war would put the infrastructure in place to make America the premier industrial nation. Lincoln took chances by promoting infant industries during the war rather than buying off European sources. Not only did it prove smart business, but by war's end, the Union controlled its own destiny, immune to foreign boycotts or pricing. In the end, Union manufacturing overwhelmed the South.

Lincoln used tariffs to raise money for the war as well, which was a basic use of tariffs as proposed by the Federalists earlier. Lincoln's economic advisor, Henry C. Carey, was a huge supporter of Clay's American System. Carey became a key political ally of Clay, forming the Pennsylvania Society for the Encouragement of Manufacture as well as the American Industry League. Carey was a prolific writer in support of tariffs throughout his career. Carey requires some note because he was the most influential economist of the 1850s, 1860s, and 1870s. He was in favor of easy money and strong tariff support, ideas supported by Clay, President James Garfield, and, later in the 1890s, President William McKinley. Carey understood the nature of the money supply as a stimulus and supported the printing of greenback dollars. Today, of course, he would be considered an inflationist, but he argued that while inflation hurt the bankers, it helped the manufacturers. He correctly identified the "enemy" as the eastern banking concerns, who, as banking monopolists, favored importation and trade. Carey argued that these bankers were actually hostile to American industrial enterprise. Carey also predicted the bankers' takeover of the railroad industry to control trade. His writings foreshadowed the rise and dominance of J. P. Morgan in the McKinley era. Carey was the major influence on Lincoln's tariff policy, which would become the policy of the Republican Party for many decades. Carey's disciples in Congress, such as the congressmen "Pig Iron" Kelley, Garfield, McKinley, and Thaddeus Stevens, carried the protectionist banner in the time period between Clay and Herbert Hoover. These men also demanded congressional oversight to assure profits gained from tariff protection were invested back into the industry creating employment.

Lincoln's presidential victory of 1860 was through his success in the old Iron Whig districts of Ohio and the other pig iron aristocracy districts in Pennsylvania, Maryland, Connecticut, and western Virginia. Lincoln's protectionism assured these districts would remain Republican for many decades. The vote in these districts set new majority records as Lincoln's protectionism played as well as his antislavery stand. The election would bring war to the nation, but prosperity to the iron districts of the North and the Midwestern manufacturing districts. It would build a long-term Republican majority and an industrial base for America's future. At the time the government's main source of income was tariffs (not income taxes). Almost all industries benefited, but the iron, glass, textile, forging, and tinplate industries, as well as mining, boomed. The protectionist representatives wrote the tariff bill, assuring iron received the highest level of protection. This political alliance would assure Republican protectionist policies for the next 70 years. Lincoln's protectionism and policy of American economic growth would peak in 1890 with the McKinley tariff bill.

*See also:* Homestead Strike of 1892; McKinley Tariff of 1890; Navigation Acts; Panic of 1857; "Report on Manufacturing"; Tariff of Abominations; *Wealth of Nations*; Whig Party Evolves

### References

Cain, Peter. *Free Trade and Protectionism: Key Nineteenth Century Journal Summaries.* London: Routledge, 1996.

McPherson, James. *Abraham Lincoln.* New York: Oxford University Press, 2010.

Skrabec, Quentin R. *William McKinley: Apostle of Protectionism.* New York: Algora, 2008.

# World's Largest Cannon/ Civil War Technology (1864)

On February 11, 1864, the world press gathered for a great event at a Pittsburgh foundry that would capture the imagination of American business and the world. Wars are economically stimulating, but few have led to advances in technology and management procedures as much as the Civil War did. This cast cannon was the world's largest and most powerful cannon, requiring new manufacturing methods to be developed. The cast cannon took 10 days to cool completely. The gun required 24 horses to move it to the Pennsylvania Railroad's special car. The weight restricted the train to 30 miles an hour on its trip to Fort Hamilton, New York. The firing of the gun showed a range of five miles. During earlier wars, a range of 400 yards was considered good. The 20-inch cannon would weigh over 50 tons and fire a half-ton projectile four miles. The estimated cost of the finished gun was over

$32,000. The Hanging Rock district of Ohio made the high-quality iron for the cannon. It was never used in the Civil War but remained on seacoast duty through World War I. The story resulted in the novel *From the Earth to the Moon* by Jules Verne, in which a projectile was shot to the moon. A few months later, the Fort Pitt Foundry cast another great 20-inch gun, the XX-Dahlgren, known as "Beelzebub." This would be the first of a series of XX-Dahlgrens: Satan, Lucifer, and Moloch. These guns were made too late for service in the Civil War but would be part of the manufacturing revolution created by the Civil War. In addition, the foundry made 645 ten-inch Rodman cannons, 90 thirteen-inch mortars, and 80 fifteen-inch Rodman cannons. The massive demand for pig iron caused a 100 percent increase in price and a world-class metal industry to evolve in Middle America. Pittsburgh's need for pig iron almost tripled during the Civil War; furthermore, war inflation took the price from $18 to $40 per ton. Most of the pig iron was coming from Youngstown's new blast furnaces and Ohio's Hocking Valley charcoal furnaces. These Youngstown furnaces were now the largest in the world. The reports on the manufacture of these great guns in *Scientific American* and *Harpers* brought metalworking to the public's attention.

The foundation of the American steel industry would be forged during the Civil War. Steel was being made by the "German method," a "high"-volume variation of crucible steel. This required pig iron to be heated in crucibles in coal-fired furnaces for days. Then carbon was re-added to produce steel. One crucible might hold only 200 to 1,000 pounds of steel. Larger castings required a simultaneous pouring and mixing of the liquid steel. Several American foundries such as Singer, Nimick, & Company were casting small rifle (three-inch) steel cannons to compete with German and British guns. By 1864, Pittsburgh's Hussey, Wells and Company, using the crucible and German method, could produce 20 tons of cast steel a day (when most steel companies were lucky to cast a ton a day). Years later, these developments in casting steel would bring George Westinghouse to Pittsburgh to pursue his railroad inventions. These events would also inspire Germany's great cannon maker, Alfred Krupp.

Abraham Lincoln took a personal interest in the development of technology, holding his famous "champagne trials," which attracted generals and diplomats from all over the world. Lincoln was America's Prince Albert in the advance of science and technology. He added America's greatest scientist, Henry Joseph, to his informal cabinet. Lincoln formed the army balloon corps to promote airships in the war. One war observer of these operations would be Count Zeppelin of Germany, who would launch the first true airships. Lincoln hired James Eads to design and build a fleet of ironclad ships. Eads would later use this technology to build America's first steel bridges. While never a factor in the war, the ironclads advanced the science of armor making and steel ships. The foundation of the Civil War technology would make the United States a world naval power in the 1890s.

The bottle-shaped Dahlgren gun aboard the ironclad *Passaic*. (Naval Historical Center)

Prior to the Civil War, bronze cannons hurled 25-pound shells a few hundred yards; after the war, huge iron cannons hurled 100-pound projectiles over four miles. At the start of the war, a well-trained soldier could fire 3 rounds a minute; at the end of the war, 50 rounds a minute were possible. Lincoln was obsessed with the development of rifles and firearms. Breech-loading rifles and machine guns were the result of the war. The potential of submarine warfare was demonstrated. The world moved from one of cellulose and wood to one of iron and steel. In communications, generals who had previously needed hours to move messages across the front could now do it in seconds. Telegraph lines went from a few hundred to thousands of miles. The news of the start of the war with the firing on Fort Sumter took three weeks to reach London; news of Lincoln's death took 10 days.

The Civil War honed the management system and the American manufacturing system. The Civil War allowed for the standardization of the practices of the Springfield Armory and the Connecticut Valley machine industry to perfect the mass production needed to supply the army. These mass-production techniques moved into all areas. Standard-sized shoes emerged due to the needs of the army. Food-canning techniques were revolutionized, with production moving from under 1 million cans in 1860 to near 25 million by the end of the war. In clothing, mass production of uniforms built the foundation for the new industry of ready-to-wear clothing using standardized sizing. The demand for and size of production moved manufacturing after the war to adopt equity stock companies over individually owned firms or partnerships. One of the more negative developments was a new form of tax known as an income tax to finance the war. The income tax lasted until 1872 but would be resurrected later in the century.

The Civil War also introduced the role of the railroad and telegraph in logistics. The importance of logistics was emphasized by naming Thomas Scott of the Pennsylvania Railroad as assistant secretary of war. The father of this logistics movement was Daniel C. McCallum, superintendent of the Erie Railroad in the 1850s. Lincoln made him superintendent of all railroads during the war. McCallum's system was to establish an organizational chart and a department structure. He used simple reports and control to maximize results. In General Sherman's March on Atlanta, McCallum moved 160 railcars a day over 360 miles of track to supply Sherman's 100,000 men and 60,000 animals. Another man who served in this great logistics organization of the War Department was Andrew Carnegie (then of the Pennsylvania Railroad), who would later use logistical science to integrate the steel industry. Carnegie would organize telegraph extensions along the railways during the war.

*See also:* Andrew Carnegie's First Steel Mill; Automated Sewing Machine; Baltimore & Ohio Railroad; Great Exhibition of 1851; Abraham Lincoln Establishes Protectionism; Overland Travel and Mail Service; Western Union Telegraph Company

### References

Bruce, Robert V. *Lincoln and the Tools of War.* Urbana: University of Illinois Press, 1989.

Hounshell, David. *From American System to Mass Production, 1800–1932, The Development of Manufacturing Technology in the United States.* Baltimore, MD: Johns Hopkins University Press, 1984.

Morris, Charles R. *The Tycoons: How Andrew Carnegie, John D. Rockefeller, Jay Gould, and J. P. Morgan Invented the American Super Economy.* New York: Henry Holt, 2005.

# Transcontinental Railroad Completed (1869)

The railroad industry, more than any other, defined the 19th-century explosion of technology and invention. It was the industry that birthed Thomas Edison, Andrew Carnegie, Cornelius Vanderbilt, Jay Gould, J. P. Morgan, Henry Bessemer, and George Westinghouse. The railroad industry maintained almost 100 years of exponential growth, driving a world industrial boom. In 1850, there were only 9,000 miles of track in America; in 1860, there were 30,626 miles of track; in 1870,

52,299 miles; in 1880, 93,262 miles; in 1890, 166,703 miles; and in 1900, 193,346 miles. The growth of railroads caused a boom in industries like coal, steel, iron, machining, and mining. Anything related to the railroad industry was a growth industry. A small invention for the railroad was a way to riches from 1870 to 1920. The initial motivation for a transcontinental railroad was to create trade with Asia and link the East Coast to the western gold fields; the benefits, however, would prove to be far greater.

The linking of the East and West Coasts via the transcontinental connection of the Union Pacific and the Central Pacific occurred on May 10, 1869, creating an economic boom. By 1890, the American railroad industry's gross income exceeded $1 billion, with the total capital invested over $10 billion. The weight of goods moved increased enormously, from 90 million tons in 1860 to 235 million tons in 1880 and 425 million tons in 1900. These are staggering numbers even by today's standards. The transcontinental railroad was no less monumental, being the largest and most ambitious project ever attempted by the nation. The vision was that of the Central Pacific Railroad's founders: Leland Stanford, Charles Crocker, Mark Hopkins, Collis Huntington, and their chief engineer, Theodore Judah. Judah did the final lobbying of Congress in 1861 for the necessary funds. It had the support of Abraham Lincoln, since he had made it a campaign promise. The old Whigs now in the Republican Party were very supportive of such national projects as well.

The Pacific Railroad Act passed in 1862. The act specified that the Central Pacific would start at Sacramento, California, moving east to meet a new company, the Union Pacific Railroad, moving west from Omaha. Thomas Durant would head the Union Pacific Railroad. The contract specified that only American iron rails could be used, even though British ones were available at a third of the cost. (British rails went directly from port, while American rails needed rail transportation first, adding another $100 per ton.) Rails made in western Pennsylvania moved east to Philadelphia and then were loaded onto ships for the 16,000-mile trip around Cape Horn to supply the Central Pacific Railroad. The project would require over 1,700 miles of track. All iron rails were to be supplied by American mills, which increased the demand for a fledgling iron and steel industry in the East. This was consistent with Lincoln's Republican policy of protectionism. The government would pay in bonds at the rate of $16,000 a mile in the flatlands, $32,000 a mile for hilly terrain, and $48,000 a mile for the mountains. In addition, the railroads received 6,400 acres of land for every mile completed, which they could sell or lease to settlers. Even with this, the companies had to issue bonds at 6 percent to cover all expenses. In all, over 30,000 workers would be involved. Labor shortages would bring thousands of Chinese laborers into the United States. By 1864, the government had to almost double the money given to save the project.

The Railroad Act of 1864 created a system of corruption that made many investors rich. This act would show the worst of government involvement in such projects. It created a new stock company called Credit Mobilier. Credit Mobilier set the supply contracts. If a shovel cost Credit Mobilier a dollar, they might charge the Union Pacific three dollars. Credit Mobilier could also overcharge for the actual cost of track laid. The project now generated a dividend for the stockholders at the expense of the government. The railroad officers and congressmen were major stockholders. Credit Mobilier was called the "gravy train." It was estimated that for every dollar spent, the Credit Mobilier made three dollars, the cost to taxpayers being near $1 million. Workers were paid about $2.50 a day ($1.20 a day if Chinese) plus food and lodging. Skilled workers, like carpenters, made $4.00 a day.

Construction was painfully slow until 1867, averaging less than a mile a day. Indians, mountains, cholera, supply shortages, turnover, and labor shortages all contributed to the construction problems. In 1867, two veterans of the Union Army's logistics miracles such as Sherman's March joined the effort. General Greenville Dodge and General Jack Casement were able to build an "army on wheels." A unique incentive program was designed where each man received a pound of tobacco for a mile of track laid. If the workers laid another half-mile, they got an extra dollar. For four miles of track, the workers got an extra two dollars. In 1867, the crews laid 245 miles of track. In 1868, they laid 425 miles, with the record of 7¾ miles in one day. Average wages went up an additional $35 a month. Frederick Taylor would apply the success of these incentive programs to manufacturing in the 1880s. Casement set up a supply train of 22 cars to supply and feed the crews as they blazed forward. Crews never waited for rails and ties with this new logistics system. In the final push to link at Promontory, Utah, a crew broke the 10-mile day.

It came at a high cost, but the transcontinental railroad launched America into the Industrial Revolution. The main motivation had been to expand trade with China and Japan, but the real benefit was economic growth. However, it was the internal growth driven by westward migration and settlement that was the major economic impact of the transcontinental railroad. Farms moved west since their grain could now be shipped to eastern and western ports. Travel from Omaha to Sacramento went from a six-month wagon trip or a one-month stagecoach journey to a six-day trip for $40 one-way (or $60 to $100 for more luxurious seating).

*See also:* Baltimore & Ohio Railroad; Clipper Ships; Overland Travel and Mail Service; Western Union Telegraph Company; Westinghouse Air Brake

### References

Ambrose, Stephen E. *Nothing Like It in the World.* New York: Simon & Schuster, 2000.

Gordon, Sarah. *Passage to Union: How the Railroads Transformed American Life.* Chicago: Ivan Dee, 1996.

Stewart, John J. *The Iron Trail to the Golden Spike.* New York: Meadow Lark, 1994.

William, John Hoyt. *A Great and Shining Road: The Epic Story of the Transcontinental Railroad.* New York: Time Books, 1988.

# Westinghouse Air Brake (1869)

The railroad industry, more than any other, defined the 19th-century explosion of technology and invention. It was the industry that birthed Thomas Edison, Andrew Carnegie, Henry Bessemer, and George Westinghouse. The railroad industry maintained almost 100 years of exponential growth, driving a world industrial boom, partially driven by Westinghouse's railroad technology. In 1850, there were only 9,000 miles of track in America; by the end of the Civil War in 1865, there were around 35,000 miles; by 1874, there were 77,740 miles; and by 1900, there were 198,964 miles. At the time of Westinghouse's death, there were over 250,000 miles of track. By 1890, the American railroad industry's gross income exceeded $1 billion with total capital invested over $10 billion. The weight of goods moved increased enormously—from 90 million tons in 1860 to 235 million in 1880 and 425 million in 1900. These are staggering numbers even by today's standards. The 19th century's richest men such as Cornelius Vanderbilt, John D. Rockefeller, Carnegie, and J. P. Morgan made their money in the railroads' growth. A small invention for the railroad was a way to riches from 1870 to 1920. One growing problem was the death of brakemen, which seemed to be a daily occurrence. These train wrecks were grabbing the headlines with the grim news of death and injury. Editorials across the nation were screaming for industry action on safety. The public was becoming fearful of rail travel. Westinghouse was typical of Victorian inventors who looked for economic rewards for inventing, and the railroad offered the most potential. Passenger safety was only one factor; the length of freight trains was another.

The biggest obstacle to larger freight and safer passenger trains was the inadequate braking systems in use. The hand brake system in place required coordination and muscle power. The locomotive engineer would start throttling down the engine as he signaled the brakemen with the whistle (known as the "down brakes whistle"). A brakeman was assigned between every two cars on the train. The brakeman would begin the process of applying friction brakes on each car by turning a hand wheel known as the horizontal wheel, located on a vertical post at the end of each car; the hand wheel multiplied the force of the brakeman's muscles. The needed strength of the brakemen was the source of the term "Armstrong system." The hand wheel pushed brake shoes on each car against the wheels. After the brakes were applied to one car, the brakeman jumped to the other car to apply the brakes. Poor coordination between the brakemen could cause "locking" and serious jolting to the passengers. Luggage was often thrown wildly inside the passenger cars, injuring the passengers. Many times brakemen were killed or injured in this difficult task as well. The danger to the brakemen was unbelievable. The average life of a brakeman on the job was estimated at seven years. The brakeman had to race from car to car, often on roofs slippery with ice, snow, and rain. Even on the best days, the swaying, bobbing, and jolting of the cars caused them to lose their footing. The statistics of the time were just as unbelievable. It was estimated that 1,000 brakemen were killed each year and another 5,000 injured. While these deaths, as horrific and numerous as they were, didn't make the headlines, railroad wrecks were front-page news. In 1853, President Franklin Pierce had a son killed, and even Charles Dickens had been in a major brake-failure wreck in 1865. Dickens, like many of the time, was fearful of rail travel. An 1856 head-on crash in central Pennsylvania had killed over 50 people, mostly children on their way to a Sunday picnic. For business, the lack of a braking system limited the length of trains to 10 freight cars. The government was also taking note of the problem as the public fear and outcry increased, and if the industry didn't address the problem, the government would regulate it.

Westinghouse already had a railroad equipment business and was looking for new products. He had been a vigorous reader of the technical and engineering journals from his earliest days at his father's plant. By 1868, the compressed air tooling was making news as new tunnels were being built all over the world. The Mont Cenis Tunnel had become a weekly report in the journals. Westinghouse immediately saw the application of compressed air to railroad braking as a means to transfer energy to a braking system. A Pittsburgh train was equipped with the Westinghouse system in September 1868. (This date has been confused with April 13, 1896, the actual date that the patent was issued.) The train left a tunnel at 30 miles per hour only to see a merchant and his cart stalled on the street crossing. The train hit the brakes, stopping in time. Having had such a spectacular demonstration, there was no question about proceeding, which they did, with other tests along the way.

If done well at 30 miles per hour, hand braking could stop a train within 1,600 feet. The Westinghouse "straight air brake" could do it within 500 feet. Word of the trial did travel quickly in local railroad circles. The railroads, however, were cautious. First, to many railroad executives, brakes were a safety issue, not a profit issue. In fact, Westinghouse's success struck fear in many because of the cost of potentially converting all existing trains. One estimate was that $40 million would have been needed in 1875 to convert the industry (more like $1 billion in today's money). In July 1869, Westinghouse Air Brake was formed with a board of directors from the enthusiastic railroad executives. The board consisted of 22-year-old Westinghouse, Robert Pitcairn, W. Card, Andrew Cassatt, Edward Williams, G. Whitcomb, and Ralph Baggaley. The capitalization was $500,000. Westinghouse sold the railroads on the air brake, showing it would be a savings versus the federal regulation that was moving through Congress. Westinghouse continued his work on the brake, showing that its use could more than triple the tonnage carried on freight trains.

In 1874, Westinghouse brakes were on 20 percent of the nation's trains. In 1876, he had his brakes on 37 percent of the existing trains, or 2,645 locomotives and 8,500 passenger cars. Westinghouse featured his braking system at the 1876 Philadelphia World's Fair. By 1879, Westinghouse had installed his system on 3,600 locomotives and 13,000 cars; mainly, these were automatic brakes. In 1893, Congress required the air brake and automatic coupler on all trains and passed the Railroad Safety Appliance Act. The safety was the result of Westinghouse and his friend William McKinley, chairman of the Ways and Means Committee (and future president). When Westinghouse started making air brakes in 1869, freight trains were 15 cars long, carrying 300 tons and averaging 30 miles per hour. At his death in 1914 they were 130 cars long, carrying 7,000 tons and averaging 60 miles per hour. The brake gave huge profits to the railroads. Statistics show that Westinghouse had put his brakes on over 3 million cars and 80,000 locomotives in this country alone by 1916. Westinghouse had as much as 70 percent of the world market.

Westinghouse needed to standardize his parts and assembly to make it a commercial success. His manufacturing system was as revolutionary as his air brake. With the booming sales of the automatic brake, Westinghouse was in need of good mechanics and machinists, but the labor market was tight. Straight hourly wages for such skilled employees were around $2.50 per hour. Westinghouse devised a piece rate system based on units or work done. Employees actually earned $4.00 an hour while supplying the world. Westinghouse preceded the famous Frederick Taylor piece-incentive system by 20 years. Westinghouse's manufacturing system was the first to offer employee pensions and health care. He developed a system of internal education and paid employees to go on to attend college. He was one of the earliest manufacturers to use women in the factory.

*See also:* Baltimore & Ohio Railroad; Centennial Exposition; Great Railroad Strike of 1877; Scientific Management

### References

Derry, T.K., and Trevor Williams. *A Short History of Technology.* New York: Oxford University Press, 1960.

Leupp, Francis. *George Westinghouse: His Life and Achievements.* Boston: Little, Brown, 1918.

Skrabec, Quentin. *George Westinghouse: Gentle Genius.* New York: Algora, 2007.

# Panic of 1873

These 1800 "panics" were just that, resulting in massive stock sell-offs and bank runs. The financial markets were unable to handle the large swings of the capitalistic economy, lacking the Federal Reserve system of today. Loans were "callable"; that is, a bank could call in a loan, demanding that all or part of the loan be repaid immediately. As the bank runs reduced the cash on hand, banks had to call in business loans to generate cash, which in turn created a downward spiral. A financial panic would last one to four years as the markets slowly worked things out. The Panic of 1873 hit the nation hard. The panic lasted five years with 30 percent unemployed and another 40 percent working less than seven months a year. Nationwide, three million people would lose their jobs while daily wages fell 25 percent. Unemployment nationally was running over 25 percent for years. Banker Thomas Mellon called the Panic of 1873 the "most disastrous and extensive collapse since that of 1819." Railroad workers suffered a 35 percent decrease in wages. Wages for Ohio coal miners dropped by half during the panic. The nation noticed an increase in "tramps" on city streets. In New York City, over 50 soup kitchens were serving over 20,000 hungry persons. Andrew Carnegie remarked that he had to step over tramps to get to his New York office. The *New York Times* suggested getting a dog with good teeth as protection against the tramps. Oil had dropped from $3.00 a barrel to $0.50 a barrel. Agricultural products had dropped a similar percentage, causing farms to fail and a dramatic decrease in railroad profits. Financial and political scandals of the period further rocked investor confidence.

Nationally, a quarter of the nation's 360 railroad companies failed as well as 20,000 other businesses. Looking back, Carnegie found the Panic of 1873 as the most difficult of the panics for capitalists: "So many of my friends needed money, that they begged me to repay them. I did so and bought out five or six of them. That gave me my leading interest in this steel business." The fact is Carnegie was one of the few to profit from the 1873 panic because he kept investing against the trend. The Carnegie strategy of buying in a panic would prove a very successful one over the years for those with faith in the American economy. Still, many see the recession of the 1870s as equivalent to that of the 1930s. It took over five years for the nation to dig out of this depression in the 1870s. The Panic of 1873 might be considered a natural part of the business cycle resulting from the expansion of the Civil War. However, inflationary pressures, scandals, speculation, and Wall Street corruption complicated it.

Like most panics, the Panic of 1873 had started in New York with investment house problems. The panic started as a bank crisis; within a few days the stock market closed for the first time in its history. The Panic of 1873 was the result of railroad speculation after the Civil War. Railroads had continued to expand with the enthusiasm created by the transcontinental railroad. The government poured new money into a new line—the Northern Pacific—and speculators followed quickly. In the early 1870s, there was a true bubble in railroad stocks. However, the railroads were undercapitalized and not producing profits. Grain prices had continued to fall, further reducing railroad profits. New York banker Jay Cooke was behind the railroad stock bubble with the overselling of Northern Pacific stock and bonds. Rumors of financial scandals with Cooke's firm started to surface. Meanwhile, the Northern Pacific was in dire need of capital, and Cooke couldn't sell bonds because of the rumors. In early September 1873, some small railroads went under, and a stock panic started to build. On September 18, 1873, known as Black Thursday, the large investment house of Jay Cooke failed. Black Friday, September 19, brought the failure of others, and a full-blown panic was initiated. The market crashed. Western Union led the crash, falling from 75 to 59 points on Black Friday.

The banks refused to help, and J. P. Morgan was happy to see the collapse of Cooke, his financial rival. Other Wall Streeters such as Jay Gould tried to take advantage of the stock crash to buy out railroad magnate Cornelius Vanderbilt. This competition ruled out the cooperation needed to prevent a further decline in the markets. Vanderbilt saved his stocks by getting loans abroad. Most banks reacted badly by refusing checks, which created a banking panic and mass withdrawals. Large banks started failing, and customers rushed to get their money out. Vanderbilt asked President Grant for help, but he initially refused. The government did eventually start to buy back railroad bonds. The panic slowed on its own while

things seemed to improve. Then, in October 1873, several investment houses collapsed over wild railroad speculation. The New York Stock Exchange was forced to close for 10 days. Similarly, many banks closed for days on end. By the end of the year, there were over 5,000 bankruptcies. Problems mounted as Europe called in American loans, as Europe had also overspeculated in the railroads. President Grant stayed out of the situation, feeling the government had no authority to act.

From a financial crisis in New York, the panic spread to America's factories over the year of 1874. The depression following the Panic of 1873 is considered second only to the Great Depression of the 1930s. Business stocks fell 32 percent versus the 55 percent decline of the 1930s. Farmers were also hit hard with declining prices and

Scene at the New York Stock Exchange on Black Friday, September 19, 1873. (Library of Congress)

capital shortages. One of the ways the government helped the country climb out of this depression was to use legislation to expand the money supply. The nation lacked a Federal Reserve and required legislative investment to pump money into the economy. The five-to-six-year length of the depression following the Panic of 1873 was about the average for these recessions over the years. The Panic of 1873 was considered a cause of the Great Railroad Strike of 1877, as the resulting unemployment remained stubbornly high until 1879. Morgan emerged from the Panic of 1873 as the nation's largest financier. Vanderbilt also saved his empire and grew stronger as did Carnegie. Carnegie would later call the expansion of plant building in panics a business strategy to be used.

*See also:* Banking Crisis and Great Recession; Federal Reserve Act; Great Railroad Strike of 1877; Jefferson Embargo; Panic of 1837; Panic of 1857; Panic of 1893; Panic of 1907; Savings and Loan Crisis; Stock Market Crash/Great Depression; Transcontinental Railroad Completed

### References

Juglar, Clement, and W. DeCourcy. *A Brief History of Panics in the United States.* Old Chelsea, NY: Cosimo, 2005.

Lubetkin, John. *Jay Cooke's Gamble: The Northern Pacific Railroad, the Sioux, and the Panic of 1873.* Norman: University of Oklahoma Press, 2006.

Surhone, Lambert, Miriam Timpledon, and Susan Marseken. *Panic of 1873: Long Depression, Jay Cooke.* Saarbrucken, Germany: Betascript, 2010.

# Andrew Carnegie's First Steel Mill (1875)

Andrew Carnegie represents the first of America's robber barons and a major beneficiary of the Panic of 1873. He would build his first steel mill during this downturn, saving tens of thousands of dollars. Carnegie was a pure capitalist, proving his genius in investing and building industry. He remained one of America's wealthiest industrialists. In business, he was a pioneer in industrial organization, motivation, and the application of new technology. He proved out the concept of supply chain management through vertical integration. Carnegie immigrated to America from Scotland as a young boy after the automated loom had destroyed his father's craft as a weaver. Young Andrew started in a Pittsburgh cotton mill, but he rapidly adopted the new technology of the telegraph. Unlike his father, Carnegie embraced the new technology and quickly moved up. He invested in the Pennsylvania Railroad where he was employed. In 1862, Carnegie then purchased a $40,000 share in an oil venture known as Columbia Oil, which would return over 400 percent by the end of the decade. Carnegie then searched for a new investment and went to England to study the emerging technology of Bessemer steelmaking. Steel was a new material and stronger than wrought iron, which was used to produce rails for the booming railroad industry. Carnegie saw a huge steel market if the cost of production could be brought down.

Carnegie planned to enter the new steel rail business by being a low-cost and high-technology producer. First, Carnegie partnered with iron manufacturers and railroad executives to penetrate potential railroad markets. This allowed him to attack the wrought iron rail market with a steel rail product. In 1875, Carnegie opened the world's largest steel mill and factory to produce steel rails for the railroad. Edgar Thomson Works at Braddock, Pennsylvania (near Pittsburgh), was named after Edgar Thomson of the Pennsylvania Railroad. Carnegie hired the best Bessemer steel engineer in the business, Alexander Holly, to build his new mill. Carnegie had competition in the steel business, but he focused on cost as his competitive advantage. Carnegie continued to build during the Panic of 1873, saving significantly on construction costs. He hired some of the best and most experienced managers to build his management organization. He brought in railroad men as partners to boost sales. Carnegie and his partners endured the Panic of 1873 to see the mill roll its first rail on September 1, 1875. Carnegie was the first in the industry to apply cost accounting, breaking out the product cost for each process step. Carnegie used this to benchmark and to improve as well as to evaluate new process technology. As motivation, Carnegie hired young managers by offering them stock and ownership in the company based on their performance. These managers, tested in the fire of competition, became the best on the American scene. Over 30 of these young managers would become multimillionaires when Carnegie sold the business. Carnegie boys would go on to control over 40 percent of America's industrial assets.

Carnegie continued to expand and improve the mill, fully integrating production of steel rails by 1883, using hot blast furnace pig iron produced at the mill rather than buying cold pig iron on the open market. Carnegie built some of the world's largest blast furnaces to drive the process cost down further. Realizing the advantage of vertical integration, Carnegie invested in coke production, using the coal-based fuel for his blast furnaces. Carnegie controlled the partnership and poured his profits into expansion of steel manufacturing versus the diversification that many suggested to him. His managers invented a new type of holding furnaces to allow liquid blast furnace iron to move to the Bessemer converter, further saving on the cost of reheating. Carnegie instituted a policy of rapid technology implementation to reduce costs throughout the process. With each improvement in process cost, Carnegie lowered the rail price to take more market share and gain economy of scale. Managers were rewarded with large percentages of cost savings to further motivate process cost reduction. Carnegie further rearranged the rolling operations to eliminate the need for intermediate heating between rolling. His cost push led him to start his own railroad to reduce plant transportation costs. Carnegie expanded the railroad to take iron ore from the Cleveland docks to his Braddock mill. Another part of his vertical integration was the buying of coalfields and coke ovens to produce his own fuel completely. By the 1890s, big railroads such as the Pennsylvania Railroad became the biggest customer of and supplier of services to the steel business. Vertical integration became one of the most successful business models of the Gilded Age. H. J. Heinz applied it in the food business, A. Busch in the beer industry, Henry Ford in auto production, and George Westinghouse in electrical appliances.

Carnegie was one of the first to talk of competitive advantage. He never let his mills lose their technological edge. At his Braddock mill, he perfected the new, clean steel production of open-hearth steelmaking. When he purchased a fairly new Bessemer steel plant at Homestead, Pennsylvania, he gutted it to convert it to the open-hearth process for tougher steel markets. He was the first American manufacturer to apply natural gas as an industrial fuel and the first to electrify his operations. He always maintained a technological edge over the competition, regardless of cost. By the end of the 1890s, Carnegie controlled the rail, structural steel, and armor plate markets. Besides cost control, technology, and vertical integration, Carnegie mastered competitive advantage by market control. He was a feared competitor. He often targeted competitors, defeating them in the marketplace and taking them over. Carnegie benefited much from the McKinley tariffs, but to his credit, he reinvested in plant equipment and expansion. His one weakness was his poor labor relations. Eventually, Carnegie was bought out voluntarily by J. P. Morgan, who formed the world's first billion-dollar corporation, United States Steel, in 1901.

*See also:* Abraham Lincoln Establishes Protectionism; First Billion-Dollar Corporation—United States Steel; Highland Park Ford Assembly Line; Homestead Strike of 1892; McKinley Tariff of 1890

### References

Bridge, James Howard. *The Inside History of Carnegie Steel Company.* New York: Aldine, 1903.

Krass, Peter. *Carnegie.* New York: Wiley, 2002.

Wall, Joseph Frazier. *Andrew Carnegie.* Pittsburgh, PA: University of Pittsburgh Press, 1970.

# Centennial Exposition (1876)

The world's fairs of the 20th century were the first form of true marketing. They offered a venue to introduce new products and concepts to the public. Products were also market tested at these fairs. A gold medal translated into major sales dollars. The Centennial International Exhibition of 1876 was the first official world's fair in the United States. Its official name was the International Exhibition of Arts, Manufacturers and Products of Soil and Mine. The idea was to celebrate the 100th anniversary of the signing of the Declaration of Independence in Philadelphia. Amazingly, 10 million visitors, roughly 20 percent of the American population, attended the fair over a six-month period in Philadelphia. There were fears of a European boycott because of high American tariffs, but European countries lined up to present products to the growing American market. President Ulysses Grant and Brazilian Emperor Dom Pedro opened the fair.

The private-sector board raised about $5 million with the U.S. government supplying a $1 million loan. The fair was huge even by modern standards. There were 200 buildings covering 256 acres at Philadelphia's Fairmont Park. There were 30,000 exhibits. The Pennsylvania Railroad scheduled special excursion trains from Chicago, Pittsburgh, New York, and Baltimore. The Main Exhibition Building was the largest in the world, covering 22 acres. The highlights included the arm and torch of the Statue of Liberty (completed in New York Harbor in 1886). There was a prototype of the first galvanized cable to be used by the Roebling brothers in the Brooklyn Bridge. A 70-foot Corliss steam engine powered the fair. The 1,500-horsepower engine powered all the machinery with 5 miles of shafting and 75 miles of belts. In all, the Corliss steam engine ran over 8,000 machines at the fair. The city of Philadelphia and the state of Pennsylvania invested heavily in the fair, hoping for huge profits for hotels, saloons, and local businesses.

As visitors got off the train at the Pennsylvania Railroad Station in Philadelphia, they would first see the new emporium of John Wanamaker. Wanamaker was a marketing genius, and this was the first true department store in the United States. It was a wonder of 120 departments staffed by perfectly dressed women, a practice that H. J. Heinz would emulate years later. The store was two-thirds of a mile long, covering three acres, with 129 counters. The store had an in-house restaurant and a men's smoking room. It augured a new age in retailing and advertising. On the way to the fair, visitors probably stopped at the small chocolate shop of Milton Hershey. Hershey would be another supporter of paternal capitalism.

The list of new products at the fair included Alexander Graham Bell's telephone, the Remington typewriter, Heinz ketchup, Hires root beer, the Westinghouse air brake, mechanical pencils, Edison's duplex telegraph, mechanical calculating machines, electric lighting, automatic screw machines, electric dynamos, the internal combustion engine, asbestos, aluminum, zippers, and the first monorail. Andrew Carnegie exhibited the longest steel rail ever rolled (72 feet long), and the German Alfred Krupp exhibited the world's largest steel cannon. Krupp had found world's fairs to be particularly successful in the sale of his cannons. The side exhibits offered the first electric dynamos, which would be the first step toward incandescent lighting. The dynamo generated an electrical current by moving a magnet back and forth in a copper wire coil. Dynamos were driven many times by Westinghouse steam engines, which represented a large market for Westinghouse Machine Company. These dynamos used this type of direct current (DC) to operate arc lights. These bluish lights were considered curiosities, but the fair spurred sales for city lighting systems. These lights came from the arcing of electricity between two electrodes. The recently patented internal combustion engine of George Brayton was shown; it would be a major step toward the automobile. A Pittsburgh bus operator would see the engine at the fair and contract it for use in a commercial bus. These fairs functioned as a meeting place for venture capitalists and inventors. Today, we have industry-focused fairs such as the Detroit Auto Show and the Las Vegas Electronic Fair to perform the same function. The 2010 World's Fair was in Shanghai, China, and cost $50 billion. Like America in 1876, China is demonstrating its arrival on the industrial scene.

Specialty foods were a major attraction at the fair. The Centennial Exposition had introduced many products such as buttered popcorn, ice cream soda fountains, and bananas. One of the most promoted sauces at the Centennial Exposition was Worcestershire sauce. Worcestershire had roots going back to the 1830s when Lord Sandy returned from India with a tangy sauce he fancied. The exact Lea & Perrins recipe is secret, but it is believed to include anchovies, shallots, cloves, malt vinegar, salt, garlic, sugar, chilies, cayenne pepper, and tamarinds (brown pods from a tropical tree). The power of fair marketing could be seen in the spread of popularity for products such as Worcestershire sauce and ketchup. The large Crosse & Blackwell specialty food company exhibit augured Heinz's future. Crosse & Blackwell had been founded in 1830 and had built a fortune on sauces. The company offered such products as chow-chow, ketchup, malt vinegar (for fish and chips), celery sauce, and preserved jellies in glass packaging. Even more impressive was the beauty of the glass containers at the fair. Crosse & Blackwell offered differentiated bulk commodities to most grocers. This new marketing concept would spread to American companies.

The fair was noted for its inspiration and advance of technology. Over 10,000 new patents were filed over the next four years. Inventors such as George Westinghouse, George Eastman, Thomas Edison, Joseph Brown, Simon Ingersoll, and Heinz all claimed inspiration from the Centennial Exposition. Many of the manufacturing systems and machines found immediate application. Heinz would see an automated canning machine at the Philadelphia Centennial Exposition, and he would apply the technology at his Pittsburgh plant. At the time a tinsmith could produce 60 to 100 tin cans a day, slower than the bottling operation for sauerkraut. But the talk in the trade from the fair was canning machines. This machine could do 55 cans in an hour! Heinz set up a tin-canning operation for sauerkraut that proved successful, and tin cans became cost effective over glass and barrels. Another fair machine that attracted manufacturers was the Brown & Sharpe grinding machine that allowed hardened steel tools to be ground to precise sizes. This would be the cornerstone of the "American system" of interchangeable parts and standardized tooling. The automatic screw machine at the fair could produce 100,000 nuts and bolts in a day versus the hand lathe rate of 8,000 a day at the time. Ingersoll-Rand exhibited the first steam-driven rock-drilling machine. The Smithsonian built the Arts and Industries Building in Washington, D.C., in 1881 to permanently house the machinery exhibits.

*See also:* Chicago World's Fair; Great Exhibition of 1851; Patent and Copyright Statutes; Television at the 1939 World's Fair

### References

Gross, Linda, and Theresa Snyder. *Philadelphia 1876 Centennial Exhibition.* Mount Pleasant, SC: Arcadia, 2005.

Rydell, Robert. *World of Fairs.* Chicago: University of Chicago Press, 1993.

Skrabec, Quentin. *The Metallurgic Age.* Jefferson, NC: McFarland, 2006.

# First Commercial Telephone (1877)

The history of the telephone is a true study in many aspects of business. Like most major inventions, the telephone was the confluence of many streams of technological developments. The telegraph had a host of potential inventors working on improvements including Thomas Edison. Much effort was being put into the multiple telegraph to allow rapid two-way communication through dots and dashes. Alexander Graham Bell and Edison were both working on the multiple telegraph with financial backing. The hope was that the multiple telegraph could break the monopoly held by Western Union Telegraph Company. Bell demonstrated the ability to "talk" with electricity in 1874, which shifted the research effort from the telegraph to the telephone. This development allowed him to have two investors, Gardiner Hubbard and Thomas Sanders, to finance the initial development work. Bell recorded the first telephone success on March 10, 1876. Bell would beat Elisha Gray to the patent office by a few hours, and a legal battle would ensue. Still, the original device needed more development for commercial application. These improvements came quickly, with the range moving from a few miles to over 50 miles within 18 months.

Bell took his invention to the Centennial Exposition in 1876 to search for financial backing for the development. The telephone demonstrations at the Centennial Exposition proved extremely popular. Seeing the phone at the exposition, Lord

Kelvin took the technology to England to sell. Bell's business model was to sell the telephone to business owners such as bankers as well as some early adopters. Bell planned a series of demonstrations in major cities. His first was at the Boston Music Hall. He connected phones five miles apart for the demonstration. Bell launched a company and was able to sell 1,700 pairs of telephones by the end of 1876. The telephones needed to be connected in pairs by an iron wire within a range of a couple miles. Initial buyers were banks and company executives who wanted to stay in touch with business operations. Because of the high equipment cost, Bell leased the telephones to develop a market, but the customer was responsible for setting up the iron wire line. The leasing model proved highly successful and would be emulated by future inventors of costly new technology. Still, the telephone saw rapid market growth because, unlike the telegraph, it required no special skills. Bell proved an outstanding marketer using word of mouth gained at the World's Fair; he followed with the Boston presentation, then more demonstrations in major cities. Using the newspaper to advertise, Bell set up at major hotels to demonstrate and sell the telephone. In late 1877 in Pittsburgh, an enthusiastic early adopter, H. J. Heinz, connected his home and his pickle factory (a distance of 15 miles) and then added a connection to his parents' home. Bell had offered to sell the telephone rights to Western Union for $100,000, but they declined. It was said that conflicting personalities killed the deal. By 1878, Bell Telephone had 10,000 phones in service.

Businesses were quick to adopt the new technology. By the end of 1877, a Californian telephone company called Ridge Telephone Company formed to service mining companies in the Californian mountains, covering distances up to 60 miles. Demand from commercial customers increased rapidly. Other companies followed, seeing that by investing in an iron wire, they could sell the service. Bell Telephone quickly took control of licensing these new companies through patent control. Some companies leased the telegraph lines to make connections, but the telegraph companies realized the competition might be detrimental and discontinued the practice. For his part, Bell wanted to behave as a monopoly and control the market through manufacture and leasing of phones. Companies quickly realized that they could start their own switching boards to connect multiple phones. A new business model of the telephone exchange company evolved, but again local companies were forced to deal with Bell. Exchange companies used shared lines (party lines) and switchboards to minimize wires and maximize customers. A long-distance call (between local exchanges) cost about 15¢ ($5 today) for five minutes. Bell had initially formed the American Telephone and Telegraph Company (AT&T) to manufacture and lease phones. He was able to establish a patent-based monopoly by leasing and selling to local subsidiaries to provide telephone service. It wasn't easy with American Bell fighting 600 lawsuits, but American Bell would win them all.

Technology flourished as the lawsuits continued. Copper wire replaced iron wire, creating another new industry. Copper wire was a much better conductor and transmitter, although more expensive. Switchboards were improved to reduce the need for wire. Edison made a major advance in 1878 with the carbon microphone. The carbon microphone/transmitter allowed high voice quality and longer-distance transmission. Edison aligned with competitor Western Union because Western Union had supplied development money to Edison as they struggled against Bell's new technology and company. Edison had actually been hired before Bell's telephone to do research and development on the telegraph. A new company, Western Electric, emerged to produce the improved Edison phone. Edison and Western Union also formed the American Speaking Telephone Company to lease phones and set up phone service.

The major challenge to Bell Telephone then came from the giant Western Union, which had the better speaker system developed by Edison. The basic system was clearly an infringement on Bell's patent. Still, Western Union put 56,000 phones in service by 1879. Western Union, through Edison Telephone, even took on British Bell Telephone in England. Western Union lost the lawsuit, but then purchased the controlling interest in Western Electric, which supplied telephones to Western Union. Bell Telephone went on to control the national network by the formation of AT&T. Bell also won the patent infringement suit in England. By 1880, the monopolistic behavior of American Bell Telephone was actually slowing market penetration. Service also was poor, which is often typical of monopolies. This was exactly the type of monopoly that Thomas Jefferson had feared. The Bell patents ran out in 1894, and the market had tired of the monopolistic behavior. When the patent expired, hundreds of companies rushed into various segments of the phone business.

Between 1894 and 1904, over 6,000 independent companies were motivated to move into the telephone business. The number of telephones jumped from 285,000 to 3,317,000 in the same time period. The rise of independent companies drove local service costs down, but new problems occurred. The national system that AT&T had been pushing slowed. AT&T had connected New York and Chicago by 1892 prior to the expiration of the patents. A call from New York to Chicago using the AT&T system cost $9 ($200 today) for five minutes. City-to-city phone calls were mainly controlled by AT&T even after the expiration of the patents, since local independent exchanges were not connected. It would take until 1915 to connect New York to San Francisco because of interconnection problems between companies. Loading coils, which would have made the connection technically possible, came in 1899. AT&T continued to have a monopoly on long-distance calls for many decades.

*See also:* Centennial Exposition; Patent and Copyright Statutes; Western Union Telegraph Company

**References**

Coe, Lewis. *The Telephone and Its Several Inventors: A History.* Jefferson, NC: McFarland, 1995.

Fisher, Claude. *America Calling: A Social History of the Telephone to 1940.* Berkeley: University of California Press, 1994.

Pretzer, William. *Working at Inventing: Thomas Edison and the Menlo Park Experience.* Baltimore, MD: Johns Hopkins University Press, 2001.

# Great Railroad Strike of 1877

This deadly national strike started in late July 1877 as the East Coast was caught in a major heat wave. The nation was still struggling with the Panic of 1873 with unemployment high throughout the nation. The stagnation of the economy had squeezed profits on the nation's railroad companies. The Pennsylvania and Baltimore & Ohio railroads laid off thousands and asked the remaining brakemen and firemen to take a 10 percent pay cut while doubling up on the work with "doubleheaders." The doubleheader was the combining of two trains and two engines (two locomotives and 34 cars instead of one locomotive and 17 cars) but with a single crew. The railroads thought they had the upper hand in that railroad wages were the highest in the nation, and the nation was in a recession. The rail workers were making five to six dollars a week compared to Westinghouse Air Brake employees, who averaged four dollars a week, and Carnegie steelworkers, who averaged three dollars a week. The workers of Baltimore & Ohio Railroad called for a strike on July 14, 1877; it spread from Maryland and West Virginia to Chicago and further west. In addition, with the poor economy, most railroad workers were getting only six months of work a year. The wage cuts came with the news that the railroad companies were increasing dividends. The strike started on July 14 at Martinsburg, West Virginia. The strike would spread to outside Baltimore at Camden Yards on July 16 with a demand to reinstate wages. The strike moved quickly along the line to West Virginia and further west. At Cumberland, Maryland, the strike turned violent. In Baltimore, 10 strikers were killed as they faced off against federal troops. On July 19, the Pennsylvania Railroad joined the strike, taking control of the Pittsburgh station and the switches. On the morning of July 20, no trains were moving in Maryland, Pennsylvania, West Virginia, Ohio, and Illinois. During the peak of the riots in Baltimore, gangs, socialists, and the unemployed joined the strikers. At major cities, the unemployed flooded the ranks of the strikers. Some estimates suggest that the national unemployment rate was over 20 percent. Pittsburgh soon became the epicenter of the violence because of its railroads and depressed industry.

The riot in Pittsburgh started on July 21, 1877, as the first doubleheaders arrived at Pittsburgh. Rioters overturned locomotives, pulled up tracks, and set the Union Depot on fire. Pittsburgh erupted in violence, and the state militia arrived. Tracks were torn up and cars burned. The unemployed and street gangs joined in the riot. Shooting broke out on both sides. By the end of the day, 20 had been killed, including the sheriff, with hundreds of wounded lying on the sidewalks. Pittsburgh's Catholic bishop Tuigg walked the streets, giving last rites to the wounded, as another nine would die in the streets. Men, women, and children joined in the pillage. The Union Depot was torched, and over 1,000 freight cars of products were looted as citizens joined in. In all, 1,383 freight cars, 104 locomotives, and 66 passenger cars were destroyed at Pittsburgh. The city had 39 buildings burnt to the ground. President Rutherford Hayes rushed federal troops to help the overwhelmed state militia. Fear seized the city. Pittsburgh's damage came to over $5 million. The strike moved west into Ohio, where the governor encouraged the formation of private police works to protect property.

Chicago also had significant riots and property damage. In many cities, the unemployed, youth, socialists, and others joined the strike and looting. A mob of over 20,000 terrorized Chicago. In Chicago, the death count reached 20 as the city was totally closed down. With the tracks torn up between Baltimore, Pittsburgh, and Chicago, the nation's industry came to a standstill. In Illinois, coal miners joined the strike; in Pittsburgh, steelworkers joined the strike. By July 24, the riots traveled to San Francisco, where unemployed Chinese immigrants joined in the strike. The country had never known such violence except in war and would never see such civil unrest again until the civil rights riots in the summer of 1967. Americans had only read about such work-related violence in Europe in the 1870s, but the European immigrants of the 1840s could well remember the unrest and riots caused by socialists. Labor historian Joseph Rayback described the effect best: "The Railway Strike of 1877 thoroughly shocked a large portion of the public. Not since slaveholders had ceased to be haunted by dreams of a slave uprising had the propertied elements been so terrified." Rich neighborhoods in Chicago and Pittsburgh

Destruction in the Pittsburgh railroad yard following the Great Railroad Strike of 1877. (Library of Congress)

hired police to secure their homes and gardens. It was the perfect storm as the recession, heat wave, unemployed, and strikers came together on July 21, 22, and 23. The strike went on for 45 days until total peace was restored. Eventually the federal and state militia prevailed. The railroads had won the wage battle but at a great cost to equipment and property. Many cities started funds to employ the unemployed for service work at one dollar a day to take people off of the streets.

The Great Railroad Strike would change the course of American unionization. Unions learned the importance of better organization. They also learned the importance of public opinion. Initially, the railroad workers had widespread public sympathy and support. As violence and riots evolved, they lost that support. The same was true of the press, which initially supported the strikers. That changed with the violence and the inclusion of socialists and communists in the movement. The public wanted no part of the socialist movement that was spreading violence across Europe. The railroad companies came to change their strong-arm approach to employee grievances, realizing the property cost of such strikes far outweighed the wage concessions. Within five years, the major railroads had injury insurance, unemployment insurance, and pensions. The railroad companies also added air brake technology to eliminate brakemen (one brakeman per two cars) and to allow for doubleheaders. City mayors and local capitalists realized the need for unemployment funds for service work to keep people from joining such riots.

*See also:* Haymarket Riot; Homestead Strike of 1892; Panic of 1873; Pullman Strike; Westinghouse Air Brake

**References**

Bellesiles, Michael. *1877: America's Year of Living Violently.* New York: New Press, 2010.

Bruce, Robert. *1877: Year of Violence.* Lanham, MD: Ivan R. Dee, 1989.

Stowell, David. *The Great Strikes of 1877.* Urbana: University of Illinois Press, 2008.

Stowell, David. *Streets, Railroads, and the Great Strike of 1877.* Chicago: University of Chicago Press, 1999.

# World's First Skyscraper (1884)

Even today, the skyscraper is the icon of American business and a symbol of economic might. The skyscraper also represented a cultural revolution in office and real estate management. The skyscraper offered a solution to the high cost of prime city real estate. For years, building height was limited by the strength of materials, insufficient water pressure, and the ability of people to climb steps to their offices. In the 1880s, buildings over six stories were rare. Buildings carried their weight through the frames versus the internal skeletal structure. The Home Insurance Building in Chicago is recognized as the first skyscraper. The Home Insurance Building was 10 stories high (138 feet). It was the first building to be supported on the outside and inside. It was also the first building to fully use steel frame technology. Skeletal support, not height, was the defining characteristic of the skyscraper. It was technically possible to build up to 10 stories with stone framing. The Flaxmill Building in Shrewsbury, England, was a cast iron–framed building in 1797 that rose 11 stories. Six-story buildings became common with wrought iron beams and the invention of Elisha Otis's safety elevator in 1854. The Otis elevator had premiered at the Great Exhibition of 1851.

Cast iron frames had become popular, but steel was needed for internal structures strong enough to carry the building weight. Cast iron was popular because of its fireproofing, since fire was a major threat to city buildings of the time. Stone and cast iron beams had been used in the early 1800s, but true internal weight-bearing construction required the strength of steel. Wrought iron beams were an intermediate material that Peter Cooper had pioneered in New York. Steel, however, offered the strongest material available. Steel has three to four times the tensile strength of cast iron. Steel was in very limited supply until the development of the Bessemer steel process in the 1860s; prior to 1870, Bessemer steel was not available in large enough quantities for building. Steel also had to prove itself, and that took place in bridge building. The demonstration of the load-carrying strength of steel would be the Eads Bridge in St. Louis in 1874. The 520-foot bridge was the brainchild of America's steel man, Andrew Carnegie. Bridge designer James Eads had to convince Carnegie that steel could be used. Carnegie, however, had no steel mills at the time and had to purchase steel for his Keystone Bridge Company. The success of the Eads Bridge would usher in the age of structural steel for construction.

Carnegie would become a believer in steel, opening up his great Bessemer steel plant at Braddock, Pennsylvania, in 1875 and following it with his massive open-hearth structural mill at Homestead, Pennsylvania, in 1890. Carnegie would supply the structural beams for the building of the Brooklyn Bridge in the early 1880s. In 1883, it would be Carnegie who would sell steel to the Home Insurance Building architect, William Le Baron Jenney. Jenney had originally planned to use wrought iron beams and had actually started with wrought iron framing. Jenney actually built six stories before Carnegie convinced him to switch to steel beams. Jenney's use of steel framing won him the title of the "father of Chicago steel construction." The use of steel dropped the cost of insurance dramatically. The second steel frame building would come in 1886 with the building of Chicago's 12-story Rookery. Carnegie would build a 15-story skyscraper in Pittsburgh in 1890 using the "Chicago skeleton."

The use of steel in skyscrapers was followed by its use in constructing fireproof factories. H. J. Heinz started his fireproof three-story factory in 1889. Most of America's cities had been devastated by fires, and insurance costs had soared by the 1880s. Fire was one of the main reasons many companies failed. Fires had destroyed many American cities such as Chicago, Boston, and Pittsburgh. H. J. Heinz Company built its factory to be completely fireproof with steel beams and concrete fill between floors, which brought significant insurance savings for the company. The infrastructure was structural steel from Carnegie Steel. The popularity of skyscrapers created a revolution in steelmaking and construction. Bessemer steel's limits were being reached in the late 1890s at around 12 stories of height. Structural beams required the higher-quality open-hearth steel to move beyond 12 stories. Carnegie purchased a brand-new Bessemer steel mill at Homestead and gutted it to make open-hearth steel for the structural steel market that would move buildings skyward.

Skyscrapers were as much a cultural as a technological advance. In the late 1890s, skyscrapers started to be viewed as real estate and rentable office space. Culturally, the New York World Building in 1899 is considered the first modern skyscraper. The New York World Building was built as commercial real estate versus a corporate headquarters. The New York World Building was financed by banker

The world's first skyscraper—the Home Insurance Building in Chicago. (Chicago History Museum/Getty Images)

August Belmont as a real estate investment. The building had 950 separate offices to rent, and 4,000 people worked there. The New York World Building was 30 stories and 391 feet high. Chicago and New York became true business centers with these huge office buildings. The World Building also featured the electric elevator of Werner von Siemens, which was also a necessary technology for 30-plus-story buildings.

The next critical step in taller skyscrapers (moving beyond 30 stories) was the production of the Bethlehem Steel I beam. The I beam was lighter, but its design gave it more strength than the structural beams used at the time. The I beam was the invention of engineer Henry Grey, but it took the financing and building of a special rolling mill to make it a reality. Charles Schwab of Bethlehem Steel in 1907 made the investments necessary to change American skylines. Schwab used his business connections to overcome the resistance of engineers and architects to using the new technology. The I beam was lighter and stronger, but it cost triple what the older H beam did. I beams gained popularity with their use in Gimbel Brothers, the Field Museum, and the Chicago Opera House. The beam quickly gained export markets. In 1909, America produced less than a million tons of I beams, but in 1929, America produced over four million tons of I beams. There were many doubters, but its use in New York's Metropolitan Life Building of 50 stories (700 feet) proved it to be a success. The Bethlehem I beam went on to change the skylines of Chicago and New York with the Chrysler Building in New York reaching 77 stories (927 feet) in 1930 and the Empire State Building reaching 102 stories (1,250 feet) in 1931. Skyscrapers are great symbols of economic might today. Today we have the 2,717-foot, 160-story Burj Khalifa in Dubai.

*See also:* Andrew Carnegie's First Steel Mill; First Billion-Dollar Corporation—United States Steel; Great Exhibition of 1851

### References

Condit, Carl. *The Chicago School of Architecture.* Chicago: University of Chicago, 1964.

Sabbagh, Karl. *Skyscrapers: The Making of a Building.* New York: Penguin Books, 1991.

Turak, Theodore. *William Le Baron Jenney: A Pioneer in Modern Architecture.* Ann Arbor: University of Michigan Press, 1986.

# War of the Currents (1885)

The war of the currents was a gigantic clash between two of America's greatest inventors and Wall Street, headed by New York bank magnate J.P. Morgan. It pitted Thomas Edison's based direct current (DC) against George Westinghouse's alternating current (AC) to supply America with energy. Edison took an early lead based on his DC lighting systems and the invention of the incandescent lightbulb. Edison's first home lighting system was for Morgan. Morgan, who had helped finance Edison initially, lined up New York customers for his Pearl Station generating plant. On September 4, 1882, Edison watched from Morgan's office as his system lit up lower New York City. By the end of 1882, the Pearl Station was lighting 3,400 lamps for 231 customers. By the next year it was lighting 14,000 lamps. Edison was also constructing a central power station in Detroit (Henry Ford would work as an engineer there). The DC system had huge technological and cost problems. The DC system had a drop in voltage as the distance expanded. DC power required double the amount of copper wire compared to the AC system, and even then, the distance was very limited. To correct this required thick copper wires at the generator tapering off to the end of the line. The cost of copper inhibited the spread of Edison's DC system. He designed a central feeder station concept to overcome the voltage drop and copper usage. While much lower in cost, it would still be more costly than AC systems. By the late 1880s, Morgan was in control of Edison General Electric and the DC system.

The battle of the 1880s was not between DC and AC power but between arc lighting and Edison's incandescent lighting. Arc and incandescent lighting actually were two separate markets by 1892. Both were growth markets. Arc lighting meant that the light was created by the electrical arc between two carbon electrodes, much like arc welding today. Arc lights were great for outdoor applications such as streetlights because of their simplicity, power, and brightness. Arc lighting also offered much more candlepower than gaslights and could light railroad yards, factories, and parks. Arc lighting was an extremely profitable business, which had attracted Westinghouse to form his Pittsburgh lighting company in 1880. Arc lighting would be a growth market into the 20th century. In 1881, there were 6,000 arc lights in service; by 1886, there were 140,000 arc lights in service; by 1895, there were 300,000; and by 1902, there were 386,000. Technically, arc lights could be run by either DC or AC power, but they tended to use DC. Westinghouse had developed a fully functional AC arc lighting system in 1886.

Edison's incandescent lighting and power generation system used DC power. DC had serious transmission problems requiring excessive amounts of copper and power stations every mile. For this reason, Edison's DC systems were favored in densely populated areas such as New York. DC held only one advantage but an important one—that of a superior commercial electric motor. The DC motor favored DC's use in streetcar systems such as those of Thomson-Houston. Westinghouse, however, would develop an AC motor with the help of Nikola Tesla. Incandescent lighting could operate on either AC or DC with certain modifications. Edison held most of the patents relating to DC, while Westinghouse owned those for AC. Edison did hold a key patent for incandescent lightbulbs, which Westinghouse needed to grow his AC system.

On Thanksgiving of 1886, Buffalo, New York, was lighted by the Westinghouse AC system. Westinghouse had now entered Morgan and Edison's territory. Morgan realized that AC was the best-cost system. In 1888, Morgan was the largest stockholder of Edison Electric, but Edison had enough stock to block Morgan from imposing management or forcing Edison to consider AC, so the war continued. Edison Electric remained the largest and most integrated producer of power and electrical lighting systems. The status of electrical power generation at the end of 1887 told the story. Edison had 121 central power (DC) plants throughout the United States but primarily in densely populated areas that lowered its distribution costs. In about a year of market operation, Westinghouse had 68 central AC plants operating or under construction. Edison tried a marketing attack based on the danger of AC. A horse and cow were electrocuted for the press. At one point Edison was searching for a circus elephant to electrocute. Edison challenged Westinghouse to an electrical duel running the two currents through their bodies. Edison supported the use of electrocution for the death penalty in New York, so he could advertise the danger of AC. In August 1890, convicted murderer William Kemmler was electrocuted. The system bungled the job, turning it into a cruel spectacle. Edison supporters promoted the term "Westinghoused" for electrical execution. The market was turning against DC despite Edison's negative ad campaign because of the economic advantages of AC power. Westinghouse was winning contracts with industry, in particular, the steel and aluminum industries. The market was moving toward AC power.

Edison would be hurt as Morgan bought enough stock to take over Edison Electric in 1890. Edison, however, kept the company DC based as Morgan started to hedge his bets. Westinghouse would gain a marketing advantage by winning the 1893 World's Fair contract and, shortly afterward, the contract to build the Niagara Falls power generating plant. Edison tried to block the World's Fair's use of AC by using his monopoly on lightbulbs, but Westinghouse countered with the manufacture of a less efficient bulb on a different patent. Westinghouse would have to hire hundreds of men to replace thousands of lightbulbs daily because of their poor quality. Morgan made one last run by blocking financial aid to Westinghouse's bid for the World's Fair. Westinghouse got the support of rival banker August Belmont. Belmont was a pure moneyman, lacking the colossal trust dreams of bankers like Morgan. Belmont's deal would bring in two companies—United States Electric Lighting Company and Consolidated Electric Company. Westinghouse's system at the 1893 World's Fair would win him the bigger victory of building an AC power plant at Niagara Falls. Morgan and General Electric actually partnered with Westinghouse in the transmission of AC power. The building of the great Niagara AC power plant would mark the end of the war of the currents.

For Morgan, the war of patent fights, advertising, and price-cutting was wasting capital and money. Morgan would always point to the patent wars between electrical companies as a sign of the wasteful practices inherent in competition and a justification for trusts. The cost of copper and the lack of long-distance transmission would doom a national DC power grid. Morgan would force Edison out completely and reorganize Edison Electric into General Electric. General Electric moved into AC power generation and use. Westinghouse Electric and General Electric continued the patent battles for years. Westinghouse refused to join Morgan's trust. Eventually, because of the leveraged loans of 1893, Morgan forced Westinghouse Electric into bankruptcy.

*See also:* ALCOA Aluminum Formed; Chicago World's Fair; Niagara Falls Power Plant; Westinghouse Air Brake

### References

Hammond, J. *Men and Volts: The Story of General Electric.* New York: J. B. Lippincott, 1941.

Jonnes, Jill. *Empires of Light.* New York: Random House, 2003.

McNichol, Tom. *AC/DC: The Savage Tale of the First Standard War.* New York: Jossey-Bass, 2006.

Seifer, Marc. *Wizard: The Life and Times of Nikola Tesla.* New York: Citadel, 1998.

# Sears Mail Order Business (1886)

Richard Sears launched his business and revolutionary business model in 1886. He would ultimately merge the booming railroad market with the expanding mail service of America's westward movement to create a new business model. His mail order business model, sales guarantee, and use of advertising were major advances in the business world. Sears's rise to a promotional genius started slowly when he was a railroad agent for the Minnesota and St. Louis Railroad. Sears had been studying the use of promotional mail that flowed through the railroad. His first business venture was to sell a lot of watches rejected by a retailer in 1886. Sears promised the wholesaler that he could sell them, and he kept any profit over $12. The watches had a retail price of $25. Sears started selling the watches at $14 through other agents along the railroad line. Sears expanded sales using promotional mail flyers. He was wildly successful, and within six months he had made a profit of $5,000.

He studied the very successful business model of Montgomery Ward, who was already selling direct with a mail order catalog with 280 pages and 10,000 illustrations. The rural market was huge as 70 percent of the population was living in small rural communities. Rural prices for goods in general were sky-high with the middleman taking large profits. Sears focused narrowly on watches and jewelry to hone his business model. He quickly sensed some resistance, much as the Internet retail companies of a few years ago did. Farmers wanted to be able to trust that the retailer was honest and financially sound. Furthermore, farmers wanted a competitive price and a chance to preview the product. Farmers wanted to see the more expensive items first. Sears moved his company to Chicago in 1887 to be at the western crossroads of the railroads. Sears used the bonded railroad agents to offer his product cash on delivery based on examination when delivered, and he would expand this over the years with the cooperation of the postal system. This would be a powerful concept for the rural selling of expensive goods.

He then started to address the other concerns of his rural market. He improved his ads to include bank references and made personal visits to rural communities. He advertised to local and rural newspapers to improve the trust in the Sears name. His early flyers were extremely well done and had a folksy appeal. He added a money-back guarantee and a repair service. He built on word of mouth of his trustworthiness and ethical business practices. In 1887, Sears's first employee was watch repairman Alvah Curtis Roebuck. Sears quickly added silverware to his line. The postal system aided the mail order business by allowing catalogs to move at one cent per pound. The catalog was 80 pages in 1888. In 1890, Sears had proven his business model and expanded to standard-size clothing and popular durable goods such as sewing machines and bicycles. Sears's money-back guarantee was a solid promise that Sears never haggled over. The policy stated: "Satisfaction Guaranteed or Your Money Back." Most important for skeptical farmers, Sears delivered on his guarantee without argument. The catalog in 1890 was 322 pages with illustrations and detailed descriptions. The postal system expanded its rural direct home delivery, which further supported the business model. Sears's advertising was aggressive, and many of his claims would not meet the test of today's Federal Trade Commission.

Sears did have tough competition from the larger Montgomery Ward in the early years. Montgomery Ward also had an alliance with the farmer's main organization—the Grange. Many country storekeepers started to lose business to Sears, and they refused to have the catalogs in the store. The catalog offered far more than the country store could hope to keep in inventory. A few stores decided to partner and form an alliance with Sears, but many stores opposed Sears publicly by negative word-of-mouth efforts. Sears's rural free delivery, ironclad money-back guarantee, and variety made it difficult for small storekeepers. Small storeowners often mounted enough political pressure to have the local newspapers refuse Sears's advertising. Sears responded by advertising in the new and popular mail magazines such as *Ladies' Home Journal*. The resistance is not unlike that of today by small storeowners against big stores such as Wal-Mart. Sears also had to initially run high inventory costs to assure availability, much as Amazon did in the early days of selling books over the Internet. From the start, however, Sears developed a strong supply chain to support his direct-selling business model. Sears's price, quality, and customer service would eventually win over the local residents who at first resisted.

Sears pioneered in advertising by offering specials and gifts. When towns actually started burning catalogs to save their local businesses, Sears developed more innovative practices. Catalogs were sent in batches to local patrons to distribute to friends. Records were kept on these new customer sales. Based on sales, catalog distributors were given prizes such as a sewing machine or stove. Sears promoted sales clubs similar to direct product sales today. Clubs would get further discounts. Sears's catalog became so popular he could charge for it, but he always sent it free to his best customers. He also would apply the $0.25 catalog fee to any order over $10.00. In 1893, the company became known as Sears, Roebuck and Company as Julius Rosenwald entered the company. Rosenwald brought extensive supply chain management to the growing business, allowing for a major expansion of the company.

The government, supported by the farm lobby and a business-experienced post-master, John Wanamaker, favored the expansion of the mail order business. Wannamaker opened the first department store in Philadelphia during the Centennial Exposition of 1876 to make his fortune. The full implementation of Rural Free Delivery in 1896 was a major boon for Sears, Roebuck and Company. Prior to Rural Free Delivery, farmers had to travel to the railroad station to get their mail. The Sears catalog continued to evolve and innovate. The company added a self-test for eyeglasses in 1896 as well as heavy products such as pianos and organs. In 1897, color was introduced to the catalog, as red and brown were added, and by 1897, additional colors such as green and gold were added. Sears started to issue specific catalogs to focus on farm equipment and clothing. Rosenwald had extensive clothing experience as well and added bigger sizes for the stout farmers. custom-made garments were added as well. Sears added a special catalog for builders, which proved another success. With $10 million in sales in 1900, Sears surpassed its biggest competitor, Montgomery Ward, which had $8 million in sales. This expansion was fueled by a volume purchasing policy that gave Sears a cost advantage in the market. Sears would remain America's largest retailer until it was overtaken by Wal-Mart in the 1990s. Known for his risk-taking, Sears added a customer credit program in 1911. Sears's strategy retained its rural focus until the 1920s when it started to open retail stores.

*See also:* Automated Sewing Machine; Centennial Exposition; Clipper Ships; First Electric Sign (Product Branding and Advertising)—H. J. Heinz; Overland Travel and Mail Service

### References
Hoge, Cecil. *The First Hundred Years Are the Toughest.* Berkeley, CA: Ten Speed, 1988.

Weil, Gordon L. *Sears, Roebuck, U.S.A.* New York: Stein and Day, 1977.

Worthy, James. *Shaping an American Institution: Robert E. Woods and Sears.* Chicago: University of Illinois Press, 1984.

# Haymarket Riot (1886)

The Haymarket Riot would change the course of unionization in the United States. It would help define the union movement and differentiate it from the union movement in Europe, and, for many, it would represent a major setback. The union movement had been building in the United States since the mid-1870s. The Great Railroad Strike of 1877 had demonstrated the power of the movement and some of the public concerns. Still, union membership was growing rapidly and was gaining support in many of the industrial cities. Working conditions at the time were abysmal. Workers often worked 12-hour days, seven days a week. Safety and benefits were nonexistent. While pay was much higher than in Europe, it was perceived as being too low. The length of the working day was considered particularly oppressive. A national labor organization—the Knights of Labor—was gaining popularity with its campaign for an eight-hour day. The Knights had even won over Bill Jones, the enlightened plant manager of the nation's largest factory, the Edgar Thomson steel plant of Andrew Carnegie. Jones had argued with Carnegie that the eight-hour day would actually increase productivity and had implemented it with great success. Prior to the Haymarket Riot, the eight-hour day had broad popular support in the United States. Under the leadership of Terence Powderly, the Knights had won a major strike against Jay Gould's Wabash Railroad in 1882. The membership of the Knights boomed to 700,000 nationally. The organization was particularly strong in the Chicago manufacturing district.

The early spring of 1886 pitted union workers at the McCormick Harvesting Machine Company against management over 12-hour-plus working days. At the same time, the Federation of Organized Trades and Labor Unions had called for a May 1 parade and march in American cities for union support. The Knights of Labor joined the national day. The march in Chicago had the strong support of German radicals as well. Chicago was the heart of German immigrants and socialists. Estimates of the crowds in Chicago on May 1 were over 80,000. Nationwide, the estimates of the May Day march were over a half million. Albert Parsons, an anarchist and founder of the International Working People's Association (a Marxist/socialist group), led the Chicago march. It was an opportune time for the locked-out workers of McCormick to form an alliance with this massive popular movement. On May 3, a protest outside of the McCormick plant resulted in a death. The McCormick plant was under the protection of outside Pinkerton guards and privately hired police, as strikebreakers had been hired to run the plant.

The death ignited an outcry among the young German radicals of the May 1 protests. Even though the strikers were Irish American, the German population rallied with them under the prodding of the socialist German radicals. These anarchists took over the McCormick strike to use for the broader purpose of the eight-hour day and socialist movement. On May 4, a crowd of 1,500 to 2,000 gathered in Chicago's Haymarket Square where farmers sold their products. The protesters had expected a crowd of 20,000, but a rainy day kept the crowd down. The main speaker was August Spies, editor of a German socialist paper in Chicago (*Arbeiter-Zeitung*). Police had gathered to break up the peaceful demonstration.

During some of the small scuffles, someone threw a pipe bomb, wounding police officers. The scene erupted in police fire. Eventually the crossfire resulted in the death of eight police and four civilians with over 100 wounded. Panic followed. Local anarchists printed flyers calling for an uprising and revenge. The violence turned the general public against the organizers of the eight-hour-day movement.

The trial that followed was covered by the nation's newspapers. Eight people, including Spies and Parsons, were charged with murder. All were anarchists, and six were German immigrants. The trial stirred up more sentiment against the Germans, socialists, and the eight-hour-day unionists. Links were made with the violent socialists of France, known as the Second International. The trial, however, was deeply faulted, polarizing the public. The defendants argued that Pinkertons had thrown the bomb to turn the public against the unionists. Another popular conspiracy theory was that eastern capitalists hired the bomber. Eventually, seven of the eight defendants received the death sentence, although it was never determined who threw the bomb. There is no doubt that the Haymarket was a major setback to the eight-hour day. In addition, the membership of the Knights of Labor plummeted after the Haymarket Riot as the unions took the blame for the violence. The American Federation of Labor did grow its membership by avoiding linkage with the anarchists. The Haymarket help steer the American union movement away from the political role that unions played in Europe. Samuel Gompers,

Police charge rioters in Old Haymarket Square in Chicago, Illinois, on May 4, 1886. (Library of Congress)

father of American unions and founder of the American Federation of Labor, saw the importance of keeping the union movement away from becoming a political movement. Gompers had been a socialist but saw the shortcomings of a union movement focused on the overthrowing of capitalism versus a movement focused on the grievances of and abuses to the workers. Gompers would start to argue for a "pure and simple" movement. Gompers's approach saw public support grow for unions and moved the American unions from the European model. It was clear that the public supported better pay and working conditions but had little stomach for violence and anticapitalist rhetoric.

The full effect of the Haymarket evolved over the years with the American labor movement itself. American unions started a path to worker representation as opposed to political change. May 1 was adopted by the International Socialists as a world day to honor workers and the "martyrs" of the Haymarket. The communists of the 20th century adopted the May Day tradition. Initially, the Haymarket strengthened public opposition to unions. A bronze statue was erected in 1889 to honor the policemen who died there. Starting in 1927, the statue began a long history of being bombed, vandalized, and moved. It became a rallying symbol again in the 1960s and 1970s for war protesters and the radical Weathermen, who destroyed the statue. It was rebuilt once again in 1992 with a politically neutral plaque, calling attention to its role in highlighting the eight-hour day. In 1893, a workers' monument was erected in a suburban cemetery to honor the workers. The workers' monument has grown in popularity over the years with unions.

*See also:* Andrew Carnegie's First Steel Mill; Great Railroad Strike of 1877; Homestead Strike of 1892; National Labor Relations Act (Wagner Act); Paternal Capitalism—Homestead and Wilmerding, Pennsylvania; Pullman Strike; Revolution, Famine, and Immigration

### References

Avrich, Paul. *The Haymarket Tragedy.* Princeton, NJ: Princeton University Press, 1984.

David, Henry. *The History of the Haymarket Affair: A Study of the American Social–Revolutionary and Labor Movements.* New York: Collier Books, 1963.

Foner, Philip S., ed. *The Autobiographies of the Haymarket Martyrs.* New York: Pathfinder, 1969.

Green, James R. *Death in the Haymarket: A Story of Chicago, the First Labor Movement and the Bombing That Divided Gilded Age America.* New York: Pantheon Books, 2006.

# ALCOA Aluminum Formed (1888)

Steel and iron were the materials used in American industry in the 19th century, but a new light metal would lead American industry into the 20th century. Aluminum is the earth's most abundant metal. Yet aluminum oxides and silicates are extremely stable oxides that are not easily smelted into aluminum metal. Industrialist Saint Claire Deville displayed these few buttons, made of very expensive aluminum, at the 1855 World's Fair in Paris. The simple display of "silver from clay" inspired Emperor Napoleon III of France. The cost was $522 a pound, or about $10,000 a pound in today's dollars. Napoleon III had aluminum tableware produced for his best guests, while lesser guests used gold and silverware. George Westinghouse used aluminum foil on the walls of his house when it had a price higher than gold in 1880. With the completion of the Washington Monument in Washington, D.C., it was decided to cap the monument with a pyramid of precious aluminum in 1884.

The real breakthrough to the commercial production of aluminum came in 1886, achieved by Charles Hall. Hall was a student at Oberlin College in Ohio working in a makeshift laboratory. He was an obsessed Edison-type chemist whose endless experimentation had unlocked the secret. Today a beautiful aluminum statue of Charles Hall at Oberlin College commemorates the discovery. Motivated by the possibility of making a fortune, he continued endless experiments on cheaper aluminum making, even as he discovered an electrolytic method to remove aluminum from its oxide. Hall had tried many different oxides, taking his Edison-like trial-and-error experimental approach to extremes. Finally he discovered that cryolite, a mineral from Greenland, would work. The Hall process was electrochemical, requiring an electric current; like Edison, Hall used a series of batteries to supply the electricity for his laboratory.

About the same time a French student, Paul Heroult, developed the same process as Hall, using chemical electrolysis. The process used a huge amount of electrical current, limiting its use until Westinghouse opened the Niagara Falls generating plant in the 1890s. The amount of energy needed to smelt just one pound of aluminum would keep a 40-watt lightbulb burning for 10 to 12 days. To state it another way, today aluminum smelting takes 3 percent of the world's electrical power. Commercialization would, however, get its start in Pittsburgh in 1888. It was there that Charles Martin Hall and Alfred Hunt would come together. Hunt was one of the country's first true metallurgists. Hunt went to the Massachusetts Institute of Technology to study metallurgy in the chemistry department. He had the capital and industrial contracts to commercialize the Hall process.

On July 31, 1888, Romaine Cole (a Pittsburgh invstor), Hunt, Howard Lash (president of Carbon Steel), Millard Hunsiker (sales manager of Carbon Steel), Robert John Scott (a Carnegie partner and superintendent of Union Mills), and W. S. Sample (chief chemist at Pittsburgh Testing) held a meeting at Hunt's home in Pittsburgh. This organizational meeting resulted in the formation of Pittsburgh Reduction Company (later the Aluminum Company of America, or ALCOA), whose name would be synonymous with the commercialization of the Hall process. Hunt asked Pittsburgh banker Andrew Mellon for a small loan to help with the operation. Like so many during the Gilded Age, Mellon was captivated by this silver-like metal. Science fiction writers such as Jules Verne and H. G. Wells hailed it as the future of metals in the 1880s in the science fiction books that a young Mellon had read. Verne used it in fictional boats, buildings, aircraft, and a space capsule for the moon. Mellon offered a much larger loan and bought $6,000 worth of stock. It was the beginning of a historic relationship.

Yet another Pittsburgher, Westinghouse, supplied two powerful Westinghouse dynamos to produce the needed electrical current for aluminum production. The 1,200 amperes and 25 volts of each steam-driven dynamo were beyond any laboratory battery and offered the potential for continuous operation. Westinghouse himself supervised the installation. Westinghouse had been experimenting with aluminum parts for several years and looked forward to having aluminum available to use in transportation applications where lightweight aluminum could offer many advantages. On Thanksgiving Day 1888, the plant, under the supervision of Charles Martin Hall, produced its first commercial batch of aluminum. By mid-1889, the Pittsburgh plant was producing about 1,000 pounds of aluminum a month at around $5 a pound. By the end of the year, the price was about $2 a pound. At this price, new uses started to appear.

The year 1893 would prove the turning point. That year ALCOA would win the many patent challenges to the process. The judge was William Taft (future president of the United States). The 1,500-page decision made it clear that Hall was the inventor. The Pittsburgh Reduction Company now controlled the patent for the only commercial process of aluminum production. The aluminum capitalists exhibited the Hall process at the Chicago World's Fair in 1893. The Pittsburgh Reduction Company was an award winner at the fair with its educational exhibit. The exhibit included some of the original small pellets made by Hall at his Oberlin laboratory. There was a scale model of the Hall process and aluminum samples. Year later at the Pittsburgh Exposition, the company demonstrated an aluminum bicycle and kitchenware such as pots and pans. The potential use of aluminum in bicycles attracted the Wright brothers, who would use an aluminum crankcase in their first plane, which would open the use of aluminum in aircraft production in the future. Baron von Zeppelin would use aluminum framing in his famous hydrogen airships. The year 1893 brought Westinghouse the Niagara Falls power project, and the Pittsburgh Reduction Company signed a contract to be the major customer of the new Niagara Falls plant. This new plant near the Niagara with a huge supply of electrical power would have the capacity to produce 10,000 pounds of aluminum a day and dropped the price to $0.75 a pound. Westinghouse's Niagara project and ALCOA's new aluminum plant would realize the dreams of science fiction writers of the previous 100 years.

The growth of the company after the Spanish-American War was phenomenal. In 1901, Pittsburgh Reduction Company organized the Aluminum Cooking

Utensil Company to sell products to housewives. Banker Mellon increased his share in the company and highlighted its use by building aluminum bathtubs and sinks in his home. The Mellon family became active in shaping the direction of ALCOA and financed companies that used aluminum. The Mellon approach was similar to Morgan's monopolies but used horizontal integration, dealing with the using finished-product companies and sales outlets. The company developed a novel plan to sell its Wear-Ever brand. College students were recruited to sell door to door by demonstrating aluminum cookware, a sales model that would be used by many companies. In 1907, Pittsburgh Reduction Company changed its name to the ALCOA (Aluminum Company of America). ALCOA continued its amazing growth, but in 1912, it ran up against the new antitrust laws. In later years, Mellon ordered the first all-aluminum cars to be made. This model of banking, horizontal integration, and industry became known as the Mellon system. Mellon had strong political ties, which allowed for favorable tariffs to protect ALCOA in its infancy. Originally, in the 1890s, aluminum had a tariff of 8¢ to 15¢ a pound under President William McKinley. The tariff for raw aluminum was reduced to 2¢ a pound in 1913, but finished aluminum products maintained a high tariff rate, which allowed Mellon and the country to horizontally integrate into aluminum products. The Mellon system of horizontal expansion and corporate control was so successful that Mellon was drafted to be secretary of the Treasury in the late 1920s.

*See also:* Chicago World's Fair; Commercial Flight; Niagara Falls Power Plant; War of the Currents; Westinghouse Air Brake

### References

Cannadine, David. *Mellon: An American Life.* New York: Knopf, 2006.

Carr, Charles C. *ALCOA: An American Enterprise.* New York: Rinehart, 1952.

Skrabec, Quentin R. *The World's Richest Neighborhood: How Pittsburgh's East Enders Forged American Industry.* New York: Algora, 2010.

# McKinley Tariff of 1890

The McKinley Tariff of 1890 was a specific bill passed by William McKinley, then chairman of the Ways and Means Committee and future president of the United States. It also represented a political policy of protection of American industry that people had been arguing about for almost 100 years in America. The famous McKinley Tariff of 1890 was the peak of decades of protectionist policy by the Republican Party and the Whig Party prior to that. America had been strongly protectionist since the presidency of Abraham Lincoln, with roots going back to

Henry Clay's "American system." The highest tariffs, averaging 40 percent of the shipped value, came with the McKinley Tariff of the 1890s, which ushered in a period of world supremacy of American manufacturing. The infamous Smoot-Hawley Tariff of 1930 was a bit larger, in that there were higher rates and more products. Smoot-Hawley added to a world trade war as the world moved into depression, but it was just one of many errors (there was a tax increase as well). The Smoot-Hawley Tariff was not a managed-trade tariff but all-out across-the-board protectionism. The McKinley approach to tariffs was based on the cornerstone of trade reciprocity to prevent trade wars. It required heavy congressional overview to assure profits were put into plant expansion and employment. The McKinley tariffs of the 1890s focused on the protection and development of infant industries such as aluminum, tinplate, and electrical products as well as the basic industrial core of steel, iron, processed food, and glass.

McKinley, a congressman from Ohio, took up the cause of Clay's American system in the 1880s. McKinley had found a simple truth in the necessity of man (human beings in general) as a maker and producer. Man's soul is in making and using tools; it is what distinguishes him from the animals. It was McKinley's belief that the level and nature of manufacture defines the level of civilization. McKinley came from a middle-class working family in the iron industry; his family had suffered unemployment caused by cheap imports. Bankers and merchants were ancillary to McKinley's economic view; McKinley's roots in a middle-class iron-making family caused him to forge an alliance with labor and capital for a common goal. The manufacturing districts such as eastern Ohio, western Pennsylvania, Illinois, Indiana, southern Michigan, and New England would become his political base.

McKinley's great Tariff of 1890 passed Congress by satisfying many Democrats with the counterbalance of the Sherman Anti-Trust Act and Interstate Commerce Act. As a third-term congressman in 1880, McKinley hailed and supported President Chester Arthur's Federal Tariff Commission. The Tariff Commission actively monitored the tariffs and their impact. McKinley adapted the trade policy of reciprocity of President Garfield's secretary of state, James Blaine. McKinley followed Garfield as chairman of the Ways and Means Committee. Congressional oversight to assure that profits were reinvested in plant expansion and increased employment was one cornerstone of the bill. The other was reciprocity requiring balancing of imports and exports from a trading partner.

McKinley also was innovative in his 1890 bill, which included a special reciprocity clause. The bill waived 99 percent of the duties on raw materials that were imported and then exported as finished goods to foreign markets. This was a creative approach to allow cheap raw materials for manufacturers while promoting American manufacturing aboard. This would allow South American wool and raw sugar to flow in and be converted by American manufacturers into clothing and refined sugar that could be exported without duties to South America. The industrialists rallied around McKinley, but eastern bankers offered stiff opposition, enjoying the profits of trade. McKinley built an unusual alliance of capitalists, laborers, people from the middle class, and immigrants. The political success of McKinley's tariffs depended on the capitalists investing their profits in plant expansion in America instead of pocketing the profits.

McKinley's bill of 1890 was maybe the best researched ever and used science and statistics to apply the tariff rates. First, McKinley argued that the revenue tariff approach was the real problem, not protective tariffs. His statistics were convincing: "Before 1820 nearly all our imports were dutiable; scarcely any were free; while in 1824 the proportion of free imports was less than 6 percent; in 1830, about 7 percent. . . . The percent of free imports from 1873 to 1883 was about 30 percent, and under the tariff revision of 1883 it averaged 33 percent." For his 1890 bill, it would be 50 percent. The difference was that it focused on the nation's needs, not the production of revenue, as tariffs had for years been the only major source of government income. The plan was fully consistent with the Federalists' and the Whigs' view of a manufacturing utopia. The McKinley plan was the result of years of study, and no one knew more about tariffs than McKinley, but he would have to make political compromises to get it passed and spend years defending it and fighting cuts.

As president, McKinley pushed for reciprocity arrangements through treaties in the 1897 Dingley tariff. Debated at the time, reciprocity gave protectionist America a perception of fairness. Many conservatives were concerned that McKinley's reciprocity arrangements would lead to an erosion of protectionism, but McKinley believed it was necessary for the future. American surplus was becoming an issue, and McKinley wanted to allow for a boom in exports. In his last speech, given at Buffalo, McKinley defined his vision: "A system which provides a mutual exchange of commodities is manifestly essential to continued and healthful growth of our export trade. . . . Reciprocity is the natural outgrowth of our wonderful industrial development under the domestic policy now firmly established. . . . The expansion of our trade and commerce is a pressing problem. Commercial wars are unprofitable. A policy of good will and friendly trade relations will prevent reprisals. Reciprocity treaties are in harmony with the spirit of the times; measures of retaliation are not."

Statistics for the decade from 1890 to 1900 support the conclusion that McKinley's tariffs were successful, as prices came down, profits rose, capital investment went up, and wages held steady or increased slightly (real wages clearly rose). The average annual manufacturing income went from $425.00 a year, or $1.44 a day, in 1890 to $432.00 a year, or $1.50 a day, in 1900. The average working day in manufacturing remained around 10 hours. Heavily protected industries such as steel fared slightly better with wages. The cost-of-living index fell during the decade from 91 to 84, about an 8 percent drop. The clothing cost of living dropped even more, from 134 to 108, or 19 percent. Food stayed about the same, but the cost of protected sugar dropped around 25 percent. The bottom line is that real wages (adjusted for the cost-of-living index) rose from $1.58 a day to $1.77 a day in 1900, about a 12 percent increase. Invention flowered during the period as companies invested in research and development to meet congressional oversight of profits. The success of this period of managed trade depended on government oversight, business cooperation, and labor support. The list of companies that built their foundation and expanded includes Libbey Glass, United States Steel, Standard Oil, ALCOA (Aluminum Company of America), H. J. Heinz (there was a 40 percent tariff on pickles), and Bethlehem Steel, to name a few.

*See also:* Abraham Lincoln Establishes Protectionism; First Japanese Auto Sold in the United States; Homestead Strike of 1892; Jefferson Embargo; Paternal Capitalism—Homestead and Wilmerding, Pennsylvania; "Report on Manufacturing"; Whig Party Evolves

### References

Gould, Lewis. *The Presidency of William McKinley.* Lawrence: University of Kansas Press, 1980.

Phillips, Kevin. *William McKinley.* Boston: Houghton Mifflin, 2003.

Skrabec, Quentin. *William McKinley: Apostle of Protectionism.* New York: Algora, 2008.

Zieger, Robert. *Republicans and Labor.* Lexington: University of Kentucky Press, 1969.

# Homestead Strike of 1892

The Homestead Strike of 1892 is the labor/management classic for today's manager. It would determine the path and the nature of industrial unions, as well as management–union and public–union relations. The Homestead Strike would leave an indelible mark on American business. The roots of mistrust, biased press coverage, political intervention, and overly strong stands would be planted on the river floodplain of Homestead across from Pittsburgh. The struggle would bring good and bad. It forced all Americans to look at the nature of work, business, jobs, and the economy. It is rare that when Americans shed blood, real change does not come. The relationship between socialism and American trade unionism would be forged in the blood of the workers and managers of Homestead. American unionism would become distinct from that of Europe after Homestead. The concerns and views of both union leaders and managers at Homestead have a familiar ring today.

The gathering of forces at Homestead would lead to an end of many icons in America. It would be here that America's strongest union would face America's largest company, Carnegie Steel. Industrialists Henry Clay Frick and Andrew Carnegie would have their Waterloo. It would be the beginning of the end of the Amalgamated Association of the Iron and Steel Workers, but, like the Alamo, it would be the rallying cry of American unionization for decades. The Homestead Strike changed management's, the union's, and the public's view of concepts like property rights and European-style union socialism.

Both the Carnegie empire and the Amalgamated union approached July 1892 at the peak of their power. Carnegie was the richest man in the world, and his company was the biggest and most profitable. Homestead was one of America's great melting pots as Slavs and Hungarians poured in to fill the thousands of unskilled jobs created in America's largest factory. The local natives, skilled Western European Americans, were angered by this new influx of unskilled workers. The Amalgamated union was a skilled crafts union that excluded the majority of the unskilled labors in the workforce. The ethnic mix would become a major complication in the struggle. This strike was far from America's bloodiest or biggest, but it is one of the most remembered.

The buildup to the 1892 Homestead Strike started at the 1891 convention of the Amalgamated Association of Iron and Steel Workers, held a few miles downriver at Pittsburgh. The convention had 261 delegates representing 24,068 members. It was America's largest crafts union, representing the skilled crafts workers of the iron and steel industry. The union, however, was fighting the changes inherent in industrialization and technological automation. The Amalgamated union was opposing disturbing trends that eroded the skilled crafts system infrastructure. The union was holding to its skilled apprenticeship system of seniority, control over the amount of production that could be scheduled, and bans on overtime unless all crafts workers were employed. The union remained opposed to the entry of any Eastern Europeans such as Slovaks and Hungarians, who were the unskilled fraction of the workforce. As the possible strike approached in July 1892, hundreds from the national press filled Pittsburgh hotels as both sides fought for public support of their views. National politicians came also as they framed the conflict as part of the tariffs-versus-free trade debate of the time. The Democrats cited Carnegie's profits and poor wages as evidence that years of protective steel tariffs had failed to help the workers. Homestead had been recognized by both Carnegie and the union as the location of Armageddon for the showdown of labor and steel management.

The real battle was, for the most part, against the advance of technology, which was reducing the skill level needed. Homestead represented a stand for management as well as reinforcement of property rights and control of the means of production. Carnegie had purchased the failed Homestead Bessemer steel mill and gutted it, putting in the latest technology. Carnegie and Frick, his general manager, had eliminated hundreds of skilled workers. Carnegie had brought in thousands of unskilled Eastern European workers and was expanding their role in the operations. Furthermore, the economy of 1892 was now in a downturn, which gave Carnegie the upper hand that he had played so well in the past.

For most, the facts of Homestead are surprising. The unionized skilled workers at Homestead numbered 800 out of about 3,800 total employees. The Amalgamated Association of Iron and Steel Workers represented an even smaller group, 325 highly paid and skilled workers. The wage argument was initially with those 325 workers. Even more surprising might be that the average American worker at the time made $8.50 a week, while a union steelworker at Homestead averaged $35.00 a week. In terms of a wage cuts, the new proposal from Carnegie meant a cut from 40 percent to 20 percent. The 3,000-plus unskilled laborers joined the strike, having no place to go.

In early June, Carnegie wisely left Pittsburgh for a vacation in Scotland. On June 25, 1892, Frick closed off negotiations and started plans for a lockout. Meantime, reporters from around the world were flooding into Pittsburgh. One paper estimated there were at least 135 journalists from all over the globe. Homestead was a story waiting to happen.

Frick set up an 18-foot wooden fence with barbed wire and allegedly with rifle slots. Sewers leading from the mill were provided with gratings. Arc light searchlights were also installed on 12-foot towers. It was rumored (falsely) that the barbed wire was electrified, using Westinghouse's new alternating current. In early June, Frick had contracted with the Pinkerton Company, which supplied hired armed guards for industry and others, for an army of 300 guards. The hiring of Pinkerton guards, while unpopular, was not unusual. However, the number needed for America's largest industrial plant was unusual. Pinkerton was short on trained guards because of prolonged strikes in the mines of Utah and Colorado. Pinkerton had been advertising in western cities for armed guards at five dollars a day plus

Union strikers drive Pinkerton guards from the Homestead Steel plant during the Homestead Strike in July 1892. (Library of Congress)

food and lodging. They mustered these raw recruits in Chicago, a mix of college students, drifters, and laid-off workers. The union similarly prepared its forces, which included the unskilled workers. They patrolled the river, the railroad tracks, and the bridges. They assumed scabs would be sent in, so scouts on horses were sent up and down the river to warn the town of any approaching company men.

Things had reached the breaking point in Homestead as the saloons filled up and effigies of Carnegie, Frick, and others were hung on telegraph poles. Frick laid out his plan to have the Pinkerton guards enter the works, turning it into a fort. They would enter via the Ohio and Monongahela Rivers. The union had managed to gain the support of the unskilled workers, which surprised Frick and Carnegie, but it was a weak alliance. The unskilled workers were caught in the middle and could only hope for a quick settlement. By July 4, 1892, the workers had gotten word of men being hired by Pinkerton in Chicago. On July 5, the workers pushed down the fence and surged into the mill. Local authorities were overwhelmed.

The Pinkertons moved to the Homestead plant by two river barges on the Ohio River. The barges had been purchased and converted into covered troop carriers. These were floating forts described as "Noah's Arks." They were equipped with dining halls and kitchens, complete with a hired steward and 20 waiters. Winchester rifles were in closed boxes to be opened only by command. As the barges moved toward the plant, fog and early morning darkness helped cover their approach. A horseman spotted the barges and was sent to awake Homestead. At 2:30 A.M., the Homestead Electric Works sounded a whistle alarm. Residents and workers, like the minutemen of old, got out of bed and picked up old family guns. There was some pushing at the mill, and then shots rang out. Three steelworkers were killed on the spot and dozens wounded. An old 20-pounder Revolutionary War cannon was fired, missing the barges and hitting and killing a steelworker. The Pinkertons had some wounded as well and retreated to their floating forts. Inaccurate cannon fire and shots continued as the Pinkertons huddled in their floating forts. The Pinkertons had some protection but lacked air-conditioning, and the barges were becoming sweaty iron furnaces. The Pinkertons were not professionals, so they doubted the value of their lives in this strange action. In Pittsburgh, Frick tried to use the courts to put pressure on the governor to send troops. Homesteaders added to the barrage by tossing dynamite. Telegraph wire reports to Washington and Congress brought calls to repeal the tariffs that had helped Carnegie Steel. Meanwhile, the Homesteaders poured oil on the Monongahela River and started a few surface fires. By 7:00 P.M., the Pinkertons had had it and raised a white flag. The count was 13 dead and 36 wounded. Captured Pinkertons were forced through a crowd of angry workers who freely beat them with clubs.

The sheriff struggled to find deputies, and the union leadership in Homestead struggled to regain control of the town. Union men in Chicago talked about sending men and guns. The Congress debated daily. The governor finally sent troops after Pittsburgh political bosses pulled every string possible; still, the troops were not greeted in Homestead. Rails were torn up to slow the trains, but the troops were in place by July 12. With the town under military control, Congress sent a special committee to hold hearings. With Homestead peaceful and under martial law, the advantage passed to Carnegie's company. Union president Hugh O'Donnell called unsuccessfully for a national boycott of Carnegie steel products, and Samuel Gompers came to help support the unsuccessful boycott. O'Donnell appealed by letter on July 16 to the Republican vice-presidential candidate, Whitelaw Reid, to allow the union to save some face by reopening the negotiations. A strong-willed Frick, however, refused, sensing he had a victory. On July 14, O'Donnell went to New York City to try to win over the Republicans, who were counting on the labor vote for high tariffs in the fall presidential election. While O'Donnell was in New York with the Republicans, Frick started to advertise for scabs, according to the long-range plan. Things changed again as the socialists entered the crisis from places like New York and Chicago. On July 23, a clean-cut socialist and activist in a suit, Alexander Berkman, entered Frick's office at the *Chronicle-Telegraph* building on Pittsburgh's Fifth Avenue.

The socialist and anarchist movements in the United States had been following the action at Homestead and hoped to use it to their political gain. The most radical left fringe was the anarchists, who even rejected the minor organizational bent of Karl Marx. The anarchists had always looked for opportunities to get involved in labor scuffles. They were best known for the Haymarket Riot in Chicago. For them, the capitalists were the evil of the world. Berkman had arrived alone in Pittsburgh around July 16 with little money and a gun, wearing the suit his girlfriend, Emma Goldman, had suggested. Frick was in the office with his partner and second in command, John Leishman. Berkman rushed in and fired, hitting Frick in the shoulder. Frick fell, and Berkman fired again, hitting Frick in the neck. Berkman's entrance into the crisis changed things. The union wanted no part of Berkman's act. While the press continued to villainize Frick, they also hailed his courage and nerve. Frick survived and remained in control from his bedroom. His courage and resolve were amazing. The religion of the workers was Catholicism, and the local priests and press saw more evil in anarchists than capitalists. An editorial in the *Catholic World* in 1893 noted: "The distribution of wealth is frightful in its very inequalities. Still I do believe that the social system is radically and hopelessly wrong. I do believe that the American workmen can right their wrongs by the machinery at their disposal and without violating any rights or any law, human or divine." The public across the nation was concerned about the existence of anarchist cells in major cities and the rising tide of socialism, which forced unions to expel known socialists. The public turned against the union. Still, the public had little stomach for the use of Pinkertons and troops in labor disputes. For the next few years, Homestead would be debated in major newspapers across the nation.

Pennsylvania governor Robert Patterson was a Democrat, and the Homestead uprising played into the politics to break the workers' support for Republicans, which had been due to the Republicans' tariffs. The White House was watching the problems at Homestead closely. President Benjamin Harrison was struggling and needed the labor vote, while the Democrats were linking Homestead to the Republicans. Harrison privately was opposed to the use of armed Pinkertons, but Frick would not end the strike even "if President Harrison himself should personally request him to do so." Frick had gone too far to consider a change. Harrison sent in troops to end the strike, and Frick replaced the striking workers. By October, Frick was in charge of the mill, and it was operating again. Democrats felt they could carry western Pennsylvania for the first time since the formation of the Republican Party in the 1850s. Torchlight parades in Homestead had floats portraying "protectionism" as a black sheep, as politicians injected their own brand of racism into the crisis. Senate Democrats came to Homestead to hold hearings. Homestead cost Harrison and the Republicans the election, and the Democrats would effectively repeal the great protective Tariff of 1890. However, the union was crushed, and it would not be until the 1930s that Pittsburgh mills would again be unionized. The American union movement moved away from the socialism, violence, and political role of unionization seen in Europe. Unions also realized the importance of full representation and solidarity.

*See also*: Railroad Strike of 1877

### References

Krass, Peter. *Carnegie.* New York: Wiley, 2002.

Krause, Paul. *Battle of Homestead.* Pittsburgh, PA: University of Pittsburgh Press, 1992.

Skrabec, Quentin. *Henry Clay Frick: The Life of a Perfect Capitalist.* Jefferson, NC: McFarland, 2010.

Wall, Joseph Frazier. *Andrew Carnegie.* Pittsburgh: University of Pittsburgh Press, 1970.

# Panic of 1893

The Panic of 1893 had started as a financial crisis with the banks. The root cause remains debatable to this day, but some key factors are known. Part of the problem was a reduction of European investment in America. In 1890, the famous British investment firm Baring Brothers went bankrupt. Baring Brothers was a major stockholder in American firms. This financial failing caused investment to dry up in America. Another analysis is that Europeans pulled money out of

America because the Sherman Silver Act caused them to lose confidence. Europeans were moving from bimetallism to a gold standard. Certainly that was a factor, but another, more debatable view is that J. P. Morgan created it because he would benefit from it by building his railroad trust and electrical trust. Most of the failed railroads would come under Morgan's control during the panic. There was also a drain on Treasury gold, which Morgan attributed again to the Sherman Silver Act. This act held America on a bimetallic monetary system in which 16 ounces of silver was the equivalent of 1 ounce of gold. Another theory was that the generosity of the Republican pensions for veterans drained the Treasury. In fairness, however, the tariff revenues from the McKinley Tariff more than covered the pensions.

In any case, the first signs of a panic came 10 days before President Grover Cleveland took office, with the failure of the Philadelphia and Reading Railroad. By summer, the stock market had crashed. Cleveland and Morgan blamed the Sherman Silver Act and called for a repeal. Cleveland, a Democrat, pressured the Democrats to hold them in line but at a great cost to the party. He stood with Morgan on gold, which resulted in a split in the Democratic Party. The Silver Act was repealed. Some of the problem was the world's resistance to leaving the gold standard, and since most exports went to countries using the gold standard, accounts were settled in gold. In addition, Cleveland blamed the Tariff of 1890 and moved quickly to reduce duties, but he wanted the gold standard. Moving to the gold standard had the effect of tightening the money supply in a recession, which most economists today would view as problematic.

Layoffs in the fall of 1893 were approaching a million, and 141 banks had failed. The smokestacks of the Mahoning Valley and Pittsburgh were cold. Two old steel companies—Pennsylvania Steel and Oliver Iron and Steel—went bankrupt. Railroads, which were the nation's largest employer, failed almost monthly, forcing massive unemployment. One of the claims was that the railroads had overextended once again. Unemployment was probably around 25 percent. Wage cuts were causing a rash of strikes as well, and the country declined further into a depression. The year 1894 would be the darkest of the panic. Union leader Samuel Gompers estimated that three million people were out of work in 1894.

Historian Henry Adams chronicled the times: "Winter is here and my perpetual miracle is that people somehow seem to go on living without work or money or food or clothes or fire. One or two million people are out of work; thousands of rich are cleaned out to the last shoe leather; not one human being is known to be making a living." It is considered the deepest depression other than that of the 1930s. Jacob Sechler Coxey of Massillon formed the idea of a massive march on Washington to highlight the rising unemployment. Coxey had also run for Congress as a Populist candidate. The depression had idled his coal mining operation for months. Coxey had some unique ideas that would augur those applied in the 1930s. Coxey hoped to form a Christian nation based on charity. He called also for an eight-hour day and a minimum wage of $1.50 as well as a national bond issue to support the unemployed. Coxey suggested a massive influx of money and public works for the unemployed, but it was the idea of a national march that struck fear in the hearts of Congress. The march reportedly reached 20,000 at its peak in western Pennsylvania. Coxey and his "officers" rode horses at the front of the column as a band marched alongside. Hugh O'Donnell, one of the Homestead leaders, led the way. Headlines seemed to rally more from all parts of the country. Coxey's Ohio army followed roughly today's Route 30 to Pittsburgh. Towns offered food as the armies passed through. As the army reached Pittsburgh, it swelled to 300,000 in the city.

Hobo towns lined the great railroads leading into Washington, and the streets were filled with beggars. Immigrants in tent cities struggled to stay warm and eat. The rich suburbs of Chicago, New York, Pittsburgh, Baltimore, and Washington lived in constant fear of looting or attack. Rich suburbs hired their own guards to protect their neighborhoods. The cities had emptied their coffers to supply relief. Andrew Carnegie kicked in an equal amount of about $125,000, and other capitalists chipped in another $100,000 in Pittsburgh. The money was used for city work projects like those Coxey had been calling for, like the work projects of the federal government in the 1930s. In Maryland, roads were mud from a rainy spring, and the army bogged down. Food became scarce and towns less supportive. Mounted police had an easy time intimidating the weary army in Washington, D.C. Populists in Congress read Coxey's petitions, and a bill was unsuccessfully introduced in the Senate. The New Deal in the 1930s would finally see many of Coxey's ideas implemented, and Coxey's march would be a model for the civil rights movement.

Before the Panic of 1893 ended, a quarter of America's railroads would fail, and steel prices would crash. In 1893 alone, 15,000 businesses failed, along with 158 banks. Of America's 253 blast furnaces, 116 shut down in 1893. There were many strikes in the steel, railroad, and mining industries. Wage reductions at Chicago's Pullman Company resulted in a violent strike in 1894. In the long run, the public increased its demand to get gold for their silver certificates, which drained the Treasury to the crisis point. President Cleveland, the Democrats and Republicans, the Senate, and the House all lacked a complete answer to the panic. The Panic of 1893 was very deep but also short. The effects of the panic would last until 1895 as the Republicans won massive congressional elections and William McKinley took the presidency in 1896. High tariff rates were restored. Depression turned to boom as gold finds around the world inflated the money supply. In addition, the Spanish-American War created more inflation and demand.

*See also:* Banking Crisis and Great Recession; McKinley Tariff of 1890; Panic of 1857; Panic of 1873; Panic of 1907; Pullman Strike; Stock Market Crash/Great Depression

**References**

Gillmore, Jesse. *Disastrous Financial Panics*. Charleston, SC: BiblioBazaar, 2009.

Lauch, Jett. *The Causes of the Panic of 1893*. Charleston, SC: Nabu, 2010.

Steeples, Douglas, and David Whitten. *Democracy in Desperation: The Depression of 1893*. Santa Barbara, CA: Greenwood, 1998.

# Chicago World's Fair (1893)

World's fairs of the period were major marketing and trade opportunities; with millions of visitors, they brought major commercial opportunities for the host city. The Columbian Exposition was to celebrate the 400th anniversary of Columbus's discovery of America. The cities of New York, Washington, D.C., St. Louis, and Chicago were all in contention to host it. Chicago won out on April 25, 1890. The competition caused a New York editor to call Chicago "that windy city." President Harrison signed the act, designating 630 acres in Jackson Park and the Midway for the World's Fair. Financial problems, organizational problems, and the presidential election caused it to be a year late. Its scale and grandeur exceeded all previous and most future fairs. The fair would be a triumph of alternating current electric lights as George Westinghouse won the contract to light it up over Thomas Edison. The fair is considered the last and winning battle in the famous "war of the currents" between, on the one hand, the partners Nikola Tesla and George Westinghouse and, on the other, the combination of Thomas Edison and J. P. Morgan. The fair would need three times the power used for the whole city of Chicago. Almost 93,000 incandescent lights and 5,000 powerful arc lights would light the "White City." The use of electric power at the fair eliminated some of the public fear of the technology and ushered in the widespread use of electrical power. The fair marked the movement of America from an agrarian-dominated market to one of industry. The railroads offered special "Exposition Flyers" that brought visitors to the fair at the amazing speed of 80 miles per hour.

President Grover Cleveland would throw the switch to light up the fair. The dominant symbol of the fair was to be George Ferris's invention—the Ferris Wheel. The wheel was 264 feet high and had 36 cars, which held 60 people each. The fair would have over 28 million visitors. General admission to the fair cost 50¢ for an adult and 25¢ for children. The fair would inspire the Emerald City of L. Frank Baum's *Land of Oz*. It would be remembered for the introduction of Cream of Wheat, Juicy Fruit gum, Pabst beer, Aunt Jemima syrup, Shredded Wheat, Libbey cut glass, Cracker Jack, Tiffany lamps, Heinz ketchup, neon lights, carbonated soda, picture postcards, and the hamburger. The gold medals and ribbons given in almost endless categories were immediately adopted by company advertising departments for years of sales campaigns. The cultural impact included Columbus Day, ragtime music, and the Pledge of Allegiance. It was a demonstration of culture and business merging to create consumerism. The Chicago World's Fair was the realization of the importance of mass marketing in American business.

The fair proved the power of mass marketing, and the companies of Libbey Glass and H. J. Heinz became known for advancing the science of marketing. Heinz introduced his famous pickle pin, which became an American icon, at the Columbian Exposition. The Heinz exhibit was on the second floor, while European firms such as Crosse & Blackwell and Lea & Perrins were on the first floor. The enormous size of the fair and amount of walking made visitors reluctant to walk up the stairs of the large Agricultural Building. Heinz also had a small ground-floor exhibit in the Horticultural Building, which he used to hand out coupons for his pickle pin as a free souvenir. Actually these were watch chain ornaments, which Heinz had first introduced in 1889 for early fairs, factory visits, and local events. He also sent out boys to pass out free coupons. The green pickle was made out of the natural plastic gutta-percha. Heinz noted that over one million of these pickle charms were given away. The foreign food exhibitors claimed, to little avail, that Heinz was using unfair practices. The advertising success inspired others at the fair to use popular souvenirs as advertising.

Columbian Exposition of 1893 bathed in the white light of electricity. (Library of Congress)

Edward D. Libbey also introduced one of his personal projects to the world at the Chicago fair. Like any good marketer, Libbey had a love for new products. For months, Libbey had secretly been developing "spun glass." One marketing angle was to create a spun-glass dress for Georgia Cayvan, a famous actress of the time. It was a marketing ploy by Libbey. Cayvan tried to wear the dress several times, but it was too brittle for regular use. The dress did attract fairgoer Princess Eulalie of Spain, who had a large entourage of press following her and her friend, Duke de Veragua, a relative of Christopher Columbus. The princess had a duplicate dress made for her, and Libbey became the official glasscutter for Spain. While spun glass did not take off, Libbey got extensive publicity in Europe and America. Libbey needed $250,000 to implement his vision of spun glass. His contract, which cost him $5,000, gave him the exclusive right to sell glassware on the fairgrounds. This assured him a central location on the Midway for his factory. Libbey hired Toledo architect D. L. Stine to design the beautiful factory building to house his cut-glass operations. The factory was really a beautiful Italianate pavilion on the Midway Plaisance. A large dome was designed to hide the smokestack required by the glass furnaces. It would also have living quarters on the second floor for Libbey and Florence, his wife. The building had a palace-like look of stone, but like most of the fair's prestigious buildings, it had a stucco façade. Libbey actually made a profit on his fair exhibition. His success at the fair made the company the premier cut-glass manufacturer in the world. Libbey used his profits to launch an electric lightbulb factory and start research on the automatic glass bottle–making machine. The fair was considered inspirational to many such as Henry Ford, who studied the first gasoline engine on exhibit.

The fair is often considered the triumph of American consumerism. It proved a huge entertainment draw and would be the model for Coney Island in New York, Heinz Pier in Atlantic City, Hershey Park, and later Disneyland in California. The Midway made famous shows such as the Buffalo Bill Wild West Show. The fair showed that merging entertainment and consumerism could change culture and society. Many today point to Walt Disney World's EPCOT (Experimental Prototype Community of Tomorrow) as the legacy of the Columbian Exposition's entertainment and applied business model.

*See also:* Centennial Exposition; Great Exhibition of 1851; War of the Currents; Television at the 1939 World's Fair

### References

Appelbaum, Stanley. *The Chicago World's Fair of 1893.* New York: Dover, 1980.

Badger, Reid. *The Great American Fair: The World's Columbian Exposition and American Culture.* Chicago: Nelson Hall, 1979.

Findling, John E. *Chicago's Great World's Fair.* Manchester, UK: Manchester University Press, 1994.

# Pullman Strike (1894)

The once-hailed utopian Pullman Company and town would be the location of a major labor strike that would spread like the Great Railroad Strike of 1877. Pullman City was 14 miles south of downtown Chicago near Lake Calumet. At its peak, the strike would involve over 250,000 in 27 states, and it lasted three weeks. The violence resulted in the death of 13 strikers and over 60 wounded with property damage of more than $340,000 (about $9 million today). The strike was the effort of the American Railways Union, headed by the socialist Eugene V. Debs. The trouble started in May 1894 when 3,000 of Pullman's 5,800 employees at the Chicago plant were laid off. In an effort to save jobs, George Pullman cut the wages of the remaining employees by 25 percent. Pullman had seen orders for his railcars plummet as a result of the Panic of 1893. Pullman was labor friendly, but he was hardheaded and a poor communicator. He had even been hailed by many as a paternal capitalist, but Pullman was no Andrew Carnegie or George Westinghouse. He ran Pullman City as a profit center. Workers were required to live in Pullman City, in which Pullman ran all utilities and services and charged rent for a profit. Pullman charged rents 25 percent higher than those in surrounding neighborhoods. In addition, he purchased water from Chicago at 4¢ per 1,000 gallons and sold it to his town at 10¢. Clergy were charged rent on churches, and the library charged a fee, too.

Members of the American Railways Union asked that the rents in the Pullman worker town be reduced. Pullman ended up firing the union representatives, which brought Debs, the union president, into the disagreement. Pullman then locked out the employees. Things escalated quickly to a strike, as Pullman Company announced it would pay a regular dividend to its stockholders. The strike slowly started to evolve along related railways, as three-quarters of the rails moving in and out of Chicago closed. The union called for a nationwide boycott of Pullman cars. Railroad workers across the nation refused to switch Pullman cars. The General Managers Association managed the combination of rail lines and companies. The association had strong ties in the Grover Cleveland administration as well as with J. P. Morgan.

With the depression of 1893 reaching a peak, the situation was volatile. Not wanting another Haymarket Riot or Railroad Strike of 1877, President Cleveland got involved, hiring 3,600 special deputies and sending 6,000 troops to Pullman City. The troops had the full protection of the U.S. government. The newspapers supported Cleveland initially, but it was short-lived. Pullman used scabs and strikebreakers at the factory, which caused violence. Federal involvement inspired more rioting by the workers as the unemployed joined in. On July 7, the strike erupted into shootings and deaths as troops clashed with workers in Chicago. The strike started to spread across the country along the railroads. Cleveland was forced to get an injunction against the strikers. The federal injunction was based on the fact the strike interfered with delivery of the U.S. mail. It was the first time the federal government had used an injunction to stop a strike. However, the strikers stood their ground.

Chicago began to attract socialists and anarchists to "help." Ray Baker, second in command of Jacob Sechler Coxey's army of marchers (the cross-country labor march for jobs), showed up in Chicago. The country seemed split between fear and outrage. Pullman refused arbitration, and New York and other large cities supported him, characterizing the strike as an attack on society. As famous socialists and anarchists such as Emma Goldman joined the effort, many feared a rebellion in America's large cities. The timing was poor for the strikers, as an anarchist had just assassinated the president of France. Republican industrialist Mark Hanna, however, supported the workers, calling Pullman a "damn idiot." Hanna would be one of those to expose Pullman's "utopia." Other paternal capitalists such as Andrew Carnegie and John Rockefeller were appalled at the extent of Pullman's profit making on his worker city. Debs was an outstanding speaker and pulled in socialists such as Goldman to Chicago. Goldman was an anarchist, socialist, Russian immigrant, and revolutionary. Goldman would later inspire Leon Czolgosz, President McKinley's future assassin. Earlier she had been the girlfriend of the attempted assassin of Henry Clay Frick during the Homestead Strike. The strike was reaching the level of the Railroad Strike of 1877. Mayors from over 50 cities asked Pullman to accept arbitration.

Samuel Gompers, one of the most enlightened labor leaders of the time, tried to mediate a settlement. He sent a telegram to President Cleveland only to have it rejected. Cleveland commented, "If it takes the entire army and navy of the United States to deliver a postal card in Chicago, that card will be delivered." Cleveland sent 14,000 federal troops, and the anger now turned toward him. Cleveland sent the federal troops without notifying Governor Altgeld of Illinois and against his wishes. Governor Altgeld stated in a letter made public, "I am advised that you have ordered federal troops to go into service in the State of Illinois. Surely, matters have not been correctly presented to you in this case or you would not have taken the step, for it is entirely unnecessary and, as it seems to me unjustifiable." Cleveland's use of federal troops was considered anti-workingman, when even capitalists had condemned Pullman for his hardheaded approach.

The strike ended with the heavy federal crackdown, but the courts took over to take revenge for the upheaval. The result of the "Debs Strike" would change the landscape of American politics. Debs was sentenced to six months in prison for disobeying the injunction; he would later form the American Socialist Party. The Sherman Anti-Trust Act was used to support the conviction, and the Supreme Court upheld its use against labor. In addition, the Supreme Court upheld the use of a federal injunction because of interruptions to the U.S. mail. The Supreme Court of Illinois in 1897 forced the Pullman Company to divest itself of the City of Pullman. The U.S. Senate launched investigations that resulted in a condemnation of Pullman's use of paternalism for profit. Thanks to the oratory of Debs and the exposed abuses of Pullman, the public sided with the workers. The socialists gained back much of what they had lost in the Haymarket Riot. Socialists would oust Gompers as president of the American Federation of Labor for his middle-of-the-road approach. Debs would run for president a number of times, getting as high as 6 percent of the vote in 1912. President Cleveland, a Democrat, lost the support of his party in 1896 and would be forced to run as a third-party candidate. The Democratic majority lay in ruins, and the elections of 1894 and 1896 would sweep in a Republican majority. In general, the federal government and companies gained enormous power to stop national strikes, which would not be adjusted until the passing of the National Relations Act (Wagner Act) of 1935. For his part, Debs made the Socialist Party part of the American scene for years to come.

*See also:* Great Railroad Strike of 1877; Haymarket Riot; Homestead Strike of 1892; National Labor Relations Act (Wagner Act); Panic of 1893; Paternal Capitalism—Homestead and Wilmerding, Pennsylvania; Steel Strike of 1959

### References

Hirsch, Susan. *After the Strike: A Century of Labor Struggle at Pullman.* Urbana: University of Illinois, 2003.

Lindsay, Almont. *The Pullman Strike: The Story of a Unique Experiment and of a Great Labor Upheaval.* Chicago: University of Chicago Press, 1943.

Papke, Ray. *The Pullman Case: The Clash of Labor and Capital in Industrial America.* Lawrence: University of Kansas, 1999.

# Niagara Falls Power Plant (1896)

The Niagara Falls power plant would begin the world's electrical age. It would be the first plant to supply massive amounts of electrical power to consumers at reasonable prices. It would spur the electrical appliance, aluminum, and electrochemical industries. The power of Niagara Falls was obvious to the earliest settlers. The falls have an almost unbelievable average flow of 100,000 cubic feet per second, with a peak of 225,000 cubic feet per second. There is a peak period of flow from April to November. There is even a daily variation in the flow, with the peak flow at 9 A.M. and the lowest flow at 9 P.M. German electrical engineer Sir Werner von Siemens estimated in 1888 that "the amount of water falling over Niagara is equal to 100,000,000 tons of coal an hour." Sir Siemens calculated that "if steam boilers could be erected vast enough to exhaust daily the whole coal output of the earth, the steam generated would barely suffice to pump back again the water flowing over Niagara Falls." The power of waterfalls remains preeminent in electrical generation throughout the world. Even today, it accounts for a major part of all hydroelectric power generated in the United States.

The battle for the Niagara power plant contract went on between J. P. Morgan and Thomas Edison's direct current (DC) system versus George Westinghouse's alternating current (AC). A commission was formed in 1890 to explore whether DC or AC power generation should be selected. The long-distance transmission of AC power to cities such as Telluride, Colorado, and Frankfurt, Germany, helped the commission to select AC and the Westinghouse system. Finally, the success of Westinghouse's "White City" at the 1893 Chicago World's Fair was the tipping point. In 1893, Westinghouse's AC system was selected with a contract to build two 5,000-horsepower generators. Although Westinghouse got the largest part of the contract, General Electric also ended up with some lucrative contracts for transformers and transmission lines. General Electric's work on the transformers became critical to Niagara's success. The AC system and transformers allowed for long-distance transmission of power, which a DC system could not achieve. These transformers stepped up the voltage from a generated 2,000 volts to 10,000 volts as well as changing the two-phase current to three phases. The current at 10,000 volts was then transmitted through bare copper cable (on thousands of insulated wooden poles) to Buffalo, New York, 26 miles away. Full transmission would begin in 1896. General Electric transformers then stepped down the voltage to 110 volts for general lighting and 370 volts for Buffalo's street-railway system. In the end, Westinghouse's great victory generated vital profits for General Electric as the Panic of 1893 continued until 1896. General Electric and Westinghouse started to work together for the good of the Niagara project. Morgan also realized that any further internal competition would cost the overall project and his syndicate money. Morgan knew the war over AC versus DC technology was over, and it was time to move on. Niagara was to be the world's largest engineering project, requiring Morgan to bring in other financiers such as August Belmont, John Astor, and the Vanderbilts as investors. With Thomas Edison bought out, Morgan converted General Electric to AC technology.

The real man behind the Niagara power project was neither Westinghouse nor Edison nor Morgan, but Nikola Tesla. It was Tesla's patents that supplied the AC power technology. Tesla's patents had made AC technology the future. The first power came on at Niagara on August 26, 1895. On that August day, Dynamo No. 2 went online, supplying current to the Pittsburgh Reduction Company. The initial power went to the electrochemical plants nearby. Dynamo No. 1 didn't come on stream until September 30, at which time the directors of Cataract

Construction Company and Westinghouse, plus assorted millionaires, came to celebrate. Two important figures were not present—Morgan, who came later in October, and Tesla. As the plaque at the falls would reflect, Westinghouse gave all the credit to Tesla. In total, 13 of Tesla's patents were used in the creation of the Niagara power plant. Still, the bitterness of the war of the currents had created a bias against Tesla in the New York press controlled by Morgan. The *New York Times* found a way to hail the event without mentioning Tesla, while most other papers hailed Tesla as the equal of Edison in the triumph of the falls. It was a great victory for Westinghouse Electric, but Westinghouse spent time at Pittsburgh Reduction Company, further studying the wonders of aluminum smelting rather than celebrating.

One of the great results of the Niagara power station was the rise of the American electrochemical industry. The two biggest customers of Niagara were the Pittsburgh Reduction Company and the Carborundum Company. The Pittsburgh Reduction Company (the future Aluminum Company of America, or ALCOA) contracted for 5,000 of the 15,000 available horsepower. Niagara finally made the production and use of aluminum economically feasible. Niagara power's other big customer was the Carborundum Company. Carborundum was an artificial abrasive composed of aluminum oxide. These alumina crystals were produced by electrochemical processing, as pure aluminum was. Larger, colored alumina crystals found in nature are sapphires and rubies. These fine artificial alumina crystals are extremely hard, making them ideal for grinding and cutting wheels. Within a year a massive electrochemical industry grew up around Niagara, including plants producing sodium, soda ash, sodium peroxide, and calcium carbide. By 1897, 12,500 of the 13,500 horsepower available for local consumption went to electrochemical plants. Westinghouse enjoyed visiting these plants, since he always had a fascination with metallurgy. The aluminum industry owes a great deal to Westinghouse.

Within a few years, Niagara had become a major production area for steelmaking ferroalloys, such as ferrosilicon and ferrochrome. These ferroalloys required power levels for production that were unavailable until the Niagara Falls power plant. The massive amount of workers needed to build the power system and operate the electrochemical plants required a planned worker town of houses, which would be the first in the country to be lighted and heated by electricity. Industrialist William Love hoped to emulate Westinghouse's industrial utopian town of Wilmerding, Pennsylvania, by creating an industrial utopia for electrochemical workers. The effort resulted in a mile-long town along the wastewater canal known as the Love Canal. The town failed to grow and became the LaSalle area of Niagara. It would become famous for the old toxic electrochemicals that caused a strange "outbreak" of cancer in the 1970s and an example of the costly legal battles created by industrial pollution.

Buffalo, New York, had originally been the reason for the Niagara project. Buffalo received the necessary amount of current to be applied in street arc lights, incandescent lights in homes, and electric motors in factories, as well as used by the Buffalo Railway Company for streetcars. In 1901, the Pan-American Exposition came to Buffalo to show the world the future of electricity. The exposition highlighted electrical appliances that were in use in Buffalo such as sewing machines, home lighting, neon lights, electric elevators, and laundry machines.

*See also:* ALCOA Aluminum Formed; Automated Sewing Machine; Chicago World's Fair; War of the Currents

### References

Jonnes, Jill. *Empires of Light.* New York: Random House, 2003.

MacLaren, Malcolm. *The Rise of the Electrical Industry during the Nineteenth Century.* Princeton, NJ: Princeton University Press, 1943.

Seifer, Marc. *Wizard: The Life and Times of Nikola Tesla.* New York: Citadel, 1998.

# Paternal Capitalism—Homestead and Wilmerding, Pennsylvania (1896)

The full incorporation of the company town Wilmerding, Pennsylvania, would be symbolic of the peak of American industrial paternalism. American paternal capitalism became its own mix of German paternalism, communal manufacturing, and philanthropy. American philanthropy also reached its peak in the 1890s with the building of a Carnegie Library in Homestead, Pennsylvania, in hopes of appeasing the old wounds of the Homestead Strike. Paternal capitalism was the philosophy of the capitalists of the day such as Peter Cooper, the Vanderbilts, Andrew Carnegie, John D. Rockefeller, Marshall Field, H. J. Heinz, George Pullman, Philip Armour, and George Westinghouse. Their philanthropy was expressed in a wide range of applications such as libraries, unemployment funds, food banks, community hospitals, nursing homes, company housing, schools, and whole towns. It included company towns such as the coal-mining towns of Pennsylvania, Pullman City in Illinois, Love Canal in New York, the steel slums of Carnegie, and Westinghouse's company town of Wilmerding. Wilmerding would become an international model for industrial towns, as Pullman City had served as an example of fraud within this movement. In Wilmerding's early years, reporters from all over the world flooded to it. Built by the capitalist Westinghouse, it was hailed by reformers and socialists as the ideal model for industrial towns. It was despised by the bankers of the time, as well as Carnegie, as misguided capitalism. Rockefeller viewed it as corporate socialism. It stood in stark contrast to the many nearby steel town slums in Homestead, Pennsylvania—a true tale of two cities.

Paternal capitalism spans the gap before government took over the development of social services, cultural events, and the social safety net. It was viewed at its best as philanthropy and at its worst as plantation slavery of workers. Depending on one's perspective it was called paternal capitalism, welfare capitalism, corporate socialism, wealth redistribution, or triumphant capitalism. The paternal capitalists were called robber barons or philanthropists. Its roots were deep, however; the application of paternal capitalism in America was a direct response to labor and social unrest in Europe in the mid-1800s. In America, it was seen in the Great Railroad Strike of 1877, the Homestead Strike, and the Pullman Strike. Newspapers of the 1890s printed stories of stark economic contrasts of wealth differences in America. That gap of economic success could not be muted by the fact that American laborers made four to five times what those in Europe did. Successful capitalists realized philanthropy as an alternative to unrest, while the labor movement fought for better working conditions.

Many American capitalists looked to Europe for answers, since revolutions made social change there during the late 1840s. Two approaches existed in Europe and America. There was the communal model of an industrial community, such as New Lanark, Scotland, and the company town model of German chocolate king Franz Stollwerck. Robert Owen had designed the model industrial community in New Lanark, Scotland. Owen had caused much discussion in the industrial world with his early success at New Lanark, and the town was visited by American industrialists such as Carnegie and Heinz. From the start, the New Lanark community had been a planned community for the worker. The American Management Association today considers Owen's 1813 address to manufacturers a classic in management. Owen moved to America in the 1840s to found industrial communities in Kentucky, Indiana, and Pennsylvania. One Owen manufacturing community town was Economy, Pennsylvania, located within 50 miles of Homestead and Wilmerding.

Similarly, German capitalists favored working communities. The German Stollwerck Brothers chocolate factory was, at the time, one of the world's largest candy factories. Stollwerck was one of the best of a long line of German paternalists such as steel king Alfred Krupp. The German company town was neofeudal with houses built around the master's mansion. Roald Dahl's book *Charlie and the Chocolate Factory* was a parody of the German capitalist communities.

Westinghouse's approach to employee housing was much different from that of others. Westinghouse wanted to build a better house for his workers in the Wilmerding project. His approach focused on true ownership by the employee. Initially, in the 1890s, Westinghouse Air Brake purchased the land and built individual houses. The houses were then sold to the employees at a cost of around $6,000 to $8,000. The mortgages were adjusted to the employee's income and allowed for payments over 15 years. The houses were also covered by a type of mutual insurance that protected the owner in times of unemployment, disability, and death. This stood in stark contrast to the nearby company mining towns where, when a death occurred, the company quickly foreclosed on the house. Westinghouse hired many hundreds of young engineers for his nearby Wilmerding brake plant and his electrical turbine plant. He organized the Tonnaleuka Club for professional young men in the engineering and technical trades. In 1901, Westinghouse purchased the Glen Hotel building on Marguerite Avenue in Wilmerding. Westinghouse reworked the building, expanding and adding living rooms and dining rooms. In addition, there were smoking rooms, a billiard room, a bowling alley, and a library. A club was formed so that these young men could enjoy this higher class of temporary living; additionally, an associate type of membership was developed for others to enjoy the excellent recreation rooms and fellowship.

New immigrants in Wilmerding were trained in citizenship. At the beginning the emphasis was on English classes. In addition, extensive American history programs prepared in seven languages were offered. This cooperative networking was fundamental to the character of the town. This foreign program became the

Westinghouse plant at Wilmerding, Pennsylvania, in 1905. (Library of Congress)

model for the whole United States. The YMCA (Young Men's Christian Association) shared facilities with Westinghouse Air Brake management until 1907. In 1907, Westinghouse completed the "Welfare Building" for use by the YMCA, and shortly afterward he built a building for the women (YWCA). These buildings had world-class swimming pools and gymnasiums. The Wilmerding YMCA became the second largest in Pennsylvania by 1910. Westinghouse partnered with community organizations and churches.

Pullman had discredited this type of paternal capitalism with his corrupt management of Pullman City for his own profit. Wilmerding was truly an ideal model of paternal capitalism. Westinghouse's bankers opposed the "socialism" of Wilmerding and helped end most support for it in the Panic of 1907. New York banker J. P. Morgan called it "corporate socialism and welfare." Carnegie, in particular, saw Westinghouse's views as too close to socialism, yet they shared a similar belief system. Fundamental to both men's views was the idea that you need to help those who help themselves. Both men believed in competition and capitalism, and neither believed in unions. Westinghouse was a paternal capitalist but in a different vein from Carnegie. Carnegie believed that he and certain others were destined to be public trustees of capital. Carnegie was more patriarchal than paternal. Westinghouse was more like the father who teaches his sons by buying them tools and training them how to use them. To Carnegie's credit, he helped found over 3,000 libraries, both in his steel towns such as labor-torn Homestead and worldwide. Carnegie donated the library buildings but required the community to purchase the books. Rockefeller was similar in giving his money to universities, museums, and social services.

Carnegie and Rockefeller and many paternal capitalists saw their role as designated distributors of wealth. They believed they knew best what was needed by society. In fairness, these paternal capitalists supplied the social safety net of unemployment insurance, health care, and social services that are provided by the government today. Their gifts of libraries, museums, hospitals, and welfare homes were honestly based on helping, but to many, these gifts were built on the backs of workers. As the wealthiest man in the world, Carnegie did give away all of his money—some $300 million. He left only enough for his immediate heirs to live their lives out in style, leaving nothing to pass on, believing money would destroy the ambition of future Carnegie generations. Rockefeller did most of his giving as a corporate manager, carefully increasing his philanthropy as his income increased. Rockefeller preferred giving to established social and cultural organizations. He hired people to review thousands of requests by organizations, churches, and even individuals. Paternal capitalism tended to die out as companies became entities in the 1950s and government took over the role, but it still lives today with individuals such as Bill Gates and Warren Buffett. It is also remembered in the continued giving by small American businesses to local community activities.

*See also:* Homestead Strike of 1892; Panic of 1893; Panic of 1907; Pullman Strike; Revolution, Famine, and Immigration; Social Security Act

### References

Chernow, Ron. *Titan: The Life of John D. Rockefeller, Sr.* New York: Vintage Books, 1998.

Krass, Peter. *Carnegie.* New York: Wiley, 2002.

Merrill, Harwood. *Classics in Management.* New York: American Management Association, 1960.

Skrabec, Quentin. *George Westinghouse: Gentle Genius.* New York: Algora, 2007.

# First Electric Sign (Product Branding and Advertising)—H. J. Heinz (1900)

H. J. Heinz's first electric sign in Times Square would usher in a new era in American business known as the advertising age. Heinz invented a revolutionary business model for processed foods and their distribution. Most food products in the 1800s were sold as unbranded commodities in barrels, jars, and bags. Manufacturers sold to wholesalers who then distributed barrels of pickles, ketchup, flour, and so on to local stores. Heinz pioneered ideas on the role of branding, advertising, and packaging and was one of the first to patent a bottle design and shape. While he knew the art of salesmanship, he was one of the first to comprehend the idea of a market. He adjusted his package, price, and product for various markets. He truly understood his markets and did not treat them as abstract groupings. The idea was to have the consumer demand that the grocer offer Heinz products. Heinz's concept of a market led him to the methodology of branding. Heinz sold pickles and things like ketchup under the Heinz name rather than in barrels. He differentiated his products as superior to those of the unlabeled competitors. Heinz became a national brand name that the customer recognized. Heinz combined trademarks and slogans with perceived product attributes. He saw quality, purity, and convenience as core competencies for his products. Quality extended to the grocer's shelf where bad or suspect product was removed, since the Heinz name was now on the line. Companies like Sam Adams beer today have developed a similar strategy. Salesmen did more than sell; they studied the market and fed information back to the factory. This approach added customization to manufactured products. Heinz believed in vertical integration and pioneered the idea of supply chain control before Andrew Carnegie and Henry Ford. Quality was emphasized throughout the supply chain. All of these advances led to an integrated approach to marketing.

Heinz moved toward branding by quality levels in his early days to maintain a quality image while fully maximizing material use. From the earliest days, Heinz had used two quality levels as a sales strategy. In the late 1880s, his sales volume allowed him to approach this as a coordinated business strategy. In many of his products, such as ketchup, Heinz moved to a three-tier strategy of branding with a fancy label (Keystone Extra Fancy), a standard label (Howard's Brand), and a lower level (Duquesne Brand). While the recipes varied, the branding strategy was a combination of raw material quality and market pricing. He could divert lower-quality batches of raw material to a lower-quality brand. For example, in the 1890s, Fancy Ketchup sold for 45¢ a bottle; standard brand cost 25¢ a bottle; and Duquesne Brand sold at 15¢. History suggests the brand strategy initially evolved from raw material quality variation more than from a pricing strategy. A three-tier strategy helped with purchasing and process flexibility while increasing volume. The three-tier grade strategy actually improved Heinz's ability to maintain quality standards by grading during the process. His competitors' common strategy at the time was to specialize in a quality or grade level. Often the fight was for the high-quality market, ignoring price. Today, producers often manufacture for a generic line or a lower-quality competitor's line to maximize raw material and production. Heinz was one of the first to tap into the rise of American consumerism with value pricing and branding.

Product branding required Heinz to develop his own advertising and marketing department in 1900. Heinz used billboards as early as 1882 to advertise in Pittsburgh, but he limited the advertising so as not to upset the population. There was a great deal of resistance to billboards because they detracted from the beauty of buildings. Heinz had the propensity to go overboard with his advertising. In 1900, he had a 38-foot-high by 60-foot-long billboard sign on the Rhine River. At the time Heinz had very little business in Germany, but it was the first part of a name-brand strategy. At his old home in Sharpsburg, overlooking the Allegheny River, he put up "Heinz 57" on the hillside in large concrete lettering. The concrete letters outraged the citizens but created a lot of free publicity. Heinz loved to use locations that had high volumes of passersby. Eventually, many of his signs were removed, but many people believed he got more publicity through the controversy.

Heinz initially pushed signs on his beautiful horse-drawn wagons. He even had wagons shaped as ketchup bottles and pickles. He had a horse-drawn float for parades on which women employees demonstrated the bottling of pickles. As volume grew in the 1900s, Heinz painted the railroad cars that carried his vegetables to Pittsburgh and his products around the country. He was the first to paint signs along America's busiest railroads. Heinz believed in the importance of national brand advertising, and he never missed an opportunity to hang a sign, paint a building, or use electric signs. In 1898, his Heinz Pier at Atlantic City was a major attraction with free pickle pins and postcards to send home. It would be the business model for Busch Gardens and Hershey Park. Heinz's signs and samples were available at county fairs, community and church picnics, and regional exhibitions. He was the first to push the nutritional value of his products as a selling point. Beans were advertised as a cheap source of protein for families in the Panic of 1907. Heinz successfully advertised preservative-free ketchup as a major health benefit over competing ketchups.

A lot of Heinz's success in advertising can be attributed to his New York branch. As early as 1892, Heinz was using souvenirs such as calendars, pickle charms, and pickle postcards at his store displays. In 1892, his advertising budget for New York alone exceeded $10,000 ($185,000 today). A souvenir collector himself, Heinz found thousands of customers who loved souvenirs and curios. In 1893, a simple souvenir had made the Heinz exhibit the most popular at the Columbian Exposition at Chicago. His most famous advertising included the first electric sign in Manhattan, on his store at the corner of Fifth Avenue and 23rd Street in 1900 (the present location of the Flatiron Building); he distributed pickle pins there. The sign was six stories high and lit with 1,200 incandescent bulbs. It flashed on a slow cycle, emphasizing the sign; after a short period of complete darkness, a second advertisement appeared. This arrangement allowed two different messages to be flashed in a matter of minutes. The electric bill was $90 a night. The "Heinz-57 Varieties—Exhibited Heinz Pier Atlantic City" slogan was displayed. The sign was changed several times. It brought tens of thousands of visitors to his Atlantic City pier every year. A year later he added an advertisement for the Buffalo World's Fair exhibit. By 1907, Heinz was employing flood lighting for his railroad track billboards, another advertising first. For the 1915 World's Fair, he built a flashing 30-foot-high "57" sign on San Francisco Bay.

By 1900, Heinz had a large print shop and staff of artists. Writers were also added, making the first corporate advertising department. Heinz's creativity surfaced in the application of art in advertising. None of his competitors were as dedicated to print advertising, and few understood Heinz's brand strategy. The print shop also painted wagons and made streetcar signs and train car signs. Many times the print shop developed beautiful pieces of art for Heinz products. The print shop also created new labels and endless literature, posters, signs, and pamphlets. Heinz pushed court cases to protect labels and his trademarks. In the Supreme Court, he won copyright protection of labels. In 1901, Heinz created back labels that offered recipes and uses for products. These back labels also gave directions on product storage. The print shop handled the literature mailing. From the 1890s on, Heinz's magazine advertisements encouraged the reader to mail a postcard for literature and even free samples. These were creative and novel approaches far ahead of the competition. Heinz developed the concept of the story-line advertisement to support specific campaigns. The story-line advertisement offered a discussion of product benefits or the history of the product. His 1906 baked bean campaign, in particular, highlighted the story advertisement. He created product uses, such as "beans and toast" in England, which remain popular today after 110 years. While he didn't refer to his advertising for products as campaigns, that is what they would be called today. Heinz would often launch coordinated and targeted advertising for a product or product line. This would include literature on "Kitchen Tips," "The Spice of Life," and "The Joy of Living." Heinz was the first to create marketing and advertising departments.

*See also:* Chicago World's Fair; Sears Mail Order Business

### References

Albert, Robert. *The Good Provider.* Boston: Houghton Mifflin, 1973.

Hooker, Richard. *The History of Food and Drink in America.* New York: Bobbs-Merrill, 1981.

Skrabec, Quentin. *H. J. Heinz.* Jefferson, NC: McFarland, 2009.

Smith, Andrew. *Pure Ketchup.* Washington, DC: Smithsonian Institution, 2001.

# First Billion-Dollar Corporation— United States Steel (1901)

The formation of United States Steel brought together the nation's wealthiest capitalists: J. P. Morgan, John D. Rockefeller, Andrew Carnegie, and a long list of other millionaires. It required the tacit approval of two U.S. presidents—William McKinley and Theodore Roosevelt. Its mastermind was Morgan, the New York banking magnate. The amazing formation of United States Steel created a company that produced more steel than Great Britain and Germany combined; it yielded nearly a quarter of the world's production, with a capacity of seven million tons annually. It represented about two-thirds of the total production in the United States. It was the first billion-dollar corporation in history, and it was the first time the phrase "billion dollar" entered the average American's lexicon. The company's $1.4 billion capitalization was four times the federal budget of $350 million in 1900 and a full 7 percent of the gross national product. It had over 160,000 employees and was the world's largest employer. United States Steel would control around 70 percent of the American steel industry and 30 percent of the world's industry. Its sheer size required new approaches in management, sales, and finance.

Morgan had become interested in the steel industry due to the huge profits of Carnegie Steel. Through trusts and mergers, Morgan had taken the competition out of the banking, railroad, and electrical industries. Morgan believed in price "stabilization," not competition, for market share was the way to profitability. He believed he could increase profits in the steel industry with a similar approach. Morgan had gained control of Illinois Steel in 1898 and merged with a number of Chicago steel companies to create Federal Steel, but Carnegie's competitive practices remained the roadblock to industry stabilization. This new, integrated Federal Steel Company had advantages on a par with Carnegie Steel. Morgan's Federal Steel was formed around Illinois Steel and Minnesota Mining but was fully integrated, like its competitor Carnegie Steel, including coke ovens, ore mines, and finishing companies such as Lorain Steel. Judge Elbert Gary was elected president of Federal Steel. Carnegie had operated under a limited partnership to maintain full control of Carnegie Steel and prevent takeover bids.

Morgan started talks with Rockefeller, who owned most of the nation's iron ore, to form a bigger trust. They aimed at buying out Carnegie, who was talking of retiring. Morgan was less interested in market share and more in reaching the point where he could control steel prices. Morgan saw that the price-cutting and market-share competition between Federal Steel and Carnegie Steel was cutting into the profits of both companies. Morgan wanted to institute his cooperative-advantage model in the steel industry.

The role of a Morgan trust was not to raise prices but to stabilize them. The Morgan approach is similar to that of the nationally owned companies of China and the huge integrated companies of Japan. It called for cooperative advantage over competitive advantage. Morgan argued that competition between companies within an industry cost millions in patent battles alone. This had been particularly true with the Bessemer steel patent, coke-making patents, and rolling mill patents, which had taken years to settle. Furthermore, United States Steel would own the ore ships, docks, coal mines, railroads, and transportation links in the company, which resulted in huge cost savings. It also owned most of the operations making finished products from steel.

J. P. Morgan—America's greatest banker. (Library of Congress)

Morgan bought out Carnegie for $320 million to merge Carnegie Steel with Federal Steel. In addition, Morgan bought the companies of American Bridge, American Sheet, American Steel, American Steel & Wire, American Tin Plate, National Steel, National Tube, and Lake Superior Ore for a book value of over $1 billion. No corporation of such a massive size had ever been seen. The steel behemoth had real assets of $682 million against $303 million of bonds, $510 million in preferred stock, and $508 million in common stock. Judge Gary was to be chairman of the board with a salary of $100,000, and Charles Schwab was to be president of the new corporation with a salary of $100,000 and a 1 percent profit-sharing bonus. With the bonus, and because of his endless spending, it was rumoured that Schwab made a million-dollar salary. Rockefeller was a major shareholder, and the board of United States Steel reflected this: it included Rockefeller, John Rockefeller Jr., and Henry Rogers. Other board directors included Gary, Schwab, Henry Clay Frick, Robert Bacon (Morgan's partner), Marshall Field, James Reed (Carnegie Steel's lawyer), William Moore (former owner, National Steel), Edmund Converse (former owner, National Tube), Francis Peabody, Charles Steele, Norman Ream, Peter Widener, William Edenborn (former owner, American Steel and Wire), Daniel Reid (former owner, American Tin Plate), Alford Clifford (former owner, American Steel and Wire), Clement Griscom, William Dodge, Nathaniel Thayer, Percival Roberts (former owner, American Bridge), George Baker (former owner, First National Bank), and Abram Hewitt. Carnegie's 35 old (but also many young) partners became instant multimillionaires. Carnegie's old partner Frick had $61 million of stock that became $88 million in a few days as the prices of the new company's shares rose. And Schwab of Carnegie Steel made over $30 million.

The management of such a large organization had never been attempted before. The company would become the model for corporate America. The structure of United States Steel was based on the model of Frick and Rockefeller, who believed in committee infrastructure rather than a powerful autocrat. The committee structure was borrowed from Rockefeller's Standard Oil (the only other megacorporation of the time) and applied to United States Steel, which had an executive committee consisting of Gary (chairman), Reid, Edenborn, Converse, Roberts, and Steele. The executive committee was the real power in the new corporation. President Schwab needed to clear major decisions through the executive committee. There was also a finance committee to control spending and investment throughout the company. Clearly, Chairman Gary had all the real management in the structure. The committees further assigned special subcommittees, usually consisting of three members, to look at specific projects and purchases. Divisions such as Carnegie Steel and Federal Steel were run as separate companies except for sales policy, capital investment requirements, and human relations, which were set at the corporate level. The division presidents at Illinois Steel and Carnegie Steel lacked the power to spend the capital needed to upgrade their operations. The committee structure allowed for conservative review of capital expenditures. The system favored avoidance of mistakes versus aggressive management, which worked well when the company basically controlled the market and industry.

Morgan and United States Steel brought peace to the steel industry. United States Steel had a huge cost advantage, and stable prices meant huge profits. Morgan even allowed smaller steel companies to gain market share. He managed to stay under 50 percent of market share to avoid the trust-busting movement in the early 1900s. United States Steel's only fully integrated competitor was Bethlehem Steel. Many argued that the lack of competition slowed technology advances in the steel industry. United States Steel continued to grow in future decades. In the 1940s, United States Steel had over 370,000 employees and made more steel than the combined output of Germany, Japan, and Italy during World War II. The company built huge steel mills in surrounding cities such as Gary, Indiana; Philadelphia (Fairless Works); and Geneva, Utah.

*See also:* Andrew Carnegie's First Steel Mill; Homestead Strike of 1892; McKinley Tariff of 1890; Steel Strike of 1959

### References

Apelt, Brian. *The Corporation: A Centennial Biography of United States Steel Corporation.* Pittsburgh, PA: University of Pittsburgh Press, 2000.

Cotter, Arundel. *The Authentic History of the United States Steel Corporation.* New York: Moody, 1916.

Skrabec, Quentin. *Henry Clay Frick: The Life of a Perfect Capitalist.* Jefferson, NC: McFarland, 2010.

Warren, Kenneth. *Big Steel: The First Century of the United States Steel Corporation 1901–2001.* Pittsburgh, PA: University of Pittsburgh Press, 2001.

# Henry Ford Wins Race of the Century (1901)

On October 10, 1901, an automobile race between Alexander Winton and Henry Ford would set the future of the American automobile. It was a clash of business models and alternative fuels that dominated the auto world of 1901. It offers many insights into the competition of automotive fuels today as well as an understanding of the roots of auto industry business models. In 1901 steam, electric, and hydrocarbon/gasoline fuels fueled automobiles. There were over 100 manufacturers, mostly building a handful of cars each year. Production was based on the crafts system of manufacturing. Electric cars were the leading sales type, but they had limitations with a range of 20 miles, a cost of $2,000, and top speeds around 15 miles per hour. In 1901, when President William McKinley was shot at the World's Fair, a Riker Electric ambulance took him to the hospital. Steamers were the most popular car. The stock market was betting that electric cars would emerge victorious. Steamers held the speed records and could reach over 100 miles per hour. They cost around $2,500 but could carry four to six people. Steamers could have trouble starting in bad weather. The gasoline-type cars were just coming into their own. They were cheaper ($1,000) and ran on kerosene or ethanol. Customers had been slow to adopt them because they required hand cranking to start. Winton, a Cleveland industrialist, was changing the competition in 1901. Winton had moved from bicycle making to automobiles in 1897 and had an automobile factory in Cleveland, Ohio. At the time most of the gasoline-type cars were imported, such as Benz, Panhard-Levassor, and Daimler. These imported diesel engine cars ran on peanut oil. In 1901, the Cleveland Company of Winton Motor Carriage Company started to increase market share in gasoline-type cars with advertising, new technology such as the electric starter and Goodrich rubber tires, and car-racing publicity.

Out of almost 60 gasoline-type car manufacturers, Winton had taken the lead with sales of around 300 cars in 1901. The McKinley Tariff had a 40 percent tariff on imports to allow American auto manufacturers to grow, but buyers seeking high quality and wealthy customers still preferred imports. The total market was around 5,000 cars, and imports controlled most of that. The auto market was a tough place in 1901. Ford's first company, the Detroit Automobile Company, had just gone bankrupt because it was unable to maintain product reliability, quality, and a lower price tag. The Winton was hand built and was often customized for specific buyers. The lowest-cost Winton was advertised in newspapers for $1,000. More expensive models had padded leather seats and other extras and ran as high as $5,000. Winton cars were the best on the road, with Winton having 100 patents. Industrialists like John D. Rockefeller and Andrew Carnegie owned Wintons. The industrialists Cornelius Vanderbilt and H. J. Heinz preferred the French-built Panhard-Levassor with a price tag of $21,000. Wintons had cruising speeds of 30 to 40 miles per hour, but poor dirt roads reduced these speeds even further. The next most popular gasoline-type car was the Duryea in New England. Steamers were heavier and able to maintain road speeds better. Stanley steamers alone outsold all gasoline-type cars from 1899 to 1906. Winton had gone into racing to prove the durability and operation of his cars. These races proved extremely popular with the public and increased sales.

In October 1901, Ford was looking for venture capital for a new auto-manufacturing company. Winton was coming to a racetrack in Grosse Pointe, Michigan, and it was an opportunity for Ford to show his car to the public. Ford had been building prototypes since he saw his first auto at the Chicago World's Fair of 1893. His cars tended to be very light; while fuel-efficient, these Fords made poor racers. Ford had to get permission to use a Winton steering system in his car. It was a 10-mile race on a dirt track, and about 8,000 would see the race. The prize was $1,000 and a cut-glass punch bowl, but the potential was what Ford really needed. It was a lot of money, but Ford already had $5,000 invested in making his race car. Ford's car appeared too light to most investors, who saw the future in heavy, high-horsepower models like Wintons. Winton's car was 50 horsepower while Ford's was 26 horsepower. The Winton weighed about 5,000 pounds while the Ford was 2,200 pounds.

The October 10 race was to have 10 entries with the main attraction being the Winton against the French Panhard-Levassor. At race time there was only Winton and the local boy Ford. Ford would win in the last lap as Winton had mechanical problems. Ford immediately found investors for his new company. One of the investors at the race that day was coal baron Alexander Malcomson. Ford built two more heavy racers to promote his new car company of "Ford and Malcomson." Ford's commercial vision was a car for the masses, which was a different approach from most manufacturers of the time, who aimed at the wealthy. To start up, however, Ford would have still to supply the wealthier customers. The Ford racers continued to popularize Ford in the new partnership with Malcomson, but he struggled to produce a commercial prototype. Ford's "999" racer set the world speed record in 1903 at 60 miles per hour, and a year later, he set a new record at 90 miles per hour. The car company was not as successful in its commercial manufacturing.

The partnership struggled as it signed a contract with the Dodge brothers of Niles, Michigan, to supply 250 engines. In 1903, Ford Motor was formed and capitalized at $100,000. Ford Motor had 125 workers and made 1,700 cars in three different models. Ford was leasing a machine shop from the Dodge brothers. Ford looked to emulate Winton's success using advertising and dealerships. Ford was not pleased with the company's early direction toward selling higher-priced cars. Ford wanted to follow the mass-production model of Ransom Olds, who was producing 5,000 cars a year at a price of $700 each. Ford's right-hand man at the time was James Couzens, a former employee of Malcomson. Couzens and Ford worked relentlessly to bring down the cost and price. They standardized parts and automated handling to drive costs down. Ford would not achieve his dream until the release of the Model T in 1907. The Model T would weigh 1,200 pounds and cost $825. It could run on a variety of hydrocarbon fuels such as kerosene and ethanol. In 1907, Ford Motor decided to hand-make 10 Model T's. The cost of hand building the Model T would equal more than $250,000 today!

*See also:* Chicago World's Fair; First Japanese Auto Sold in the United States; General Motors Corporation Formed; Highland Park Ford Assembly Line

**References**

Brinkley, Douglas. *Wheels for the World: Henry Ford, His Company, and a Century of Progress.* New York: Viking, 2003.

Rae, John B. *The American Automobile.* Chicago: University of Chicago Press, 1965.

Watts, Steven. *The People's Tycoon: Henry Ford and the American Century.* New York: Knopf, 2005.

# Owens Automated Glass Bottle–Making Machine (1904)

Edward D. Libbey's Toledo Glass Company was the developer of the automated bottle machine. Michael Owens gets the credit (rightfully so for the invention), but its full development and implementation required the organization of Toledo Glass, and Libbey gets credit for that. Glass making had hardly changed in 3,000 years until the invention of the bottle-making machine. The automatic bottle-making machine would be a true manufacturing revolution comparable to the effect of Eli Whitney's cotton gin on the cotton industry. Even more, the bottle machine changed society and culture. A 15th-century Venetian would have felt right at home in an 1870 glasshouse prior to the automation of Libbey and Owens. The automatic bottle machine led to a revolution in packaging such as milk bottles, beer bottles, pop bottles, baby bottles, and glass jars. Business friends Libbey Adolphus Bush and H. J. Heinz were pioneering glass packaging for beer and vegetables but lacked volume glass bottle suppliers. At first, the cost of production using the bottle machine was around $0.10 a gross (144 bottles) versus $1.52 per gross for hand production of bottles. The lowered costs quickly opened up new markets for the use of glass bottles and jars. The automated bottle machine led to automated filling machines in industries such as ketchup making. The bottle machine guaranteed standard and equivalent weights and measures, paving the way for the Pure Food and Drug Act of 1906. An ancillary effect was the eventual elimination of child labor in the glass industry.

Libbey built Toledo Glass to do development work, and without it, Owens could not have made the bottle-making machine commercial. Libbey hired the draftsmen, mechanics, and engineers needed to build the machine. Owens, working from a model he developed while at the Chicago World's Fair of 1893, functioned as project manager. The bottle machine was every bit as much an organizational triumph as an engineering triumph. It required an army of technical experts and Libbey's leadership.

The bottle machine had nearly 10,000 individual parts, while the 1907 Model T had fewer than 3,000 parts. These parts had to be designed and manufactured.

Every part required a two-dimensional blueprint, so it could be machined or cast. Amazingly, Owens could not read blueprints. If more than one machine was to be made, it would require standardized parts, blueprints, and processes. Blueprints allowed Libbey to standardize his parts supply chain. Owens was incapable of such an engineering task, but Libbey supplied the necessary engineering backup. It was a huge undertaking beyond the ability of any individual. It was Libbey's style of organization and Libbey as CEO that allowed the invention of the bottle machine to progress. Libbey not only held the organization together but also funded the vision when the board of directors wavered. The bottle machine as well as later inventions was the first real team invention. It marked the end of the lone Victorian scientist making a breakthrough. Thomas Edison had an organization as support, while Libbey had a true developmental organization integrated into the effort. Libbey approached research and development as a craft, with engineers being innovation craftsmen. Libbey's developmental company would become the model for corporate development in years to come.

The development of the automated bottle took years from Owens's first semi-automated machine in 1898. The semi-automatic process could make bottles at 75¢ a gross (144 bottles). The commercial version in 1905, known as machine A, could produce 12 beer bottles per minute, or 17,280 in a 24-hour period. Compare this to hand production of 2,880 bottles per day using a crew of six men and boys. Such production capacity and lower costs quickly opened up the markets for beer and ketchup bottles. The national market in 1900 was about three million bottles of ketchup alone. These were hand-blown bottles, and since ketchup was sold in barrels as well, the potential market was probably near seven million bottles. The beer bottle market in 1900 was about twice that size. Libbey made the decision not to become either a machine manufacturer or a bottle manufacturer but developed a different type of company for the leasing of machines to end users. Leasing was a revolutionary business model that Libbey perfected.

The first license of the machine was with Baldwin-Travis (Thatcher Manufacturing) in September 1904. Thatcher was licensed to make milk bottles only. It cost Thatcher $250,000 for the license. The payment was made with $150,000 in cash, $50,000 in preferred stock, and $50,000 in common stock. Royalties were based on a per-bottle calculation of labor savings from the machine. One-half of the savings would go to the Owens Bottle Machine Company. Libbey would select companies exclusively for beer bottles, ale bottles, wine bottles, soda pop bottles, brandy bottles, and so on. The royalties for Thatcher in 1904 were 50 cents a gross. The Thatcher machine required modifications for their thick-walled square bottle. In addition, Libbey would supply Owens to help in the machine startup and installation. Owens quickly became a thorn in the side to a broad segment of the glass industry.

Licensing was the most important of these strategic issues of Libbey. Libbey personally took to selling licenses. Robotics companies are using the Libbey model of licensing and leasing today. Libbey and Owens believed the machine had a major advantage in the longneck bottles favored by beer bottles. Iron City Brewing in Pittsburgh had been one of the first to come to Toledo to see the machine. In 1903, Libbey was in negotiations with a group of Pittsburgh beer bottle manufacturers but was getting nowhere. The group had negotiated together, fearing that the machine would give any one of them an unfair advantage. Libbey secretly approached one of them, Edward Everett, after negotiations broke down. He started a secret exchange of letters using fictitious names. Libbey and Everett joined together to take over three bottle plants in Ohio (Newark, Massillon, and Wooster). The new company became Ohio Bottle Company. Ohio Bottle Company was then given an exclusive license for beer, porter, ale, and soda bottles. This company would be the major supplier to Pittsburgh Brewing Company (Iron City Beer). So, by 1905, Libbey controlled a complex web of glass companies that had avoided the image of a monopoly.

Libbey would become America's most adept monopolist, controlling the bottle market, while the government seemed unable to understand his control. Leasing gave him market control, which he could sell as a premium to companies. Once a company had first leasing rights such as Thatcher in milk bottles and Heinz in ketchup bottles, Libbey refused to lease to their competitors. With Kent Machine as his manufacturing company, Libbey had started a process of vertical integration controlling the supply chain, but his horizontal integration of markets was overwhelming. In 1905, Libbey had control of the cut-glass, bottle, and container markets. In the bottle and container markets, he was in a position to control pricing and production. He realized that the automatic bottle machine had the potential to cause disarray in the marketplace. Libbey chose to slowly change the market while maintaining price levels. This would also allow for an orderly transfer from skilled glassblowers and gathers to machine operators. Still, Libbey's tactics were every bit as monopolistic in nature as those of J. P. Morgan. Libbey, in fact, had the power to decide segment winners because he sold exclusive rights in segments such as beer bottles, vegetable jars, milk bottles, and others.

Libbey also moved quickly on expanding licensing to Europe with trips in 1904 and 1905. Owens European Bottle Machine Company was formed to sell licenses. Beer king Adolphus Busch, who had first seen the machine in 1903, became a stockholder in the European Bottle Machine. Other than Busch and Julius Prince of Germany's Apollinaris Company, the board of Owens European Bottle Machine Company was the same as that of Toledo Glass. Owens European Bottle Machine had exclusive rights for Europe, Central America, South America, Africa, Cuba, and Australasia.

One of the unexpected results of the Owens bottle machine was a huge reduction in child labor. A typical glass factory might have 100 boys working at low wages to make bottles. Wages were from $0.30 to $0.50 a day, often with room and board not included. While a boy might make $3 to $6 a week, he might be charged $2 to $3 a week for room and board. Company boarding houses were common in Ohio. Orphans were often shipped from eastern cities to take jobs in the glasshouses of Ohio where labor was in short supply. The Owens bottle machine effectively reduced the workforce to high-paid machine operators. In 1910, Libbey would repeat the developmental and marketing process with the invention and application of an automated flat glass machine.

*See also:* Chicago World's Fair

### References

Skrabec, Quentin. *Edward Drummond Libbey: A Biography of an American Glassmaker.* Jefferson, NC: McFarland, 2010.

# Upton Sinclair's *Jungle* (1905)

The publication of Upton Sinclair's *The Jungle* in 1905 would be the result of decades of failed efforts at regulation in the processed food industry. Sinclair's exposé of the meat industry and the unsanitary conditions sent a shock wave across the country. At the time, Sinclair was a Chicago socialist active in the movement. His earlier works had been failures, but *The Jungle* would make him an overnight sensation. For months in 1904, Sinclair worked a 12-hour shift in the Chicago stockyards while living in a hut. Sinclair's novel was meant to send a socialist message of the oppression of immigrant workers. It was a pessimistic novel of immigrants living as animals and dying the same. He ends the novel with a socialist orator shouting: "Organize! Organize! Organize! Chicago will be ours!" Sinclair would be disappointed with his success, as his anticapitalist message was lost. Sinclair noted, "I aimed at their hearts and by accident I hit their stomach." In fact, most Americans had no stomach for socialism. His socialist message had held up the publication of *The Jungle* with big publishers. It was first published in 1904 in a socialist paper but then picked up by Doubleday in 1906.

It was the eight pages describing the handling of processed meat that caught the public. President Theodore Roosevelt, who questioned Sinclair's politics, was sickened by the descriptions in the book. At one point Sinclair even described workers falling into the rendering tanks and being ground up. While this proved to be unfounded, many of the other descriptions of unsanitary conditions were right on. Rotting meat was clearly being used in many products. Dirt, insects, and even rats did make it into the tanks. Basically, the American food industry had no regulation. Dirty conditions had been reported, but the industry had been able to deflect critics until Sinclair's novel. Still, regulation usually comes after industrialization (and scandals). We see the same issues in China today as they struggle to regulate safety in their booming factories.

Europeans were also pushing to limit American processed food because of impurities found in it. France was banning all American food products. The controversy heated up in 1894 when a congressional committee found extensive abuses in purity levels in the food industry. At the same time, state legislatures were investigating similar abuses. Until 1898, the movement lacked leadership. Then, in 1898, Harvey Wiley, the Department of Agriculture's chief chemist, took up the flag. Wiley also added science as a weapon in the battle. He combined his scientific knowledge with his gifted writing ability to recruit an army to the cause. Alice Lakey, head of the Consumers' League joined in the battle. Wiley also brought state chemists and agriculture departments into the fight. In 1899, the Senate held its first hearing on pure food legislation. Wiley, however, lacked industry and political support. In particular, the controlling Republican Party opposed such a movement on a states' rights basis and individual freedoms.

Food purity had been a growing topic slowly building momentum for decades. The quest for food purity had started with magazines such as *McClure's, Ladies' Home Journal,* and *Collier's Weekly.* The stories of sweeping the pieces and trimmings off the floor to put in the product were eye opening. These exposés started in the 1880s, but housewives had been suspicious of commercial foods since their beginnings in the 1860s. The National Canning Association had earlier on joined the campaign for purity, realizing the need to overcome resistance to canned foods. Still, these processes were not perfect, and some packages such as barrels were not sterilized. Exploding ketchup and pickle barrels from bacteria-produced gas were not uncommon. Another issue was ethical in that consumers were paying for fillers such as sawdust. Companies such as Campbell Soups, Busch, and Heinz had actually found success in targeting the poor quality of their competitors. They even opened their factories to public tours to demonstrate their cleanliness.

Sinclair's *Jungle* created a public outpouring of calls for inspections. By 1905, public outcry had reached the ears of the politicians. The food industry and Wiley organized a select committee of six to call on President Roosevelt in 1905. Another important organization, the American Medical Association, joined the alliance. The committee would call on Roosevelt several times, but the president remained unconvinced. Roosevelt had called for an unannounced inspection of the Chicago stockyards. The findings confirmed poor practices, but Roosevelt hesitated because of Sinclair's politics. Still, *The Jungle* pushed progressive Republicans in Congress to force legislation.

Roosevelt's mind was changed over a glass of whiskey. Wiley took his portable chemistry set to a meeting with President Roosevelt. Wiley was able to use dyes and flavoring to manufacture Roosevelt's favorite 10-year-old bourbon with freshly made grain alcohol. The legend suggests that Roosevelt's response was "If a man can't get a good drink of whiskey in the evening when he comes home from work, there ought to be a law to see that he does." While a great anecdote, Roosevelt was feeling the pressure, and the congressional Republicans were ready to address at least the meat industry. Roosevelt was at the political breaking point, but he still hesitated. He also didn't care much for the showy Wiley (probably their egos clashed). In addition, Roosevelt had countries such as France banning all American food products. Finally, the public outcry forced Congress's hand, caused by the popularity of *The Jungle*. The Pure Food and Drug Act became law in June 1906. But the Pure Food and Drug Act mainly addressed meat inspection and the shipping of adulterated food. The battle against preservatives in food would follow. The Food and Drug Act of 1914 addressed canned and jarred foods. Packaged horseradish, for ex-

Advertizing poster for Upton Sinclair's *The Jungle*. (Library of Congress)

ample, was filled with cheap extenders such as grated turnip, sawdust, and floor sweepings, to say nothing of insects, sand, dirt, and animal waste.

*See also:* First Electric Sign (Product Branding and Advertising)—H. J. Heinz

### References

Arthur, Anthony. *Radical Innocent: Upton Sinclair.* New York: Random House, 2006.

Hooker, Richard. *A History of Food and Drink in America.* New York: Bobbs-Merrill, 1981.

Wiener, Gary. *Workers' Rights in Upton Sinclair's The Jungle.* Detroit: Greenhaven, 2008.

# Panic of 1907

The Panic of 1907 was typical of the boom-and-bust cycle that had evolved with capitalism. The year 1905 was representative of the situation that industrialists, capitalists, and the country found themselves in. Times had been good since the end of the Panic of 1893, but dark clouds were gathering. The booming stock market had covered the lack of capitalization in many of the mergers. The economic expansion was showing the signs of extravagance, and scandals were breaking out with excess money. The merger mania had brought the progressive government of Theodore Roosevelt into the trust-busting era. Spending was over the top in all areas, but for the country, these were truly "the best and the worst of times." Factories were running full out, and in New York, the stock market was booming. United States Steel's stock hit $50 per share. Steel production in the United States had jumped an amazing one million tons in 1905 (3,192,347 tons in 1905 compared to 2,137,347 tons in 1904). Steel production would peak in 1906 at 3,791,459 tons.

America's focus, however, appeared to be on the lives of the rich and famous, as well as the booming stock market. On January 31, 1905, the greatest ball of the Gilded Age would occur. It was the infamous ball of James Hazen Hyde at New York's Sherry's Hotel. Hazen was the young heir of the insurance fortune built by his father. The 28-year-old Hazen had become the major stockholder and director of the Equitable Life Assurance Society. The Equitable Life Assurance Society was one of America's largest insurance companies at the time, with over 300,000 policyholders and over $1 billion in force. Scandal would hit Equitable Life shortly after the ball, and it would fail, leading to a weakening of the stock market and the financial market. Insurance companies were the major holders of corporate stocks at the time.

On October 14, 1907, the stock of United Copper fell from $62 to $15 a share. The stock loss forced owner F. A. Heinze to pull money from his Butte, Montana, savings and loan, which affected a chain of banks. Nine banks pooled their resources to aid in the United Copper problems, but it was too late. Then a run started on the insurance company Knickerbocker Trust Company, because of its president Charles Barney's close relationship with Heinze. Depositors withdrew over $8 million in less than four hours. On Friday, October 18, the run reached a point at which all backers pulled out, thereby assuring its failure. The stock market saw a number of companies go under that Friday as well as United Copper. The weekend added to the tension as stories of bank failures hit the nation's press. The next week saw major companies such as Westinghouse Electric unable to cover calls on loans. In this period, when banks became short on money, they called in corporate loans, creating a downward cycle of corporate bankruptcies and bank failures. In this time before the Federal Reserve, the market depended on major bankers such as J. P. Morgan to pool assets together to put money into the system. Morgan, however, could gain much by buying up companies and letting competitors to his electrical and steel trusts fail. The collapse in the financial markets headed quickly to Main Street. Orders were quickly pulled from factories by the end of October.

The press reported the comings and goings around Morgan's New York library where he was managing operations. Only Morgan was in a position to decide the course of this panic. The monthly profits of United States Steel reflected the plunge in orders—profits in October were $17.05 million, $10.47 million in November, and $5 million in December. The morning of October 17, the news came by telegraph that Knickerbocker Insurance had failed, which meant the banks would be calling in loans. Insurance companies at the time were the country's major stockholders. Again, Morgan, America's banker, stood on the sidelines, except to assure cash for United States Steel's operations. J. P. Morgan & Company officers served as directors in 114 corporations with a capitalization of $22.5 billion, while the total capitalization for all of the New York Stock Exchange was $26.5 billion. President Roosevelt asked Morgan to inject cash into the system. Morgan did pool bankers but at a cost. The federal government would turn its back on Morgan taking over Tennessee Coal & Iron Company to add to his steel trust. They would also allow Westinghouse to go bankrupt, which was the only competitor to Morgan's electrical trust of General Electric. The federal government had to back Morgan's pool with bonds as well. It was a hard lesson, but the government would address it in the future with the Federal Reserve Act.

John Moody charged that Morgan and associates stopped the panic by "taking a few dollars out of one pocket and putting millions into another." Upton Sinclair used the panic as the basis for his novel *The Money Changers* to illustrate Morgan's ruthlessness. In the novel, a Morgan-like character orchestrates a financial crisis for private gain while destroying ordinary people across the nation. The Senate committee investigating the panic for years concluded Morgan had taken advantage of the situation. Congress believed that United States Steel paid a mere $30 million for a $90 million company, Tennessee Coal & Iron. No longer in office as president, Roosevelt testified in 1909 that he had given tacit approval to Morgan to proceed for the good of the country.

The Panic of 1907 was not deep in terms of the degree of recession, but it uncovered major shortcomings in the banking system. Congress created a Monetary Commission to study the banking system. The conclusion was that the country should not be held by individual bankers in times of crisis. This would eventually lead to the Federal Reserve Act of 1913.

*See also:* Banking Crisis and Great Recession; Federal Reserve Act; Panic of 1837; Panic of 1857; Panic of 1873; Panic of 1893; Savings and Loan Crisis; Stock Market Crash/Great Depression

### References

Bruner, Robert, and Sean Carr. *The Panic of 1907: Lessons Learned from the Market's Perfect Storm.* Hoboken, NJ: Wiley, 2009.

Calamiris, Charles, and Gary Gorton. *The Origins of Banking Panics: Models, Facts, and Bank Regulation.* Chicago: University of Chicago Press, 1992.

Chernow, Ron. *House of Morgan: An American Banking Dynasty and the Rise of Modern Finance.* New York: Grove, 1990.

Kindleberger, Charles P., and Robert Aliber. *Manias, Panics, and Crashes: A History of Financial Crises.* Hoboken, NJ: Wiley, 2005.

# Highland Park Ford Assembly Line (1910)

One of the continuing myths of industry is that Henry Ford invented the assembly line. The roots of the assembly line actually go back to the Arsenal of Venice in the 1400s. Adam Smith in his *Wealth of Nations* had outlined the idea of labor specialization, which is basic to the assembly line. It can be said that Ford Motor made the assembly line operational and economical, but a lot of credit must go to Charles Emil Sorensen (1882–1968). Sorensen was a production genius and a loyal lieutenant of Ford. Sorensen was the mastermind behind the assembly line at Ford's Highland Park plant. Even Sorensen, however, cannot take full credit as it was a team of Ford managers that worked out the system. The assembly line was created out of the crafts system as production requirements increased. Cars were originally built as a single unit by a team of mechanics. In 1910, there were over 200 manufacturers across the United States. Oldsmobile had the best factory, with a production of over 3,000 cars per year. Ford always had the dream of selling a car for the masses, but in 1910 he was bunched with all the other producers with no cost advantage.

The Highland Park assembly line really began with the inefficiencies of the second Ford plant at Piquette Avenue. Piquette Avenue was bigger than the first Mack Avenue plant Ford left in 1904, but little thought, other than size, had been put into the layout. The cost of the 1904 Piquette plant was $76,000. There were several buildings, requiring a lot of material and subassembly handling. The main focus at the Piquette plant was product development, which laid the groundwork for the 1908 launch of the Model T. Autos, in general, were hand-built using the crafts method prior to Highland Park. Generally, the crafts method had cars being built in stalls and parts being brought to the car. Using the crafts system, one to two cars could be produced in a day at best. Ford's second plant at Piquette took production to over 14,000 a year, which was believed to be the limit of the crafts method. The base cost was around $600 to $800. Ford started to design a new plant to achieve his dream of a car for the masses. The inherent problems were paramount when, in 1907, Ford started to plan the Highland Park plant. The Highland Park plant was designed to make the Model T.

Ford hired an experienced industrial architect in Albert Kahn, who had designed the 1903 Packard Motor plant in Detroit. The Highland Park plant was comprised of two separate, four-story assembly buildings. The building's design relied on logic: Raw materials were delivered to the top floor, and as finished parts were forged and machined, they made their way down the floors through more than 1,000 openings. Ford and Kahn had incorporated gravity for chutes, conveyors, and tubes. The plant was designed to efficiently take in and distribute boxcars of supplied parts. The Highland Park plant opened in 1910, but it remained in a state of development and expansion for many years. This was done on purpose as part of a continuous improvement plan. In 1910, the new assembly plant struggled to make 19,000 cars. It was far from an assembly line in 1910, but it had the best materials-handling system in the world.

Even for Ford Motor Company, the assembly line was more evolutionary. Sorensen noted, "The essential tools and the final assembly line with its many integrated feeders resulted from an organization which continually used experimenting and improvising to get better production." One key advance was the conveyer system to bring radiators to the main line. Before that, radiators were moved by hand and muscle from the docks to the line. Gravity chute conveyance systems were designed and modeled after those in food factories such as Busch Beer in St. Louis and H. J. Heinz in Pittsburgh. Kahn and Ford found the gravity conveyance system so efficient that parts plants were built up to 10 stories high to fully utilize such a system. Ford slowly learned that one-floor conveyor systems worked better. Conveyors started to be used for other parts and subassemblies. Assistant

Flywheel assembly line at the Ford Highland Park plant in 1913. (AP/Wide World Photos)

superintendent Clarence Avery achieved another key advance. Experience allowed Avery to work out the timing schedules of each operation of the assembly line, which was necessary before installation of conveyor assembly systems for motors, fenders, magnetos, and transmissions. Next, Ford had to standardize parts from his supply chain using blueprints. Supply chain development played a critical role in full implementation of the assembly line process. Ford Motor was able to cut manufacturing costs by 50 percent over a two-year period by implementing these types of improvements.

Ford didn't apply the integrated assembly line system until April 1913 when the company used it to build flywheel magneto assemblies for the Model T. Ford then moved to an assembly line for crankshafts. Conversion of the Highland Park plant to the assembly line method started in 1913. Prior to this, Ford was using an intermediate phase of 50 workstations. It took an estimated 12.5 man-hours to build a car. In 1913, Ford moved the chassis to a single chain-pulled line, which cut the time to about 9 man-hours. Within a year, Ford doubled production and cut the cost in half. Employment went to 13,000 in 1914 as the total investment at Highland Park went over $200 million. The doubling of production in 1913 created a new problem. The work had been specialized to the point Adam Smith had hailed as revolutionary.

The problem was that the boring routine work caused absenteeism to reach over 10 percent and turnover more than 300 percent! Human issues were now the limitation rather than technology. Ford's solution was to double the wage to five dollars a day, which worked. Costs came down, and the production rate hit a car every three minutes. The wage of five dollars a day did have restrictions as Ford tried to select the best assembly workers. The requirements included that a man should be married or a woman should be the sole supporter of the family, which Ford felt was necessary for productive work. Ford also required the person have "thrifty habits." He went as far as implementing a sociological department to monitor employees and help them develop thrift and family values. By the end of 1914, Ford had an amazing cost advantage over his competitors. He had no competition in cars priced under $500.

*See also:* General Motors Corporation Formed; Owens Automated Glass Bottle–Making Machine; Henry Ford Wins Race of Century; *Wealth of Nations*

## References

Brinkley, Douglas. *Wheels for the World: Henry Ford, His Company, and a Century of Progress.* New York: Viking, 2003.

Olsen, Byron, and Joseph Cabadas. *The American Auto Factory.* St. Paul, MN: MBI, 2002.

Sorenson, Charles. *My Forty Years with Ford.* Detroit: Wayne State University Press, 2006.

# Scientific Management (1911)

Frederick Winslow Taylor (1856–1915) published his famous book, *The Principles of Scientific Management,* in 1911. It represented the peak of the industrial efficiency movement of the prior decades. Taylorism, as it became known, was the application of the scientific method to management practices. Scientific management looked to optimize the way tasks were performed by simplifying the jobs so that workers could be trained to perform their specialized sequence of operational tasks in the most efficient way. Taylor had been working on the approach since the 1880s at companies such as Midvale Steel and Bethlehem Steel. In 1908, Harvard Business School based its first-year curriculum on Taylor's scientific management. Henry Ford was an early adopter of scientific management, as was Louis Brandeis in the railroad industry. Management writer Peter Drucker ranked Taylor among Darwin and Freud as one of the seminal thinkers of modern times. Taylorism became the first management fad by 1911, and after America's success in World War I, it spread throughout the world. No single management system has achieved such broad acclaim with the possible exception of W. Edwards Deming's statistical process control of the late 20th century. France and Russia, in particular, mandated the use of Taylorism in industry after World War I. It is considered the foundation of industrial engineering. Taylorism remained basic to American management until the 1980s, when it came under attack by Japanese-oriented management. Taylorism became linked incorrectly with the basic problems of the American factory system. Much of Taylor's approach was adopted and modified by 20th-century quality guru Deming. Taylor's methods have had a renaissance with the spread of the international standard ISO 9000.

Taylor, the father of scientific management, started as an apprentice pattern maker at Midvale Steel. He worked at night school to earn a degree in mechanical engineering from Stevens Institute of Technology in Philadelphia. Taylor worked his way up from the factory floor into management. In 1890, he joined a consulting firm for "systematizing of shop management." He later joined Bethlehem Steel to implement his system, but he also proved himself a famous metallurgist by applying his methods to engineering. He teamed up with Maunsel White to invent high-speed tool steels. Taylor's early work on scientific management was a scientific search for the best methods to do things. He worked with better handling and work techniques for laborers. He perfected his methods like a scientist doing experiments to determine the best results. He was best known for his famous shoveling experiment, combining the factors of shovel size and the worker's physical attributes with material density. This type of factor analysis would lead to the use of statistical analysis to optimize factors, such analysis of variance (ANOVA) in the 1970s.

Taylor would also become known for incorporating time study and inventive programs in his approach. Taylor published his best-known paper, "A Piece-Rate System, Being a Step toward Partial Solution of the Labor Problem," in 1895. Taylor went back into consulting in 1901 and fine-tuned his theories. He eventually became a business professor at Dartmouth College. Taylor became the preacher of the scientific management gospel, which was furthered by Henry L. Gantt (1861–1919), Carl Barth (1860–1939), and Frank Gilbreth (1868–1924) and Lillian Gilbreth (1878–1972). Taylor was often brought in to testify and function as a consultant for the U.S. Congress. In this capacity he studied and reported on industrial safety and the efficiency of the railroads.

Taylor took the approach used in science and adapted it to management. He recommended that a manager fully study an operation prior to developing work procedures. Taylor was one of the first to argue that much of the inefficiency in industry was related to poor management. Scientific management centered on four principles detailed in Taylor's book:

1. Replace rule-of-thumb work methods and procedures with methods based on the scientific method;
2. Scientifically select, train, and develop each employee rather than passively leaving them to train themselves;
3. Provide detailed instruction for each worker in the performance of his or her tasks;
4. Divide work equally between managers and workers, so that the managers apply scientific management principles to planning the work and workers actually perform the tasks.

These basic principles proved particularly well suited to convert unskilled immigrant labor into skilled labor. Scientific management proved very effective for the definition and implementation of assembly line work.

Taylorism and scientific management became the basis for the development of industrial engineering, industrial psychology, and shop scheduling. Taylor argued that factories and companies should have a planning department. Scientific management revolutionized the machining industry with its scientific approach to the speeds and feeds of automated machines. Taylor required the use of a strong cost system and analysis. Its most powerful impact was the use of SOPs—standard operating procedures. This came as a break from a crafts-driven system where procedures were passed verbally from a master craftsman to an apprentice. In general, scientific management was a critical step in the transition from the crafts model to that of the Industrial Revolution. The scientific management approach made for easy training of new workers. It created process and product consistency. Taylor stressed standardization throughout the operation including all tools, implements, and methods used in the trades.

Taylorism and scientific management came and continued to come under heated criticism. Taylor's use of the stopwatch and time study often found resistance from unions. Other management scientists argued it dehumanized work, creating monotony. While Taylorism proved good at breaking down tasks to run assembly lines, it proved a poor technique for overall job design, which requires the analysis of skill variety, task significance, autonomy, and feedback. Many Japanese business analysts rejected Taylor's approach, incorrectly blaming it for the decline of American quality in the 1970s and the rise of Japanese quality. Today, managers are again looking for the proper place of Taylorism in management practices. Certainly, the use of well-defined and written procedures has found a place in the international operating standard of ISO 9000. The roots of Taylorism can even be found today in the Kanban inventory management system.

*See also:* W. Edwards Deming Publishes *Out of the Crisis*; General Motors Corporation Formed; Highland Park Ford Assembly Line; Maslow's Theory of Needs

### References

Kanigel, Robert. *The One Best Way: Frederick Winslow Taylor and the Enigma of Efficiency.* New York: Viking, 1997.

Nelson, Daniel. *Frederick W. Taylor and the Rise of Scientific Management.* Madison: University of Wisconsin Press, 1980.

Nelson, Daniel. *A Mental Revolution: Scientific Management since Taylor.* Columbus: Ohio State University Press, 1992.

Taylor, Frederick Winslow. *Principles of Scientific Management.* New York: Harper & Brothers, 1911.

# Standard Oil Antitrust Lawsuit (1911)

Standard Oil was established in 1870 as an integrated oil company. The company started as a partnership—with many partners— controlled by John D. Rockefeller in Ohio. Rockefeller proved an aggressive organizer, combining oil production, transportation, and oil refining. He absorbed and destroyed his competition over the years. Rockefeller's methods were highly competitive and cutthroat, but the 50 percent drop in the price of kerosene was a favorable result. Rockefeller applied the following techniques: (1) undercutting of prices to drive the competition out of business, (2) special arrangements with railroads to hurt the competition, (3) use of volume to control transportation deals with pipelines and railroads, (4) spies and use of placed officials to disrupt the competition, (5) use of thugs for threats, and (6) control of steel barrel production to prevent competitors from moving oil to customers. The effects of Rockefeller's competitive practices changed the oil industry forever. For example, Rockefeller froze out the oil-refining and oil market center from Pittsburgh (at the time nearest to oil fields) to Cleveland.

Rockefeller had taken 80 percent of the oil market by the 1874. He focused first on horizontal integration by gaining control of the nation's refineries. Rockefeller then moved vertically to own barrel manufacturers, railroad tank cars, pipelines, and distribution centers. In 1882, Standard Oil created a holding company with 47 companies including Standard Oil of Ohio. It was a giant trust controlling these companies through interlocking directors on the various company boards. It was the first time that a trust created negotiable securities. A trust is defined as an arrangement whereby the stockholders of individual companies transfer their shares to a set of trustees of a holding company. The arrangement allows for central control and for the individual companies to function in unison as a highly disciplined monopoly. To unify this universe of 47 companies, Rockefeller created a system of managing committees to assure uniform processes, procedures, quality, and a coordinated mission. The committee system was amazing in uniting the trust. The Rockefeller committee system became a model for large American corporations such as the first billion-dollar corporation ever formed, United States Steel. Big business and control were becoming a major political issue, and in 1890, Congress passed the Sherman antitrust law that forbade the restraint of trade by schemes, contracts, deals, and conspiracies. The Sherman Anti-Trust Act had strong public support, passing unanimously in the House and 51–1 in the Senate.

By 1890, Standard Oil had over 90 percent of the oil-refining capacity in the United States. Its size and power allowed it to continuously cut costs and price, crushing the competition. The United States sued, using the Sherman Anti-Trust Act of 1890. In 1892, the Supreme Court ruled Standard Oil an illegal monopoly. Standard Oil superficially complied but retained control of the boards of the individual companies. In 1899, the company reorganized in New Jersey, where state law allowed a parent company to own stock of other companies. William McKinley's administration (1896–1901) chose to ignore the court action.

Standard Oil of New Jersey returned to its control of the market. The Standard Oil debate was hotly contended in the early 1900s. Standard Oil had been good to consumers, having driven down prices (at least temporarily), being a product innovator, improving quality, and making oil refining highly efficient. It was the type of government-allowed monopoly that American companies compete against today in the international arena. Standard Oil at the time was suffering from public distrust in a period of muckraking. Standard Oil's huge profits and cutthroat methods caught the public eye in an age of trust-busting. In 1904, Ida Tarbell, whose father had been bankrupted competing with Standard Oil, published the exposé, *The History of the Standard Oil Company*. It was a story of greed that turned the public against all trusts. The trust-busting administration of Theodore Roosevelt took on Standard Oil of New Jersey in 1904. One of the motivations was to prevent Standard Oil from controlling the new oil finds in Texas and Oklahoma. Once again using the Sherman Anti-Trust Act of 1890, the case focused on the ruthless practices of Standard Oil in destroying competition. In 1904, Standard Oil controlled over 91 percent of oil refining as well as over 80 percent of the American and 55 percent of the world market of finished products.

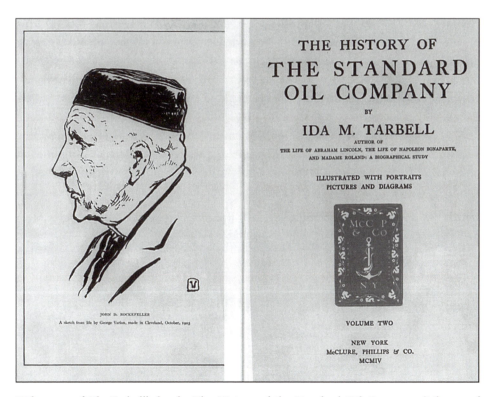

Title page of Ida Tarbell's book, *The History of the Standard Oil Company*. (Library of Congress)

The court case proved complex and lasted years, until 1911. The ruling found that Standard Oil violated the Sherman Anti-Trust Act, stating that Standard Oil's dominant position in the industry was due "to unfair practices, to abuse of the control of pipelines, to railroad discriminations, and to unfair methods of competition." Interestingly, all of these unfair practices were true but had mostly ended by 1902. In fact, Standard Oil's market share had dropped to under 65 percent by 1911. The importance of the decision, *Standard Oil Company of New Jersey v. United States,* was its use of the "rule of reason." The rule of reason stated that large size and market control were not in themselves necessarily bad or a violation of the Sherman Anti-Trust Act, but that the use of abusive tactics to attain and preserve such a monopoly was illegal. The concept of rule of reason appealed even to the business community as a fair ruling and something all could live with. Most historians believe the ruling was an important step toward free competition.

The Supreme Court ordered Standard Oil to dismantle its trust of companies. The order broke up the trust ties, but eight of the companies maintained the name Standard Oil. In themselves, they were very large vertical companies. The ruling did open up the oil industry to new competitors such as Gulf Oil and Texaco. In retrospect, the ruling created a healthy and competitive market that was very innovative. Oil exploration was greatly expanded as fortune hunters entered the market. The ruling created a debate about paternal capitalism versus better wages as a means of distributing wealth. The rule of reason was established as a legal precedent, but the ruling left an American public and government biased against companies with a large market share and monopolies. In 1984, American Telephone and Telegraph (AT&T) would be broken up based on market share. Today, this bias hurts American companies that compete against international monopolies in a new world economic market. Japan and China allow and even encourage what would be considered trusts in this country.

*See also:* Baltimore & Ohio Railroad; First Billion-Dollar Corporation—United States Steel; McKinley Tariff of 1890; "Report on Manufacturing"

### References

Bringhurst, Bruce. *Antitrust and the Oil Trust: The Standard Oil Cases, 1890–1911.* New York: Greenwood, 1979.

Chernow, Ron. *Titan: The Life of John D. Rockefeller, Sr.* New York: Vintage, 1998.

Wall, Bennett H. *Growth in a Changing Environment: A History of Standard Oil Company (New Jersey), Exxon Corporation, 1950–1975.* New York: HarperCollins, 1989.

Yergin, Daniel. *The Prize: The Epic Quest for Oil, Money, and Power.* New York: Simon & Schuster, 1991.

# Income Tax (1913)

Having been born in part from a tax revolution, the United States was slow to implement any form of taxation. Taxation has been at the heart of American business and politics since the very beginning. Over 90 percent of the early federal government was financed by tariffs. The first use of an excise tax on whiskey had resulted in the Whiskey Rebellion in 1794, and a military action was required to enforce the tax. The government did expand sales and excise taxes to finance the War of 1812, only to have all of these repealed in 1817. Congress was considering an income tax for the War of 1812 when it ended. From 1817 to 1861, the United States was funded by tariffs on incoming goods and, to a small degree, excise taxes. The Civil War, however, required huge expenditures by the federal government. The Revenue Act of 1861 imposed an income tax on all incomes over $600. The tax rate was 3 percent, graduated up to 5 percent for the very few who earned over $10,000 a year. This income tax targeted the very wealthiest of Americans and accounted for only a fifth of the necessary income for the war. This tax was repealed in 1872. During the 1880s, many states passed inheritance taxes, which had popular support. Surprisingly, the inheritance tax and a luxury tax had the support of wealthy industrialists such as Andrew Carnegie and John D. Rockefeller.

In 1894, Democrats in Congress were able to pass first peacetime income tax as part of the Wilson-Gorman Tariff. The Democrats reduced tariffs at the same time to help farmers, who complained of the high price of sugar and household products. Tariffs were considered a "tax" on the average consumer, who paid more for imported products. This new income tax was 2 percent on incomes over $10,000, which addressed less than 10 percent of households. In 1895, the U.S. Supreme Court, in its ruling *Pollock v. Farmers' Loan and Trust Company,* held such an income tax to be unconstitutional. The court ruled the income tax a direct tax, which was inhibited by the constitution under Article I, Section 9, which stated that "no capitation, or other direct tax shall be laid, unless in proportion to the census." With tariff incomes rising in the late 1890s, Congress decided not to challenge the court decision with a new tax initiative. The reduction of tariff rates in the early 1900s and rising public awareness of the excesses of the wealthy created pressure again for an income tax. This was consistent with the progressive movement of the time in both political parties. Congress first passed a corporate income tax of 1 percent on the income over $5,000 (about $110,000 today). In 1913, there was a clear demand to reduce tariffs and impose an income tax. The Underwood Tariff Act of 1913 ended the protectionist tariffs that had existed since the earliest days of the United States. With popular support, Congress moved to have the 16th Amendment passed by the states.

The 16th Amendment stated, "The Congress shall have power to lay and collect taxes on incomes, from whatever source derived, without apportionment among the several States, and without regard to any census or enumeration." Politicians sold the amendment, saying it would result in a tax only on America's wealthiest (a pledge quickly forgotten once the power to tax was given). The 16th Amendment was ratified in 1913, and Congress passed the Revenue Act of 1913. This Act levied a 1 percent tax on incomes above $3,000 with a surtax of 6 percent on those with incomes above $500,000. This meant a top rate of 7 percent. At the time roughly 2 percent of the population paid the income tax. The 1916 Supreme Court decision *Brushaber v. Union Pacific* actually expanded the meaning of "income" to include profit and gain from any source. The government's need to finance World War I quickly caused the top rate to increase to 77 percent. Democrats created an excess profit tax for corporations as well to finance the war. Total tax revenues increased to over a billion dollars in 1918. Popular support eroded as the government began to expand taxation on all fronts for the war, but the genie was out of the bottle.

The government produced a series of hundreds of bills over the years to adjust the tax for various groups and types of income; the first of these created progressive steps of income to be taxed at increasing marginal rates. The top marginal rate was cut to 58 percent in 1922. From 1913 to 1921, capital gains were taxed as ordinary income. Many argued that this treatment took away the incentive to invest in American stocks. The Revenue Act of 1921 allowed assets held for two years to be taxed at 12.5 percent instead of the then top rate of 77 percent. Capital gains taxes were adjusted and excluded with various laws until the present day. These treatments became very complex as economic models used taxes as incentives for government economic intervention. These economic uses of taxes to control behavior and the economy were popular with followers of economist John Maynard Keynes. The 1930s brought more taxation by the federal government, including a progressive tax on business profits.

Major changes came during World War II when the income tax expanded to the middle class. Franklin Roosevelt also increased the top marginal rate to 91 percent. The system was still very disorganized and full of tax fraud. Roosevelt increased enforcement as a means to increase revenue. The Revenue Act of 1942 was until that time considered the most expansive in our history. Congress also enacted payroll withholding with the Current Tax Payment Act of 1943. Congress also increased the base and rates with a "surtax." Rates ranged from 13 percent on the first $2,000 of income to 81 percent on $200,000, up to a maximum of 91 percent. The withholding tax, while extremely unpopular, greatly increased revenue. It was sold as a patriotic sacrifice during World War II. The number of taxpayers went from 3.9 million in 1939 to 42.6 million in 1945, so that 60 percent of households paid an income tax. For the same period collections went from $3.2 billion to $35.1 billion. Politicians wisely called this broad expansion of taxations and rates a "defense tax." Corporate taxes were also increased to 50 percent.

Taxes have become a political issue, with the tax code used to affect the economy and control consumer behavior. The 1940s saw the expansion of a tax code of exemptions, deductions, and credits, making the collection and maintenance of the system complex. With this complexity came business opportunities such as H&R Block to help taxpayers. Today, the income tax (Internal Revenue Service) falls under the Department of the Treasury. It represents one of the government's largest bureaucracies. Today, because of the huge government expenditures involved in maintaining, managing, and enforcing the income tax, some politicians are arguing for a flat tax on sales. This had actually been considered during the debate over the Revenue Act of 1942.

*See also:* McKinley Tariff of 1890; Social Security Act; Tariff of Abominations; *Wealth of Nations*; Whig Party Evolves; Whiskey Rebellion

### References

Brownlee, Elliot. *Federal Taxation in America: A Short History.* Cambridge: Cambridge University Press, 2004.

Joseph, Richard. *Origin of the American Income Tax: The Revenue Act of 1894.* Syracuse, NY: Syracuse University Press, 2004.

# Federal Reserve Act (1913)

The financial panics of America had always been made worse by the lack of a central bank. A panic moved quickly as runs on banks created calls on loans, which in turn created more runs. In America's early history, it did have a national bank from 1791 to 1836 (the First and Second Bank of the United States), but this mainly addressed loans for business expansion. In the Panic of 1837, the lack of a central bank once again allowed a panic to deepen. A weak alliance of banks was formed by the Banking Act of 1863, but it proved insignificant in the panics of 1873, 1893, and 1907. For the most part, money was spread around the country and immobile, being inelastic and inflexible. The very severe Panic of 1907 was particularly disturbing, requiring the federal government to trade favors for J. P. Morgan to pool major banks to act together. The immediate effect of the Panic of 1907 was the formation of the 1908 Monetary Commission. The investigation of the Panic of 1907 highlighted some of the main problems. Hearings continued in

1912 with the "Pugo" hearings of the House Banking and Currency Committee. These hearings finally led to a public outcry for reform, especially because of the revelations by former president Theodore Roosevelt of the dealings with bankers. Congressional Republicans tried to pass a private solution to the problem, but it failed in 1912. The full Monetary Commission gave its report to Congress in 1913, which was now controlled by progressive Democrats wanting full government control.

There was a general consensus that some form of central bank was needed to prevent panics. The nature of that central bank became the issue of a heated political battle between regions, political parties, bankers, and politicians. The progressive Democratic Party, under the leadership of their newly elected president Woodrow Wilson, led the charge for a central bank. The Democrats now controlled the presidency and both houses of Congress. This alone created fear among the Republicans of a takeover of the private banking sector. Still, the debate resulted in a uniquely American solution with checks and balances. The result was a hybrid of private and government banking. The 1913 act was to address control of the currency and banking mobility to slow panics. The bill established that President Wilson would appoint a Federal Reserve Board of five bankers (today seven members) to be known as the Board of Governors, which would then be independent of government control (similar to the Supreme Court justices). The Senate would approve these members. In addition, the bill called for an Organization Committee to be appointed by the secretary of the Treasury, the secretary of agriculture, and the comptroller of the currency. This temporary Organization Committee was to form district lines and name the cities for 12 Reserve Banks. The selection of the cities took almost two years as regional politics played out. Eventually the 12 were selected and approved by Congress in 1914; the Reserve Banks were located in Boston, New York, Philadelphia, Cleveland, Richmond, Atlanta, Chicago, St. Louis, Minneapolis, Kansas City, Dallas, and San Francisco (they remain the same today). Member banks would then subscribe to stock in their regional bank. Not surprisingly, progressive President Wilson's nominations were faced with tough nomination hearings in the Senate.

Another important function of the Federal Reserve was the Federal Open Market Committee, which today functions as the principal tool for monetary control, such as interest rates. The original act of 1913 gave the Open Market Committee the power to control monetary policy; it was varied over the years. Today it has evolved to control of the federal funds rate, the discount rate, and the sale of Treasury bills. The Federal Open Market Committee consists of the seven members of the Board of Governors and five of the presidents of the regional Federal Reserve banks. The role of the Federal Reserve has evolved as recessions exposed shortcomings. The Federal Reserve Act of 1913 failed to fully stop panics and bank runs in the 1930s. This weakness forced the government to address psychological

First Federal Reserve Board of Governors, 1914. (Library of Congress)

issues in panics such as fear and herd mentality. Bank runs in the 1930s were so severe that they overwhelmed the Federal Reserve system. To address public confidence, Congress passed the Glass-Steagall Act of 1933, establishing the Federal Deposit Insurance Corporation to insure savings accounts. This assured savings and smooth transfer in the case of bank failures. The Depression of the 1930s further exposed weaknesses in the Federal Reserve, and Congress expanded the role of the Federal Open Market Committee in the Banking Act of 1935.

The Federal Reserve system controls the monetary policy by targeting the federal funds rate. The federal funds rate is the rate that banks charge each other for overnight loans of federal funds from the reserve system. The rate is actually controlled by the purchase and sale of Treasury bills. The Federal Reserve also controls the discount rate, the rate that the Federal Reserve charges directly for overnight loans. Both the discount rate and the federal funds rate influence the prime rate, which is roughly 3 percent higher. The prime rate in return is the basis for mortgage rates, credit card rates, and commercial loan rates. The Federal Reserve also sets the reserve requirements for member banks, which can help control the ease of credit and the money supply.

The role of the Federal Reserve has continued from 1913 as weaknesses appear and new problems and issues have arisen. Recessions, bubbles, and inflationary periods have motivated further improvements. Key acts have included the Bank Holding Company Act of 1956, the Federal Reserve Reform Act of 1977, and the Monetary Control Act of 1980. More recently, the powers of the Federal Reserve were increased through the Emergency Economic Stabilization Act of 2008. Part of the changes brought on by the 2008 crisis was the payment of interest on depositor bank reserves, which allows for better credit control in the banking system. Recently, the Federal Reserve has added "quantitative policy" to its tools. Quantitative easing is when the Federal Reserve buys back government debt with newly printed money. The debate over political, private, and government control continues, going back to 1913. Many argue that its independence gives the Federal Reserve the power to control interest rates and the economic cycle without the consent of elected representatives. Other critics worry about the Federal Reserve's ability to increase the money supply, leading to 1970s-type inflation.

*See also:* Banking Crisis and Great Recession; Panic of 1837; Panic of 1857; Panic of 1893; Panic of 1907; "Report on Manufacturing"; Stock Market Crash/Great Depression; Wage and Price Controls; Whig Party Evolves

### References

Link, Arthur S. *Woodrow Wilson and the Progressive Era.* New York: Harper Books, 1954.

Meltzer, Allan. *A History of the Federal Reserve.* Vol. 1, *1913–1951.* Chicago: University of Chicago Press, 2004.

Wells, Donald R. *Federal Reserve System: A History.* Jefferson, NC: McFarland, 2004.

# Commercial Flight (1914)

Little noted at the time, the December 17, 1903, flight of the Wright Brothers created little excitement and cannot be classified as a commercial event. This, however, is not unusual, as suggested by the development of earlier technology. Investors require commercial demonstrations. The distance of 852 feet in 59 seconds failed to interest investors or businessmen. The Wright Brothers' motorized glider inspired few investors. There had already been and would continue to be a long line of "first" flights until the Smithsonian Institute declared the Wright Brothers the first after almost 10 years. Still, other than government grants, these early aviation pioneers found little venture capital for their work. Things were a bit different in Europe, where the hydrogen dirigibles of the Zeppelin Corporation had caught the imagination of businessmen as early as 1906. Zeppelin dirigibles were being used by a number of entrepreneurs to carry paying customers as well as the mail. While even Zeppelin Corporation was highly subsidized by the German government, success did bring in private venture capital. Government interest in possible military uses went back to the balloon corps of the Civil War, but there was little commercial interest in the early years. For most of the 10 years after the Wright Brothers' flight, technology improved through sporting contests around the world. Still, commercial applications were slow and investors even slower.

Commercial applications were coming from the bottom up, with wealthy people wanting to get places faster. The breakthrough commercial events came in little-noticed steps. A group of entrepreneurs formed the dirigible company Deutsche Luftschiffahrt Aktien Gesellschaft (DELAG) and started carrying rich passengers around Germany in 1909. This company carried 35,000 passengers between 1909 and 1914, recording a profit. Still, most airplanes of this early period had only two seats and had to take off and land in water. The approaching war in Europe brought interest in aviation in the government and military. Aircraft development was moving much faster in Europe, which was on the verge of war. In 1911, the Italians were using airplanes for carrying orders, reconnaissance, and bombing during the Italian-Turkish War. The U.S. government was observing. The U.S. government did, however, play an important role. In 1911, the Post Office Department staged several experiments of moving mail via aircraft. The experiments proved very successful, but an appropriation bill for $50,000 to develop airmail service was turned down in Congress in 1912.

A hobby pilot, Tony Jannus, got the idea he could make a dollar by shuffling rich passengers from St. Petersburg, Florida, across Tampa Bay to Tampa (a 21-mile trip) in 1914. In January 1914, Jannus started the service with great success. It was only a two-person (pilot and passenger) bi-wing plane known as a flying boat. This simple flying service carried over 1,000 in its first few months of operation, making a profit. Pilots like Jannus were hard to find before World War I because of the mechanical skill set and training needed. The success inspired more business capitalists and politicians. The international scientific magazines were now covering every event, inspiring inventors and daredevils. These events once again demonstrated potential, but the state of the technology was still questionable. Jannus's plane flew at 15 feet in good weather, and breakdowns were common. The flying boat concept did allow a margin of safety. The limited success inspired a similar water route between Oakland and San Francisco. The Russians were inspired and ran an experimental passenger flight later in 1914 that carried 16 passengers and traveled over 100 miles. The coming Russian Revolution would prevent further commercial development. In 1919, another group of Florida entrepreneurs started Chalk's International Airlines with scheduled flights between Miami and the Bahamas. But the real impetus from these first commercial flights was the possibility of faster mail.

In the United States, the development of the airplane was being slowed by endless litigation and patent wars. It took the war to break the technological logjam. Another problem was the lack of pilots, such as Jannus, due to the lack of commercial incentive. As for the National Road of 1811, the Overland Road of 1850, and Federal Express in the 1970s, a better commercial business plan developed around the U.S. mail. The military and Congress continued to believe in the commercial use of aircraft, thanks to commercial pioneers such as Jannus. In 1916, Congress made funds available from an appropriation for steamboat service. The government asked for bids for airmail service in Alaska and Massachusetts but received no bids for the proposed service. World War I brought heightened military interest.

The first routine airmail service came on May 15, 1918, with the cooperation of the War Department. The War Department supplied the planes and badly needed pilots. This route was established between New York City and Washington, D.C., with a stop in Philadelphia to change planes. This 218-mile trip was made once daily with a return trip. President Woodrow Wilson attended the inaugural service, giving a new priority for development. This was a clear example of the visions of Alexander Hamilton and Henry Clay that government has a role to play in economic development. The war created a surplus of trained pilots. In mid-1918, a number of air routes and train routes were combined to move mail faster. The plan was for a coordinated effort to develop links such as from New York to Chicago and from Chicago to St. Louis in what would become a transcontinental service. Full service from New York to San Francisco was completed in 1920. Government contracts for these mail routes evolved into passenger airline companies such Pan Am, Delta Air, Northwest, and others. Finally, in 1925, Ford Motor purchased Stout Aircraft Company to start production of the all-metal Ford Trimotor. The Trimotors could carry 12 passengers, making passenger routes profitable.

*See also:* Clipper Ships; Erie Canal; National Road; Transcontinental Railroad Completed

## References

Davies, R. E. *A History of the World's Airlines.* Oxford: Oxford University Press, 1964.

Solberg, Carl. *Conquest of the Skies: A History of Commercial Aviation in America.* Boston: Little, Brown, 1979.

Tobin, James. *To Conquer the Air: The Wright Brothers and the Great Race for Flight.* New York: Free Press, 2003.

# Panama Canal Opens (1914)

The importance of the Panama Canal was demonstrated by its premature opening in 1914 to support the movement of materials for World War I. Speed at moving goods, people, and the mail across the nation was central to economic growth. World trade depended on a shortcut through the South American isthmus versus the long trip around the horn. In the 1840s, thousands of prospectors took a 50-mile road trip between the Atlantic and Pacific Oceans to save weeks in going around the horn. This isthmus road cut 7,800 miles out of the trip. In the 1850s, the Panama Railway was completed and carried the heaviest volume of freight per unit length of any railroad in the world. The Panama Railway would actually be the foundation in the building of the canal. However, unloading and loading cargo from ship to railroad and then back to ship was expensive and time-consuming. A canal could save much cost and time. The dream of a South American canal had been an old one, with Spain and Scotland considering the possibility in the 1700s.

It would be France that would first see the real engineering and financial possibility of such a canal. The French had completed the Suez Canal in 1869 and were enjoying many economic benefits. In 1881, the French began a sea-level canal across Colombia. The idea that they could build a sea-level canal would doom the project. The area's mountains, rivers, and jungles made it impossible. The task consumed its builders, and eventually malaria and yellow fever overwhelmed them. By 1889, over 16,000 workers had died. With almost $300 million spent, the French company went bankrupt in 1889 with about only two-fifths of the canal complete. In 1901, U.S. President Theodore Roosevelt organized a study commission. The commission recommended taking over the French canal by applying a lock system in place of a sea-level canal. It wasn't until 1905 that Congress approved the American project. Congress approved $40 million to buy French assets and another $10 million to pay Panama for rights. American work began in 1905.

The lock system of the American design would solve the technical problems, and Americans had experience in building lock canals going back to the Erie Canal. It was to be an excavation on an epic scale, moving over 232 million cubic yards of earth (20 times the volume of the Channel Tunnel project). Every day the supporting railroad moved over 600 trains of dirt and supplies. A train consisted of an average of 20 cars. In the busiest month of March 1912, some 65,555 railroad cars of earth were removed. The canal would take over nine years to complete. Still, the bigger problem would be that of malaria and yellow fever. The project would ultimately require over 100,000 workers to be recruited from all over the world. A worker panic over an outbreak of yellow fever almost ended the project in 1905.

Much of the credit for success would go to Chief Engineer George Goethals, appointed by Roosevelt. Goethals exhibited outstanding skills as both an engineer

Opening of the Panama Canal, August 15, 1914. (Library of Congress)

and a manager in this difficult project. Workers came from all over the world and were paid about 5 percent above American home wages. The commission supplied free housing and maid and medical services. In addition to their base pay, the workers got 9 paid holidays, a 42-day vacation, and 30 days of sick leave. Three meals a day cost $0.30. The average pay for workers was $150 a month. Teachers got $60 per month, locomotive operators got $180 a month, and steam-shovel operators got $310 a month. The lowest-paid unskilled laborer got $30 a month working 10-hour days. Most of the unskilled laborers were from the West Indies. Workers were paid in gold and silver coins. The commission spent $2.5 million per year on recreation, which included dances, sports, movies, concerts, clubs, and special activities. The commission applied the best of American labor practices such as employee meetings and newsletters. The YMCA was brought in to manage recreational activities. The safety regulations for canal construction exceeded those of American factories.

The other key man in the project was Chief Medical Officer William Gorgas. Gorgas managed a staff of 4,000 sanitation workers. Gorgas addressed yellow fever and malaria at their source—the mosquito. He burnt and sprayed many square miles of jungle. Garbage and waste handling was improved and drainage ditches controlled. Certain types of mosquito larva–eating fish were imported. The more deadly yellow fever was all but eliminated and malaria greatly reduced. Quinine was given to workers daily to prevent their blood from harboring the malaria parasite. Death from all sources for the nine years was 5,700 compared to 20,000 during the French operation.

The canal project would be largest construction project in U.S. history up until that time. It remains today the greatest amount of material excavated for a project. Americans fought through a number of major setbacks including the breaking of dams, landslides, and accidental explosions. The French paper twice predicted these setbacks would doom the American project. The commission overcame all problems and setbacks. In fact, America's greatest accomplishment proved its ability to manage endless crisis and not give in. New designs of locks, concrete production, and concrete pouring evolved. To emphasize their achievement against all odds, President Roosevelt had employee medals minted from copper, bronze, and tin scraps salvaged from old French equipment.

The final cost was over $375 million, but amazingly it was below the original budget by $12 million. The commission formed the break-even Panama Canal Company to manage the canal. Law set the toll at $0.90 per ton of cargo. It was not until 1973, when the canal lost money, that the toll was increased to $1.08 a ton. The highest toll paid to date was $313,200 by Disney's Magic liner in 2008. Transit time takes from 10 to 20 hours. President Jimmy Carter signed the canal over to Panama in 1977, and full control by Panama was achieved in 2000. Over 300 million tons of cargo pass through the canal each year.

*See also:* Clipper Ships; Erie Canal; National Road; Transcontinental Railroad Completed

### References

Greene, Julie. *Canal Builders: Making America's Empire at the Panama Canal.* New York: Penguin, 2009.

McCullough, David. *The Path between Seas: The Creation of the Panama Canal, 1870–1914.* New York: Simon & Schuster, 1977.

# General Motors Corporation Formed (1916)

General Motors Corporation offers a study in corporate management and development for today and the future. In addition, the early General Motors Corporation would define the modern marketing approach of the American automotive industry. On October 13, 1916, General Motors was incorporated under the leadership and management of William C. Durant and Pierre S. DuPont. The actual birth can be traced back to a holding company for Buick in 1908. Durant had started his career as a Ford dealer and the owner of Durant-Dort Carriage Company in Flint, Michigan. It would be Durant who formed General Motors Company in 1908. Durant had three profitable manufacturing units in Buick, Cadillac, and Oakland. Durant brought in Oldsmobile and Reliant Motor before losing control to a bankers' trust by overextending his debt. Durant left to form Chevrolet Motor Company with Louis Chevrolet. In 1916, Durant, with the financial backing of DuPont, president of DuPont Company, and Louis Kaufman of Chatham and Phenix Bank, took back General Motors. In 1916, General Motors sold 124,834 cars compared to 735,000 for Ford Motor. Durant controlled not only General Motors but also Chevrolet and United Motors. Durant's dream was to make General Motors (or one of his companies) the major competitor to Ford Motor.

With its incorporation in 1916, General Motors formed divisions, with its corporate headquarters in Flint, Michigan. After the incorporation of General Motors, Durant brought two key managers into his organizations. Walter Chrysler became president of Buick. Alfred Sloan became president of United Motors, which Durant brought into General Motors in 1918. Durant brought all his manufacturing assets together in 1918, forming the divisions of Chevrolet, Buick, Oldsmobile, Cadillac, and Oakland (Pontiac). The modern divisions of General Motors were now in place. Lacking any management model to manage a large corporation, Durant let the divisions function as separate companies with him as the king and autocrat. In 1918, General Motors purchased several companies in Canada to form General Motors of Canada. Durant also purchased several tractor companies, creating a tractor division following the success of Henry Ford in tractors. Durant continued to look for opportunities in all areas of manufacturing. In 1919, Durant bought out Guardian Frigerator, which would become Frigidaire Division of General Motors. Durant had actually purchased Guardian with his own funds prior to selling it to General Motors. Durant was clearly the genius in the formation of General Motors, but he lacked the administrative and managerial skills to lead this huge and diverse corporation. General Motors' board and DuPont were becoming concerned about Durant overextending the corporation again. The organization was unwieldy and uncoordinated, as the organizational structure was a piecework resulting from the various mergers.

General Motors struggled with the recession following World War I; it had operating and cost problems. In 1920, Durant was forced out by the DuPont family, which now had the majority ownership. This would begin the next phase of General Motors and its contributions to American business. DuPont had been highly successful in applying operational and operating procedures at DuPont Powder Company. DuPont was committed to the use of scientific management and the principles of Frederick Taylor. DuPont had also developed a corporate management structure of line and staff functions and methods of decentralizing authority. He applied aggressive cost accounting methods from Andrew Carnegie's organizations. He used the performance system of scientific management throughout the corporation. DuPont applied his pioneering approaches in psychological tests for personnel selection and return-on-investment performance measures for departments.

In 1920, DuPont promoted a key man as his assistant, Alfred Sloan Jr., to groom him for the presidency in 1923. Sloan was a graduate of Massachusetts Institute of Technology and had built a $100-million ball-bearing company, which Durant had brought into General Motors. Sloan would first apply scientific management corporate-wide, defining scientific management as "a constant search for facts, the true actualities, their intelligent, unprejudiced analysis." Sloan invested heavily in the development of cost accounting throughout the corporation. However, General Motors' product diversity prevented it from the type of cost savings that Ford found by staying with one model. General Motors' cheapest car was $795 in 1923 compared to $370 for a Ford Model T. To overcome this cost disadvantage, Sloan applied marketing as a management science. In marketing, Sloan used surveys to obtain facts about customers. He introduced an array of colors to compete with Ford's standard black based on one of these surveys of customer wants.

Sloan would address the lack of structure and coordination. He would become known as the 20th century's most original CEO and organizational thinker. Sloan set up an organizational structure he called "federal decentralization." This structure would become the model for all future large corporations. He instituted strategic planning throughout the divisions. Divisions were even given a great deal of operational latitude. Financial control was centralized, and division performance was monitored based on return on investment.

Sloan was just as creative in product development. He introduced the annual model change and allowed division models to compete with each other. This strategy effectively ended the era of Ford's Model T and made the annual model change an industry standard to this day. His overall market strategy was a model for every purse and purpose. This strategy would unseat Ford with his cost and price advantage; it is known today as mass customization. Sloan expanded the idea of corporate financing to help customers buy cars via the General Motors Acceptance Corporation (GMAC), which allowed for easy installment payments. Sloan developed a new concept of a design department, bringing in future corvette and LaSalle designer Harvey Earl to head it. He did the first major survey of customer preferences and used the results to develop new models. By 1927, General Motors had overtaken Ford Motor Company. While Sloan and Durant's organizational structure is still a model for corporations, it has been criticized today for its rigidity. Still, the strategy of mass customization is a major part of the industrial-consumer business model.

*See also:* First Billion-Dollar Corporation—United States Steel; First Japanese Auto Sold in the United States; Highland Park Ford Assembly Line; Scientific Management

### References

Gustin, Lawrence R. *Billy Durant: Creator of General Motors.* Ann Arbor: University of Michigan Press, 1973.

Sloan, Alfred. *My Years at General Motors.* New York: Crown Business, 1990.

# Great Steel Strike of 1919

America's greatest industry had been marred by labor problems for decades, such as conflicts over the 12-hour day, seven-day week, and low pay. Labor and management had failed to make any progress. During World War I, President Woodrow Wilson's progressive view led him to create a special agency in 1918 for handling labor disputes in the war industries. This agency was known as the National War Labor Board (NWLB). The NWLB had limited authority, requiring the president to force compliance. The top priority was to prevent production disruption caused by strikes and lockouts. However, the NWLB stated their principles as the right of labor to organize, no action by the companies against organizing efforts, the right of union shops to exist, the right of the worker to a "living wage," and the use of regional "prevailing wages." The Wilson administration often used these broad principles to award contracts to companies. Even more disturbing for the steel companies was the government's propensity to support union activity and collective bargaining as a contract requirement.

The American Federation of Labor saw the NWLB as an opportunity to expand organizing in the steel industry. Samuel Gompers, who headed the American Federation of Labor, had the strong support of President Wilson. The NWLB was able to get nonunion contractors to form shop representation committees. Contracts started to require some type of collective bargaining. The government was going to impose collective bargaining and the union on companies. All the companies were doing was delaying government action; they badly needed an industry solution to government-imposed solutions. These companies now looked to the progressive Midvale Steel to design an alternative that the government might accept. The issue would accelerate at Midvale in April 1918 with a challenge from the International Association of Machinists (IAM). The IAM had started an organizing drive at Midvale. Midvale was critical to war production, and the government, through the NWLB, would certainly force collective bargaining. Midvale produced the naval guns and shells needed by the Allies. Bethlehem was also having problems with the

IAM. Midvale and Bethlehem were coordinating their approaches. *Iron Age,* the steel industry magazine, warned that the NWLB intent "will encourage union leaders to seize upon the national war emergency to organize every plant heretofore maintained as a non-union or open-shop."

In August 1918, the Midvale case came before the NWLB for review. The demands were collective bargaining, the eight-hour day, elimination of the present piece rate system, and elimination of the beneficial insurance program, which was forced on the employees by the company. These, of course, were industry-wide issues. The NWLB made recommendations for an employee representation plan, but Midvale Steel delayed any immediate action. United States Steel saw the threat of government intervention and called an industry meeting of steel executives at New York's Waldorf-Astoria. An industry plan was designed so the 8-hour day would be the base day, allowing workers to work 12 hours but at a time-and-a-half rate over 8 hours. The arrangement was popular with the average immigrant worker, who realized a pay increase. National reformers such as Gompers on the union side and Midvale Steel from the management side did not like the solution. Social reformers, priests, ministers, and community leaders saw the approach as a reinforcement of the 12-hour day. It had the effect of slowing real reform from the union or management reformers. Still, the issue of collective bargaining remained the real issue with the government.

Midvale was still under government pressure to settle the issues of collective bargaining at their Nicetown plant. The Midvale board approved a company plan for collective bargaining by Midvale Steel. The board believed there was no choice but to implement their own plan or have the government impose one. Midvale Steel had been studying the employee representation plan of Colorado Fuel and Iron after the labor problems there in 1916. The Colorado Fuel and Iron's "employee representation plan" or "Rockefeller plan" was considered a favorable model by the Wilson administration. Initially (but briefly), the United Mine Workers even accepted the Colorado plan, which had originated from the violent strike at John D. Rockefeller's Colorado Fuel and Iron mines in 1905. Critics called it

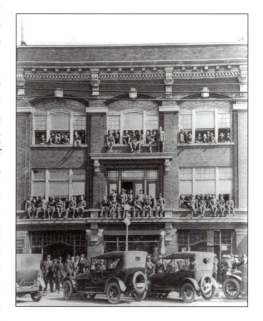

Troops in Gary, Indiana, during the 1919 Great Steel Strike. (Calument Regional Archives, Indiana University N.W.)

a "company union," and unions saw it as union busting. But in any case, it was accept-able to NWLB and Wilson administration.

In the fall of 1918, Midvale Steel and Bethlehem Steel simultaneously adopted the Midvale Steel employee representation plan. United States Steel did not follow. The Midvale Steel plan called for employee representation committees to bargain collectively while maintaining the right of the company to set overall policy. In par-ticular, hiring and layoffs for economic reasons were the right of the company. The employee representatives on the plant committee would be elected on the basis of 1 per 300 employees. It was hoped that such plans would prevent unionization.

The end of the war brought new twists on the troubled labor front. The political victories of the Republicans, the end of the war, and President Wilson's priority of a League of Nations ended the NWLB and its meddling. However, the end of the war brought an even more aggressive union organizing effort. There was a loose al-liance of the American Federation of Labor and the Amalgamated Association of Iron, Steel, and Tin Workers that created the National Committee to Organize the Iron and Steel Workers. The American Federation of Labor, headed by Gompers, was very successful in organizing immigrant steelworkers in Chicago, Youngstown, Buffalo, Cleveland, and Wheeling. Wages for immigrant steelworkers were $1,466 a year, while subsistence level for a family of five was $1,575 in 1919.

In June 1919, hundreds of the Midvale's 2,000-plus workforce walked out. The Labor Department, the navy, and the NWLB descended on the plant. The navy got things going again, but the issue was now to be settled by the NWLB. Midvale Steel was asked to speed up work on an alternative plan. Midvale Steel, however, was more interested in an industry-wide solution. United States Steel was actually pre-paring for all-out war with the union. The old tricks of using company spies, local political pressure, and harassing union leaders were renewed. Judge Elbert Gary, chairman of United States Steel, would have nothing to do with collective bargain-ing, wage increases, or the elimination of the 12-hour day. An American Federation of Labor conference in Pittsburgh had discussed and approved a fall strike. The con-ference resolution called for collective bargaining, the eight-hour day, double-time pay for overtime, one day's rest in seven, abolition of the 20-hour-long shift used to rotate the men, seniority-based wages, and the abolition of company unions.

After Labor Day in 1919, the trouble started in Pittsburgh. Union organizers could not rent meeting rooms, and local police and private guards seized literature and ran others out of town. The economic downturn gave the companies the upper hand, and the unrest soon spread to the Chicago district. The union appealed to Wilson and was counting on his support. Judge Gary of United States Steel refused to deal with the union. Charles Schwab at Bethlehem and William Corey at Mid-vale were counting on their employee representation plans to protect them. On September 22, when Gary refused to negotiate further, a national walkout started. President Wilson would have a stroke on September 26, 1919, which many believe prevented government intervention. With him incapacitated, Wilson's advisors held back. But Wilson had been rejected in the midterm elections, and public support was not with him. Furthermore, Wilson was looking for steel money and support for his League of Nations.

The strike initially hit United States Steel hard, with the majority of workers out in Pittsburgh, Chicago, Cleveland, Lackawanna, and Youngstown. Bethlehem Steel continued to work with their employee representation plans in place. These employee representation plans were company unions meant to slow the organizing efforts of the unions. The steelworkers' resolve was strong, but the public opinion remained mixed. Estimates on September 30 suggested as many as 360,000 steelworkers were on strike. The owners and local politicians formed large armies of deputy sheriffs to prevent violence. The owners used the postwar Red Scare of the Russian Revolution of 1917. Newspapers openly worried about the influence of communists in the union. Still, the steelworkers held together. The union pulled public sympathy with the push for an eight-hour day. The strike was fought in the trenches. Local violence, beatings, and raids were commonplace. Hundreds of strikers were jailed on local fronts. The Pennsylvania state police proved particularly brutal on picketers.

The companies moved to strikebreaking, using between 30,000 and 40,000 black and Mexican American laborers. Strikebreaking at United States Steel's Gary, Indiana, plant turned violent on October 6. The governor declared martial law and brought in the National Guard. The violence spread to United States Steel's nearby Indiana Harbor. The Guard completely suppressed the strikers; it ended in Indiana but dragged on around the nation. In Pennsylvania and Ohio, the violence had a racial element against black strikebreakers and their families. By 1920, the strike was over. Most considered it a complete victory by Gary and the owners. Not a single concession was given, 20 died, and over $112 million was lost in wages. However, within two years, with pressure from President Warren Harding, Gary and United States Steel were finally forced to accept the eight-hour day and six-day week. Many believe it created a racist element within the steel industry and unions for years to come. The unionization of the steelworkers would not occur until 1937.

*See also:* Great Railroad Strike of 1877; Haymarket Riot; Homestead Strike of 1892; National Labor Relations Act (Wagner Act); Pullman Strike; Steel Strike of 1959

## References

Eggert, Gerald. *Steelmasters and Labor Reform, 1886–1923.* Pittsburgh, PA: University of Pittsburgh Press, 1981.

Foster, William Z. *The Great Steel Strike and Its Lessons.* Charleston, SC: BiblioBazaar, 2009.

Warren, Kenneth. *Big Steel: The First Century of United States Steel Corporation 1901–2001.* Pittsburgh, PA: University of Pittsburgh Press, 2001.

# First Commercial Radio (1921)

The technological history of the invention of the radio remains hotly debated to this day, but the commercial history has a bit more clarity. Most point to the broadcast of the heavyweight boxing championship between Jack Dempsey and Georges Carpentier on July 2, 1921, as the beginning of commercial radio. The beginning of radio was really a confluence of ideas as seen in earlier inventions. Government would also play a role in the development of radio as it had with the telegraph and telephone. Nikola Tesla made most of the technical breakthroughs in the late 1890s, followed by the work and visions of Guglielmo Marconi to make radio practical. The Supreme Court would actually declare Tesla the inventor, years after both men died. Marconi was clearly the first to make money from the technology, building a company to implement shore-to-ship radio communication in 1898. Marconi monopolized the necessary equipment and technology. The U.S. Navy quickly realized the potential of radio and started to equip the entire fleet in 1905. There was a real boom in ship-to-ship radio communications after the sinking of the *Titanic* in 1912. Also in 1912, the U.S. government started to invest in radio research. In this case, it was the Department of Agriculture looking to broadcast weather reports for farmers. While government had a positive impact, it also had a negative impact with the passage of the Radio Act of 1912, which outlawed private radio broadcast companies until 1920. The idea was that the government needed to limit use of the broadcasting frequencies to defense and public safety issues.

As radio's potential in military and shipping applications had been proven, the American government wanted to break Marconi's international monopoly. In 1919, Marconi's American assets were sold to General Electric. Westinghouse Electric had also entered the radio field before World War I. Westinghouse had made major advances in transmission during the war with the invention of the vacuum tube and the pooling of patents for defense reasons. By 1920, the technology of long-distance commercial radio broadcasting was in place, but a business model of how to make money was still missing. Westinghouse was issued the first commercial radio license by the government in November 1920, for the station KDKA. Westinghouse broadcast the results of Harding-Cox presidential election for free but took out newspaper ads to sell radios to hear the broadcast. General Electric quickly entered the broadcasting area by forming the Radio Corporation of America (RCA).

Another business or moneymaking model emerged with the broadcast of the 1921 Dempsey fight. The fight was the first broadcast of the production company of RCA. The fight took place in Hoboken, New Jersey, and was broadcast locally on WJY, a temporary station set up for the broadcast. In addition, the fight commentary was telegraphed to KDKA in Pittsburgh, and then KDKA broadcast the commentary. KDKA had just become the first commercially licensed broadcasting station in October 1920. Westinghouse Electric, a radio receiver producer, had started and financed KDKA. Still, there were few radio receivers, and charities, organizations, and churches set up halls and charged admission. For a few years, General Electric with their broadcasting company and Westinghouse Electric with its Westinghouse broadcasting expanded radio stations with the intent to sell radios. In early 1922, American Telephone and Telegraph (AT&T) entered the broadcasting market. AT&T not only improved broadcasting technology but also created the idea of leasing its airtime in a business model called "toll broadcasting."

Westinghouse Electric still believed the real money to be in selling radios and started to expand stations and broadcasting content. Westinghouse used unpaid amateurs to read serial books and stories. Community events used the radio as well. Storybooks such as *Tom Swift and the Wireless Message* created a huge audience of children. Radio sales boomed in 1922 as even President Warren Harding and Queen Victoria became listeners. The number of stations went from 67 at the start of 1922 to over 500 by the end of the year. AT&T expanded the audience by developing radio broadcast networks. AT&T could now connect its national telephone line system to move broadcasts around the nation. Westinghouse and RCA expanded into networks as well. However, AT&T controlled the telephone lines, putting the others at a disadvantage and forcing them to research new techniques for long-distance wireless transmission, using such things as short-wave radios. In addition, costs were increasing, with government licensing costs and wire transmission. AT&T continued to expand their revenue model of toll broadcasting to selling commercial time at a dollar per minute.

The late 1920s saw over 50 percent of households having radios. In 1930, over a million and a half cars were equipped with radios. The size of the market brought in advertising revenues but also new problems. The problem of competing bandwidths and frequencies created a need for government intervention. The Radio Act of 1927 ended the overlapping frequencies and drowning out of smaller stations. The act declared radio waves to be public property, which would impact telecommunications to the present. Interestingly, government regulation of radio waves would inhibit the development of cell phones in this country because they use radio waves. By the 1930s, radio broadcasting was a much bigger business than making radios. Patent battles between manufacturers had driven costs to unprofitability. The radio companies such as Westinghouse, General Electric, RCA, and AT&T set up a "patent allies group," which decided all radios would be manufactured under the RCA label with a 60–40 split between them; RCA received 60 percent and all other parties received 40 percent. AT&T would manufacture radio transmitters. This monopoly failed, as they could not effectively control all manufacturing patents. Broadcasting proved even more competitive, with new alliances and companies. By the 1940s, broadcasting content became a major factor in revenues, as entertainment shows took over the airways. The business model for radio today remains the same with some variations.

*See also:* First Commercial Telephone; Patent and Copyright Statutes; Transatlantic Cable; Western Union Telegraph Company

### References

Douglas, George. *The Early Years of Radio Broadcasting.* Jefferson, NC: McFarland, 1987.

Douglas, Susan. *Inventing American Broadcasting, 1899–1922.* Baltimore, MD: Johns Hopkins University Press, 1987.

Jackway, Gwenyth L. *Media of War: Radio's Challenge to the Newspapers, 1924–1939.* Westport, CT: Praeger, 1995.

Smulyan, Susan. *Selling Radio: The Commercialization of American Broadcasting, 1920–1934.* Washington, DC: Smithsonian Institution Press, 1994.

# Hawthorne Studies Begin (1924)

The Hawthorne studies represent one of the greatest advances in the science of management. At the end of their 10-year quest, the studies would merge the principles of scientific management with the progressive social movement in industry. The behavioral school of management would evolve out of these studies. The studies started in 1924 to analyze several factors using the principles of scientific management. The first experiments were at the Hawthorne plant of Western Electric, which was the equipment-manufacturing arm of American Telephone and Telegraph (AT&T). Like many of America's companies, AT&T adopted the approach of scientific management. The initial experiment was to explore the modest effect of workplace illumination on worker productivity. The study was designed with a number of professors from the Electrical Engineering Department at Massachusetts Institute of Technology. Experiments used groups and control groups to study the effect of illumination on coil-winding operator productivity. A number of variables were studied over a three-year period. The conclusion was that the productivity of all groups with various intervening variables went up regardless of the level of illumination. The lead researcher was Homer Hibarger, who still believed there were other variables at play and developed another set of experiments in the relay-assembly test room. Professor Clair Turner from the Public Health Department at the Massachusetts Institute of Technology was brought in. Once again, these experimental groups showed across-the-board increases in productivity.

Turner attributed these productivity increases to (1) small group identity, (2) positive supervision, (3) increased earnings, (4) the novelty of the project, and

(5) the attention given to the workers. The importance of management attention came to be known as the "Hawthorne effect." The output of assemblers increased by an amazing 35 to 50 percent. Some old-school Taylorites argued that all could be explained by the increase in wages, which led to further studies. George Elton Mayo was brought in from Harvard to help analyze the results. Mayo started a detailed survey of the workers. The result would be a revolutionary new approach to management. He concluded that emotional factors were more important than physical factors in determining productivity and efficiency. Mayo's interviews further concluded that supervisors had a major impact on worker productivity. In particular, supervisors should be more people oriented and less aloof. Mayo argued that a human relations style of leader was needed. This conclusion would go against traditional scientific management thinking. The conclusion created some concern among the foremen at the Hawthorne plant, who believed that the surveys were designed to reflect negatively on them. Turner also believed that the results reflected group factors rather than supervision.

The complaints of the foremen led to a new experiment by Turner and Mayo. This study was to focus on additional factors that affect group productivity. Observers would also be kept in the background. The study looked at the relationships between the jobs, productivity measures, incentives, and groups of workers. Group management approaches showed that workers distorted production by various methods. The results showed that workers functioned according to an informal group organization. The researchers even identified two cliques of workers with informal standards of work behavior. It was the first time that managers recognized that nonlogical factors based on informal social systems could overwhelm scientific management approaches. It posed a new management problem where the formal organizational goals might not be aligned with the informal social system. It explained why it was so important to develop a deep-seated corporate culture. Hard-driving organizations might be successful, as seen in Andrew Carnegie's mills of the 20th century, if a culture of performance is accepted by the social worker system. On the other hand, factories without corporate cultures might fail to achieve their goals if the social worker system does not support them.

Mayo took the study and its conclusions further. He suggested a radical new approach based on human relations, psychoanalysis, a philosophical rationale, and the psychopathological analysis of industrial life. Mayo argued that managers believed the solutions to industrial problems were rooted in logical and rational behavior and could be found by scientific experiments, when the problems were actually of a social nature. He believed industrial operations had destroyed the ability to satisfy the social needs of the individual and, in turn, lowered morale and achievement. This conclusion was consistent with the emerging progressive view in American thinking. Mayo's conclusions would lead to a human relations–oriented program for training managers. Mayo favored a liberal arts background for managers over technical expertise. He also favored psychological testing for potential supervisors. The popularity of psychological testing of new managers grew in the 1940s and 1950s.

This new behavioral-school approach to management would develop in the thinking of Oliver Sheldon, Mary Parker Follett, Hugo Munsterberg, and Chester Barnard. While scientific management had given birth to the field of industrial engineering, the field of industrial psychology emerged out of Mayo's behavioral school. Organizational behavior and leadership courses were added to management curriculum at business schools. More recently, the behavioral school has led to the application of employee teams and groups in the workplace. Today, we see the evolution of the behavioral school in the area of employee participation in management.

*See also:* Andrew Carnegie's First Steel Mill; Maslow's Theory of Needs; Paternal Capitalism—Homestead and Wilmerding, Pennsylvania; Scientific Management

**References**

Mayo, Elton. *The Human Problems of an Industrial Civilization.* New York: Macmillan, 1933.
Turner, Clair. *I Remember.* New York: Vantage, 1974.
Wren, Daniel A. *The History of Management Thought.* New York: Wiley, 2005.

# Talking Movies— *The Jazz Singer* (1927)

The 1927 Warner Brothers movie *The Jazz Singer* became the first feature-length motion picture with synchronized dialogue sequences. This "talkie" would become the most profitable movie to date, but, more important, it augured the potential drawing power of talking movies. This new potential was transformed into a new industry business model. The innovative scheme was that of Warner Brothers' Sam Morris. The cost of talkie production required this new model. *The Jazz Singer* cost $422,000, a huge sum for the time. The lead actor, Al Jolson, got $75,000 for the eight weeks of filming. The approach was to have Warner Brothers take a percentage of the gate rather than the usual flat rental fee. The new model called for theaters to book in full weeks versus split weeks. In addition, a sliding scale was implemented, which favored holding the films for longer runs. It would be the marketing scheme that assured the profitability of *The Jazz Singer* and the eventual spread of talking movies. *The Jazz Singer* proved extremely profitable by charging from 25¢ to 50¢ for a ticket.

The history of the movie business is the foundation of today's entertainment business, representing the confluence of communications, culture, and entertainment. Its birth goes back to American inventors, Thomas Edison, and the company, Eastman Kodak. The process was patented in 1891 using Edison's camera, the Kinetograph, which took a series of instantaneous photographs on a new Eastman Kodak celluloid emulsion film. The film was played back using a Kinetoscope. Edison introduced the new movie process at the Chicago World's Fair of 1893. Edison was the first to go into movie production at his Orange, New Jersey, laboratory. A great marketer, Edison took these short films to be marketed in a movie parlor known as a "nickelodeon," which debuted in 1905 in Pittsburgh. Nickelodeons exploded, with 4,000 opening in two years. The moneymaking potential seemed unlimited.

Edison had a virtual monopoly on the film business until 1908. Still, patent challenges and litigation bottled up the whole industry. In 1908, the major companies, including Edison, joined in a combine known as the Motion Picture Patents Company (MPPC). Eastman Kodak agreed to supply film only to MPPC. Even so, a government antitrust suit was not needed as MPPC failed to monopolize the emerging market, especially as foreign companies entered the competition. The MPPC suffered from its own methodology, which required short feature films, lacked marketing, and ignored customer wants. It was an engineering-driven business model. Movies were limited by MPPC to a reel of film (about 1,000 feet), which lasted for about 30 minutes. This was yet another example, like early autos, of the engineering aspects, rather than the consumers, defining the market.

European film companies were demonstrating the market popularity of feature-length (greater than 30 minutes) historic epic films such as *The Fall of Troy* (1911) and *Quo Vadis?* (1912). The American independents formed together under the Universal Film Manufacturing Company to produce feature-length films in 1912. In 1914, a new film distribution company, Paramount Pictures, emerged to distribute independent films. Another company, Triangle Corporation, proved the market potential of feature-length films with *The Birth of a Nation* (1915), which was a two-and-a-half-hour film. This film also brought film production into the realm of creative art. The film, *The Birth of a Nation,* used the new filming techniques of D. W. Griffith, which increased the need for directors and producers. Directors such as Cecil B. DeMille emerged in 1915 with films like *The Cheat.*

World War I created a shortage of European silent movies, which led to the rise of Hollywood. Hollywood injected the science of marketing into film production. Prior to 1914, most movie production took place in New York because of Edison's dominance, but the year-round filming opportunities in Hollywood won out. Film production became more consumer oriented as former nickelodeon and theater owners such as Warner Brothers, Universal Studios, and Paramount entered the movie business. Studio production allowed for feature film production. The

Al Jolson in *The Jazz Singer,* 1927. (Library of Congress)

studios looked to new themes such as the comedies of Charlie Chaplin and Buster Keaton, the westerns of Tom Mix, and the adventures of Douglas Fairbanks. Output boomed, reaching over 800 feature films by the early 1920s, with Hollywood studios accounting for over 80 percent of the world production.

The big breakthrough augured by the success of *The Jazz Singer* was that of sound. The technological breakthrough came out of Western Electric's Bell Laboratories in New York. It was a "sound on disc" system called Vitaphone. The sound track was not on the film but on a separate 16-inch phonograph. Warner Brothers purchased the Vitaphone and used it on their feature film, *Don Juan,* to add music and sound effects but no dialogue. Prior to this, theaters often hired musicians to provide background music at the theater. While having restricted technical specifications, the Vitaphone did launch the talkie with the 1927 *Jazz Singer.* The talkie turned the financial fortunes of Warner Brothers around, making them competitive with the "Big Five" studios: First National, Paramount, MGM, Universal, and Producers Distributing. Like so many pioneers, the Vitaphone inspired new inventions because of the market success of talking films. Within a few years, better sound-on-film processes emerged such as the Fox Movietone and RCA Photophone system.

The use of sound caused major changes in the market. More complex mystery films evolved such as Alfred Hitchcock's *Blackmail* (1929). Of course, the classic Hollywood musicals appeared such as *The Broadway Melody* (1929) and *42nd Street* (1933). Wall Street took notice, with a major loan by Goldman Sachs to Warner Brothers. Warner Brothers pioneered the first all-color, all-talking movie, *On with the Show* (1929), which would become the industry standard. As the cost of producing rose, advertising increased to improve the gate take.

*See also:* Chicago World's Fair; First Commercial Radio; Patent and Copyright Statutes

### References

Carringer, Robert L. *The Jazz Singer*. Madison: University of Wisconsin Press, 1979.

Crafton, Donald. *The Talkies: American Cinema's Transition to Sound*. Berkeley: University of California Press, 1999.

Eyman, Scott. *The Speed of Sound: Hollywood and the Talkie Revolution, 1926–1930*. New York: Simon and Schuster, 1997.

Finler, Joel W. *The Hollywood Story*. New York: Crown, 1988.

# Stock Market Crash/ Great Depression (1929)

While the stock market crash of 1929 did not cause the Great Depression, it is the most-remembered harbinger of America's worst financial crisis. The depression that followed would be a decade of unemployment and hard times. Unemployment became a way of life for as much as 25 percent of the American workforce. The national gross product dropped 30 percent, and industrial production dropped by 40 percent. The nation's steel mills worked only two to three days per week for years. Corporate investment went negative with capital investment being below depreciation. The Depression also exhibited a "double dip," returning in 1937 after some improvement. From 1929 to 1941 unemployment was above 10 percent, and underemployment was as high as 50 percent. The estimated number of homeless in New York City alone was 15,000. The stock market dropped over 50 percent. The Depression changed the American psyche and economic thinking to this day. The Keynesian economic approach, named after John Maynard Keynes, which emphasized government spending and consumers, became the dominant approach. Tariff policy would be changed after centuries of tariff protection because of fear of trade wars. The Depression would also initiate a decade of social and economic legislation to build a safety net. Banking laws were strengthened to protect consumers, and the union movement was strengthened to help workers. The Depression also changed the political landscape of the nation into this century. An endless array of laws, including stock market controls, was implemented to address the causes and effects of the Depression.

The stock market crash did contribute to the Depression. Stock market losses caused a pullback in consumer spending, and the Federal Reserve increased interest rates. The roots of the Great Depression go back to a few years earlier and resulted from what many consider the perfect economic storm. Factors included the business cycle, overspeculation, a stock bubble, massive crop failures, trade wars, and government intervention. Still, most would agree that the taproot and beginning of the Great Depression was the stock market crash of 1929. The beginning of 1929 saw a nation in a boom economy with a record gross national product. Car production in 1929 had doubled from its 1923 level. Real income per capita had reached new highs, and the newspapers were filled with stories of excessive spending. Speculation was also at an all-time high. Margin-leveraged accounts were at record highs as well. To facilitate investment, the Federal Reserve had been following a strategy of easy money for years. Consumer credit was rising dramatically. Interest rates for margin accounts were moving higher, reaching over 20 percent. Many small investors were speculating as many stocks were selling at more than 30 times the company's earnings. People were talking of a new economic model in which all would become rich in the endless growth of the American economy. Clearly there was a stock market bubble.

On September 3, 1929, the Dow Jones Industrial Average hit a record high of 381. The Federal Reserve had issued warnings about overspeculation and had started to tighten money; unfortunately, the New York Federal Reserve broke ranks, injecting massive amounts of cash for margin stock accounts (this type of rogue bank behavior would be addressed after the Depression). The availability of call money made big investors overconfident about the stock market setbacks in September 1929. The market started to show true signs of instability in October 1929. On Black Thursday, October 24, the market moved lower on a record 13 million shares traded. The big and mostly widely traded companies lost an average of over 10 percent, triggering the first wave of calls on margin loans. President Herbert Hoover and major industrialists jumped in with positive statements. Then, on Black Tuesday, October 29, 1929, the market crashed to 40 percent of its high a month earlier. As banks recalled loans, panic set in, and the great crash entered into American legend. The Federal Reserve, business leaders, and politicians made the right moves to stop the economy from going over the cliff. Things did stabilize as the economy moved into 1930.

The quick easing of money put off bank runs and failures until later in 1930. There was even a brief recovery in the first six months of 1930. However, the indicators were showing a decline in economic activity. By the end of 1930 and into 1931, bank failures and panics started, with the now-famous lines of panicked

Crowds gather outside the New York Stock Exchange in the wake of the great stock market crash of 1929. (Library of Congress)

depositors. The number of banks that failed was 659 in 1929, 1,350 in 1930, and 2,293 in 1931. The banking problems spread in 1931 with a doubling of bank failures and mortgage bankruptcies. The New York money crisis had once again spread across the country and Europe as seen in previous panics. Deflation rapidly lowered house prices and reduced grain prices, which hurt farmers. Farm prices had dropped 40 percent from their 1926 high. The government tried to pour money into creating demand. Social problems started to mount as unemployment hit 17 percent in 1931. Congress passed the Smoot-Hawley Tariff Act creating historically high tariff rates. Still, it was not the American tariff rates so much as a rush by all countries to protect their home markets. The combination of deflation, low farm prices, and tariffs cut imports over 40 percent. In 1932, as the Dow hit 95, America looked for a political solution with the election of Franklin Roosevelt and the New Deal Democrats.

In 1933, Roosevelt imposed a bank holiday to stop panics and build new confidence in the banking system. More dramatic was the creation of the National Recovery Administration (NRA), which had sweeping powers to control wages and prices. The NRA created a national industry, similar to that of Stalin in Russia. The

NRA would be found unconstitutional in 1935. In hindsight, most economists today see it as ineffective and a mistake. Still, at least it stabilized unemployment and confidence. The Dow moved up from a low of 58. The Civilian Conservation Corps hired over 250,000 young men and at least prevented social unrest in the worst of the Depression. From 1933 to 1934, Roosevelt used the time to implement sweeping social legislation such as the National Labor Relations Board, which enforced the use of collective bargaining. Roosevelt tried a long array of approaches, including moving off and on the gold standard, credit regulation, mortgage aid, work projects, trade laws, reduced tariffs, increases in taxes, new banking regulations, and expansion of credit programs. In 1935, the New Deal Democrats looked for a long-term social safety net, enacting Social Security. The National Labor Relations Act of 1935 unionized the steel, rubber, and automotive industries as well as creating widespread collective bargaining. The government had successfully moved into energy production with the Hoover Dam and the Tennessee Valley Authority.

Things never really improved, and in 1937, the economy slipped into a "depression within a depression." This setback came as the multitude of social programs took large amounts of money out of circulation. Taxes slowed capital investment. And union-creating laws had caused wages to jump 11 to 33 percent, making things costly and bringing down demand. Another complication was the devastation of American agriculture by the Dust Bowl. The climb out of this second dip was slow. Unemployment went from 18 percent in 1938 to 14 percent in 1940, as war production would finally bring American industry back to life. Arguments about and analyses of the causes and solutions for the Great Depression continue to this day. Its impact on the nature of American business was, however, deep and lasting.

*See also:* Banking Crisis and Great Recession; Federal Reserve Act; Jefferson Embargo; Panic of 1837; Panic of 1857; Panic of 1873; Panic of 1893; Panic of 1907; Wage and Price Controls

## References

Chandler, William U. *America's Greatest Depression, 1929–1941.* New York: Harper & Row, 1970.

Friedman, Milton, and Anna Schwartz. *A Monetary History of the United States, 1867–1960.* Princeton, NJ: Princeton University Press, 1971.

Galbraith, John Kenneth. *The Great Crash: 1929.* Boston: Houghton Mifflin, 1988.

Kindleberger, Charles P. *The World in Depression: 1929–1939.* Berkeley: University of California Press, 1986.

Shlaes, Amity. *The Forgotten Man: A New History of the Great Depression.* New York: Harper Perennial, 2007.

# Hoover Dam (1931)

Hoover Dam (originally known as Boulder Dam) was built on the Colorado River between Arizona and Nevada to control flooding, provide irrigation, and generate electric power for the West. It would become one of the largest construction projects of the 20th century and one of the most successful government projects. It came in well under budget and two years ahead of schedule. Its success would be a model for other construction projects of the New Deal such as the Tennessee Valley Authority. It was started in 1931 and finished early in 1935. The actual history of the dam goes back even further to a 1922 study of a dam project for then secretary of commerce Herbert Hoover. Because the dam affected the watersheds of seven states—California, Nevada, Arizona, Utah, New Mexico, Colorado, and Wyoming—a seven-state compact was suggested. The legality of such a compact was questioned, and fear of litigation slowed it down. Hoover did get a signed compact in late 1922, but federal funding stalled.

The proposed cost of more than $100 million for a system including a total of three dams found little national support in the early 1920s. Slowly, over the years, support grew for the dam. Finally, at the end of 1928, a bill was passed and signed by President Calvin Coolidge. The bill, called the Boulder Canyon Project Act, appropriated $165 million for three dams. The bill required at least six of the seven states to approve the compact. In March 1929, six states approved it, with Arizona withholding approval until 1944. With the beginning of the Depression, President Hoover called for bids to go out on January 10, 1931. Pressure from the rising unemployment forced the contract to exclude the use of Chinese labor that had been used in the old railroad days. The winning bid was for a joint venture of construction companies known as the Six Companies. The Six Companies' bid for Hoover Dam was $48,890,955, well below the government estimate. The Bureau of Reclamation, which was in charge of Western irrigation, was the government department in charge of the overall project. President Hoover ordered the start of construction in March 1931 instead of waiting for the initial start date in October.

The contract was based on the Carnegie "drive" system used by Charles Schwab of Bethlehem Steel to produce ships for the Allies during World War I. The contract not only had penalties for running behind schedule but also provided incentive bonuses for performance measures. These incentives created a rapid pace and an atmosphere of efficiency rarely seen in such government megaprojects. Penalties and bonuses were based on major event timelines. The Six Companies showed creativity and innovative approaches to avoid various $3,000-a-day penalties. The project overcame an array of problems including heat over 100 degrees, inability to obtain steel pipe, labor problems, fatal accidents, and the largest application of concrete ever attempted. The Six Companies overcame a number of strike challenges and an organizational drive by the Communist Industrial Workers of the World.

The Hoover Dam was the earliest and largest government work program of the Great Depression. It was started and expedited by Presidents Hoover and Roosevelt to help address national unemployment. Thousands of unemployed descended on the construction site, which employed a total of 20,000 over the period but only about 5,000 at any one time. Wages varied from $0.50 to $1.25 per hour. The average of $0.80 was more than double the national average. Camp towns were built for the workers and their families; however, the camp towns were often cited for poor living conditions. Some workers did make the 30-mile daily commute from Las Vegas. The company camps did not allow gambling or drinking. The heat was oppressive, with work-site temperatures commonly hitting 120 degrees and over 140 degrees in the tunnel system. A large number of the project's 96 deaths were heat related. Safety remained a major concern. Tar-impregnated hardhats were developed for the high wall workers known as "high scalers," which would become an industry standard. The outstanding performance of meeting interim benchmarks kept the government out of the project.

Hoover Dam is still regarded as one of America's greatest engineering accomplishments. Before construction, two 56-foot-diameter three-mile-long tunnels had to be built to divert the river. In 21 months, an average workforce of 5,000 men built a structure greater than Egypt's greatest pyramid, which took 100,000 men working 20 years. It is an arch-gravity design that distributes the pressure into the canyon walls. Special cooling tubes were designed to speed up the cooling of the concrete, which would otherwise have taken more than a century. A huge refrigeration plant was built on site. The design and engineering specifications were considered conservative. The Six Companies worked as management and the government played a limited role as regulator and inspector. The government stayed out of labor problems and pay issues, focusing on engineering and design. The quality of the concrete was outstanding and is not subject to the alkali-silica deterioration that has caused considerable deterioration in similar-aged dams. To overcome transportation issues, pipe-fabricating and cement plants were built on site. At 726 feet in height, Hoover Dam was the tallest at the time. It produces over 2,000 megawatts of power for the American West. Overall, there is no better example of a well-managed megaproject than Hoover Dam.

*See also:* Erie Canal; Panama Canal Opens; Stock Market Crash/Great Depression; Transcontinental Railroad Completed; Whig Party Evolves

### References

Dunar, Andrew, and Dennis McBride. *Building Hoover Dam: An Oral History of the Great Depression.* Reno: University of Nevada Press, 2001.

Hiltzik, Michael. *Colossus: Hoover Dam and the Making of the American Century.* New York: Free Press, 2010.

Stevens, Joseph E. *Hoover Dam: An American Adventure.* Norman: University of Oklahoma Press, 1956.

# National Labor Relations Act (Wagner Act) (1935)

The National Labor Relations Act, known as the Wagner Act after Senator Robert Wagner of New York, was the cornerstone of President Franklin D. Roosevelt's New Deal social legislation. It would end decades of struggle to unionize employees in the steel and related heavy industries. This act changed the very landscape of labor in the United States in hopes of avoiding widespread social unrest during the Great Depression. The Wagner Act would usher in a wave of unionization in the steel, automotive, rubber, mining, and electrical industries. At the start of the 1930s, less than 10 percent of America's labor force was unionized; after the 1935 passage of the Wagner Act, the decade ended with 35 percent of the labor force unionized. The act changed the role of government in labor policy. The act declared that democracy must apply in the workplace. Furthermore, the act declared that the means to this democracy was the right of workers to organize and bargain collectively through employee representatives. The act established the National Labor Relations Board (NLRB) to implement and oversee the Wagner Act.

Unionization in America had had a very difficult path over the years prior to the 1935 passage of the Wagner Act. In steel, unionization had been beaten back in the 1892 Homestead Strike and the Great Steel Strike of 1919. Unionization had been declining in all industries since 1919. The automotive industry had less of a bloody history, but unionization had also been stalled. The electrical industry also had many failed attempts at unionization. Progressive liberal Democrats had continued the fight, but even Woodrow Wilson's War Labor Boards with war powers could not overcome the industrial owners. The Great Depression brought more social unrest and union activity. New York, in particular, was a hotbed of unions, socialists, and communists. Progressives and conservatives alike feared the influence of European socialists and communists. Many complained that the companies were using spies, firing union organizers, and blacklisting workers. Even enlightened managers such as John D. Rockefeller and Charles Schwab realized that somehow employees needed to be brought into wage and work disputes. Even the union movement was fractured, with John Lewis's Committee for Industrial Organization (CIO) fighting with the American Federation of Labor (AFL) for the representation rights in the steel and automotive industries. The New Deal Democrats and progressive Republicans thought it was necessary to take a bold step into labor policy. The economic downturn and the rise of communism in Europe raised many fears that unless labor issues were addressed, more serious social unrest might come to the United States.

Interestingly, the act does not apply to supervisors and government workers. Federal workers remain today one area where strikes have been restricted. The National Labor Relations Act was, to some degree, an overreaction, while balance would be achieved after years of debate and amending. The act's anticipated role of improving the economy by increasing wages was never achieved. Unions saw it as a real opportunity. The first major union success came in 1937 with the victory of the CIO union over General Motors, followed by the unionization of United States Steel.

The heart of the act is section 7: "Employees shall have the right to form, join, or assist labor organizations, to bargain collectively through representatives of their own choosing, and to engage in other concerted activities for the purpose of collective bargaining or other mutual aid and protection." The key was a secret ballot election of the union under the auspices of the NLRB. Since the passage of the Wagner Act, there have been over 360,000 secret ballot elections. The NLRB has five members, who are appointed by the president with Senate oversight. Early on, employers and the AFL, which argued that CIO unions were favored, questioned the neutrality of the NLRB. Neutrality had proved difficult over the years. Even President Roosevelt was concerned that the act went too far. Still, companies had also gone too far in restricting employee representation. The National Labor Relations Act would face 20 years of challenges in the Congress. Two major amendments would be the Taft-Hartley Act in 1947 and the Landrum-Griffin Act in 1959. The NLRB today remains a type of court for employee complaints.

The Wagner Act had many critics, but in the end the Supreme Court upheld it in 1937 (*NLRB v. Jones & Laughlin Steel*). The argument over individual choice did continue, and President Roosevelt did try to counterbalance some of the extreme activist supporters who were trying to expand the intent of the act to support unions even more. Still, the act created a number of issues that continue to this day. One is the terminology of collective bargaining as a right. Opponents maintain that collective bargaining is not a right; collective bargaining is but one method of employee representation. This argument has once again surfaced today with large government unions. Another issue was the so-called closed shop. Once a union was certified by the NLRB election, it could not be removed. Furthermore, workers would be required to join the union to stay working at the shop. In 1947, the Taft-Hartley Act limited the application of a true closed shop. It allowed "union shop," which is a form of closed shop. However, under the Taft-Hartley Act, states could pass right-to-work laws to make even union shops illegal. Today, we see the spread of right-to-work laws in southern and western states. These right-to-work laws have caused northern factories to move south. The Taft-Hartley Act also addressed some abuses of unions such as secondary boycotts and mass picketing. The Taft-Hartley Act would be challenged in the national steel strike of 1959.

*See also:* Great Railroad Strike of 1877; Great Steel Strike of 1919; Haymarket Riot; Homestead Strike of 1892; Steel Strike of 1959; Whig Party Evolves

### References

Edsforth, Ronald. *The New Deal: America's Response to the Great Depression.* London: Blackwell, 2000.

Morris, Charles. *The Blue Eagle at Work: Reclaiming Democratic Rights in the American Workplace.* Ithaca, NY: Cornell University Press, 2004.

# Social Security Act (1935)

Following up on a campaign pledge, President Franklin D. Roosevelt formed the Committee on Economic Security in June 1934. This committee solicited opinions from the grass roots using a national town hall format. The committee proposal passed quickly through Congress. On August 14, 1935, President Roosevelt signed the Social Security Act, which was a social insurance program designed to pay retired workers, age 65 or older, a continuing income after retirement. It was not originally planned to be a full retirement fund but to maintain the income of the elderly above poverty levels. It would be amended and expanded in its evolution to the current program. Today, it stands as the largest government program in the world and forms the single greatest expenditure in the federal budget. In the year 2009, over 51 million American received more than $650 billion in Social Security.

The concept of social security can be considered far more evolutionary than revolutionary, with the earliest roots going back to the English Poor Law of 1601, which established a legal basis for the responsibility of the state to provide for the welfare of its citizens. Historically, in colonial America, Scotch-Irish communities taxed citizens for the establishment of poorhouses. In addition, many American fraternal organizations such as the Odd Fellows, Elks, Eagles, and Moose took on the role of helping the less fortunate in society. The first federal program in the area of social security was Civil War pensions. In 1862, pension legislation created pensions for disabled soldiers. By 1890, this was expanded to soldiers whose disabilities came later in life, making them eligible for a pension after their service. By 1906, Civil War veterans were old enough to qualify for pensions. In Germany in the 1800s, some social security laws were passed; some employers such as George Westinghouse, H. J. Heinz, and Alfred Dolge (a piano builder) offered company pensions in the late 1800s.

The decades of the 1920s and 1930s created a tipping point in demographics with more people living in cities, people living much longer, and a collapse in the economy. The old nuclear farming family had taken care of the disabled and old, but with urban centers, nuclear families no longer had the resources to do so. During the time period from 1910 to 1930, public health programs caused a rapid increase in life spans. The life span increased an amazing 10 years. By 1930, there were over seven million people older than 65, and an estimated 50 percent of these were living below the poverty level. The unemployment of the Depression created hordes of older and disabled unemployed. Older employees tended to be the first to be laid off in an industrial environment dependent on strong muscles. The huge numbers strained the private funds available to handle these hordes. Churches quickly found themselves short on money. In addition, urban nuclear families did not have the resources they had had on the farm. Cities turned to work projects, creating jobs paying a dollar a day as they had in the Panics of 1893 and 1907, but the length of the Great Depression soon exhausted these funds. States such as California tried to address the issues, led by social crusader and novelist Upton Sinclair. Most of these socialist programs failed to get full state support, but as the Depression continued, it was clear the problem was overwhelming and required federal programs. Union support for a federal program grew by 1933. The struggle for legislation started under Roosevelt's New Deal, but at the time, it was a long-term vision more than immediate relief.

The severity of the Depression made the Social Security Act very popular at the time. It was also designed as social insurance to protect the elderly, not a retirement plan. The plan was to buy insurance through equal employer and employee payroll taxes for it. In 1937, the payroll taxes were 1 percent for the employer and 1 percent for the employee. Payroll deductions were mandated under the Federal Insurance Contribution Act (FICA). Amendments to the act in 1939 increased family protection to include help to wives and dependent children. The first benefit payment was not paid until 1940. Amendments in 1954 increased the base of employees covered by including workers like domestic workers. In 1956, the Social Security payroll tax was increased to 2 percent for the employer and 2 percent for the employee. In 1965, an amendment added Medicare and Medicaid under President Lyndon Johnson's Great Society program. In 1972, an amendment added cost-of-living adjustments to Social Security benefits.

Early Supreme Court challenges in the 1930s supported the Social Security Act while striking down much of the New Deal legislation. The initial program had many exclusions and covered less than half the workforce. It favored workers in heavy industries and large, unionized factories. Interestingly, one of the program's eventual problems would uphold its constitutionality. *Helvering v. Davis* (1937) held that since the funds were not earmarked and went into the general fund, it was a mere exercise of the Congress's general taxation powers. That lack of specificity

President Franklin D. Roosevelt signs the Social Security Act on August 14, 1935. (Library of Congress)

and general fund application allowed the money to be used for other things over the years. In 1939, an amendment required surpluses to go into a trust fund; then, as the program expanded, surpluses became small. Finally, in a 1965 "New Society" amendment, Social Security funds were again fully applied to the general fund for congressional use. The argument remains today that this problem could have been avoided if the plan had initially been given to a private insurance company and regulated by the government. The huge benefit payout with declining payroll income has put the solvency of the program in the spotlight today.

*See also:* Haymarket Riot; Income Tax; National Labor Relations Act (Wagner Act)

### References

Altman, Nancy. *The Battle for Social Security: From FDR's Vision to Bush's Gamble.* New York: Wiley, 2005.

Beland, Daniel. *Social Security: History and Politics from the New Deal to the Privatization Debate.* Lawrence: University of Kansas, 2007.

Dobelstein, Andrew. *Understanding the Social Security Act: The Foundation of Social Welfare for America in the Twenty-First Century.* Oxford: Oxford University Press, 2009.

# Television at the 1939 World's Fair

In the past, world's fairs had always been an augur of new business opportunities. The 1851 London World's Fair gave us automated machine tools, the sewing machine, rubber products, and steelmaking; the 1876 World's Fair gave us the telephone, typewriter, and electric dynamos. The World's Fair of Paris in 1877 gave us Edison's electric lightbulb, and Chicago's 1893 World's Fair gave us Heinz ketchup, Cracker Jack, Cream of Wheat, Westinghouse's alternating current distribution, Tiffany glass, and Juicy Fruit gum. The 1939 New York World's Fair will always be remembered for its introduction of television. The 1939 fair might have been lost to history because it occurred during the Great Depression, yet it was a key event in the development of commercial television. Television was the first true invention of the 20th century in that it was a collective and corporate evolution that cannot truly be assigned to any one inventor. It was perfected in corporate research centers versus the individual laboratory. It represented a new business model for product development and innovation.

To fully trace the invention of television would take a long study on the development of various electronic devices. The first step, however, was the vision that commercial television could be a useful tool as demonstrated by the sales and success of the telegraph, telephone, and radio. The market potential attracted investment by Westinghouse Electric, American Telephone and Telegraph (AT&T)'s Bell Telephone Laboratories, Radio Corporation of America (RCA), and others in development work at their research centers. The first development work centered on the mechanical models of telegraphy and transmission used for the telephone and radio. The amplification tube technology of Lee DeForest, Arthur Korn, and A. Fournier set the basis for mechanical television in 1909. This first success was limited to still pictures on a rotating mirror drum. Still, RCA did some experimental broadcasts of these silhouette images, but they were never popular. Clearly, the commercial network in this case was ahead of the marketable technology.

Electronic television also has a long history, with competing inventors and three major corporate laboratories: RCA, EMI Engineering (England), and Westinghouse Electric. During the second half of the 1920s, the individual patent rights on a crude version came down to Philo Farnsworth and Vladimir Zworykin of Russia. Farnsworth won the court battle, and RCA bought the patent rights to Farnsworth's "Image Dissector" to add to its many related devices. With its radio-broadcasting subsidiary, the National Broadcasting Company (NBC), RCA had the marketing network to exploit the very limited technology. In 1937 and 1938, NBC in New York and Los Angeles had irregularly scheduled broadcasts of electronic television. General Electric was also starting limited broadcasting, but RCA was planning a major launch through its pavilion at the 1939 New York World's Fair.

The New York Fair was more low-key with the Depression and World War II on the horizon. The RCA Television Exhibit was one of the most popular with the 45 million fairgoers. The opening ceremonies were televised, but the New York area had only a few television sets. Franklin D. Roosevelt's opening speech and a talk by Albert Einstein were televised at the opening by New York's W2XBS (now WNBC). The cost of a television receiver was around $500 to $600, or equivalent to the cost of a new car at the time. A small three-inch screen was available for around $150 at the time. These early broadcasts had no advertising support, but most of the manufacturers were in radio and knew the potential. Small stations grew around the world, but the sets developed only small markets. During the war years of 1940 to 1946, both the market and the technology lay dormant. In fact, the War Board actually halted the manufacture of television sets until 1945.

Television took off after 1945 as America went on a spending boom. In 1949, about 3 percent of American homes had television sets, but by 1954, over 50 percent of American homes had one; and by 1962 over 90 percent of American homes had them. Motorola entered television set production in 1947, bringing the price down to $190. NBC and Columbia Broadcasting System (CBS) arose as the major networks, with affiliates in larger cities. Broadcasting was by radio waves, so distances were restricted in the early decades to a 50-mile radius. The Federal Communications Commission (FCC) determined radio frequencies and power. After the war, Americans rushed to the new technology with all its drawbacks. Most of the television sets before 1970 were vacuum tube technology with poor reliability. Tubes were constantly burning out. One of America's fastest-growing small businesses was the TV repairman. Even television repair was a booming trade education market. The introduction of solid state technology in the 1970s would eliminate this small business niche.

Initially in the 1950s, local stations would sign exclusive affiliation agreements with the major networks such as CBS and NBC. Under these agreements, the stations carried national programming in the evening, allowing local content at other times. Most television stations broadcast between the hours of 7 A.M. and 11 P.M. Advertising rapidly took over the business of national programming. Tobacco companies were early advertisers. Advertisers also had enormous control over program content. Most shows were live, with the comedy hours of men like Milton Merle and Jack Benny being some of the most popular. News shows were there from the earliest days but were considered as losing money. Still, the networks kept news shows to fulfill government requirements for public service. Color television came in the 1960s but didn't hit the 50 percent of homes mark until after 1972.

*See also:* First Commercial Telephone; First Commercial Radio; Talking Movies—*The Jazz Singer*; Western Union Telegraph Company

**References**

Abramson, Albert. *The History of Television, 1880 to 1941.* Jefferson, NC: McFarland, 1987.

Everson, George. *The Story of Television, The Life of Philo T. Farnsworth.* New York: Norton, 1945.

# Maslow's Theory of Needs (1946)

In 1946, psychologist Abraham Maslow completed a series of articles following the publication of his 1934 thesis on motivation. The most famous of the series was "A Theory of Human Motivation" in the *Psychological Review.* The theory would have a latent effect on the science of management, slowly building into a core part of business analysis by the late 1960s. Maslow's theory became known as "humanistic psychology"; it was also known as the Third Force in psychology. In his field, his humanistic psychology approach was considered revolutionary and an alternative to behavioral motivation. His theory was based on a hierarchy of needs that were satisfied in the order of human importance. Many have suggested that Maslow rediscovered a 19th-century branch of economics, plutology (named after Plutus, the Greek god of wealth), which maintained a hierarchy of human needs that changed once lower needs were fulfilled. There were five tiers of needs from the bottom up: physiological, safety and security, love and belonging, esteem, and self-actualization. Using Maslow's hierarchy of needs, managers could design better motivational programs and incentive plans and improve workplace productivity. It would truly help the field of industrial psychology advance past the simple principles of Frederick Taylor's scientific management. Maslow's theory of needs continues to be the most versatile management theory, adaptable to even the most recent studies in motivation.

Maslow received his BA, MA, and PhD in psychology from the University of Wisconsin in the 1930s. His original studies were based on the study of monkeys, which he observed let some needs take precedence over others. It all started with the confirmed observation that the need for water took precedence over food. His research was considered almost trivial but had powerful consequences. He would do most of his later research at Columbia University. At Columbia, Maslow worked with Alfred Adler, one of Sigmund Freud's associates, and Gestalt psychologist Max Wertheimer. In 1962, he formally began his business consulting efforts with Non-Linear Systems of Del Mar, California. At Non-Linear Systems, Maslow kept a journal of what motivated workers in various work settings. He studied the individual needs of the workers involved, a revolutionary approach. In 1965, he published a book, *Eupsychian Management,* based on these journals. *Eupsychian* was a new word standing for "healthward" or "moving toward psychological health."

Maslow's theory works as a foundational pyramid of needs to be fulfilled. First are the very basic needs—that is, physiological needs for water, food, and sex. Maslow reasoned these had to be fulfilled first before humans are motivated to higher levels. Missionaries of the early 1900s had learned, for example, that they had to supply food and water before they could preach the gospel. Even the early Egyptians and Romans had learned the value of well-fed slave labor. Next are the needs for safety and security, such as shelter. Early industrialists had learned the importance of supplying this to immigrant workers and their families to improve factory production. Once humans have fulfilled their needs for water, food, and shelter, they look for the advanced needs of belonging (sometimes called social needs). Even the evil-based design of American slavery developed a system known as the "task system," which allowed for basic human needs to be fulfilled and thus increased productivity. These needs for belonging are for things like relationships and community or even fraternal organizations. The paternal capitalists such as H. J. Heinz, Andrew Carnegie, and George Westinghouse supported community centers, employee clubs, and churches for the workforce. Once social needs are in place, then the esteem needs for achievement, status, and rewards should be met. Finally, there are the extremely complex needs of self-actualization, which Maslow believed that few ever fully achieved and would apply to some futuristic work-force. Maslow did suggest that the goal for all humans (while rarely achieved) was self-actualization; thus managers should search for ways to help workers achieve self-actualization in the workplace. Maslow saw creativity as a key attribute of self-actualization. While Maslow's theory seemed too simplistic for the social sciences, it was quickly adopted in education and later in business.

Maslow's work and the passage of the Wagner Act inspired new ways to look at labor relations. A number of labor institutes were developed including the School of Industrial and Labor Relations at Cornell (1945), the Institute of Labor and Industrial Relations at the University of Illinois (1946), and the Institute for Social Research at the University of Michigan (1947). These universities also added curriculum in industrial psychology. Out of these efforts evolved new approaches to business leadership such as the work done by Rensis Likert. More practical programs evolving out of Maslow's work included new industrial relations programs focused on human needs such as the Scanlon plans at Lincoln Electric and Adamson Company.

Maslow's theory also became the Rosetta stone to understanding new data and studies, beginning from 1970 to the present. One of these studies was that of Fredrick Herzberg in the 1950s, which showed that money was not a motivator but that things like achievement rewards and positive feedback were. Herzberg's results conflicted with the results of the early scientific managers, who had demonstrated that money was a motivator. In particular, money had been shown to be a powerful motivator in factory incentive systems in the 1920s and 1930s. Maslow's hierarchy of needs could reconcile the conflicting results. In the case of Herzberg, he had used thousands of engineers in his study. Engineers were highly paid employees with most of their physiological, safety, and belonging needs met by their high salaries. For these engineers, it was the esteem needs that needed to be satisfied. The early scientific management studies used factory workers, who often needed more money to supply the basic needs of housing, food, and community. While many of Maslow's ideas have fallen out of vogue in the social sciences, they remain today the cornerstone of motivational theory for business managers.

*See also:* Privatization of the Plymouth Colony; Scientific Management; *Wealth of Nations*

### References

Herzberg, Frederick, Bernard Mausner, and Barbara Snyderman. *The Motivation to Work.* New York: Wiley, 1959.

Kaufman, Bruce E. *The Origins and Evolution of the Field of Industrial Relations.* Ithaca, NY: ILR Press, 1993.

Maslow, Abraham. *Eupsychian Management.* Homewood, IL: Richard D. Irwin, 1965.

# General Agreement on Tariffs and Trade (GATT) (1947)

The General Agreement on Tariffs and Trade (GATT) was implemented by the western nations after World War II to regulate trade and assure world economic recovery, but the roots were in the Great Depression. World economists believed the Great Depression led to two problems: (1) the shutdown of trade, which crippled countries such as England and America, and (2) the rise of fascism in Germany and Italy. The conclusion was that trade restrictions were the root cause. This was based on the high tariffs of the Smoot-Hawley Tariff Act of 1930 in the United States and the high-tariff countermoves of Europe. GATT was negotiated to assure open international trade through the reduction of tariffs, quotas, and subsidies. The original idea would assure the free flow of American manufactured products into the European market. The impact of GATT remains today, since it established the American dollar as the international currency and America as the leader in free trade. It has also created a flood of products into the United States as the rebuilt economies of Europe and Asia strengthened. GATT also established the institutions of the World Bank and the International Monetary Fund. GATT would govern international trade from 1947 until 1995, when the World Trade Organization (WTO) replaced it formally. GATT's guiding principles, however, remain in effect today.

After World War II, it was clearly to the advantage of the United States to promote a strong dollar and free trade. The United States was sitting in a unique position as the only country with a powerful manufacturing base standing. England's and Russia's manufacturing was crippled, and Germany, Japan, Italy, and most of the world's manufacturing lay in ruins. The United States could take advantage of free trade by shipping manufactured goods throughout the world and bringing in cheap raw materials and minor products. In addition, the United States had a huge shipping merchant marine in place to benefit from expanded world trade. Europe and Japan would have to go to the United States for manufactured goods even though a high dollar made them expensive. Of course, the other incentive for the agreement would be to promote peace through trade. There was also a group of politicians who believed, incorrectly, that tariffs had caused the Great Depression. The writings of Adam Smith had also come back into vogue with world economists. Economist John Maynard Keynes was one of the leading proponents of GATT.

The original GATT Treaty of 1947 and its 23 members tried to achieve fair trade through reciprocity and negotiated trade deals. GATT created a reversal of the American policy of applied and scientific tariffs that had been in place from the birth of the nation. GATT did try for the reciprocity that William McKinley had added to his famous 1890 Tariff Act. GATT, at least in its stated mission, was not "free" trade but the elimination of "discriminatory treatment" and "barriers to trade." GATT would later address "antidumping" practices; the British began dumping practices with iron products after the War of 1812. While trade after GATT remained a type of economic chess game, the agreement did lead to a remarkable amount of trade liberalization between nations. GATT was a negotiation-based multilateral instrument more than a formal treaty. Most considered it a de facto international organization. GATT was a series of eight "rounds" of meetings starting in 1947 in Geneva and ending in Uruguay in 1986. These "rounds" lasted from 5 to 87 months in duration. The rounds produced unique sets of agreements and tariff levels. The Kennedy round (1964–1967) resulted in a 35 percent reduction in tariff rates between members, which is the largest in the history of the world. By the Uruguay round in 1986, membership had reached 123 members.

The Uruguay round, which ended in 1994, created a new organization, the WTO. The WTO has 153 members representing 97 percent of the world's population. It evolved out of GATT into an international administrator and arbitrator of trade. It does provide a forum for negotiations for settling disputes. The WTO established a type of trade organization with its "most-favored-nation" rule. Most-favored nations are assured equality in trade requirements among other members. Another rule of the WTO is the "nondiscrimination" rule, which eliminates the use of nontariff restrictions such as technical standards. This rule evolved into the international manufacturing standard known as ISO 9000 to eliminate technical trade barriers. WTO members are required to have transparency in publishing their trade regulations. The WTO also facilitates "binding and enforceable commitments." The WTO has a formal dispute process to research and rule on member violations.

The WTO still has its issues. Labor has questioned whether these tariff-free arrangements have forced lower wages in the industrial countries. It is a key political issue, which many call "fair trade." The question centers on countries like the United States, where product prices reflect pensions, health care costs, and living wages, competing against products of countries such as China and India where these worker benefits are lacking. Many Americans argue that the WTO has resulted in a loss of sovereignty. An ongoing debate continues on intellectual rights and the use of agricultural subsidies. More recently, environmental issues have been part of the discussions. Again, the environmental costs of products can put American products at a disadvantage with those from countries with lower regulations.

*See also:* Jefferson Embargo; Abraham Lincoln Establishes Protectionism; McKinley Tariff of 1890; Navigation Acts; "Report on Manufacturing"; Stock Market Crash/Great Depression; Tariff of Abominations; *Wealth of Nations*; Whig Party Evolves

### References

Bagwell, Kyle, and Robert W. Staiger. "An Economic Theory of GATT." *American Economic Review,* 89, no. 1 (March 1999): 215–248.

Hudec, Robert. *The GATT Legal System and World Trade Diplomacy.* New York: Praeger, 1990.

# First Credit Card (1950)

The first credit card charge was made on February 8, 1950, by Frank McNamara, Ralph Schneider, and Matty Simmons at Major's Cabin Grill in New York City. The event is still known as the "first supper." The credit card was Diners Club, developed by McNamara and Schneider. The Diners Club was a cardboard card. It was a closed loop system between the issuer, consumer, and merchant. While the purchase was made on credit, the bill had to be paid at the end of the month. The concept caught on fast for charging travel expenses, and Diners Club had 20,000 members by the end of 1951. By 1958, American Express entered the credit card business with a plastic card. With American Express's financial base, it moved into other countries, making it popular with traveling businessmen. In 1960, Hilton Hotels followed the credit card business model with Carte Blanche. With the backing of the Hilton name, Carte Blanche was considered the most prestigious card and developed an international market. Banks got into the business in 1959 with Bank of America's BankAmericard, which was open loop, allowing the bank to charge interest on revolving credit. Credit cards revolutionized merchandising around the world. The customer gained convenience and safety, but prices increased, and high interest rates were also a result. Merchants benefited with increased sales and secure transactions, but the merchant was charged a fee for the privilege of accepting cards and a small transaction fee. Today there are many variations of the original business model.

The business model for the credit card evolved in a short window before paper checks reached full popularity. Paper checks took days to clear the bank, and until magnetic inks were developed in 1959, the banks had limited ability to handle any volume of paper checks. Merchants were not willing to accept the risk of a bounced check from a traveler. Most small business transactions remained in cash before the 1950s. Some hotel chains and oil companies had experimented with their own charge card for their products and services in the 1920s prior to the Depression. American Express had been looking at credit cards as early as 1946, but the success of Diners Card quickly brought them into the market. American Express changed the business model a bit, since the company had a strong financial background and identity. American Express had pioneered money orders with the Pony Express in the 1850s. In the 1870s, American Express was using the telegraph to move money across the nation. In 1890, American Express had an established business in travelers' checks. It entered the market as a premium card over Diners Card, charging the consumer six dollars versus the five dollars for Diners Card. The reputation of American Express allowed the company to have a higher fee for the merchant as well. This fee, known as the discount rate, was around 1 percent and was increased to 1.9 percent if the bank offered credit beyond the monthly billing. Still, American Express was basically a closed loop system with limited revolving credit, although they were the first to experiment with open loops. Bank networks expanded the business model to make money from revolving credit, or the open loop system.

Frank McNamara invented the Diners Club card, America's first credit card. (Roy Stevens/Time Life Pictures/Getty Images)

In 1959, Bank of America entered the business with BankAmericard, which offered revolving credit through a third-party bank. Barclaycard (England) in 1966 became the first credit card outside the United States. A group of Californian banks, seeing the credit possibilities for profit, offered MasterCard to compete with BankAmericard. Similarly, Citibank got into the revolving credit card with its Everything Card in 1967. Banks realized large profits from the revolving credit card, and a type of competition started. Citibank and MasterCard merged in 1967 to create Master Charge. BankAmericard started a mass mailing campaign in 1969 to selected "good" credit risks, which was to become the marketing standard for the industry. Interest rates allowed this type of business to be the bank's most profitable. Interest rates were limited by the states, but some states such as Delaware, with weak usury laws, and South Dakota, which had no limits, soon became headquarters for these operations.

The closed loop system created controlling organizations or associations for the bank, merchants, and users. These associations such as MasterCard and Visa were really controlled by the banks. American Express and Diners Card remained closed loops outside banking networks. In 1986, Discover Card entered the business with a new, merchant-oriented approach. Discover was part of Sears, which at the time was America's largest retailer. Discover Card was consumer friendly with no customer fee charged, lower merchant fees, cash-back rewards, and higher credit limits. While Discover Card was never as successful as Visa or MasterCard, its innovations impacted how the credit card business functioned. The banks tried to hold Discover Card out, and in 2004, the U.S. government won an antitrust court ruling against MasterCard. The ruling forced banks to offer customers American Express and Discover Card in addition to MasterCard.

While the credit card has injected billions of dollars of credit into the economy, it remains controversial but popular. Antitrust suits continue in America and Europe. The Fair Credit Billing Act in 1975 (amended in 1986) addressed customer liability (limited to $50) in fault. A 2010 ruling of the Supreme Court allows merchants to charge different prices based on the type of card. The courts and Congress continue to battle over items such as interest rates charged, late penalty fees, and hidden fees.

*See also:* Overland Travel and Mail Service; Western Union Telegraph Company

### References

Mandell, Lewis. *Credit Card Industry: A History.* New York: Macmillan, 1990.

Simmons, Matty. *The Credit Card Catastrophe: The 20th Century Phenomenon That Changed the World.* Fort Lee, NJ: Barricade, 1995.

# UNIVAC I (1951)

The UNIVAC I computer (Universal Automatic Computer I) was the first commercial computer produced in the United States and the world. At a cost of over $1.5 million, it was first delivered to the U.S. Census Bureau on March 31, 1951. The development of the computer required the vast financial resources only available through government help. The UNIVAC I was designed by J. Presper Eckert and John Mauchly, who had built an earlier computer known as ENIAC. Remington Rand built the UNIVAC. The cost limited it to government agencies that could afford the million-plus-dollar cost. The Census Bureau had paid for most of the development work. After the Census Bureau, the Air Force, Army, Navy, and Atomic Energy Commission purchased it. In 1954, General Electric, United States Steel, Westinghouse, Metropolitan Life, and DuPont became the first companies to purchase the UNIVAC. These companies used the UNIVAC I to do big number-crunching jobs such as payroll calculations and sales analysis. This meant that the first trained business users were from corporate accounting departments. The UNIVAC captured the public when CBS used it to predict the presidential election of Dwight Eisenhower in 1952, based on a population sample of only 1 percent.

The UNIVAC I used vacuum tubes as on/off switches (bits) to do electronic digital binary computing. It was a massive machine, 25 feet by 50 feet in size and weighing 29,000 pounds. Its family tree goes back to the earliest electronic digital computer, known as ABC and built in 1937 by John Atanasoff of Iowa State University. The ABC computer led to the development of the ENIAC (Electronic Numerical Integrator and Computer) in 1946. The ENIAC was financed by the U.S. Army to be used to calculate artillery-firing tables. The ENIAC was housed at the University of Pennsylvania and cost over half a million dollars. The designers were Eckert and Mauchly of the Electrical Engineering Department. The ENIAC had over 17,000 vacuum tubes, five or more of which burned out each day; they required 30 minutes to locate and replace and effectively limited the use of the ENIAC. Still, the ENIAC could calculate a trajectory in 30 minutes that it would take 12 hours for a human to calculate. The ENIAC was based on the program memory design of John von Neumann, who had been responsible for the British computer known as Colossus, which broke the German code in 1943. The release of the ENIAC started a long history of legal battles.

Eckert and Mauchly left the University of Pennsylvania in 1946 to form the Eckert-Mauchly Computer Corporation (EMCC). This company first built a computer known as BINAC (Binary Automatic Computer) for Northrop Aviation. The BINAC was a failure and hardly used. In 1949, EMCC was sold to the typewriter company Remington Rand. The UNIVAC came out in 1951, and by 1954, 20 of them had been built and sold. The UNIVAC used about 5,000 vacuum tubes with greatly improved tube life over the ENIAC. The UNIVAC was also the first "stored program" computer using magnetic tape rather than punched cards for memory and data storage. This stored program approach allowed it to greatly reduce the vacuum tubes needed in the ENIAC. The UNIVAC also was the first to have a magnetic tape memory, greatly expanding its application. The UNIVAC was in direct competition with IBM's electromechanical calculating machines that had been used by the Census Bureau in 1890. UNIVAC's first business application came in October 1954 when it was used to produce payroll checks for General Electric's Appliance Park employees. Not surprisingly, UNIVAC was being sold on its ability to reduce salaried clerks and overhead, but its high price tag limited it to only a handful of large companies.

IBM countered in 1952 with its own electronic computer, the IBM 701, based on von Neumann's work, who was hired as a consultant. IBM employed an improved vacuum tube, which made it four times faster than the UNIVAC. IBM sold its first 701 to the Los Alamos nuclear weapons laboratory in 1952. The battle between the IBM 701 and the UNIVAC was a short one, with IBM releasing model 702. IBM had a powerful marketing and business sales network in place, having been in the calculator business since 1890. Furthermore, IBM used a business model similar to that of Libbey Glass with the bottle-making machine. IBM rented their machines at $3,500 a month in 1955, which opened up a huge market. By 1956, IBM overtook the UNIVAC. With the rental business model, IBM looked away from government projects to the commercial business market. In 1954, IBM offered a new model for an expanded commercial market. The IBM 704 with its FORTRAN programming allowed it to be used for engineering calculations in addition to number-crunching business applications.

The UNIVAC computer is considered typical of the first generation of computer using vacuum tubes. The next generation of computers came in the 1960s with the application of transistors in place of vacuum tubes. Transistors greatly reduced the size of computers. More minimization came in the 1970s with the use of the integrated circuit or silicon chip. In 1973, electronic digital computer technology became public domain in the 1973 landmark court case *Honeywell v. Sperry*. This court case overturned the 1964 patent for the ENIAC, making the ABC computer of 1939 the valid patent and putting the technology in the public domain.

*See also:* IBM 360 Computer; Patent and Copyright Statutes; The Year of the PC

### References

Ceruzzi, Paul E. *A History of Modern Computing.* Cambridge, MA: MIT Press, 2003.

McCartney, Scott. *ENIAC: The Triumphs and Tragedies of the World's First Computer.* New York: Walker, 1999.

Stern, Nancy. *From ENIAC to UNIVAC: An Appraisal of the Echert-Mauchly Computers.* Bedford, MA: Digital Press, 1981.

# Shippingport Atomic Power Station (1956)

The Shippingport Atomic Power Station in western Pennsylvania would be the first full-scale nuclear electric power plant exclusively for peacetime uses. Its location was the Beaver Valley, about 25 miles from downtown Pittsburgh. Pittsburgh's Westinghouse Electric built the reactor. It was managed by Duquesne Light Company and went on the grid in August 1956. The power station was built in 32 months at a cost of $72.5 million. It was an experimental reactor known as a light water thermal breeder and was distinguished by its ability to transmute inexpensive thorium 232 to a fissile fuel, uranium 233. Shippingport had a modest capacity of 60,000 kilowatts. Its basic function was creating heat from nuclear fuel fission to generate steam to turn turbines, thus generating electricity. It was the first result of President Dwight Eisenhower's Atoms for Peace program. After 25 years of successful service, Shippingport became the first nuclear reactor to be successfully decommissioned (completed in 1985). Atoms for Peace was one of the successful government and business programs that founders Alexander Hamilton and Henry Clay had envisioned, and it ranks with the Erie Canal, National Road, Hoover Dam, and the 1960s space program.

The high cost involved in research and development and construction required an alliance of business and government. Duquesne Light teamed up with the new Atomic Energy Commission of the Eisenhower administration and committed $30 million to the project over five years. Duquesne Light's commitment came from its use of coal in the already smog-filled skies of the steel city of Pittsburgh, which often had the sun blotted out by smog in the afternoon. Smog and soot had plagued the area for over a century. Shippingport was a blend of efforts by the navy's Admiral Hyman Rickover, Duquesne Light Company, Westinghouse Electric, and the Bettis Atomic Power Laboratory under the political leadership of President Eisenhower. Such a government/corporate alliance would take strong leadership, and that strong project leadership is attributed to Admiral Rickover. The Atomic Energy Commission did supply 90 percent of the overall costs and assumed the legal liability for the project. Westinghouse Electric functioned as the general contractor for the construction. The project required government support because fossil fuels were abundant at the time.

Admiral Rickover would leave a distinctive mark on America's nuclear energy. He had been working with Westinghouse Electric since the early 1950s to develop nuclear submarines and aircraft carriers for the navy. Rickover had been behind the building of the Bettis Atomic Power Laboratory outside Pittsburgh in 1948. It was here that the Mark I submarine nuclear reactor was built at a cost of

$30 million. Rickover's success made him the logical candidate to head up the Atomic Energy Commission in 1953. Rickover approached Shippingport as an example of peaceful uses for atomic energy. He demanded reliability and safety throughout the design and construction phase. In addition, he required low-grade fuel versus enriched uranium in order to prevent diversion of nuclear fuel elements from use in nuclear weapons. The Shippingport plant was built specifically to advance the use of nuclear power, and it was to be a model for the future. Rickover's attention to the safety mission and his autocratic management style won over the public from their concerns about nuclear energy. Rickover continued the development of nuclear submarines using the same technology. As construction started at Shippingport in 1954, the USS *Nautilus*, the nation's first nuclear submarine, was launched. The design of the nation's first nuclear aircraft carrier, the USS *Enterprise*, was started in 1954 as well, and it launched in 1960. The navy's outstanding safety record in nuclear propulsion remains part of the Rickover legacy.

Positive publicity was a key goal of both Atoms for Peace and the construction of the Shippingport plant. On September 6, 1954, President Eisenhower waved a neutron wand in Denver, Colorado, to signal a bulldozer in Shippingport to start construction. Eisenhower's address was televised to workers and guests at the construction site. Shippingport functioned faultlessly up to 1964 when it was shut down to install a new core to expand the capacity to 100,000 kilowatts. In 1974,

Delivery of a nuclear reactor to the Shippingport, Pennsylvania, power station. (Library of Congress)

the plant was shut down for a mechanical problem in the turbine. The Department of Energy used the time to convert Shippingport to a light water breeder reactor. President Jimmy Carter dedicated the new reactor in 1977. Carter was a nuclear engineer and a graduate of the Navy's nuclear submarine program. The plant was decommissioned in 1982 after 25 years of very successful operation. General Electric was hired to be the general contractor to do the shutdown, deconstruction, and cleanup. Final deconstruction was completed in 1985 at a total cost of $98 million. The site was graded, seeded for grass, and turned over for unrestricted use.

Shippingport proved the economic feasibility of breeder technology. The breeder reactor concept was based on the scientific principle that the reactor using low-grade fuel could produce more nuclear fuel than it consumed. However, the cheap availability of enriched uranium allowed more conventional reactors to dominate the future market for nuclear power plants. The safety record of the plant was near perfect, thanks to redundant containment design, which assured no escape of radiation to the environment. The design used low-pressure steam to be created in a secondary exchange of heat, which isolated this secondary water from the radioactive inner system. In general, nuclear power gained wide acceptance, thanks to Shippingport, until the Three Mile Island accident in 1979 (ironically 80 miles east of the Pittsburgh area).

*See also:* America Targets the Moon; Erie Canal; Hoover Dam; National Road; Panama Canal Opens; "Report on Manufacturing"; Three Mile Island Nuclear Failure; Whig Party Evolves

## References

Beaver, William. *Nuclear Power Goes On-Line: A History of Shippingport.* Westport, CT: Greenwood, 1990.

Cravens, Gwyneth. *Power to Save the World: The Truth about Nuclear Energy.* New York: Knopf, 2007.

# Federal Aid Highway Act of 1956

The interstate highway system had long been envisioned as a way to improve America's commerce and defense, but it took the political will of President Dwight D. Eisenhower to get it built. The Federal Aid Highway Act of 1956 (popularly known as the National Interstate and Defense Highways Act) would supply the federal funds for over 42,000 miles of highway. The act appropriated $25 billion over 12 years for the entire system. It would actually cost $114 billion over 35 years. The money for the system came from an established Highway Trust Fund to be paid for by taxes on gasoline and diesel fuel. The federal government paid for 90 percent of the system with the balance being paid for by the states. The system made profound changes in American business and life, such as the increase in long-distance truck hauling (which overtook the railroads), the growth of suburbs, the rise of mega-vacation sites, and new business ideas such as motels, station wagons, fast food, and campgrounds.

The history of an interstate system is traceable to the first National Road (Route 40) in the late 1700s. For the most part, roads remained a local responsibility until the mass production of the automobile created a new demand for paved roads for travel. The first national effort came with the Federal Aid Highway Act of 1916, which appropriated $50 million to improve rural roads for mail delivery. The 1916 act was a form of federalism that required a 50–50 split in the funding of roads between the federal and state governments. The federal government established the Bureau of Public Roads, giving it design approval and inspection authority over the states through the 1916 act. The act allowed for funding appropriations to be given to the Bureau of Public Roads. By 1923, funding had reached $75 million a year and covered nearly 10 percent of U.S. roads. Major expansions included U.S. Route 1 and U.S. Route 2, which followed the Canadian border in New England. Still, the road network lacked a vision, overall planning, and focused funding until President Eisenhower addressed the need in 1956 and championed a true interstate system.

Lieutenant Colonel Dwight Eisenhower had been a participant in the army's Transcontinental Motor Convoy to assess the nation's roads in 1919. The trip took over 60 days with one chapter of the report by Eisenhower titled "Through Darkest America with Truck and Tank." In the 1930s, President Franklin D. Roosevelt looked at highway construction as part of his New Deal, but the lack of planning never allowed a national system to evolve into a funded program. In 1944, Congress passed the Federal Highway Act of 1944, which only maintained the status quo. During World War II, General Eisenhower gained respect for Hitler's German autobahn as a national defense tool. In 1952, General Motors was pushing for an interstate system to support the growth of the auto industry. President Eisenhower selected Charles Wilson, president of General Motors, as his secretary of defense. The Eisenhower administration moved the interstate to a national priority for Congress.

Eisenhower established a committee in 1954 to develop a grand plan that could be sent to Congress. The plan would be defeated a number of times before passing in 1956. Opposition centered on funding, overall costs, the gas tax, and local and state resistance to superhighways. Even after the bill passed, local opposition from affected neighborhoods and early environmentalists continued opposition into the 1960s. Funding was to be through the gasoline tax. The plan was to develop a federal highway over a 20-year period; the time period would later be extended. The plan called for a series of east-west routes (even numbered) and north-south routes (odd numbered) to be developed. The system would incorporate toll roads such as the Pennsylvania Turnpike. The design addressed national defense needs like the linking of seaports, railroad centers, and airports across the nation.

While construction started in 1956, a lot of issues remained unresolved. The American Association of State Highways and Transportation Officials (AASHTO) and the Federal Highway Administration were formed to hammer out standards and regulations. Once standards were set, new interstate highways required the approval of the Federal Highway Administration. The Federal Highway Administration and the AASHTO set not only construction standards but also limits for truckloads and speeds. The first new construction was on U.S. 40 (I-70) in Kansas.

The interstate highway system would have an impact on American culture and business that rivaled that of the railroads. One result of the interstate system was a reduction of 20 to 30 percent in the travel time between cities. The population moved to the suburbs, starting the decline of city business districts. Shopping malls moved further out to serve the suburban population. Reduced times and better roads were boons to the trucking industry. New related industries such as motels and fast-service restaurants to serve long-distance travelers emerged. Truck stops grew quickly with the increase in long-distance trucking. Oil companies moved into the truck stop business and other services. Vacation destinations in Florida, California, and New York boomed with the increase in vacationers and visitors.

*See also:* Baltimore & Ohio Railroad; National Road; Overland Travel and Mail Service; Transcontinental Railroad Completed; Whig Party Evolves

### References

Lewis, Thomas. *Divided Highways: Building the Interstate Highways, Transforming American Life.* New York: Penguin, 1999.

McNichol, Dan. *The Roads That Built America: The Incredible Story of the U.S. Interstate System.* New York: Sterling, 2006.

# First Mass-Produced Transistor Radio (1957)

For the engineer, December 23, 1947, is immortalized as the day of the invention of the transistor. Others may point to 1954 and the release of the Regency TR-1 transistor radio, but for the businessperson, it was the breakthrough Japanese transistor radio in 1957 that had the greatest impact on American business. The Sony TR-63 would be the first "pocket-sized" portable radio. For a few years American manufacturers dominated the transistor radio market, since it was Bell Laboratories that gave us the transistor. The transistor radio, however, proved a perfect combination for Japanese manufacturers. The Japanese Ministry of International Trade and Industry had been searching for new industries to develop in Japan after the war. The ministry helped finance a $25,000 licensing agreement for Tokyo Telecommunications, which grew from seven employees to become Sony Corporation (originally Tokyo Tsushin Kogyo) with over 500 employees. Sony used its advantage in low labor costs to release the smaller, lower-priced TR-63 transistor radio to the American market.

The 1906 development of the vacuum tube had moved electronics a huge step forward, but the vacuum tube's size and reliability limited its product application. After World War II, America's largest industrial laboratory, American Telephone and Telegraph's Bell Laboratories, started a research project to develop a better electronic switch and amplifier for the telephone. The method was the goal-oriented research and development of Thomas Edison. It was an extension of earlier research on semiconductors. A research team was assigned under Bill Shockley to develop a semiconductor switch. In 1947, the transistor came into being. The transistor team of Bill Shockley, John Bardeen, and Walter Brittian would win the 1956 Nobel Prize for their work. In 1954, Texas Instruments developed the first silicon transistor as companies around the world were now looking at product development. Texas Instruments was producing transistors for military applications but started to look for more profitable commercial applications. A year earlier, Masaru Ibuka, cofounder of Sony, traveled to the United States to study transistors and was able to purchase a license to produce them. Ibuka started a commercial product development team back in Japan with his partner, physicist Akio Morita. Japan would emulate this strategy of buying or copying basic research to invest in product development in many industries.

Texas Instruments teamed up with Industrial Development Engineering Associates and Regency Electronics to manufacture the Regency TR-1, the first transistor radio, in 1954. The TR-1 was designed to be as small as possible, based on a market analysis of a 20 million-unit market. The TR-1 struggled with quality problems and a price tag of $49.95 (over $360 in today's dollars). Sales did reach 100,000 a year. Raytheon's 8-TP-1 and Sony's TR-55 entered the market in 1955. The Raytheon radio had better quality and reliability but was larger and carried an $80.00 price tag. Sony's had the lowest price at $39.99 and was the smallest; still, the sales were around 100,000. The size was not considered pocket-size yet. The Sony effort was a total failure, but as was typical of the Japanese product development model, they learned from their mistakes and introduced a new product quickly. The Sony TR-55 also lacked advertising because Sony was still a small company with limited capital. Sony advertised the product only in trade magazines. Sony looked to miniaturize its product and advertise more.

In 1957, they introduced the TR-63 to the American market. The TR-63 cracked the transistor radio market wide open. Its size was roughly 4.5 by 3 by 2.5 inches. It utilized a nine-volt battery to reduce the size. The company quickly got the price down to under $25, which opened up more market. By 1962, the price was $15. Sony advertised the radio as pocket-size, although it was a very uncomfortable fit. Sony also hired an advertising agency, and a cartoon character "Atchan" was created to advertise the radio. Market success and low Japanese labor costs quickly brought competitors such as Toshiba and Sharp into the business. It would be the transistor that would be the root of these electronic giants of today.

Many cultural forces combined to make the transistor radio a major commercial success. These included the huge youthful population segment (baby boomers), high disposable income after World War II, and the growing popularity of rock 'n' roll music. In addition, the Japanese learned marketing. They started to produce colorful and novel plastic cases to attract the youthful market. They also produced radios with corporate logos for the business promotional market. In many ways, the transistor radio business taught the Japanese how to be successful with products in the United States. The Japanese applied this simple business model to overtake market after market in the United States. By the late 1960s, production had left Japan for Hong Kong because of lower labor costs there. Today, China is the major producer of transistor radios, although American Zenith did hold on to the upper end of the market for years. The transistor radio success inspired the Japanese to move into the American market with other products, including cars. The transistor radio today remains the most popular communications device in history, with estimates that seven billion were produced.

*See also:* First Japanese Auto Sold in the United States; Talking Movies—*The Jazz Singer*; UNIVAC I

### References

Morita, Akio, and Sony Corporation. *Made in Japan.* New York: HarperCollins, 1994.

Nathan, John. *Sony: The Private Life.* New York: Houghton Mifflin, 1999.

Schiffer, Michael Brian. *The Portable Radio in American Life.* Tucson: University of Arizona Press, 1991.

# First Japanese Auto Sold in the United States (1958)

The story of the rise of Japanese imports and Toyota in America really is one of America's entrance into the global economy. The first sale of the Toyota Toyopet in

1958 hardly started a flood of imports; in fact, the Toyopet proved unsuccessful in the American market. The real point was the determination of Toyota to become an international manufacturer. The Toyopet was sold at America's first Toyota dealer in San Francisco, up the coast from its newly opened headquarters in Hollywood. A small but growing import market arose in postwar America with the entrance of the Volkswagen Beetle, which started in 1949. While the sale of a Toyota was hardly noticed by the American press, it was a huge corporate event for Toyota. It was a strategic project, not a tactical move, to sell a few more cars and expand Japanese manufacturing. America, which had invested heavily in the rebuilding of Japan, hailed the Japanese imports as a triumph of capitalism.

Toyota proved more flexible than American manufacturers. The Toyopet had a top speed of merely 55 miles per hour and a small 27-horsepower engine. When the Toyopet bombed in the United States, Toyota took it off the market to have it redesigned. Toyota was considered a joke in America and was producing only 60,000 cars a year in Japan. Still, the company had set its vision on being an international company, opening a manufacturing plant in 1959 in Brazil after redesigning for the Brazilian market. The idea of testing, redesigning for a specific model, and eventually localizing production became its business model as a global company.

Toyota and the Japanese automakers have roots going back to the early 1930s with a government push for national industrialization. In 1936, the Japanese government passed the Automobile Manufacturing Industries Act with the express purpose of breaking the American car monopoly. Toyota and Datsun took the lead in this effort. World War II caused Japanese automakers to focus on truck production. After the war, Toyota was given permission by the United States to resume auto production. The depressed domestic market and limited manufacturing capacity required a far different approach to manufacturing than that used in the United States. The very weakness of their auto industry would, in the long run, become the basis of its strength today. The total monthly production of Toyota was around 10,000 units, or roughly a day's production by one American auto plant. In addition, Toyota had to produce all kinds of products such as trucks, car, taxis, and fire engines. The market and limited capacity resulted in a much more flexible approach to manufacturing, which can be seen today in lean manufacturing. While American assembly lines focused on economies of scale from volume, Japanese assembly lines focused on product flexibility, rapid tooling change, efficiency, and continuous cost-cutting. The company maintained an aggressive vision of becoming an international manufacturer even in these early days. In the late 1940s, Toyota sent engineers and managers to study Ford Motor Company. Company owner Toyota Toyoda visited Henry Ford and his River Rouge plant personally.

First shipment of Toyota Toyopets at the port of San Francisco in 1958. (AP Photo/American President Line Photo)

In the late 1950s, the small size of Toyota's and Nissan's cars offered little threat to the big luxury market of the United States. The failure of the Toyopet model inspired the development of the Toyota Corona for the American market in 1964. The Corona was a six-passenger car with a lower price tag, higher quality, and better gas mileage than the sedans of the Big Three. In 1965, Toyota Corona sales hit 6,400 vehicles, but by 1967, sales reached 71,000 vehicles and continued to double every year to 1971. With a growing reputation for quality, Toyota introduced the Crown, a semiluxury car. In 1969, Toyota imported the Corolla, which would become the best import seller and America's favorite small car. By 1973, Toyota had hurt Volkswagen more than it had the Big Three. The Big Three still considered the Japanese cars a niche market, albeit a growing one. One overlooked factor was the improving Japanese quality and declining American quality, which was having an impact with young, upscale buyers. The major advantage of good gas mileage meant less in times of cheap oil prices.

The big breakthrough for the small car-market dominant Japanese auto producers came when America got a taste of the oil crisis in 1973. The Organization of

Petroleum Exporting Countries (OPEC) in 1973 punished the United States for its support of Israel in the Yom Kippur War. The cost of oil increased 70 percent, and the Arabs imposed an oil embargo. American motorists were forced into long lines and feared not being able to get to work as gasoline supplies tightened. The crisis caused a major market shift to small cars that would remain, to some degree, after the embargo ended. American manufacturers started to switch to smaller cars, but quality issues hurt them in this segment of the import market. The market shift brought more Japanese auto products into the market such as Honda. The Japanese had lower labor costs, government support, and good products. Honda took on the rising calls for protectionism by building a manufacturing plant in Marysville, Ohio, in 1981. Toyota followed in a joint manufacturing venture with General Motors known as NUMMI (New United Motor Manufacturing) in Fremont, California.

American manufacturers looked to the government for trade relief, but the commitment to and U.S. leadership in the General Agreement on Tariffs and Trade restricted any political help. In the 1980s, continued American quality problems, poor gas mileage, and price problems opened up the luxury segment of the American market for imports. The Japanese used their manufacturing and efficiency advantages to move into the luxury and truck markets. The booming sales, in general, generated cash for the Japanese to automate factories as well. Toyota moved into the luxury market with its Lexus brand in 1989. Honda followed with the Acura in 1991. Today, Toyota's lean manufacturing has replaced the earlier assembly line of Ford.

*See also:* General Agreement on Tariffs and Trade (GATT); Highland Park Ford Assembly Line; General Motors Corporation Formed; General Motors Bankruptcy; Jefferson Embargo; McKinley Tariff of 1890; *Wealth of Nations*

### References

Liker, Jeffery. *The Toyota Way.* New York: McGraw-Hill, 2003.

Liker, Jeffery, Michael Hoseus, and Center for Quality, People, and Organization. *Toyota Culture: The Heart and Soul of the Toyota Way.* New York: McGraw-Hill, 2008.

# Steel Strike of 1959

The Steel Strike of 1959 was the nation's longest, at 116 days. The steel industry at the time was the nation's largest industry with 540,000 United Steelworkers of America (USWA). The root of the strike would be over management control and contract clauses in the workplace. In particular, management maintained the right to assign the number of workers to a task, reduce the workforce with machinery, and introduce new work rules. It became a bitter battle in a nation totally dependent on domestic sources for steel. The strike ended with President Dwight D. Eisenhower invoking the 1947 Taft-Hartley Act. The union challenged the Taft-Hartley Act, but the Supreme Court upheld it. The union eventually retained contract clauses on work rules and won a small wage increase. In retrospect, the strike was a disaster for the union, management, and government. The strike led to significant steel imports into the nation, which would devastate domestic production.

The steel industry had been unionized in the 1930s and continued to make major gains through the 1940s. The passage of the Taft-Hartley Act in 1947, which amended the Wagner Act, slowed the progressive government support of unions. The Taft-Hartley Act had outlawed closed shops but permitted union shops, which required union membership after a period of time. The Taft-Hartley Act did allow states to pass right-to-work laws. It also allowed the president to intervene in strikes that posed a national emergency. The Taft-Hartley Act had been hard fought, with President Harry Truman vetoing it and the Congress overriding the veto. The big test of the Taft-Hartley Act would be the 1959 steel strike.

The United Steelworkers focused on negotiations to expand benefits, pensions, and unemployment protection. They were successful at including clauses in contracts to protect jobs and hours worked. The Taft-Hartley Act had started to slow union gains through the 1950s. The war had shown the strong need for domestic steel, and the government invested millions to expand production. The government even built a $200 million steel mill in Utah, which United States Steel purchased from them in 1947. The steel industry never got a rest as the Korean War created even more demand. American steel was at the peak of its power, but its very strength became a weakness. At its 1940s peak, the American steel industry made over 60 percent of the world's steel. The steel industry overexpanded in the 1950s. Imports into the United States were less than 3 percent of the domestic market. After the 1959 strike, U.S. steel production was 26 percent of the total world market (the lowest since the 1870s). Steel prosperity in the early 1950s resulted in favorable contracts to the steel unions. In 1956, the United Steelworkers had won large wage increases of 4 to 6 percent per year. In 1957, American steelworkers were earning $2.92 an hour compared to $0.75 an hour in Germany and $0.45 an hour in Japan. The industry approached 1959 with overcapacity, high costs, and imports starting to come into the market.

Still, the first-quarter profits for the industry were at a near record of $375 million with an 11.7 percent return on stockholder's investment. This was partly a result of a huge inventory buildup in steel-dependent industries fearing a strike. The underlying problems were masked by profits reflecting the end of a boom. The government was anxious about the 1959 steel negotiations because inflation was rising, and the steel settlement would lead other big industries in wage increases. The 6 percent wage increase in 1956 had created major increases in the prices of manufactured goods overall. In 1956, the union also unionized 40,000 white-collar workers in the steel industry. Steel management felt the time was right in 1959 to take a stand over years of wage increases. The huge inventory buildup forced the management to take a strike or suffer a major downturn. As the deadline approached, the Eisenhower administration was active in the negotiations, and cabinet members were able to broker an extension with union chief David McDonald. The strike, however, started on July 15, 1959, as negotiations broke down. The strike was national against all American steel producers.

The strike would drag on for 116 days, bringing most American industry to a halt. Over 150,000 autoworkers and another 150,000 in the railroad industry were laid off. Europe and Japan rebuilt steel mills, and imported steel surged into the United States. Even worse, the American steel industry had foreign steel pouring in at greatly reduced prices, so if the union got a wage increase and prices went up, a large segment of the market was gone. As the strike reached the critical stage, President Eisenhower invoked the Taft-Hartley Act to bring the workers back for 80 days of negotiations for the government to broker a deal. Eisenhower sent Vice-President Richard Nixon to get directly involved. The government was successful but at a high cost. The total package was worth about $0.40 an hour and boosted steel prices by $16 a ton. Imports remained at double the 1959 level. Two years later, in 1961, American steel started a long slide, losing market share to lower-priced imported steel.

In 1962, inflation and the effects of the 1959 strikes caused more price increases, which the government used public pressure to prevent. Now, inflation and wages had combined with lost market share to reduce industry profitability. In the 1980s, the seeds of the 1959 strike brought the end of the American steel industry. In 1982, there were days when the great Monongahela River steel valley produced no steel (the first time that had happened since 1840). This was a far cry from 1944 when the Monongahela Valley steel mills outproduced the mills of Germany, Japan, and Italy combined.

*See also:* Andrew Carnegie's First Steel Mill; Great Steel Strike of 1919; Homestead Strike of 1892; National Labor Relations Act (Wagner Act)

## References

Apelt, Brian. *The Corporation: A Centennial Biography of United States Steel Corporation.* Pittsburgh, PA: University of Pittsburgh Press, 2000.

Millis, Harry, and Emily Brown Clark. *From the Wagner Act to Taft-Hartley: A Study of National Labor Policy and Labor Relations.* Chicago: University of Chicago Press, 1950.

# America Targets the Moon (1961)

The American space program is one of the best models of cooperation between business, industry, and government. The program impacted all phases of American business. On October 4, 1957, the Russian satellite Sputnik rocked the United States. Sputnik galvanized and strengthened America's resolve to compete with the Soviet Union in a space race. The nation's fears and security became channeled in the Cold War space race, which united the nation's resources. In 1958, the government created the National Aeronautics and Space Administration (NASA) and launched its first satellite. The real race began in 1961. With America continuing to fall further behind, President John F. Kennedy announced America's goal to reach the moon. Outside of war, rarely has a nation been so set on a national goal as America in the space race. The space race would increase business and commerce for every tax dollar spent. The manned space program was the largest-ever government investment, surpassing the Panama Canal, but unlike the canal, commercial value was measured in spin-offs versus the end goal. The commercial spin-offs included solar batteries, new materials, computer advances, improved communications, new robotics, and weapons systems. The program made major advances in manufacturing design and management approaches to product improvements. NASA's organizational infrastructure of process and project management proved highly successful to coordinate private (schools and industry) and military enterprises.

Most would agree that the space program had deep roots in Nazi Germany and its V-2 missile that terrorized London in World War II. The American army had brought V-2s and the lead German rocket scientist, Werner von Braun, back to the United States. The launch of Sputnik moved the United States to create the National Advisory Committee for Aeronautics, which quickly evolved into NASA in 1958. On July 29, 1958, President Eisenhower signed the National Aeronautics and Space Act with an annual budget of $100 million and 8,000 employees. The Army Ballistic Missile Agency headed by von Braun and his team of German engineers was absorbed into NASA. The United States was able to counter the Russians with its first artificial satellite, Explorer, on January 31, 1958. NASA was designed as a civilian organization, while the military continued the arms race with nuclear ballistic missiles. NASA proved the ideal mix of government overview and regulation for a massive national industrial project. The teamwork of private industry and democratic government proved superior to the government/military-controlled project management of the Soviet Union.

The next shock to the Americans came with the launch of Russian Yuri Gagarin into space on April 12, 1961. Gagarin orbited the earth for 108 minutes. A few weeks

Buzz Aldrin on the moon, July 20, 1969. (National Aeronautics and Space Administration)

later America launched Alan Shepard for a brief 15-minute shot into space. Still, to the public, America seemed to be behind the Russians, and that was a threat to national defense. President Kennedy realized this and called for a national program on a scale never seen before. On May 25, 1961, Kennedy set the national goal of a man reaching the moon by 1970. The only previous national program on such a scale was the Panama Canal. Within three years, Kennedy increased the budget to $10 billion a year. It was a huge industrial project employing over 35,000 NASA employees and another 500,000 employees as contractors. Subcontracting rippled through the nation's industry with almost all cities and towns having a factory involved. Almost any factory could claim some part of the national project, as subcontracting was extensive. Universities were awarded large research grants to solve engineering and scientific problems. One early result was the American use of solar power for satellites versus the old battery technology of the Russians.

A related program in 1958 was the Advanced Research Projects Agency (ARPA), which was created to develop space technology for military applications. ARPA would lead to revolutionary breakthroughs in communications and computer technology. The new focus on engineering and science strengthened American universities. Science toys became popular throughout the 1950s and 1960s. Space would dominate the national scene through the 1980s. The NASA program initially focused on a step-by-step effort to put a man on the moon. The simplified mission statement was the powerful statement "everything we do is to get there." The program included manned vehicle development and satellites. The mission was accomplished on July 20, 1969, with the moon landing of astronauts Neil Armstrong and Edwin Aldrin. The space program found renewal in the 1980s with the space shuttle, but support declined as the Cold War moved toward an end.

NASA estimates that for every dollar spent in the space program, the country receives seven dollars in increased jobs and income. There is no question that the space program has proven to be the best economic stimulus for American business. Spin-offs became a new business-government model. The space program's impact went far beyond directly measured benefits. There was an inspirational factor not seen in projects like the Panama Canal and the Hoover Dam. In the 1960s, under von Braun, NASA launched a publicity relations program that advanced science and engineering education across the nation. This campaign built a national interest in science that paid huge dividends in the 1960s, 1970s, and 1980s. Some of the scientific developments of NASA such as fuel cells had yet to realize full commercialization, but the future still holds many benefits from the space program. NASA contributed much to the field of engineering and business in its approach to commercial design. One approach is that of failure mode effect analysis (FMEA), which studies potential product failure modes to improve design and has been a standard approach in manufacturing. It could be argued that the program had entered a period of diminishing returns after the 1960s, 1970s, and 1980s. There is a strong argument today that the space program should be turned over to the private sector because there is a growing business in satellite communications that is attracting the private sector.

*See also:* ARPAnet (Earliest Internet) Formed; Erie Canal; Federal Aid Highway Act of 1956; Hoover Dam; National Road; Panama Canal Opens

### References

Bromberg, Joan Lisa. *NASA and Space Industry.* Baltimore, MD: Johns Hopkins University Press, 2000.

Kranz, Gene. *Failure Is Not an Option: Mission Control from Mercury to Apollo 13 and Beyond.* New York: Simon & Schuster, 2009.

Pellerin, Charles. *How NASA Builds Teams: Mission Critical Soft Skills for Scientists, Engineers and Project Teams.* New York: Wiley, 2009.

# McDonald's Launches Golden Arches (1962)

McDonald's has a long history going back to 1940 in San Bernardino, California, but it was in 1962 that it launched its world-famous Golden Arches logo, which made the company an American icon. In the preceding year Ray Kroc had bought out the

McDonald brothers for $2.7 million with the specific vision of making it the number-one fast-food chain. Kroc showed American business how to incorporate an operating concept into an international business. McDonald's developed a franchise business model that would be the standard for American business. Kroc's growth was historical. By 1965, McDonald's went public at $22 a share. In 1985, McDonald's became part of the Dow Jones Industrial Average. Besides business models for franchising and standardized operations, McDonald's developed the concept of corporate culture with its Hamburger University in 1961.

McDonald's is an amazing story of the development and evolution of a new business model. The history of McDonald's goes back to 1937 when patriarch Patrick McDonald opened the Airdrome restaurant in 1937 at Monrovia, California. The Airdrome restaurant was a carhop operation. It was based on 10¢ hamburgers and all-you-can-drink orange drink for 5¢. Patrick's sons, Maurice and Richard, came into the business in the 1940s. The brothers quickly realized the importance of speed in such an operation. In 1948, they eliminated the carhops and moved to a business model they called the "speedee service system." This was a self-service system specializing in a limited menu of hamburgers, cheeseburgers, French fries, shakes, soft drinks, and apples. They redesigned the kitchen to assure speed in order preparation. They probably borrowed from the first pioneer of fast food, Walter Anderson of White Castle, in the 1920s. White Castle focused on hamburger-cooking speed and supply costs, forcing customers to add their own condiments. McDonald's added more variety and kitchen organization to its operation. Both McDonald's and White Castle were franchising their systems in the 1950s (White Castle was franchising in the late 1930s). The McDonald brothers were starting to offer franchises in the late 1940s but lacked the necessary sales and marketing skills. Another weakness of the McDonald's at the time was an aversion to advertising, which White Castle had mastered.

Things changed in 1952 when Kroc, a milkshake-mixer salesman and marketer, entered the employ of the McDonald brothers. Kroc had the best knowledge of the then infant fast-food industry and offered to franchise their system and introduce a marketing program. It was a loose business arrangement for Kroc, but he was able to franchise the first McDonald's restaurant at Des Plains, Illinois, in 1955. Kroc's marketing quickly took the number of restaurants to over 100 in 1959. The demographics of suburban growth helped fuel the McDonald's franchise. Kroc and the McDonald brothers grew further apart, and in 1961, Kroc bought out the chain for $2.7 million. After the sale, the brothers briefly went into competition with Kroc, but Kroc drove them out of business. He retained the operating system but now added a powerful marketing campaign. Kroc's business model stated that marketing and operations had to be coordinated to support each other. This marketing and operations coordination would always distinguish McDonald's from the competition.

Kroc also varied from the McDonald brothers' model of a limited menu, but cautiously. Kroc used test locations to add a Lenten season special of the Filet-O-Fish, which was successful, but his meatless "hulaburger" was a failure. A Pittsburgh franchise successfully developed and marketed the Big Mac in 1968. Kroc aggressively used billboard advertising to spur local sales. He targeted families with his Ronald McDonald advertising campaign in 1963. Kroc also reinforced cleanliness standards at his franchises to support the family image. By 1964, McDonald's had sold over a billion hamburgers. In 1969, McDonald's was in all 50 states with over 1,000 restaurants, allowing Kroc to launch a national advertising campaign. The campaign is in the Smithsonian Institute today and is known as "You Deserve a Break Today." It was a national jingle written by Barry Manilow that took the nation.

The company built on its basic business model to fuel its growth in the 1970s. McDonald's cautiously introduced new products such as the Quarter Pounder, Happy Meals, and fast breakfast items that did not compromise its speed-based system. In 1972, McDonald's pioneered the fast-food breakfast with the introduction of the Egg McMuffin. McDonald's opened its first drive-through in 1975 with the goal of service in 50 seconds or less. To build on its family image, McDonald's started its Ronald McDonald Houses in 1974 for families with children in nearby hospitals. McDonald's started to move into Canada, Asia, and Europe. By 1976, sales surpassed $3 billion, and the company paid its first dividend, making it a mature growth company.

McDonald's success brought in new competition to the fast-food industry such as Burger King and Wendy's. Burger King tried to take market share by adding variety with their "have it your way" campaign. McDonald's proved flexible while maintaining the roots of its "speedee" system while countering Burger King's strong advertising. McDonald's added more products such as Chicken McNuggets and health-conscious foods such as salads and lean burgers. In addition, McDonald's built on their advertising and marketing strengths to win the "burger wars" of the 1980s. As the burger market matured in the 1990s, McDonald's marketing programs moved to promotional giveaways such as movie-related toys. McDonald's countered its slow growth in America by moving into new markets such as Russia and China. The phenomenal growth would end in 2002 as McDonald's reported its first quarterly loss. McDonald's is today reinventing itself around its core competencies of fast service, healthy fast food, kids, and quality.

*See also:* Chicago World's Fair; First Electric Sign (Product Branding and Advertising)—H. J. Heinz; Upton Sinclair's *Jungle*

### References

Facella, Paul. *Everything I Know about Business I Learned at McDonald's: The 7 Leadership Principles That Drive and Break Success.* New York: McGraw-Hill, 2008.

Kroc, Ray. *Grinding It Out: Making of McDonald's.* New York: St. Martin's, 1992.

Love, John F. *McDonald's: Behind the Arches.* New York: Bantam Books, 1995.

# Telstar Communications Satellites (1962)

While the manned space program took the headlines and America's imagination, the communications satellite program was quietly revolutionizing business. Telstar, not *Apollo 11*, would impact business in a direct and major way in the 1960s. Satellite communications from the very beginning was commercial technology and a joint venture of private industry and government. On July 10, 1962, Telstar I was launched and relayed television pictures and telephone calls through space. Telstar was unique because it was a privately sponsored space launch. Telstar represented a working alliance between American Telephone and Telegraph (AT&T), Bell Telephone, the National Aeronautics and Space Administration (NASA), the British Post Office, and the French Post Office. Telstar was new technology in that it was an "active" or "repeater" satellite that amplified the signal using solar cells to power it. Government and military satellites as well as those of the Russians focused on reflecting surfaces, but in the 1950s, AT&T had started repeater technology because of the huge potential payback in television and telephone transmissions. Telstar I could handle 1,000 simultaneous telephone calls compared to 36 simultaneous calls via the transatlantic cable. Telstar technology would be the start of today's massive space communications system.

When AT&T petitioned the Federal Communications Commission for permission to launch a communications satellite in 1960, the Kennedy administration opposed it. The reasoning was that it would create a space communications monopoly. The launch was allowed, but NASA issued contracts to other companies such as Radio Corporation of America (RCA) and Hughes Aircraft. To assure that AT&T would not withhold key technology, the Kennedy administration created the Communications Satellite Corporation (COMSTAT) with ownership shared by the government and private companies—AT&T, RCA, Western Union, and International Telephone and Telegraph (ITT). This was covered in the 1962 Communications Satellite Act. The arrangement diffused the AT&T technology among all the telecommunications companies. This government/business model would be expanded to an international approach through the International Telecommunications Satellite Corporation (INTELSAT). The origin of satellite communications, however, came from the private sector.

The idea for a communications satellite was born in 1954 at AT&T's Bell Laboratories. John R. Pierce of Bell Laboratories predicted that a communications space network could be worth a billion dollars, which launched the project. The design plan was to be a satellite able to relay and amplify signals. This AT&T team invented the tube transponder to relay and amplify signals and developed solar panels to power the satellite. The transponder was used to relay sent data (originally a television channel) back to earth. Bell Laboratories had invented the silicon solar cell in 1954 and had successfully tested it in the Navy satellite, Vanguard I, in 1958. Solar power gave the United States an important edge over Soviet battery-powered communications satellites that lasted short periods. Telstar offered a major improvement over passive or reflective satellites such as Echo I, launched in 1960.

The satellite was ready by 1960 when AT&T petitioned the government for a space launch. Telstar was a 170-pound 34.5-inch sphere designed to fit NASA's Delta rockets. Its 14-watt power system required large ground antenna stations to be built as part of the system. These antennas were 177 feet long and were housed in huge 14-story structures. Each country in the alliance would be responsible for building ground stations. Bell Laboratories built its station at Andover, Maine. England and France also built ground stations to receive signals. Telstar was a non-geosynchronous orbiting satellite, which limited its availability for transatlantic signals to 20 minutes in each 180 minute orbit.

The Telstar I was launched from Cape Canaveral on July 10, 1962. The first television pictures were broadcast on July 11, and a public broadcast was featured on CBS, ABC, and NBC. They had hoped to broadcast a speech by President Kennedy, but as for many of the early satellite broadcasts to follow, the timing was

Artist's rendering of the 1962 Telstar satellite. (National Aeronautics and Space Administration/ Glenn Research Center)

not synchronized with the start of the speech. The first long broadcast was the 1964 Tokyo Olympics, which was covered by all the communications including the newly launched Telstar II. Telstar suffered from radiation blackouts from the Van Allen belt (from nuclear bomb tests), which augured future problems with space radiation. By October 1963, radiation had burned out its fragile new transistors.

Despite some radiation-related setbacks, Telstar was off to a successful start. Telstar became an integral part of culture when a 1962 instrumental song named "Telstar" rose to the top of the charts. In 1965, the first commercial geosynchronous satellite (Intelsat) was launched, allowing for long uninterrupted broadcasts. The costs for transatlantic telephone calls were cut by one-tenth by the mid-1960s by using geosynchronous satellites instead of transatlantic cable transmissions. Fiber-optic cable in the 1980s would once again lower the cable transmission cost below that of satellites,

As part of the COMSTAT agreement, by 1964 there were two Telstar satellites (AT&T), two Relay satellites (RCA), and two Syncom satellites (Hughes Aircraft). Satellite technology improved rapidly as NASA developed bigger missiles capable of launching large satellites. Improved solar panels and geosynchronous orbits improved transmissions. Lower-orbit satellites now avoid the problems of the Van Allen radiation belt. These low-earth-orbit satellites (LEOs) are key to cell phone transmission. Bigger, more powerful satellites reduced the large cost of big antenna ground stations. Satellite communications is a multibillion-dollar industry today. Each year 10–20 communications satellites are launched at a cost of $75 million each. AT&T and Hughes Corporation are still in the business, and the government remains in the business as well.

*See also:* America Targets the Moon; First Commercial Telephone; Transatlantic Cable; Western Union Telegraph Company

### References

Gavaghan, Helen. *Something New under the Sun: Satellites and the Beginning of the Space Age.* New York: Springer, 1997.

Labrador, Virgil. *Heavens Fill with Commerce—A Brief History of the Satellite Communications Industry.* Sonoma, CA: Satnews, 2005.

Whalen, David J. *The Origins of Satellite Communications, 1945–1965.* Washington, DC: Smithsonian Institution Press, 2002.

# First Wal-Mart (and Kmart) Open (1962)

The year 1962 in retrospect would become the foundation of modern retailing with the opening of the first Wal-Mart, Kmart, and Target stores. The roots were in a much older American iconic business model, that of the five-and-ten stores. Kmart had evolved out of S. S. Kresge Corporation, founded in 1897 as a five-and-ten store chain. American demographics had many moving away from the cities. S. S. Kresge moved with them to the suburbs in stand-alone stores or in malls. S. S. Kresge was facing sales declines at its urban five-and-ten stores and looked to reinvent itself. The first Kmart opened in March 1962 in Garden City, Michigan, followed by the first Wal-Mart in Rogers, Arkansas. Kmart got off to a very fast start by opening 18 stores in the first year, pioneering the discount store nationally. The core con-cept of discount stores was to offer discounted products to consumers by cutting margins and costs by volume selling. Wal-Mart maintained a strategy and goal of low cost throughout its history. The business model would evolve to include sub-urban locations, mass advertising, volume purchasing, and sales promotions. By the 1990s, Wal-Mart overtook Kmart to become a world leader in retailing and America's largest employer. Interestingly, in 1962, Dayton Corporation, a depart-ment store chain, saw a future in having some discount stores and opened Target in Minnesota.

The business model of Wal-Mart has, at its core, the business beliefs of its founder, Sam Walton. Walton earned a degree in economics from the University of Missouri in 1940. His first retailing experience was with J.C. Penney in Iowa. From J.C. Penney he learned the importance of employees and managers to the success of retailing. After World War II, Walton returned to open his first store on bor-rowed money. Walton's store was a Ben Franklin franchise, but he called it the Walton 5 & 10. Walton and his brother owned 16 of these variety stores by 1962. The stores were located in Arkansas and surrounding states. Walton also focused on stand-alone "family center" stores. He often looked to successful retailing managers from his competition to staff his new stores. He could use these seasoned managers to build successful organizations. Walton focused on the importance of loyal man-agers and made them limited partners by asking them to invest $1,000 of their own in the stores. He also focused on satisfying the new demographics of the suburbs with later store hours and sales promotions for holidays. He started to experiment with discount purchasing through quantity buys from wholesalers. He developed various store layouts to speed customer purchases and reduce overhead. He devel-oped what he called "self-service," which moved general checkouts to the front of the store. Customers used lightweight baskets to bring their goods to the checkout. This was a much different business model than the clerk-and-counter layout of five-and-ten stores of prior decades.

Kmart eclipsed Wal-Mart's steady early growth. The decade of the 1970s be-longed to the aggressive growth of Kmart in discount marketing. The company used mass purchasing power to develop its own brands. Wal-Mart expanded more conservatively, but both companies added auto centers and pharmacies, challeng-ing Sears in the auto-service area. Kmart was able to drive early discounters such as Zayre, Ames, and TG&Y stores out of business and take sales away from Sears. Wal-Mart expanded in the South as Kmart expanded in the Midwest and East. Besides honing the operations and corporate marketing, Walton was very focused on profitability, which made Wal-Mart the favorite of Wall Street. In the 1970s, Walton promoted community and American-made products, which were popular in the South. In business, he added people greeters to his stores. Stores gave to local charities and community events in an effort to calm fears of local merchants. Wal-Mart operations became the industry benchmark for inventory control and mass purchasing with an enthusiastic following on Wall Street.

In the 1980s, Wal-Mart overtook Kmart in sales. Kmart and Wal-Mart came into direct geographic competition. Wal-Mart aggressively located near Kmart to drive them out of business. Wal-Mart's success was as much a result of Kmart's failure to focus on its stores as it was a superior discount business model. Wal-Mart fine-tuned its discount business, expanding only in a variation of discount retailing with Sam's Club. Kmart, on the other hand, started to move into other businesses such as Waldenbooks, Kmart Food Stores, Borders Books, OfficeMax, and Builders Square. Kmart stores started to look outdated and even decaying as Wal-Mart moved into competing sites. Its remaining Kresge stores were also holding Kmart back. Wal-Mart management continued to innovate in their discount stores, providing one-hour photo processing, adding pharmacies, implementing bar coding, partnering with fast-food chains for in-store operations, opening superstores, and moving into international markets. Wal-Mart became an industry leader in inventory control techniques and technology, further reducing costs. In the 1990s, Kmart tried to reinvent itself, but it was too late as Wal-Mart had established itself in Kmart's markets. Kmart went into a higher-priced quality segment closer to that of Target. Kmart's move up in quality to value rather than discount actually hurt it in the competition with Wal-Mart. In 2002, Kmart filed for bankruptcy and would eventually merge with the failed Sears Corporation.

Wal-Mart continues today to build from its core competencies as a discount retailer. It is expanding into banking, tax services, dentist offices, and so on, all built around its basic stores. It presently has limited competition on the national level. Target (which opened its first store the same year as Wal-Mart) competes on the high end of Wal-Mart's market segment. Target focuses successfully on value (the relationship of cost and quality) while Wal-Mart maintains its low-cost focus. There is some regional chain competition for Wal-Mart from Meijer stores in Michigan and Ohio. Wal-Mart continues to face lawsuits and public opposition with its low-cost operations strategy. It has resisted unionization nationally, which has made it a political target. Its low-cost purchasing, however, has made it a major importer of Chinese products. Wal-Mart also faces tough political resistance from local merchants. Still, it appears that while nobody wants a Wal-Mart next door, almost everyone wants to shop at one.

*See also:* Automated Sewing Machine; Sears Mail Order Business

### References

Fishman, Charles. *The Wal-Mart Effect: How the World's Most Powerful Company Really Works—and How It's Transforming the American Economy.* New York: Penguin, 2006.

Walton, Sam. *Sam Walton: Made in America.* New York: Bantam, 1993.

# IBM 360 Computer (1964)

The 1964 New York World's Fair would be the launching point for a revolution in business computing. The crown jewel of the IBM pavilion was the million-dollar-plus IBM 360 computer and a dramatic introduction of the computer to the general public. The IBM 360 family of computers was designed to do a variety of computer tasks for businesses, including administrative and engineering tasks. IBM promised that there would be basic software that would allow for future upgrades. This common instruction-set architecture was revolutionary for the time. This type of architecture is taken for granted today. The IBM pavilion at the World's Fair had a 500-seat theater on hydraulic lifting rams, pushing the audience to the rooftop to view a nine-screen film on the workings of a computer. The fair had over 10 million visitors. The exhibit allowed the first interaction with a computer. Questions about history were asked for the computer to respond to. The development costs of the IBM 360 computers were in the billions, exceeding the development costs for the nuclear bomb. IBM believed the 360 series would open up the commercial market for the computer, which had been dominated by government and military contracts. It would be an investment that would assure IBM's dominance in business computers for decades. The original price ranged from $135,000 to $500,000. The first commercial customers were insurance companies, banks, and the accounting departments of large manufacturing companies such as United States Steel.

While the IBM 360 was a revolutionary product, it was an evolutionary result of IBM's business model. In fact, IBM's business model is one of evolving business machines for decades, moving from hand calculators to electromechanical devices to electronic calculators. IBM had a long history in data analysis and business calculations, going back to the 1890 census. Herman Hollerith had designed a punched data card to tabulate experimental counts for the 1880 Tabulating Machine Company. The company won government contracts to analyze census data but looked for commercial business applications for the machines at companies such as the railroads. In 1914 Thomas Watson was brought in from National Cash Register to head the then Computing Tabulating Recording Company. Computing Tabulating Recording Company had been formed in 1911, which is the official formation date of IBM; the name was changed to International Business Machines Corporation in 1924. In 1920, IBM introduced its first machine—the printing tabulator.

Like high-tech companies today, IBM formed educational and creativity programs for employees to develop new products. By the 1930s, IBM was making time clocks, job recorders, time stamps, and dial recorders. In 1935, IBM won the contract for the world's biggest accounting project, known as the Social Security Act, using its "super-computing machine." IBM had also introduced the first electric typewriter, which would be a core product for the company for decades. These two technologies would be key roots to the evolution of the IBM 360. The two technologies were merged to create the first electromechanical calculator in the late 1930s. During World War II, IBM invested heavily in research, resulting in the release of the IBM 603, the first commercial product to use electronic arithmetic circuits. In the 1950s, IBM started the use of magnetic tape as storage for its calculators. While large computers such as the Universal Automated Computer (UNIVAC) were focused on specific applications, IBM wanted flexibility in its large computers. A programming language known as FORTRAN was released in 1957, allowing the computer to be used for different operations based on formula calculations. This would be a key evolutionary step in the development of the IBM 360.

The 1960s brought huge investment in research and development, which resulted in applications such as its report program generator. The 1962 IBM 7090 was developed to help airlines manage their reservation systems. The work on this project would lead to the IBM 360. IBM was then the largest computer company in the world with over 100,000 employees and controlling 70 percent of the market. The company was gambling billions in research for its IBM 360 system. The competition of Burroughs, National Cash Register (NCR), Eckert–Mauchly Computer Corporation (makers of UNIVAC), Control Data, General Electric, Radio Corporation of America (RCA), and Honeywell, known as the "seven dwarfs," were letting IBM take the research lead. The research and development costs for the IBM 360 are still considered the highest for any product development project by a private company. Many inside IBM thought the IBM 360 would never recoup the huge investment. The risk was really overstated, since IBM had been taking steps toward the IBM 360 for over 50 years. Its evolutionary-step research business model would become the standard for corporate research managers. Using this approach to research a project would produce a development tree of new products. The IBM 360 would be a huge success, and research on the project would lead to the magnetic tape typewriter, NASA computer systems, memory chips, and fractals, which would lead to computer animation. The IBM 360 became the heart of America's space program. It found a home in most of America's accounting and engineering departments. IBM sales increased more than fivefold. The company was so dominant that its architecture became a standard. The cloning of the IBM 360 by Soviet spies assured that the IBM architecture would become a world standard. The IBM

360's success brought the number of employees to 270,000 and over $7 billion in sales by 1970.

The gigantic success of the IBM 360 would bring a new problem. The U.S. government filed an antitrust suit in 1969, stating IBM violated the Sherman Anti-Trust Act. The case would drag out for 13 years (*U.S. v. IBM*) and impact IBM's managerial and product decisions. Eventually, the government would drop the case, but IBM did open its systems and training, allowing for the development of independent companies to provide services for IBM hardware. With its failed entry into the copier market, IBM showed that size alone did not guarantee new product success. Finally, in the 1980s, Apple and Microsoft took down the giant of the PC business.

*See also:* CD-ROM; First Billion-Dollar Corporation—United States Steel; First Mass-Produced Transistor Radio; Patent and Copyright Statutes; Social Security Act; UNIVAC I; The Year of the PC

**References**

Austrian, Geoffrey. *Herman Hollerith: Forgotten Giant of Information Processing.* New York: Columbia University Press, 1982.

Maney, Kevin. *The Maverick and His Machine: Thomas Watson, Sr. and the Making of IBM.* New York: Wiley, 2004.

Pugh, Emerson. *Building IBM: Shaping an Industry and Its Technology.* Cambridge, MA: MIT Press, 1995.

# *Unsafe at Any Speed* (1965)

It is not uncommon for books to combine with culture to change the nature of business. Upton Sinclair's *Jungle* in 1905 changed the food industry and gave birth to extensive legislation. *Unsafe at Any Speed* by Ralph Nader would do the same thing in the automotive industry in the 1960s. The book centered on the oversight of the automotive industry to address safety and, in some cases, even sacrifice safety for economic reasons. The book would create an activist movement leading to the National Traffic and Motor Vehicle Safety Act of 1966. Auto manufacturers would be required to install seat belts, use crash testing, and set requirements for recalls. It would hurt the initial effort of American automakers to meet the rising challenge from Japanese imports. For Nader, it launched a long career of consumer activism and the implementation of more consumer legislation.

Nader had a law degree from Harvard and worked for Assistant Secretary of Labor Daniel Patrick Moynihan in the Johnson administration. In Washington, Nader also became an advisor to the Senate subcommittee on car safety. Even earlier in his career, Nader published an article for *The Nation* in 1959 called "The Safe Car You Can't Buy." Nader was head of a consumer safety movement after World War II. The failed Tucker Motors had tried to reach this market segment with the inclusion of seat belts in cars. There had been a growing drumbeat of complaints about safety being traded for economy. The death rate from automotive crashes had been rising for years, alerting the public to possible problems. Still, the issue of safety was considered a decision to be made by the consumers with their selection of a model. The big three automakers of the 1960s were highly profitable and were often the target of consumer groups because of their size. The slow but steady growth of Japanese imports required a business response. In 1960, General Motors countered with its Chevrolet Corvair. The Corvair's poor safety record would create a public outcry.

The Corvair had an air-cooled engine and rear-wheel drive (like the popular Volkswagen Beetle). The Corvair pioneered economical design features. The rear air-cooled engine greatly improved fuel economy and ride quality. The car had many revolutionary design elements and was named *Motor Trend*'s Car of the Year for 1960. It was also on a 1960 cover of *Time* magazine, which hailed its engineering. Even with all the safety concerns, the Corvair proved highly successful, selling 1.8 million cars during the 1960s. In the first four years, the Corvair was hit with over 100 lawsuits, but these remained below the public's radar until 1965 with the publication of Nader's *Unsafe at Any Speed*. These early lawsuits provided the original research material for his book. Nader's advising role to Congress on car safety also allowed him access to the overview of the national safety problem. Nader was convinced that the big automakers could drag out lawsuits, allowing the problem to be shelved as in the past. In addition, Nader felt that powerful auto-state legislators and lobbyists would prevent real action on the industry. Nader believed his book would be a breakthrough for the safety of the American consumer. He also probably realized that safety activists were looking for a leader for their growing numbers.

*Unsafe at Any Speed* would make Nader a household name and turn the safety movement into a political force. Nader was able to draw on insider information not available to the public. He used the growing safety-problem headlines about the Corvair as a foundation for the book. Nader was able to build on the growing handling and stability problems of the Corvair. Nader's attack would eventually destroy the sales of the Corvair by 1967, even though in 1972 the Corvair would be vindicated by an independent government report. The book was far more than an attack on the Corvair. *Unsafe at Any Speed* addressed the safety problems of industry and government, claiming the problem bordered on a conspiracy. Nader argued the whole system was about car manufacture and profits with no concern about the driver. Nader was right, but the problem was even deeper, with customers who demanded economy and style over safety features. American customers, unlike

Ralph Nader testifies before Congress, 1966. (AP Photo)

German customers, were not willing to pay for safety features. Nader even broke new ground with a chapter dedicated to the car's impact on air pollution and smog. In particular, it was focused on the problems of Los Angeles.

The initial industry and government response was to attack Nader. The harassment campaign slowed as the book's sales rose. Nader had friends in Congress, and in 1966, the president of General Motors, James Roche, was forced to apologize to Nader publicly. Nader later successfully sued General Motors for invasion of privacy, winning $280,000. Nader used the money to launch a center for consumer activism. He moved into a number of environmental and consumer issues as a result of the book's success.

The major impact of the book would be the unanimous passage of the 1966 National Traffic and Motor Vehicle Safety Act. The act addressed the rising fatalities and injuries of the 1960s. The act represented a major shift in safety responsibility from the individual consumer to the federal government. The act forced the auto manufacturers to add features such as safety belts and stronger shatter-resistant windshields. The act created the National Highway Safety Bureau, which led to improved highway construction. Construction improvements included breakaway signs, breakaway posts, better road illumination, improved traffic separation, and guardrails. By 1970, death rates were on the decline. More recently, the government has focused on consumer behavior such as seat belt use, alcohol limits, child-safety devices, and motorcycle helmets.

*See also:* Federal Aid Highway Act of 1956; First Japanese Auto Sold in the United States; General Motors Bankruptcy

### References

Marcello, Patricia Cronin. *Ralph Nader: A Biography.* Westport, CT: Greenwood, 2004.

Mashaw, Jerry. *The Struggle for Auto Safety.* Cambridge, MA: Harvard University Press, 1990.

Nader, Ralph. *Unsafe at Any Speed.* New York: Grossman, 1965.

# ARPAnet (Earliest Internet) Formed (1969)

The Advanced Research Projects Agency Network (ARPAnet) set the infrastructure that would become the Internet. ARPAnet began as a network of connected university computers. The ARPAnet was funded by the Defense Advanced Research Projects Agency (DARPA). The original intent was to develop a network for military command and control after a nuclear attack. The computer network was based on telephone lines and required a new technology known as packet switching to move data on telephone lines between computers. After its startup in 1969, ARPAnet evolved into several innovations in the early 1970s such as e-mail, a file transfer protocol that allows data to be sent in bulk, and a remote connecting service for network computers. This network grew to connect universities with defense funding across the nation. When the Defense Department pulled out of the project in 1990, it had laid the groundwork for today's worldwide Internet. Universities continued the old network as the National Science Foundation network (NSFnet) as it had expanded to individuals with the advent of the personal computer.

The roots of the ARPAnet go back to the funding of DARPA, which was formed in 1957 as a response to the launching of Sputnik. DARPA was created as a very special research group for the Department of Defense. The name was changed in 1958 to Advanced Research Projects Agency (ARPA). ARPA had an $12 million annual budget and much flexibility on spending it. Its first project was to look at a communications network that could operate after a nuclear attack on the United States. This bombproof network would allow distant military centers to communicate. ARPA adapted the early work by Paul Baran of the Rand Institute in the 1960s. This early network research had been financed by the Air Force. Baran's work was on a packet-switching system that would allow information to be routed on any available electronic lines such as telephone lines. Baran's packet-switching concept was a revolutionary idea of breaking data or messages in packets to flow along available lines and then be reassembled at the destination machine. This differed from a traditional phone call, which used circuit switching to form a dedicated circuit for the duration of the communication session. Packet switching allows data to flow on a fractured network unable to develop a dedicated or "direct" hookup. Packet switching is a special computer protocol allowing computers to exchange information (network control protocol).

Baran's packet-switching network offered another possibility of connecting universities involved in research for the Defense Department. At the time even computers in the same room could not talk to each other, let alone computers at different universities. Packet switching along telephone lines would be a necessity to move large blocks of research data. These connections would allow huge amounts of data to be transported between universities. Beyond packet switching, some hardware to handle the messages had to be developed. Since ARPA was a small core group, it contracted out the work to BNN Technologies. To connect distant computers, each location required a gateway computer known as an interface message processor (IMP, or router as it is known today). The first IMP was built by Honeywell and could service four local computers. The first network connected computers at the University of California, Los Angeles (UCLA) and the Stanford Research Institute in September 1969. UCLA and Stanford both had Scientific Data Systems (SDS) computers. Initially, after the user typed "login," the system shut down; it took another month to work out the bugs for a message, which was ultimately sent at 10:30 P.M. on October 29, 1969.

By the end of 1969, an IBM 360 at the University of California, Santa Barbara, and a DEC at the University of Utah were added to the network. The Massachusetts Institute of Technology was added to the network in March 1970. In 1971, the first e-mail was sent; by 1973 there were over 40 sites, and e-mail made up 75 percent of the traffic, which augured the future of the Internet. To send a message on the ARPAnet required a computer to break the message into packets using an Internet protocol (IP). The packets also received a digital identification because individual packets might take different paths. Individual packets are routed based on traffic. When the individual packet envelopes reach the destination computer, transmission control protocol (TCP) reassembled the message in the correct order. The network was slow, running at 50 to 200 kilobits per second. The year 1971 also brought the use of a terminal interface processor (TIP) capable of adding over 60 slave terminals to the host computer. By the mid-1970s, huge databases were being passed between universities using file transfer protocol (FTP). The ARPAnet had achieved its goal and was supporting both military and civilian research applications. In 1983, the ARPAnet was split into the NSFnet and the classified military network (MILnet). ARPAnet continued as a communication system between certain research pockets at various universities until most of the IMP routers became obsolete in 1989.

The NSFnet used local area networks (LANs) to link whole universities internally and externally. The NSFnet started to look for more funding as the ARPAnet shut down in 1990. In 1991, Senator Albert Gore crafted and the Congress passed the High Performance Computing and Communication Act. The bill created and funded a super information highway for research, which evolved into the Internet of today. Today's Internet is made up of the same infrastructure of routers and protocols. The Internet, regardless of its government origins, remained firmly rooted in private industry.

*See also:* Bill Gates Internet Memo; Google Incorporated; IBM 360 Computer; UNIVAC I; The Year of the PC

### References

Abbate, Janet. *Inventing the Internet.* Cambridge, MA: MIT Press, 1999.

Banks, Michael. *On the Way to the Web: The Secret History of the Internet and Its Founders.* New York: Apress, 2010.

Hafner, Katie. *Where Wizards Stay Up Late: Origins of the Internet.* New York: Simon & Schuster, 1998.

# Wage and Price Controls (1971)

On August 15, 1971, President Richard Nixon announced a series of economic measures to address accelerating inflation, which was approaching 6 percent. The controls and the removal of the gold standard created major short-term and long-term economic changes, but inflation would not be fully resolved until the 1980s (it would peak at 15 percent in March 1980). The period would become the standard reference point for the impact of inflationary pressures on American business. While wage and price controls had mixed results, the event marked the problem of inflation that marred the decade of the 1970s. The wage and price controls bought time for Nixon to win the election, but the decade long inflationary trend continued unabated for years. It would take a recession in 1980 and a tight money policy by the Federal Reserve to end the brutal inflation of the 1970s. In the short run, the effort would lead economists to use monetary policy to address inflation. In the long term, the removal of the gold standard would lead to free-floating currency values.

The origin of the crisis goes back to the 1960s. The late 1960s saw a surge of spending for the Vietnam War and the Great Society of President Lyndon Johnson. By 1969, inflation was on the rise. The public had a mixed view of inflation. The big unions and big business were protected with cost-of-living adjustments to wages and salaries. People on fixed incomes or employees lacking cost-of-living adjustments faced a major loss in purchasing power. Most were pleased with the rise in housing prices; however, new owners were being blocked out of the market. Price increases for food, cars, and consumer goods were looked at as a major negative. Still, others enjoyed the savings rate of return. The government was running large deficits, but the economy was picking up as the Federal Reserve was easing monetary policies. Inflation was causing major problems in international markets as the United States was also moving off the gold standard. More accurately, there was a de facto gold standard that allowed the Federal Reserve to continue to print money beyond a 100 percent gold backing. The dollar was losing value, causing Arab oil barons to see their petrodollars devalued. The gold coverage of the dollar dropped to 22 percent, which created a lack of confidence in the dollar by foreign countries. The dollar was further eroding as foreign countries demanded gold for dollars, and the U.S. Treasury was being drained of gold reserves. Germany was the only country aggressively addressing inflation, since they feared it more than deflation, having suffered super-inflation in the 1930s.

Starting in 1969, the United States entered a period of high prices and shortages. The news fueled the fire with stories of price gouging. The public worried as countries such as France called in the dollar to take gold out of the United States. The value of the dollar fell, and headlines blamed the problems on a foreign-caused exchange crisis. The huge increase in the money supply was being overlooked as the administration wanted both low interest rates and low unemployment. High housing costs were causing the postwar baby boomers to have trouble entering the market. Public opinion was demanding that some action take place.

Nixon's announcement on August 15, 1971, was a three-pronged approach—a wage and price freeze, a 10 percent import surcharge, and an end to the dollar's convertibility to gold. In the short run, the approach worked, but it had many long-term ramifications. By 1976, the major currencies were floating and no longer under government control. The long-term impact on the American economy is clouded by other major economic shocks such as the Arab Oil Embargo. Historically, the fixing of prices has shown few positive effects. This had been tried on a major scale by the ancient Romans, the Soviet Union, and European countries during the French Revolution and World War II. The results were a black market in goods and material shortages. For decades, the black market was a way of life in the price-controlled Soviet Union. Adam Smith had predicted this 200 years earlier. Even America had learned a hard lesson after World War II with price controls on meat. These controls eventually led to scarcity. Consumers even rejected it, realizing that cheap meat was of little value if there was none available to buy. Nixon was well aware that price controls would create shortages, but the political environment required some action. Nixon's wage and price controls were short-lived, but the gold issue remained the long-term legacy. The great wave of inflation returned in 1974, fueled by the Arab

Oil Embargo and the pushing of the money supply to keep unemployment low. The elimination of the gold standard freed the Federal Reserve to pump unlimited amounts of money into the system.

The wage and price controls did little to change the underlying causes of the 1970s inflation. Another result of the 1970s inflation and stagflation was a rethinking of Keynesian economic policies. Prior to the 1970s, Keynesian economists believed that inflation and unemployment were inversely related, that is, that high inflation meant low unemployment. This relationship was known as the Philips curve. The basis was that the high demand of inflation (reflected in high prices) required more workers to be hired, thus driving down unemployment. The stagflation of the 1970s showed that high inflation and high unemployment could coexist. Milton Friedman led the rethinking of Keynesian theories. Friedman showed that the Philips curve shifted in the 1970s as businesses adapted to long periods of inflation. Workers and management started to take inflation into account in their wage negotiations. The bottom line of the 1971 wage and price controls was that they signaled the beginning, not the end, of an economic crisis. Inflation would continue into double digits, and a new condition of stagflation occurred with a recession with inflation.

*See also:* Arab Oil Embargo; Banking Crisis and Great Recession; Jefferson Embargo; Navigation Acts; Panic of 1837; Panic of 1857; Panic of 1873; Panic of 1893; Panic of 1907; Savings and Loan Crisis

### References

Gali, Jordi. *Monetary Policy, Inflation, and the Business Cycle: An Introduction to the New Keynesian Economics.* Princeton, NJ: Princeton University Press: 2008.

Rockoff, Hugh. *Drastic Measures: A History of Wage and Price Controls in the United States.* Cambridge, MA: Cambridge University Press, 2004.

# Arab Oil Embargo (1973)

The Arab Oil Embargo would be the true beginning of the energy crisis. The root cause was the rising power of the Organization of Petroleum Exporting Countries (OPEC), controlled by Arab countries to use oil as a political force. The industrialized nations were dependent on Arab oil producers. The U.S. support of the Israeli military in the Yom Kippur War in October 1973 created a political backlash in the Arab nations. Arab oil-producing countries imposed an oil embargo on the United States and increased prices to its European allies by 70 percent. Oil jumped from $3 a barrel to over $5 a barrel overnight. By the end of the embargo it had reached $11 a barrel. The United States relied on foreign countries for 36 percent of its oil in 1973. The embargo caused consumer panics, with stations running out of gas and mile-long lines. Rationing became necessary. The American auto industry was caught off guard with large gas-guzzlers in their showrooms. Sales of imported gas-efficient cars surged; even though the embargo lasted only six months, buying patterns were changed forever. At the end of the six-month embargo, oil would be $18 a barrel. The shock of the embargo helped secure the passage of the trans-Alaska pipeline in 1973 and expanded oil exploration. Mass transit projects, carpooling, and other conservation projects came into vogue. In addition, the huge jump in oil prices created a worldwide recession.

The real problem had been growing for years. American dependence on foreign oil had increased through the 1960s from under 20 percent to 32 percent. Demand for oil was growing at 5 percent annually. About 7 percent of the oil came from the Arab states by 1973. The root of the 1973 oil crisis goes back to the formation of OPEC in 1960 as a cartel to control the supply and prices. The members by 1973 were Iran, Iraq, Kuwait, Saudi Arabia, Venezuela, the United Arab Emirates, Qatar, Indonesia, Libya, Nigeria, and Algeria. OPEC was the supplier for 45 percent of the world market by 1973. The price of oil had remained around $1.00 a barrel for most of the 1960s and was $1.30 a barrel at the start of 1970. President Nixon's move of not allowing dollars to be converted to gold in 1971, which OPEC was unable to adjust for, caused a devaluation of the dollar. The inflation of the 1970s was putting pressure on OPEC to increase their prices, but it would be politics more than supply or demand that created the energy crisis. OPEC had for a decade proved ineffective at holding or raising prices due to the cartel members' tendency to cheat.

On October 6, 1973, Syria and Egypt launched a surprise attack on Israel, beginning what became known as the Yom Kippur War. A week later, the United States began an airlift to supply Israel in response to the supplying of Syria and Egypt by the Soviet Union. On October 16, OPEC raised the price of oil to $5.11 a barrel. The Arab states of OPEC announced that they would continue to increase the price of oil in 5 percent increments until their political goals were met. When Congress voted for a $2.2 billion relief package for Israel on October 20, the Arab states quickly announced a boycott against the United States. Oil prices rose to $12 a barrel and continued at this level through the 1970s. Prices at the pump went from $0.30 a gallon to $1.30 a gallon. The United States initially absorbed the impact with limited pain from the higher prices. On November 5, the Arab states announced a 25 percent output cut, which started to put pressure on supplies in the United States.

The November output cut took the crisis to the Main Streets of the United States as gasoline station lines grew and reports of stations running out of gas created panics. President Nixon responded with a ban on Sunday gasoline sales, and daylight savings time was extended into winter to save fuel. Because consumers were topping off and keeping gas tanks full, odd-even sales days were implemented based on license plate numbers. Various other voluntary conservation moves were also implemented. Still, local panics occurred in highly populated areas. The government prepared to use ration coupons but never had to use the system, as the embargo ended in March 1974. Secondary effects included a national trucker strike over the cost of fuel and toilet paper panics based on oil shortages in the paper industry. Eventually the government imposed a 55-mile-per-hour speed limit.

The 45 percent increase in fuel prices caused a recession and helped contribute to what would be called stagflation. These fuel costs rippled through the economy creating higher food costs and high inflation. The 1970s would always be remembered for out-of-control inflation. The bigger and longer-lasting impact of the oil embargo was its effect on the automotive industry. The embargo was the beginning of the end of the popularity of big six-cylinder and V8 cars. Japanese four-cylinder cars such as the Toyota Corona, Toyota Corolla, Honda Civic, and Datsun 510 became popular. American manufacturers suffered from their inventory of large cars and strategic line of designs. The Big Three were forced to develop four-cylinder and smaller models such as the Ford Pinto, Chevy Vega, and Plymouth Valiant. In the longer run, a number of energy acts were passed in the late 1970s to address conservation and energy usage. The Department of Energy was created in 1977.

Long gas lines during the 1970s energy crisis. (Library of Congress)

*See also:* First Japanese Auto Sold in the United States; General Motors Bankruptcy; Jefferson Embargo; Standard Oil Antitrust Lawsuit; Wage and Price Controls

**References**

Carroll, Peter N. *It Seemed Like Nothing Happened: America in the 1970s.* New Brunswick, NJ: Rutgers University Press, 1990.

Merrill, Karen. *The Oil Crisis of 1973–1974: A Brief History with Documents.* New York: St. Martin's, 2007.

# First Customer Scan of a Bar Code (1974)

Historians have now assigned June 26, 1973, when a pack of Wrigley's Juicy Fruit Gum was scanned at a Troy, Ohio, supermarket, as the beginning of commercial bar codes by enshrining the pack of gum in the Smithsonian. However, the history of bar codes and code scanning goes back to the 1940s. Even though initial capital and equipment investments were huge—even for a single chain store it might approach $1 million—the studies showed a payback in less than three years. In addition, food processors would have to invest heavily in the new technology. With implementation, the costs of the equipment were reduced, and new applications and savings quickly surfaced. The savings, however, were hindered by the resistance of unions, manufacturers, and consumers, which slowed overall implementation. The bar code, however, is an example of a user-driven innovation. The National Association of Food Chains deserves the credit for making the bar code successful.

The bar code is a visual code in an optical machine-readable format. It has a long history going back to the late 1940s when Bernard Silver and Norman Woodland of the Drexel Institute of Technology realized there was a potential need for reading product information such as the price at the checkout registers of grocery stores. Not only prices but general sales and inventory information were critical to the profitability of supermarkets. Woodland and Silver received a patent for their system based on Morse code and an optical reading system adapted from the DeForest movie sound system, which allowed reflected data to be converted into sound. The system had serious commercial limitations, but the patent rights were sold to IBM in 1951 and to Philco and then to RCA in 1963. All of these companies became actively involved in the development of a commercial system. In the late 1950s, bar code systems were tried by the railroads to identify railroad cars in the system, with limited success.

The motivation to fully develop a bar code system came from the National Association of Food Chains. This industry group fully recognized the advantages of cost reduction and inventory control for supermarkets. In 1966, the National Association of Food Chains initiated the development of a system by RCA, owner of the Silver and Woodland patent, and Kroger offered to become a test company for the project development. The industry group also requested the help of other companies working on bar codes such as IBM, National Cash Register, and Singer. The IBM and RCA systems were tried in 1973 with limited success. In 1973, the RCA system (using an IBM coding label) was successfully tested at Marsh's Supermarket in Troy, Ohio. The IBM code would become the universal product code and the industry standard. The code was split in two halves of six digits each. The first digit differentiated products into variable or nonvariable weight. The next five digits were the manufacturer's code, the next five coded the product, and the final digit was for control. Pricing was handled in the software. For years, the product price was still on the label because customers demanded it.

The system was expensive, and the economic studies were mixed. IBM's own studies showed that it would take a bar code labeling of 70 percent of the store products to fully realize the predicted savings. The National Association of Food Chains continued its support in spite of questionable economic analyses. They were able to push compliance with food manufacturers and reach the 70 percent implementation by the end of the 1970s. Also by 1980, 8,000 supermarkets had bar-coding scanners. Unfortunately, the equipment cost, customer resistance, and technology issues did not allow the grocery industry to realize the projected savings.

Simultaneously, other industries and companies were advancing technology. Computer Identics Corporation was working on the application of codes for manufacturing industries. Its founder, David Collins, had worked in the early 1960s on the failed application of bar codes in the railroad industry. Computer Identics Corporation was using the cutting-edge technology of laser readers by 1970. These scanners were much better than the 500-watt lightbulb system of the Woodland patent. Lasers could read codes quickly and accurately. Even before the famous scan of a packet of gum, Computer Identics was using its system at General Motors to identify, monitor, and track car axles at manufacturing plants. Engineers might argue that this Computer Identics system was the first bar code system in 1969, but it lacked the standardized and uniform code that was being developed for the grocery industry. The laser technology, however, would hold the key to the bar code's full commercial success in the 1990s.

Bar coding steadily evolved and grew in the 1990s. By the late 1990s, the bar code had led to billions of dollars in savings for manufacturers and retailers, the biggest savings coming from improved inventory control, improved marketing and sales analysis, and monitoring of sales trends. Implementation also helped reduce shoplifting and reduced the number of employees. The full use of automatic checkout was slow during the 1990s as there was employee union resistance, consumer resistance, and the need for good verification systems. After 10 years, the full savings of automated checkout are being realized. Manufacturing use of bar codes for inventory control is also starting to reach full implementation. Retailing also continued to advance the technology with 2D codes in 2005. These 2D codes allow cell phone users to read bar codes, and they are linked to related websites to allow shoppers to compare prices and product information. Applications in the logistics industry for tracking have also been fully implemented. Bar codes have also spread to hospitals and research organizations.

*See also:* FCC Approves Advanced Mobile Phone System (1G); RFID at Wal-Mart; Talking Movies—*The Jazz Singer*

### References

Kato, Hiroko, Keng T. Tan, and Douglas Chai. *Barcodes for Mobile Devices.* Cambridge: Cambridge University Press, 2010.

Palmer, Roger. C. *The Bar Code Book: Fifth Edition—A Comprehensive Guide to Reading, Printing, Specifying, Evaluating, and Using Bar Code and Other Machine-Readable Symbols.* Bloomington, IN: Trafford, 2007.

# The Year of the PC (1977)

While engineers might look to an earlier date as the birth of the personal computer, for business historians, it was the year 1977 that launched the mass merchandising of the personal computer. Today the year is known as the "1977 Trinity" of Apple, Radio Shack, and Commodore computers. This trinity brought monitors, keyboards, and tape (standard cassette of the period) memory to the previous mathematical boxes and video games. In 1977, Radio Shack offered the first mass-marketed PC in the TRS-80, with prices starting at $600. Radio Shack proved that the personal computer would be a mainstream consumer product. The Commodore PET was also released in 1977 with a price of $800; and while it had limited success, it would set the stage for the highest-selling sales model ever, the Commodore 60, a few years later. Commodore would be the first to use major retail store outlets such as Kmart. Similarly, the limited release of the Apple II would herald the beginning of the personal-computing giant Apple Company. The Apple II had a price from $1,200 to $2,600 depending on the memory size. Apple chose to develop its own retail outlets. The TRS-80 through Radio Shack would set the business sales model for companies, while the Apple II would set the consumer design model for mass merchandising of the personal computer.

The commercial history of the personal computer can be traced to the 1975 release of the Altair computer kit in *Popular Electronics.* The Altair kit cost around $400 and was little more than a box with switches. While the Altair with the Intel 8080 chip delivered little, it did spark a burst of creativity in the marketplace. One incubator of this creativity was the Homebrew Computer Club near Stanford University. Apple founders Steve Jobs and Steve Wozniak, future founders of Apple

Computer, were members of this hobbyist group. Wozniak would test out his ideas at the Homebrew Club for his Apple computer. Jobs, his partner, injected the business and marketing assets into personal computer design. Wozniak worked hard to reduce the chips needed for a personal computer from over 50 to just 5. The Apple II had a monitor for graphical display, which was lacking with the Altair. Out of the trinity of personal computers in 1977, the Apple II was the first to use a color monitor. From the start, Jobs incorporated his vision of "user friendliness" that would come to characterize Apple products. The team of Jobs and Wozniak proved the perfect balance of technology and business sense. Apple II was the best customer-oriented product with a ready-to-use computer out of the box. The Apple II sales started off slow, lacking the mass marketing of larger companies, but proved the impact of word of mouth in the consumer base among hobbyists and gamers.

The Radio Shack TSR-80 was the first personal computer produced by a major company, which was Tandy Corporation, owner of 3,000 retail stores and a national mailing list. Tandy used its engineering staff to hold down costs, realizing that the market would be price sensitive. Tandy Corporation tried to move beyond the electronics hobbyists by offering software applications on cassette tape. It gave blackjack and backgammon software for free and offered additional applications such as personal finance and small business payroll management. Tandy's marketing had identified a market potential of the personal computer in small businesses. Tandy's marketing pushed sales over 10,000 in the first two months.

The Commodore PET (Personal Electronic Transactor) was aimed at educators and calculator users of the time. Commodore's experience was in calculators. In the early 1970s, there was a brisk market in programmable calculators sold by Texas Instruments, Hewlett-Packard, and Commodore. These programmable calculators sold for around $800 but were popular with engineers and educators. The PET's price of $800 made it very competitive in the calculator market. It had a tough, single-unit design (monitor, processor, and keyboard) that made it popular with schools in which Commodore's marketing group had inroads. The calculator-based keyboard,

Steve Jobs with the Apple II, 1977. (AP Photo/Apple Computers Inc.)

however, limited its general popularity. The Commodore PET never matched the sales of the TRS-80 or Apple II, but it did set the platform for the Commodore 64, which addressed its market shortcomings. In the 1980s, the Commodore 64 sold through outlets like Kmart and made it the Model T of personal computers and the world's best-selling personal computer model of all time. Commodore proved that the personal computer would be a mass-produced consumer product.

This trinity of personal computers with their various business models would evolve into a huge consumer market combining hobbyists, gamers, engineers, small businesspeople, scientists, and educators. Two developments during the next two years would expand the market and sales of the personal computer. The first was the use of floppy drives versus the slow standard cassette drives. Floppy drives had been invented in 1967 by IBM, and hobbyists were using them with their Altairs. A floppy drive could read 100,000 bits per second versus a mere 1,000 bits per second for a cassette drive. Floppy drives allowed a market to develop in software applications. Cassette storage had limited the personal computer to small, simple programs. The next development was that of a breakthrough application. The trinity of personal computers still attracted people who were proficient in writing programs.

The limited applications for small business and professionals were restricting the market. Interestingly, the software became a separate industry as initial companies like Apple focused on the hardware. Still, to a large degree, the lack of software was the limiting factor in early hardware sales. The breakthrough application was VisiCalc, a spreadsheet application for accounting and financial calculations. Daniel Bricklin and Robert Frankston developed it on an Apple II computer. They began selling this application for $200, and the software became the driving force for Apple sales. Apple's sales boomed, and the stock went public in December 1980. Still, the major use of personal computers in business would await the introduction of the IBM personal computer in early 1982.

*See also:* ARPAnet (Earliest Internet) Formed; First Mass-Produced Transistor Radio; IBM 360 Computer; UNIVAC I

### References

Ceruzzi, Paul E. *A History of Modern Computing.* Cambridge, MA: MIT Press, 2003.

Wozniak, Steve. *IWoz: Computer Geek to Cult Icon.* New York: Norton, 2006.

# Three Mile Island Nuclear Failure (1979)

The commercial success of the Shippingport Nuclear Plant and the safety record of American nuclear submarines contributed to a boon in nuclear plant expansion in the 1960s. By the 1970s, growth had slowed, as the industry became the target of environmental activists and inflation made building nuclear plants extremely costly compared to coal plants. Government-driven nuclear energy had supported the building boom of the 1960s, which also created abundant electrical supplies as the stagflation of the 1970s reduced demand. The crushing blow for the nuclear industry would come in 1979 at a nuclear plant on the Susquehanna River near Harrisburg, Pennsylvania. On March 28, 1979, a cooling-water valve closed, setting off a series of malfunctions and human errors that led to a near full meltdown. The incident threatened the public with radioactive contamination, and the headlines worldwide reflected these fears. The resultant panic would raise doubts as to the safety of the nuclear industry and would halt nuclear plant construction in the United States for decades. Of course, the Three Mile incident was only a catalyst for backing out of overexpansion and problems created by stagflation in the 1970s.

Public acceptance of nuclear power had always been problematic. The bombing of Hiroshima in 1945 had demonstrated the destructive power of nuclear energy. The 1950s had brought nuclear power plants on stream in the United States, England, and Russia. The Atomic Energy Commission had been created in 1946 by Congress and had launched a public relations effort early on. The first commercial nuclear plant came on line in 1956 in Sellafield, England. The success of the U.S. Navy's nuclear submarine program and the Shippingport Nuclear Plant in the late 1950s had won over the public. President Eisenhower's Atoms for Peace initiative in 1953 had also been successful in gaining public support. The Atomic Energy Act of 1954 turned over much of the 1940s research efforts to private companies. The United States also supported the creation of the International Atomic Energy Agency in 1957. After the government supported the building of the Shippingport Plant, the Dresden Nuclear Plant in Illinois in 1959 was the first one built without government funding.

All of these government actions created a boom in the 1960s for nuclear power plants. The 1960s also saw the launching of the world's first nuclear-powered aircraft carrier, the USS *Enterprise,* and the first nuclear power generator in space. Building of nuclear plants in the 1960s boomed, with only local opposition, so that nuclear power produced about 2.5 percent of the electricity generated in the United States in 1970. In 1973, U.S. utilities ordered a record 41 nuclear plants. President Jimmy Carter, a former nuclear engineer and navy submarine graduate, came into office in 1977 with plans to further expand nuclear development. However, the reality was that utilities had overcapacity coming on line in the late 1970s. There was also a growing concern over radioactive waste disposal and fears of nuclear weapons proliferation around the world. By 1979, nuclear power had reached 12 percent of the total electrical power in the United States. Opposition to nuclear power was on the rise with high-profile politicians entering the protests. By the early 1970s, nuclear construction had stalled as costs rocketed with inflation. Prior to the Three Mile

President Jimmy Carter visits Three Mile Island, Pennsylvania, the site of America's first nuclear accident, in 1979. (National Archives)

Island accident, 40 approved nuclear power plants had been cancelled. Then, 12 days before the accident, the release of a blockbuster movie detailing a nuclear plant accident, *The China Syndrome,* hit the theaters. The timing would create the perfect storm for the Three Mile Island accident.

The problems at the Three Mile Island plant started on March 28, 1979, in reactor 2 of the plant. A stuck valve would lead to failures in the nonnuclear secondary system followed by a failure in the primary system, causing reactor coolant to be released and a meltdown of the core. The operating crew's efforts to control the problem highlighted some reactor design problems as well as the propensity for human error in such emergencies. The news was slowly leaked to the press. Twenty-eight hours after the accident, the owner of the plant—Metropolitan Edison—and Pennsylvania's governor announced everything was under control. A few hours later a voluntary evacuation of a 5-mile radius was announced. The zone was extended to 20 miles within a day. Eventually 140,000 people left but returned within three weeks. The accident was covered internationally, creating fear. The health effects are still being debated, but no immediate deaths or health problems surfaced. Longer-term studies suggest an increase in cancer for the downwind population, although this is hotly debated.

The impact on business was felt more quickly. Orders for Babcock and Wilcox nuclear generators were immediately cancelled. At the time of Three Mile Island, 129 had been approved and planned, but only 53 of them would be completed.

However, nuclear power's proportion of electrical generation continued to rise to a peak of 22 percent in 1991 as planned capacity came on line and older plant capacities were increased. In 1984, nuclear power overtook natural gas to become second to coal in power production. In the longer range, no American nuclear power plant has been planned since the accident in 1979, but over 50 power generators came on line in the 1980s. Direct costs to insurers for evacuation and health expenses totaled over $80 million. The cleanup of Three Mile Island would cost over $1 billion. The second reactor at Three Mile Island came back on line in 1985. Internationally, the meltdown of the Soviet Union's Chernobyl plant created deaths and environmental destruction in 1986. The Chernobyl accident reactivated the old fears of Three Mile Island, and once again environmental opposition to nuclear power plants stiffened. As public fear had been subsiding, the Fukushima reactor accident in 2011 cast more doubt on nuclear energy. Germany plans to close all reactors by 2034. Still, nuclear reactors account for about 15 percent of the world's electrical generation. Nuclear power, however, offers a very clean (no carbon) option for power generation and is gaining some political favor with environmentalists.

*See also:* Niagara Falls Power Plant; Shippingport Atomic Power Station

### References

Cravens, Gwyneth. *Power to Save the World: The Truth about Nuclear Energy.* New York: Knopf, 2007.

Walker, Samuel. *Three Mile Island: A Nuclear Crisis in Historical Perspective.* Berkeley: University of California Press, 2004.

# IBM Personal Computer (1982)

For the business world, IBM's entrance into the personal computer business marked a revolution. While Apple and others had developed the personal computer, IBM held its hold on business operations with its mainframes. Personal computers had made little headway into the corporations, which were controlled by information technology (IT) departments, until IBM signaled it was OK to use personal computers for real business. The IBM personal computer would lead to two of the greatest business stories of the century—the purchase of Microsoft's operating system and the reverse engineering of the BIOS chip to clone the IBM. The introduction of spreadsheets allowed small businesses to have computers; by 1980, personal computers were infiltrating big business departments with spreadsheets and better report graphics. In 1980, IBM made the decision to move into the growing personal computer market. By utilizing parts from other manufacturers, IBM caught up on lost time, introducing a personal computer in 1982. IBM would purchase its operating system software from a small, struggling company—Microsoft. With IBM making personal computers, it became all right for big business to make large capital investments in personal computers. Lotus Development developed a new and better spreadsheet (1-2-3) for the IBM personal computer. The market mushroomed, and success brought new entries into the personal computer market. The cloning of the IBM personal computer would break open the market.

The IBM personal computer was one of the computer industry's most underestimated product launches. IBM went into the project as a defensive move in a very small segment of the overall computer business, but the company didn't realize the IBM personal computer would change and greatly expand the market for personal computers. While believing the personal computer was far from a threat to its mainframe business, IBM needed to move quickly to gain a foothold in this growing personal computer segment. IBM was a manufacturing company and made the decision to go outside for parts and software to develop a personal computer. It used an Intel 8088 chip to anchor its new personal computer. IBM built a machine for business, which meant it could utilize its extensive sales and marketing network for the new personal computer.

The IBM had a built-in operating system that was purchased from Microsoft. Microsoft supplied IBM a system they had purchased for a mere $15,000. Bill Gates would make his fortune on the simple deal he made with IBM. He settled for a $50 royalty per machine sold for the operating system PC-DOS and maintained the rights to sell his system to other manufacturers as MS-DOS. IBM went for the deal, believing the real money was in the manufacturing of the personal computer, not the software. The success of the IBM computer and Microsoft's selling to the competition created an industry standard for operating systems. The IBM personal computer was launched in 1982 with a price of $1,556. While the price was higher than for most personal computers at the time, the brand of IBM made it an instant success. Big business was now free to make major investments in what had been considered a toy. Sales quickly reached 250,000 units a month and overtook Apple sales in 1982. The great success of the IBM personal computer would barely last to the middle of the decade, but its mark remains even today.

IBM maintained control of its personal computer by its BIOS chip, which was a read-only chip with the stored code linking the machine and the operating system. The BIOS chip was protected by an army of lawyers who prosecuted any company that tried to copy it. In 1983, three Texas Instruments employees, Rod Canion, Jim Harris, and Bill Murto, started a company called Compaq. Compaq's expressed goal was to create a fully compatible IBM personal computer. They conceived of the idea of reverse engineering to produce a clone legally.

The reverse engineering of the ROM-BIOS chip was to become an industry legend. It was clear that directly copying any portion would not pass legal muster. The approach was to first hire a group of engineers who had no knowledge of the IBM

BIOS chip or the computer. These "virgins" were interviewed by lawyers to assure they were "clean." These virgins were then told to look at the BIOS chip and write down what the code did. Once these general functions were identified, another set of virgin engineers was given the code and asked to design a chip that could do those functions. Compaq was, of course, free to purchase the other parts and Microsoft's operating system (MS-DOS). In 1983, using the reverse-engineered BIOS chip, Compaq introduced a fully compatible IBM personal computer. It had a similar price with the only advantages being that it was compatible with the IBM and was more portable (it could be transported in a suitcase).

The success of Compaq and clones was due to the availability of better software applications. IBM had decided to control its operating system and application software by creating its own. In 1987, IBM introduced its OS/2 operating system. This decision was made in part to block the growth of compatible clones, but it was too late and extremely costly. Much of the cost was in converting users to a new system of commands. The huge investment failed, and software for IBM clones became a deciding factor, with IBM's effort failing and Apple software not being compatible with IBM or clones. The IBM personal computer and the clones of Compaq and others like Dell became the standard in business, holding Apple to a small segment of the big business market. Microsoft was then making profits from its operating systems, which controlled everything except Apple in the market. Furthermore, Apple computers and software were not compatible with the IBM. The major boom in software development followed the IBM and its clones. In 1989, Microsoft released Microsoft Office, the most useful office software ever released. Microsoft Office would propel the sales of the IBM clone, putting IBM out of the personal computer business and defeating Apple in the business market. By 1991, IBM clones dominated the business market, with the biggest winner being Microsoft. Apple sales declined, but the company maintained niches in education and the arts.

*See also:* Bill Gates Internet Memo; IBM 360 Computer; UNIVAC I; The Year of the PC

### References

Carroll, Paul. *Big Blues: The Unmaking of IBM.* New York: Crown, 1994.

Swedin, Eric, and David Ferro. *Computers: The Life Story of a Technology.* Baltimore, MD: Johns Hopkins University Press, 2007.

# FCC Approves Advanced Mobile Phone System (1G) (1982)

Many of the significant events of business have been driven or motivated by government action, but the development of the cell phone is a case where government regulation was a major roadblock. The technology for the cell phone has a long history and certainly could have been available in the 1970s in the United States, except for the restrictions imposed by the Federal Communications Commission (FCC)'s control over the necessary radio frequency bands. The technology had been evolving since the 1940s with military and police applications. Mobile telephones for automobiles had been in existence since the 1950s. Government control in the United States limited commercial development, while in Europe the first mobile phone network for the public was launched in 1971 in Finland. The first truly cellular network was launched in 1979 in Japan. AT&T had applied to the FCC for approval in 1971, but final approval for a U.S. network did not come until 1982. Because the advances in these network protocols and frequencies came in phases, they are referred to as generations, with 1G (first generation) being cellular phone networks, 2G being digital networks, and 3G being mobile broadband for data.

The merger of the telephone and radio telephony was complete by 1930 when it was possible to place phone calls to ocean liners. In World War II, German tanks had a tactical advantage with their two-way radio communications. Mobile car phones appeared in Finland and Sweden as early as 1946. These two-directional antenna communications were limited to short distances and restricted to a few frequency bands. The first breakthrough toward a true cellular 1G network came from Bell Laboratories, which proposed hexagonal cells with towers that could receive signals from three directions at time. Bell Laboratories continued the development of the concept so that moving phone calls could be "handed off" between towers. Europe quickly moved free of full government regulation of radio bands. There were several limited commercial trials in the United States, but the biggest application came in 1970 as Amtrak equipped trains with pay phones for the track between New York and Washington. This success led AT&T to file a proposal with the FCC for radio band frequencies for an advanced mobile phone system (AMPS) in December 1971 (it would take 10 years to be approved). This wireless analog system is considered the first-generation, or 1G, network. In the meantime, work on another necessary component, the handheld phone, was underway at Motorola and Bell Labs. In 1973, Motorola received a patent for a handheld phone, but it was the size of a large portable radio or walkie-talkie. The patent allowed Motorola to continue development, seeing eventual commercial applications.

In 1979, the size and weight of the handheld phone was cut in half as hand-off cell technology had improved to the point that the first commercial cellular network was opened in Japan and Europe. The Japanese network serviced over 20 million in densely populated Tokyo using 23 base stations. In 1981, Sweden's cellular network allowed for roaming between systems. The year 1981 brought approval for the radio bands needed for cellular systems in the United States; and a year later, Ameritech launched a full-service cellular network in Chicago using the handheld Motorola DynaTAC phone. Bell Laboratories continued to improve transmission technology through the 1980s as the industry showed linear growth, with most being in the sale of car phones. Handheld phones were often referred to as "brick" phones because of their size. Europe was experiencing much faster growth in these early years because of less government regulation.

In 1990, there were over 10 million users worldwide. Explosive growth of cell phones came in the early 1990s with the introduction of digital networks (2G). These digital networks improved call quality and reduced dropped calls, but the most important improvement was the major reduction in phone size, moving from a two- to four-pound phone to a quarter-pound phone. Besides, the digital networks and market pressure combined to result in smaller, more powerful batteries to power these phones. These 2G digital networks also allowed for text messaging. By the mid-1990s, the cell phone industry exploded, with smaller companies merging to gain markets and improve service throughout the nation. Verizon, which had roots going back to Bell Atlantic, pursued this strategy to become the largest wireless company, with over 100 million customers, and the world's largest telecommunications company (over $100 billion in sales). Bell Atlantic had been one of the seven baby Bells coming from the antitrust judgment against AT&T in 1984. The coupling of cellular technology with communications satellite networks opened the world for cell phone users. The movement of massive amounts of data in the last decade led to 3G mobile broadband networks. AT&T also rose to become a major player in cell phones and 3G networks.

*See also:* First Commercial Telephone; Television at the 1939 World's Fair; *Telstar* Communications Satellites; Western Union Telegraph Company

### References

Hanson, Jarice. *24/7 How Cell Phones and the Internet Changed How We Live, Work, and Play.* Santa Barbara, CA: Praeger, 2007.

Klemens, Guy. *The Cellphone: History of the Gadget That Changed the World.* Jefferson, NC: McFarland, 2010.

# Deindustrialization of America— General Tire Akron Closes (1982)

On March 1, 1982, General Tire announced it would close its Akron, Ohio, tire plant. General Tire was the last car tire plant in the city of Akron, Ohio, known as the Rubber City. B. F. Goodrich had stopped making car tires in the Rubber City in 1975; Goodyear closed its Akron tire plant in 1978; and Firestone had closed its Rubber City plant in 1981. Imported cars, steel, and rubber had started to cause the loss of domestic industrial business since the early 1970s. The 1982 recession would be the final nail in the coffin for much of America's heavy industry. In April 1982, LTV Steel shut down its Pittsburgh Works (formerly Jones and Laughlin Steel) after 135 years of continuous steelmaking. The plant closing ended almost 200 years of iron and steel production in the "Steel City." The steel union could not cut wages enough to compete (even if they worked for nothing). LTV Steel reported that the material cost of steelmaking at Pittsburgh was greater than the total cost of finished Japanese and Brazilian steel shipped into the United States. It was an amazing ending for a plant that once employed 20,000 steelworkers. These plant closings would be the beginning of closings affecting millions of American industrial jobs that would never return. By the 1990s, the once-great industrial cities of Youngstown, Akron, Warren, Buffalo, Wheeling, Homestead, Braddock, Duquesne, Bessemer, Birmingham, Canton, and Massillon, as well as large parts of major cities such as Cleveland, Pittsburgh, Detroit, Baltimore, and Chicago, were devastated.

The year 1982 was only the most visible sign of a trend that had started in the 1970s. The roots of the deindustrialization of America are even deeper. The beginning can be traced to a political and economic decision by the United States after World War II to become the stabilizing force in the world. Part of that decision was a high dollar policy, which would make the dollar the reserve currency of the world. This was coupled with an open trade policy to cement the stabilization of trade between nations. This combination would put basic American products at a price disadvantage. For two decades after the war, devastated steel mills, rubber factories, auto plants, and product assembly lines offered little competition. But as new factories emerged, lower-priced European and Japanese products flooded the American market. Steel was first to feel the pain in the 1960s and 1970s as steel, Japanese autos, and other basic products cut into domestic steel production. American industry and unions failed to fully understand the economic tidal wave they were facing. The Steel Strike of 1959 had been settled by the government to help the union maintain high wages and benefits. The unions' refusal to stop wage and benefit increases exacerbated the problem into 1982, when the recession was the last nail in the coffin. In 1973, the Arab Oil Embargo increased purchases of smaller imported cars, taking more of the domestic steel market. Free market economists dominated both political parties as the imports crushed the world's most powerful steel industry. The Monongahela River steel valley mills that had produced more than the total production of Germany, Italy, and Japan in the 1940s were leveled, leaving 2 blast furnaces (there had been as many as 30 operating) in 1990. The unions, management, and government never changed their behavior, seeing the industry as too big to fail. As painful as it was for the steel mills of Pennsylvania, Ohio, and Illinois, it was looked at as a regional problem in the 1970s. Meanwhile, the growing economy of Japan promoted even more government support of Japanese industries. Steel would be hit particularly hard. No one fully realized that the steel industry was only the first domino to fall.

Regional devastation was deep as the industries of major cities collapsed as did the benefit-dependent services of dentist offices and optometrists. Real estate prices crashed, as did small businesses dependent on the local economies; as an aggregate, however, the American economy absorbed the setbacks in the 1980s and 1990s. The high-technology and personal computer boom of the late 1980s helped soften the loss of heavy industry. The single-family wage earner disappeared, as families required two smaller incomes to maintain their standard of living. Steel, rubber, and glass companies tried to adjust with early buyouts to force retirements, so plants could be downsized. The highly paid flood of new retirees cushioned the blow to communities in the 1980s. Steel companies started to merge to reduce costs, and other industries sold out to foreign companies. Japanese competition pushed harder as the American heavy industries were forced into bankruptcies by the burden of huge pensions. When LTV Steel, the nation's second-largest company, filed for bankruptcy in 1987, there were five retirees on the books for every active worker. With tens of thousands of retirees, Bethlehem Steel lasted a few more years until it also filed for bankruptcy. This was typical and only promoted more Chapter 11 bankruptcies, so companies could turn their pension liabilities over to the government. By the 1990s, Chapter 11 bankruptcy was hitting the supply chains of the steel, glass, and automotive industries. Industrial communities were suffering from the loss of taxes, forcing cuts to teachers and school systems.

Most of the nation's steel mills would eventually go down, even with the initial help of Chapter 11 bankruptcy. The automotive industry fared a little better as it got some tariff relief in the 1980s; however, for their own survival, they started to buy from foreign suppliers of steel and other parts. By 1990, it was too late to save the raw material industries to any degree. The auto industry wavered, but the United States Autoworkers offered some concessions. The industry would make it to the next recession in 2007. Then, in 2009, the unthinkable happened with the bankruptcy of General Motors. The great "Rust Belt" spread from Pittsburgh and Cleveland to Detroit and Chicago. Only the American southern states with their right-to-work laws and influx of foreign manufacturers bucked the trend of deindustrialization.

*See also:* Andrew Carnegie's First Steel Mill; First Japanese Auto Sold in the United States; General Motors Bankruptcy; Great Steel Strike of 1919; Homestead Strike of 1892; National Labor Relations Act (Wagner Act); Steel Strike of 1959

### References

Hoerr, John P. *And the Wolf Finally Came: The Decline of the American Steel Industry.* Pittsburgh, PA: University of Pittsburgh Press, 1988.

Love, Steve, and David Giffels. *Wheels of Fortune: The Story of Rubber in Akron.* Akron, OH: University of Akron Press, 1999.

# CD-ROM (1985)

The compact disc (CD) is an optical disc storage system that represented a significant leap in data storage amounts. Philips, Sony, RCA, and others spearheaded its original development in the 1970s. The evolution of the CD-ROM represented a unique model of collaborative commercial development between Philips and Sony. It would be a business model for cooperative advantage. The CD consisted of data bits in a sandwich of polycarbonate, aluminum, and lacquer. The optical code is stored in the reflective aluminum layer. A laser does the optical reading. A standard formatting system allowed the disc to be used. In 1985, the format was extended to a read-only memory for computers. The CD-ROM allowed for 650 megabytes of storage compared to the 1.5 megabytes of the standard floppy disc of the time. Such massive storage would make it possible to have a full encyclopedia on a disc and would eventually lead to video storage on DVDs.

By the mid-1970s, a number of stories had surfaced on the work of Philips and RCA on an optical storage system for music using lasers. Sony had also been working secretly on a CD system since 1975. In 1979, both Philips and Sony demonstrated CD players. The quality of CD music was considered a major advance over the cassette tapes of the period. Many believed that Sony and Philips would do battle over formats and systems, but Sony had already experienced a major setback trying to dictate and control the videotape format. Sony's superior videotape quality system was being defeated by the open VHS format in the marketplace. Sony had come to realize that industry cooperation would yield high profits and limit downside losses rather than battling for competitive advantage. To this end, Sony and Philips formed a joint engineering committee on the CD in 1979 to cooperate in its commercial development.

This cooperation would be the model for the future in the electronics industry, which had suffered (along with consumers) from format wars in the industry. In the case of the CD, Philips brought their manufacturing process to the table, while Sony brought its error-correction disc technology to the table. The joint committee worked on the standardization of formats as both companies continued their product development separately. Both companies hoped to make their money from the discs and licensing of the playing machine rights. The committee standardized disc size, playing time, and coding format. Playing time was to be 80 minutes of uncompressed audio. The committee issued a set of standards known as the "red book." In 1981, the first CD recordings were released in Germany, but 1983 is known as the "Big Bang" year for CDs. In 1983, Billy Joel's *52nd Street* album was released. The high quality of the disc rapidly opened up the early-adopting audiophile market. The market grew rapidly, with 400 million CDs being produced in 1988.

In 1982, both Sony and Pioneer Electronics introduced CD players for around $1,000. Pioneer offered a car CD player in 1984. The quality allowed the CD to make fast inroads on cassette players. Germany's Benz produced the first factory-installed car CD player in 1985, followed by General Motors in 1987. For most of the 1980s, the CD was a storage medium for audio, but in 1985 Sony and Philips were looking at its potential in computers. This early technology was "read only," which put it at a major disadvantage in computers using rewritable floppy discs. Still, in 1985, the industry hammered out future standards for a CD-ROM. The standard, called the "yellow book," would become the industry standard ISO 9660. The expanding acceptance of the music CD systems continued to drive costs down. Efforts to sell the computer industry on the use of CDs stalled in the late 1980s until large data applications started to favor the CD.

It would be the game industry with its huge data storage requirements that would ultimately make the CD-ROM a popular computer storage medium. In 1993, some manufacturers were including CD drives with computers. The standard CD-ROM could hold up to 680 megabytes, or 300,000 pages of written data. The CD-ROM offered full multimedia storage for computers. This multimedia storage allowed for the encyclopedia to be fully contained on the CD-ROM, which would ultimately end the 300-year industry of encyclopedia books. Microsoft released *Microsoft Encarta*, a CD-ROM encyclopedia, in 1993, the first for a computer. The CD-ROM also allowed storage of clip art for applications. By mid-1995, CD drives were common in computers, and CDs had fully captured the music market. It took till 2008 for all computers to be equipped with CD-ROM drives; however, the sales peak was long past, as other devices such as memory flash drives became popular.

In 1985, Sony and Philips had set the standards for recordable CDs (CD-R) to address the major disadvantage of the compact disc. These recordable discs used ink instead of metal in their reflective layer. The disc could be recorded permanently (burning), which made it more useful for music recorders than computers. The recording required a machine recorder that cost $1,000 in 1992. Quality was a major issue but improved through the 1990s. The archival life of less than 10 years was another drawback. In 1997, the CD-RW (Compact Disc-Re-Writable) was used to make the CD more competitive with other storage mediums in its features. A few years earlier, the DVD format entered the video market and saw rapid growth over VHS tapes. Sales of the CD-ROM peaked in 2000 as other formats and competing technology such as flash drives and MP3s became more popular. The business mark of the CD-ROM is more its cooperative development business model than its use as a storage medium. The rise and fall of the CD highlights another important business issue in digital storage. Much data has been lost in the transition from cassette tape to five-inch discs to three-inch discs to CDs to flash drives because data was not backed up in an archival format. Many businesses pay services to store data in archival magnetic tape systems.

*See also:* IBM 360 Computer; The Year of the PC; UNIVAC I

**References**

Peek, J. B., J. Bergmans, Frank Toolenaar, and S. Stan. *Origins and Successors of the Compact Disc: Contributions of Philips to Optical Storage.* New York: Springer, 2010.

Stockwell, Foster. *A History of Information Storage and Retrieval.* Jefferson, NC: McFarland, 2007.

# Savings and Loan Crisis (1986)

The savings and loan crisis of the 1980s would represent the greatest collapse of U.S. financial institutions since the Great Depression. While it had roots in the 1970s, the face of the crisis is marked by the insolvency of the Federal Savings Loan Insurance Corporation (FSLIC) in 1987. The FSLIC was the federal insurer of savings accounts at these thrift institutions, the thrift's industry equivalent to the Federal Deposit Insurance Corporation (FDIC). By year-end 1986, 441 thrifts with $113 billion in assets were insolvent; another 533 thrifts with $453 billion were on a watch list with less than 2 percent of total assets in tangible capital. The period 1986 to 1995 would result in the failure of 1,043 thrifts with assets over $500 billion. The cost to the taxpayers was in excess of $200 billion. The savings and loan crisis would result in a number of new regulations and a 50 percent reduction in the size of the industry.

American thrifts, which became known as savings and loans, were focused on housing loans and experienced rapid growth after World War II. In the 1960s and 1970s, the savings and loans competed for savers by offering high interest rates in a time of spiraling inflation. The stagflation of the 1970s weakened the financial assets through slow growth in housing and high interest rates. In the early 1980s, lower interest rates caused savers to move to other saving options, which further weakened the savings and loans. Congress and the federal government looked at ways to help the savings and loans grow out of their problems. Congress looked to a combination of expansion of savings and loans products and deregulation.

The Depository Institutions Deregulation and Monetary Control Act of 1980 allowed savings and loans to issue credit cards, make consumer loans, invest in real estate, and offer interest-earning checking accounts. These products put savings and loans in competition with commercial banks. The Economic Recovery Tax Act of 1981 allowed savings and loans to sell their mortgage loans to Wall Street firms and allowed losses to be offset against taxes. Savings and loans began the process of bundling loans and selling them at steep discounts. Small savings and loans became overextended, and others were backed by few solid assets. The public learned of the mess in March 1985 with the failure of Home State Savings Bank of Cincinnati.

Depositors began a run on the bank's branches, causing the governor of Ohio to call for a bank holiday and closure of the state's savings and loans. Only federally backed (FSLIC) savings and loans reopened as other depositors drained the state's insurance funds. The problem soon spread to other states. As federal regulators were forced to take over these banks, the federal fund was depleted by late 1986. The federal government continued to back all insured savings and loans.

From 1986 to 1989, an additional 296 institutions were bailed out by the government. Things got worse as the Senate and House Ethics Committees uncovered political scandals affecting both parties in Congress. Five U.S. senators including Alan Cranston (D-CA), Don Riegle (D-MI), and Dennis DeConcini (D-AZ), were forced out of office, and John Glenn (D-OH) and John McCain (R-AZ) were rebuked for poor judgment and influence peddling with the Lincoln Savings and Loan failure. The scandals kept the savings and loan crisis in the news, requiring more reform by Congress. In January 1987, the Government Accounting Office declared the FSLIC officially insolvent by over $3.8 billion. Meanwhile, the whole savings and loan industry in Texas was near collapse. Texas represented over 50 percent of the industry liabilities, and the situation was worsened by a deep recession in the oil industry. In the end, 14 of the 20 biggest losses would be Texas savings and loans. The Texas savings and loan problem threatened the whole system.

Bank panic at the Old Court Savings & Loan in Randalstown, Maryland, 1985. (Marty Katz/ Time Life Pictures/Getty Images)

By 1989, the savings and loan crisis was dragging the economy into recession. In February 1989, President George H. W. Bush announced a $50 billion bailout of the savings and loan industry. In August, Congress passed the Financial Institutions Reform, Recovery, and Enforcement Act of 1989. The Savings Association Insurance Fund (SAIF) replaced the FSLIC. The Resolution Trust Corporation was created to resolve insolvent savings and loans. A new regulatory agency, the Office of Thrift Supervision, was created. Freddie Mac and Fannie Mae were given additional responsibility to support the mortgages of low-income families. By the official end of the savings and loan crisis in 1995, over 1,600 banks had closed or received substantial federal aid, representing 50 percent of the industry. Regulation helped restrict liberal practices, but many believe the root causes were never fully addressed.

*See also:* Banking Crisis and Great Recession; Panic of 1837; Panic of 1857; Panic of 1873; Panic of 1893; Panic of 1907; Stock Market Crash/Great Depression; Wage and Price Controls

### References

Curry, Timothy, and Lynn Shibut. "The Cost of the Savings and Loan Crisis: Truth and Consequences." *FDIC Banking Review,* December 2000, 2–3.

Holland, David. *When Regulation Was Too Successful—The Sixth Decade of Deposit Insurance.* Westport, CT: Greenwood, 1998.

Mayer, Martin. *The Greatest Ever Bank Robbery: The Collapse of the Savings and Loan Industry.* New York: C. Scribner's Sons, 1992.

# W. Edwards Deming Publishes *Out of the Crisis* (1986)

While the deindustrialization of America had many complex factors—such as the dollar policy, aging manufacturing plants, postwar overcapacity, trade deficits, and unions' wage and benefit demands—the decline in manufacturing quality was one of the more controllable factors at the plant level. The decline of American manufacturing quality became obvious in the 1970s in the area of automotive products, such as the quality issues of the Ford Pinto. The high comparative quality of the Japanese imports in the 1970s accelerated the market loss to small Japanese cars. The competitive losses launched a decade of soul searching. In 1980, an NBC television program entitled "If Japan Can . . . Why Can't We?" started that process. The show highlighted W. Edwards Deming as a quality guru with some answers. His popularity grew, and in 1986 Deming published his own answer in *Out of the Crisis.* The result was a massive quality movement in the United States that years later restored much of the lost quality. Today, American cars have finally reached world-class quality levels again.

The manufacturing quality problems were somewhat inherent to the focus on mass production. Quantity becomes the goal and focus of mass production with an entropic decline in quality if not countered by management. Deming would take American management and their practices to task. He argued the problem was with managers and their systems versus the worker. As part of the solution, Deming argued for the implementation of objective evaluations using statistical process control (SPC). The Deming approach would lead a movement of quality methods and philosophies that included the ideas of Philip Crosby, Walter Shewhart, Joseph Juran, Genichi Taguchi, and Kaoru Ishikawa. To some degree, these statistical methods were a logical improvement of Frederick Taylor's ideas of scientific management.

Deming had worked with Shewhart at Western Electric in the application of statistical process control. Shewhart had published the first industrial use of statistical process control in his work *Economic Control of Quality Manufactured Product* in 1931. Deming went on to apply statistics to his work at the Census Bureau; during World War II, Deming trained American manufacturers in the production of quality war materials. After the war, Deming was assigned to several projects in the rebuilding of Japan. He gained popularity with a series of lectures to the Union of Japanese Scientists and Engineers (UJSE). Deming was part of a movement by Japanese industry to become world competitive. While much credit is given to Deming's statistical techniques, the real power of Deming's approach was its focused goal of improvement that matched the national goal of returning Japan to an economic power.

Deming was followed in Japan in 1954 by other quality gurus such as Juran. Juran offered a systematic and operational approach to applying Deming's statistical methods. The Juran approach consisted of setting goals, organizing the workforce into problem-solving teams, and then applying statistics and other diagnostic methods. The success of the Japanese manufacturing miracle by the 1970s

W. Edwards Deming, America's quality guru, 1986. (AP Photo/Richard Drew)

created American companies to search for the reasons for Japan's advantage. The ideas of Deming and Juran became popular in their country of origin in the 1980s. Deming would become a consultant for organizations such as Ford Motor, General Motors, and the Department of Defense. Some original Japanese ideas on employee teams (quality circles in Japan) were added to the approaches of Deming and Juran and refined. Juran's *Quality Handbook* has become an industrial bible since its first edition in 1955.

Under cost pressures and with a declining market share, the American automotive industry was dragged into new quality initiatives such as Ford Q1, General Motors' Targets of Excellence, and Chrysler's Penstar program. In addition, a new breed of American quality gurus such as Crosby (*Quality Is Free*) and Tom Peters (*In Search of Excellence*) focused on customer satisfaction. The most important thing was that the attitude had changed by the 1990s as American quality began the slow climb back to world-class levels. Taguchi argued that the cost of quality failure, while hidden, presented a major manufacturing cost. Deming's ideas on the quality process were incorporated into the international manufacturing standard of ISO 9000. ISO 9000 forced companies to standardize processes much as Taylor had standardized products in the 20th century. ISO 9000 also added a systems approach, forcing companies to have a systematic and documented approach to problem solving. The automotive companies that wanted a stronger emphasis on statistics and specific customer requirements created additional requirements to ISO 9000, calling the standard QS 9000 in 1990. Today, the automotive version is known as TS 16949.

The United States recognized the need for national quality examples and in 1987 established the Malcolm Baldridge Award to highlight America's best example of quality manufacturing and service each year. In the 1960s, Japan had implemented the Deming Award to honor quality performance. The Reagan administration believed we needed a similar emphasis on the national level. Some early winners of the Baldridge Award included Motorola, Westinghouse Electric, and Xerox. The quality movement of the 1980s and 1990s did help restore American quality, but it could not eliminate the impact of the economic factors driving American deindustrialization. The Baldridge Award–winning programs of General Electric and Motorola morphed into the use of experimental design and statistical methods in their Six Sigma program for employee problem-solving teams. Six Sigma included the cost of quality, which Taguchi had made popular in the 1990s. Six Sigma programs combine statistical tools to allow employee teams to analyze process performance and design experiments to improve the process.

*See also:* First Japanese Auto Sold in the United States; First Mass-Produced Transistor Radio; Maslow's Theory of Needs; Scientific Management

**References**

Breyfogle, F. W. *Implementing Six Sigma.* New York: Wiley, 1999.

Deming, W. Edwards. *Out of the Crisis.* Cambridge, MA: MIT Center for Advanced Engineering Study, 1986.

Fryman, Mark A. *Quality and Process Improvement.* Albany, NY: Delmar, 2002.

# Amazon.com (1994)

The growth of the Internet in the 1990s was driven by new business models to exploit it. Amazon is credited with developing the concept of ecommerce. Amazon developed a business model for Internet success that would be used for over a decade and expanded into other internal business applications. After studying the rapid growth of the Internet, founder Jeff Bezos came up with a methodological business approach to making money with the Internet. His business plan was, however, unique in that it proposed not making a profit for five years. The business plan called for losses in an effort to gain name recognition and overcome customer resistance to buying books over the Internet. The business plan developed a perfect symbiotic relationship with the growing Internet technology. It proved very profitable in the long run but extremely frustrating to stockholders in the short run. In fact, it did not make a profit until the sixth year, reporting a $5 million profit in the first quarter of 2001. The patience of the business plan proved highly profitable, reporting a $3.9 million profit in 2002, making major inroads into the overall booksellers market. While profits have varied widely, sales reached into the billions by 2000. By 2010, Amazon had surpassed brick-and-mortar stores such as Barnes & Noble, Home Depot, Target, and Best Buy, lagging only behind such giants as Wal-Mart.

The formation of Amazon offers a classical study in how to start a business in general. Bezos was a Princeton University graduate in computer science and a former financial analyst. Seeing the hyperexponential growth of the Internet, Bezos began to look for potential business opportunities. He drew up a list including the selling of compact discs, computer hardware, books, videos, and so on. The amount of product and the lower price range favored the entry into books. Bezos formed the company in 1994, moving to Seattle because of its high-tech workforce. The first year, he invested time and money in the development of a novel website. Bezos realized he could gain an advantage over brick-and-mortar bookstores because of their high overhead costs. Still, initially, he had to manage the balance between building inventory and offering good delivery times. He started in a garage but quickly moved to a low-rent warehouse. While business took off immediately, he stocked only 2,000 of the most popular books, assuring good delivery on those titles.

The real strength and source of rapid growth was in his website and adaptability to the Internet. The website offered the type of browsing and comparison that would be difficult in a brick-and-mortar store. Customers could research areas of interest or the complete writings of an author. The website could track customer interests and previous purchases, allowing for recommendations and notification by e-mail of a new book in the customer's area of interest or by a certain author. These were services that a brick-and-mortar store could not readily offer. The website quickly won the attention of Internet servers and customers. Amazon also added customer services such as gift-wrapping. Through special services, novel digital shopping features, and discounting, Amazon began to overtake brick-and-mortar stores.

Amazon used its early understanding of the Internet to build partnerships with Internet servers and popular websites. Amazon also got authors and others involved through its associate program, which linked Amazon to individual websites and offered the associates a small commission. The associate program reached 60,000 by early 1998. Still, Bezos faced some delivery issues, finding that delivery was a key factor in expanding Internet sales. Amazon found that same-day shipping was a key metric to their success. Bezos set a corporate goal of 95 percent same-day shipping of in-stock orders. To achieve better delivery, an East Coast warehouse was opened in late 1997. The Delaware warehouse adjusted for an early shortcoming of the Seattle location, which was its distance from the East Coast center of book publishers. Amazon's growth was so fast that the business model needed to be flexible for new opportunities. By the end of 1997, Amazon became the first Internet company to reach one million customers. At the end of 1998, Amazon had become the world's third-largest bookseller by expanding to Europe.

The rapid growth allowed for more benefits to the company. They could demand larger discounts from the publishers. They also started to set up direct shipping where possible to further improve customer delivery times. They even started to earn significant interest on the float between payments to the publisher and customer credit card payments. Still, Amazon was reporting only losses, while it expanded into new markets. Amazon moved into music CDs in 1998. The music database not only was searchable but also allowed the customer to listen to a clip prior to buying. This feature was actually a competitive advantage to Amazon over brick-and-mortar stores at the time. There were some early failures of the business model. In 1999, Amazon moved into online auctions, taking on an established eBay. While Amazon failed to overtake eBay, it was able to morph services such as used books and CDs into its operations. This type of adaptability and flexibility became a hallmark of Amazon as they tested new ideas and opportunities through their Internet business.

The real strength of the Amazon business model is its ability to expand with the Internet and technology. A more generic pattern of the model reflects that of Sears in its use of the railroad in the 1800s. In 2011, Amazon was by far the largest

Internet retailer, thanks to its expansion by diversifying into similar products for Internet sales. Amazon has moved into a wide variety of products. It launched its MP3 downloads and its e-book reader Kindle in 2007 using the strength of its established ecommerce infrastructure. Amazon continues to use experiments to test new potential for its Internet infrastructure and expertise as in the past. This includes cloud computing utilizing its excess server capacity. In 2011, Amazon's success contributed to the bankruptcy of the number-two bookseller—Borders.

*See also:* ARPAnet (Earliest Internet) Formed; Bill Gates Internet Memo; Google Incorporated; Sears Mail Order Business

### References

Marcus, James. *Amazonia: Five Years at the Epicenter of the Dot.Com Juggernaut.* New York: Norton, 2004.

Osterwalder, Alexander. *Business Model Generation: A Handbook for Visionaries, Game Changers, and Challengers.* New York: Wiley, 2010.

Spector, Robert. *Amazon.com—Get Big Fast: Inside the Revolutionary Business Model That Changed the World.* San Francisco: HarperBusiness, 2000.

# Bill Gates Internet Memo (1995)

In the 400-some years of American business, it seems only fitting that the business icon of the last 70 years—the corporate memo—should have a place in history. It was a memo of an entrepreneur in transition from founder to CEO. In 1995, the 20th anniversary of Microsoft, it had become was an international company with its number of employees approaching 20,000. Its size and diverse locations had evolved beyond its early beginnings in a rundown motel. At this point, Microsoft dominated the software industry but had been caught off guard by the growth of the Internet. Bill Gates realized he had to reinvent the corporate vision and inspire a degree of urgency on the organization. Gates chose the vehicle of an Internet memo to emphasize that urgency and the importance of the new technology. The memo was a call to enter the market and to *dominate it.* On May 26, 1995, Gates released a memo to his executives pointing to "the internet tidal wave" as a new business opportunity. Gates called the Internet, in 1995, the "most important single development to come since the IBM PC was introduced in 1981." That event had been the source of Microsoft's success, and now Gates looked to recreate the same success with the Internet. The memo illustrated Gates's deeply competitive nature.

The memo itself would break most conventional rules for a good business memo. It was long (over seven pages) and broad in its scope. Yet it was well focused enough to start the discussion of a detailed action plan. It was designed to begin thought on the task, which would be followed up by an Internet retreat of his managers in a few weeks. Still, the memo was visionary and at the same time offered a practical course of action. Most important, it clearly communicated the new vision of the corporation and the benchmarks and achievements that the company would use to measure the managers. For employees, it had a biblical quality in its direction and guidance. It awoke the sleeping giant. In 1996, Netscape's Navigator controlled over 85 percent of the browser market, with Microsoft's Internet Explorer having only 10 percent. Within two years, the percentages were reversed. The memo would surface in the 1998 antitrust case against Microsoft. Interestingly, it was leaked first on the Internet. The memo laid out a multimedia vision, foreseeing the merger of television and computers into a unified broadband medium. Microsoft also entered online services with its MSN to compete with the service leader at the time—America Online. The memo had unleashed the greatest concentration of computer know-how on a focused goal. It also showed that Gates was not just a gifted geek but also a seasoned and competitive businessman.

The weakness identified in the Gates memo appeared at the peak of Microsoft strength in the operating system market. Microsoft had won its court case with Apple over the GUI (graphical user interface) operating system. Microsoft was then the world leader in operating systems, but there was a problem. The problem became obvious with the release of Windows 95, which lacked a web browser for the booming Internet, a web browser being the necessary software to retrieve, capture, and navigate through information on the Internet. At the time, Apple had a web browser, and even IBM OS/2 had one. Microsoft geeks started to warn Gates, who had been, at best, lukewarm to the Internet, which his organization reflected. A lack of a web browser threatened to resurrect IBM and Apple as competitors. In addition, personal computer clones were using Netscape's Navigator. The immediate effect of Gates's memo was the purchase of software in August 1995 from Spyglass Incorporated to use as an add-on web browser to Windows 95. The next year Microsoft bundled it in its Windows package and gave it away free. Netscape at the time was not charging for its software to noncommercial users but charged for upgrades. Microsoft's technical resources, once they had been shifted and focused, started to overtake Netscape's early technological advantages. The latter part of the 1990s would be known as the "browser wars." Microsoft edged ahead with a combination of technology and market leverage with its software. As Netscape's sales fell, so did the money available for the necessary development to keep pace with Microsoft. By 1998, America Online purchased Netscape, but its browser business was over. Netscape's browser would resurface years later as an open source product known as Mozilla Firefox, which amazingly recaptured up to 20 percent of the market.

Gates's incredible turnaround in Internet applications and services brought the filing of an antitrust suit based on its abusive tactics in the web browser war with

Netscape. The suit alleged that Microsoft abused monopoly power on its Intel-based computers with its handling of operating system and web browser sales. The suit was opposed by many economists, who lined up to support Microsoft. Most felt it was an unnecessary intrusion of government driven not by consumers but by rival companies. The initial judgment in 2002 found that Microsoft had used monopolistic practices in violation of the Sherman Act. Microsoft appealed, and eventually there was a settlement in 2002. In retrospect, there was little real impact on Microsoft, although the legal fights continue.

Another important result of the Microsoft memo and its ultimate victory in the browser wars was the realization of the codependency of Microsoft with its founder. In 1998, Gates addressed this issue and started the transition to a true corporate infrastructure. Steve Ballmer, a friend and Harvard graduate, took over as president of Microsoft while Gates remained CEO. It is a model of making the transition from a founder-driven business to corporate control. Gates's theme of never being overtaken again remains as corporate culture. Most recently, Microsoft has launched an initiative to move into search engines.

*See also:* First Billion-Dollar Corporation—United States Steel; Standard Oil Antitrust Lawsuit; The Year of the PC

### References

Gates, Bill. *Business @ the Speed of Thought: Succeeding in the Digital Economy.* New York: Warner Business Books, 2000.

Wallace, James, and Jim Erickson. *Hard Drive: Bill Gates and the Making of the Microsoft Empire.* New York: Harper Business, 1999.

# Google Incorporated (1998)

Google began at the nation's greatest technical incubator, Stanford University, as a research project by two PhD students—Larry Page and Sergey Brin. Work on what would become the Google search engine started in 1996. The project was called the Stanford Digital Library Project (SDLP). The project was originally funded by a number of government agencies including the National Science Foundation. They developed an early search engine called BackRub. It was not the first; in fact, Excite, WebCrawler, Lycos, Infoseek, and OpenText were already on the Internet. Carnegie-Mellon University's Lycos was then the most-used search engine on Netscape's list, even though Infoseek was the default search engine on Netscape. These early search engines were viewed as software to be licensed or sold, not as moneymaking ventures. The rise of Google was due to its business model rather than its technological advantage.

The history of the search engine is almost as old as the computer itself. The source of commercial search engines can be traced to Stanford University long before Google. The Internet directory and server Yahoo was formed by two Stanford students, David Filo and Jerry Yang, in 1994 and was incorporated in 1995 with $2 million in venture capital. Yahoo functioned as a full-service Internet provider with a search engine licensed from others. Even earlier, a group of Stanford undergraduates had developed a search engine using statistical analysis of word relationships in 1993. The software was released and evolved into the company known as Excite. At the time no true business model for making money from search engines had emerged except to sell to, license, or develop an Internet service. In many cases, search engines were offered for free by Internet providers. Lycos was a major search engine developed by Carnegie-Mellon University students; it was used freely on the Internet but also developed into a service company. By the late 1990s, new ideas to make money from search engines emerged.

In 1996, AltaVista and Inktomi Corporation were advancing search engine technology. AltaVista was the first to allow for natural-language queries as well as advanced search methods using Boolean logic. Inktomi had a search engine known as Hotwire, which included the best technology and the beginning of a new business model. A great deal of search engine software was available, but the

Google cofounders Larry Page (left) and Sergey Brin. (AP/Wide World Photos)

commercial rewards for further development seemed few. Inktomi saw the possibility of commercial gains by charging a flat or recurring fee for commercial websites (paid inclusion). While Inktomi pioneered paid inclusion, the market was not yet big enough to support it. Some search engines were using pop-up advertisements with limited success.

In 1998, Bill Gross, founder of Overture (initially known as GoTo.com), developed a pay-per-click business model for his search engine. The idea was that advertisers paid a fee when their websites were clicked on after an Internet search. These are known as sponsored ads. The idea generated a great deal of appeal to advertisers, who were used to broadcast advertising on television. Pay per click assured the audience was being individually targeted. Google would eventually adapt to this model and expand its application to targeted audiences. However, the success of Overture initially showed Google and potential investors the possibility of making money with search engines.

In August 1998, Google got a loan from Stanford entrepreneur and cofounder of Sun Microsystems, Andy Bechtolsheim. The next month the company formally incorporated as Google Inc. and operated out of a garage. The name came from the term *googol,* representing the number 1 followed by 100 zeros. Google quickly gained a reputation as a better search engine than Excite and Hotbot. The company moved to the now-famous incubator at 165 University Avenue in Palo Alto. The focus was to build user loyalty and technical superiority. It attracted venture capitalists such as Kleiner Perkins Caufield & Byers and Sequoia Capital. Sequoia had already made profitable investments in Apple Computer, Atari, Oracle, and Cisco. Google was able to get $25 million from the two, but Sequoia required the hiring of a CEO and a fully developed business model. Sequoia clearly brought the business discipline needed for Google to become dominant. The model was based on selling key search words to advertisers using a combination of bids and clicking-through charges. Google continued to rise in stature, and eventually America Online chose Google as its search partner, followed quickly by Yahoo. However, it would take another two years to fully overcome rivals such as Overture. The competition of search engines led to the incorporation of technology and marketing in Google AdWords.

The unique and specialized advertising model of Google AdWords revolutionized the marketing business model. AdWords is a pay-per-click system that ranks or orders search results for sponsored links. How much the advertiser ultimately pays depends on bidding on per-click rates based on keywords, and on a quality score. The quality score is a complex calculation based on historical click-through rates, relevance of keywords, the advertiser's account history, and other relevance factors. In addition, Google added location-based targeting and other frequency factors. By 2003, Google had established itself as the dominant search engine and had moved aggressively into other areas. Google went public in 2004 and controlled over 80 percent of worldwide searching. In retrospect, more than any other company, Google commercialized the Internet and took real advertising dollars from other media such as television and radio. The advertising dollars are amazing and continue to attract new entries into the search engine market. By 2005, Google had a market value of over $50 billion. In 2010, even Microsoft has entered the competition with its Bing search engine.

*See also:* ARPAnet (Earliest Internet) Formed; Sears Mail Order Business

### References

Battelle, John. *The Search: How Google and Its Rivals Rewrote the Rules of Business and Transformed Our Culture.* New York: Portfolio, 2005.

Stross, Randall. *Planet Google: One Company's Audacious Plan to Organize Everything We Know.* New York: Free Press, 2008.

# First 3G Networks and the Smartphone (2003)

The 3G network, as the third generation in mobile telecommunications is known, has a complex history because some of the engineering advances to a third generation are subjective. This third generation was driven more by standards and network protocol than by technology. This generation of telecommunications meets the international specifications International Mobile Telecommunications-2000 (IMT-2000) of the International Telecommunications Union. This new wireless communications network supports a wide range of new devices such as smartphones, mobile laptops, videophones, and mobile television. Japan was the first to launch a true 3G network in 2001. The standard allows for more broadband efficiency and allows speeds of 6 to 15 megabits per second to support smart devices, although technically the standard requires peak data rates of only 380 kilobits. The 3G networks use different radio frequencies than the 2G ones. The year 2003 stands out as the year of American 3G networks, or mobile broadband. Verizon and AT&T (Cingular at the time) introduced their 3G networks that year. The 3G network and standards needed a device to expand their use. The networks are not so much a technical breakthrough as a commercial breakthrough. The arrival of 3G expanded the use of cell phone devices to video email, mobile television, movie watching, Internet surfing, and video conferencing.

In late 2003, Cingular had its 3G wireless network ready, but it needed a breakthrough device to push network use and profits. The very first 3G phones to hit the market in 2003 were heavy and large. They were very unpopular. Wireless companies were looking for a manufacturer to popularize 3G, but these wireless providers wanted complete control over manufacturers. Their voice phone business was peaking, and profit margins were declining. The 3G offered the potential for high-profit-margin data users downloading music, books, and videos and surfing the Internet. Wireless phone carriers such as Cingular and Verizon had gotten used to defining the devices to be used. Steve Jobs at Apple Computer was looking at a much different relationship in the development of a multiuse cell phone of the future. Apple had already successfully moved into the MP3 music market with its iPod. Jobs envisioned a single device to function as an Internet, music, and phone device. It was the perfect utilization of the 3G technology. In 2005, Jobs launched a team of 200 engineers on the iPod development project while he started secret negotiations with Cingular. Jobs realized that competitors were watching, and he wanted to assure secrecy. This was a major breakthrough, and he well remembered how Microsoft had pirated his operating system. He spread out his team members and separated his hardware and software teams. Visits to Cingular were kept secret, and members signed in as employees of Infineon. He also had developed an advanced touch screen for his failed PC tablet that competitors still had not duplicated, and he planned to use it in his new iPhone. Jobs publicly denied that any work was being done on a cell phone during the whole time Apple was working with Motorola and Cingular on a music phone to be released in 2005, known as ROKR. The ROKR, with an Apple operating system and supported by its iTunes library, did come out in late 2005. The 2007 release of the iPhone made the ROKR obsolete. The iPhone was able to hold 1,500 songs versus 100 for the ROKR. The ROKR also had a bulky walkie-talkie-like appearance, which added to its unpopularity. The June 28, 2007, release of the iPhone was an amazing testament to Apple's market following. Estimates of sales for the first weekend were as high as 700,000.

The development of the iPhone was the perfect combination of Apple's search for a high-profit device and the carriers' search for a breakthrough application. The competition between carriers such as Verizon and AT&T (which purchased Cingular at its peak in 2006) allowed Apple to take leadership in the manufacturing and design of the new generation of cell phones. Jobs found himself in the driver's seat with his proposed iPhone. Jobs wanted to break the earlier cell phone model where the cell phone manufacturers profited on the sale of the device rolled into the time-specified contract. Jobs wanted higher profit margins and wanted to profit from the usage as well. Negotiating with AT&T, which at the time was losing market share to Verizon, gave Jobs huge leverage. The iPhone could offer a huge flood of new customers. Jobs even pushed AT&T (Cingular) to assure video email in the network. Jobs also demanded that he have complete commercial and manufacturing control over the iPhone. Jobs got what he wanted. Apple would make a profit of about $150 on the initial selling price of $599 and $10 a month from every AT&T bill on a two-year contract. Even after the initial price was reduced to $399, Apple still made $80 per phone.

The iPhone business model caused manufacturers to design for customer approval rather than for carrier approval as had been the case in the cell phone business model up until then. Prior to the iPhone, carriers determined the prices and features of the manufactured phones. The results lived up to every hope and dream of Apple. They sold over three million phones in the six final months of 2007, returning more than the estimated development cost of $150 million. Google's Android phone came into the market because of the exclusive initial deal with AT&T. The iPhone created a whole new industry of phone applications to develop all of the iPhone's capabilities. Carriers that lost their control over wireless devices were even looking at wireless banking to expand their services along with the iPhone's capability. The expansion of 3G networks rejuvenated the stalled technology of electronic books with devices such as Amazon's Kindle. These 3G electronic books are redefining the selling of books and accelerating the decline of brick-and-mortar stores. To date, 3G has proved to be a major commercial advance, more so than the first two generations of wireless communications.

*See also:* ARPAnet (Earliest Internet) Formed; FCC Approves Advanced Mobile Phone System (1G); Google Incorporated

### References

Elliot, Jay, and William L. Simon. *The Steve Jobs Way: iLeadership for a New Generation.* New York: Vanguard, 2011.

Vogelstein, Fred. "The Untold Story: How the iPhone Blew Up the Wireless Industry." *Wired Magazine,* January 9, 2008: 27–28.

# RFID at Wal-Mart (2005)

In January 2005, Wal-Mart, the nation's largest retailer, announced to its top 100 suppliers that radio frequency identification (RFID) labels would be required on all pallet shipments. Many consider the event the beginning of a revolution in inventory management and package tracking. RFID uses a microchip label to emit radio waves to transfer information data to an electronic reader. The RFID product tags could accurately update inventory routinely without human labor, and this accurate inventory count in seconds could reduce inventory and manage the entire ordering and delivery needs of the supply chain. Delivery tracking throughout the supply chain would be possible. And in the store, quick electronic checkout would be possible, and estimates of huge savings were possible by avoiding out-of-stock situations. Commercial experiments are now underway to tie RFID tags with smartphones for credit card purchases and other applications such as electronic toll collection. While the benefits are huge, problems with initial cost and privacy and security concerns remain.

The technology of RFID is a confluence of several streams of development. The earliest roots go back to the development of electrical transponders to identify planes at the end of World War II. The more recent history is one of miniaturization of the unit. The earliest patents occurred in the 1980s. These tags consist of a microchip with an integrated circuit for storing, processing, and sending data. Most have a small built-in battery that can be activated in the presence of a reader or can actively broadcast. Some low-cost ones are passive (having no battery) and read by a mobile sensor/reader, since broadcasting is presently limited to a few yards. The active battery-powered tags are very expensive (over $50) and therefore are applied to larger and expensive items. The passive labels being used by retailers such as Wal-Mart cost around 5¢ to 10¢ each at present.

Wal-Mart is one of the few retailers big enough to help push this implementation down the supply chain. However, in 2007, the Department of Defense also requested RFID labels on many of its purchases. The Department of Defense has since mandated it on most pallet shipments according to MIL STD 129. Wal-Mart's initial 2007 plan was to use smart labels on all pallets going to Wal-Mart stores and Sam's Club. As might be expected, suppliers were not happy and dragged their feet. Sam's Club imposed a threatening $12-per-pallet penalty, which it later reduced to $0.12 a pallet. Wal-Mart issued a full-implementation target for pallets by 2010. While the target was not reached, much progress was made. Wal-Mart was not alone, as other retailers and wholesalers have joined in on pallet shipments. Procter & Gamble is one of Wal-Mart's suppliers that have readily adopted RFID. In 2010, Wal-Mart took a larger step in implementing RFID tags on clothing. At the same time J.C. Penney was experimenting with RFID.

RFID offers potential huge savings in inventory control, reduction of lost sales due to better stocking, and reduction in theft. Wal-Mart studies suggest out-of-stock situations could be reduced as much as 30 percent, translating into more sales. Inventory control software has made big advances since the 1990s with material requirement planning (MRP). MRP systems can be a real advantage in inventory management, but they require an accurate physical count to function properly. RFID offers the accuracy to improve the function of MRP and inventory control software. The cost of hand scanning of inventory is eliminated. The ability of RFID technology to instantly provide an updated, accurate picture of inventory on hand and shipments in transit would mean large savings. In addition, the impact on theft would be just as big. One problem, however, is concern over privacy and tracking beyond the store. Another is that the in-store scanners could access digital codes embedded in credit cards or special driver's licenses.

Applications are expanding beyond retailing as well. Assets can be tagged and readily inventoried at year end. Banks such as Wells Fargo and Bank of America are using RFID tags on information technology assets. One of the earliest uses of RFID included tagging of animals after the outbreak of mad cow disease. Some casinos are using embedded RFID tags on high-value chips to detect counterfeit chips and invalidate stolen chips. One area of research continues to be automatic checkout systems and payment. Today, Intermec Technologies and Symbol Technologies (Motorola) are the major manufacturers. Tag prices are coming down, which will encourage more implementation. Interestingly, the path forward can be found in the implementation of bar code technology.

*See also:* First Customer Scan of a Bar Code

### References

Bustillo, Miguel. "Wal-Mart Radio Tags to Track Clothing." *Wall Street Journal,* July 23, 2010.

Lahiri, Sandip. *RFID Sourcebook.* Amonk: NY: IBM Press, 2011.

# Banking Crisis and Great Recession (2008)

The Great Recession has approached the misery of the 1930s, and full analysis of the causes will continue for years. Still, the Great Recession has many similarities to previous recessions in its origins and effects. The official start of the Great Recession has been tagged as December 2007 after a real estate bubble evolved into a financial crisis. This initial crisis, known as the subprime crisis, was a result of low-quality mortgages failing throughout the banking system. While the subprime crisis had its roots in America, bundled financial packages containing these mortgages had been sold throughout the world, and it quickly became a worldwide crisis. The full accounting of the recession is not complete, but based on the drop in gross national product (GNP), it is the greatest recession since the 1930s. Banking failures and housing declines have been the largest since the 1930s. In many areas, house prices have experienced declines never seen before. In 2008, the government had to take over the country's largest mortgage companies, Fannie Mae and Freddie Mac. Large financial firms went to the brink, with Lehman Brothers filing for bankruptcy and the world's largest insurance company, AIG, needing to be bailed out by the government for amounts in excess of $150 billion. The end of 2008 required federal bailouts of Citigroup and other large banks. General Motors and Chrysler would require billions in bailout money and structured bankruptcies. The Federal Reserve jumped in with billions of dollars worth of cash bailouts and Congress passed a $787 billion stimulus package. While the analysis of the causes and effects is incomplete, the place of the Great Recession in the top 100 major business events is assured.

One feature of the pre-recession problems was the rise of a worldwide housing bubble. In the United States, decades of government policy had focused on increasing house ownership. That policy, coupled with commodity inflation, drove housing prices sky-high. From 1997 to 2007, many American home prices more than doubled. The rapid rise in prices created a speculation bubble in the high-priced segment of the market. The lower- and middle-priced homes were driven up by excess money and the government policy of loosening credit requirements. One issue was the lowering of interest rates by the Federal Reserve. Subprime mortgages were also at the root of the housing bubble. *Subprime* refers to the poor quality of the borrower's credit record. Standards for mortgages were almost nonexistent for these subprime loans. The drive to expand these subprime loans came from government-sponsored agencies such as Fannie Mae and Freddie Mac. Clearly, the government was applying pressure to take on more subprime mortgages. When Fannie Mae and Freddie Mac were forced into receivership in September 2008, they had over $5 trillion in mortgage obligations.

The problem had spread throughout the American and world banking systems due to lack of regulation and innovative new financial products. These innovative products were complex and confused the actual stream of mortgage payments. They included the bundling of subprime mortgages into mortgage-backed securities (MBS) and collateralized debt obligations (CDO) for sale to investors. These derivatives increased the distance from the underlying assets as they were sold all over

Lehman Brothers headquarters on September 15, 2008, the day the 158-year-old financial institution filed for bankruptcy. (AP Photo/Louis Lanzano)

the world. This type of derivatives and the asset distance allowed for frequent illegal acts and loss of accountability. It also allowed for loose standards on credit, since the mortgages were sold off in these derivatives. Major banks had billions of these creative derivatives on their books. The pricing of these risky investments became an issue as the system broke down.

In 2007, the whole system started to unravel. The Bush administration had discovered the subprime weakness in 2006, but Congress was not ready to act. Credit agencies were also aware of the problem and started to downgrade bonds related to subprime mortgages in June 2007. European banks were hit first in the fall of 2007 with several runs on French and British banks. By the spring of 2008, the crisis moved to the source in the United States. Bear Stearns was rescued from bankruptcy in March 2008. Fannie Mae and Freddie Mac had to be rescued in August 2008, while Lehman Brothers went bankrupt in September 2008. At the same time Merrill Lynch was rescued by being purchased by Bank of America in a deal brokered by the government. Black September continued with an emergency loan to AIG, which was deemed "too big to fail." The financial crisis moved into the stock market, and the market fell 777 points on September 29, the largest one-day drop in history. Congress was in the midst of a great debate on an economic bailout. Many of the lessons of the 1930s were again discussed.

October continued the stock market slide and bank failures. In November 2008, the crisis came to Main Street as unemployment claims jumped to a seven-year high. More money was needed by AIG, and Congress was looking at loans for American carmakers as they faced potential bankruptcy. Citigroup needed a government loan of $20 billion to keep it from going under. The carmakers got their loans in December, and Citigroup was forced to merge with Morgan Stanley. The stock market declined into 2009, plunging to a low of under 7,000 on the Dow. Runs on money market mutual funds required the government to insure them. The Federal Reserve used all its tools to flood cash into the system. Finally, Congress passed and President Obama signed the bank relief legislation on January 28. European countries had to implement similar bailouts. This huge influx of funds into the system was based on the lessons of the Great Depression when the government was slow to react.

The problems of the recession would continue even as the banking system stabilized. Bloomberg News estimated that over $14 trillion of global company value was eliminated in 2009. While the recession continued worldwide into 2010, China, South Korea, and India appear to have avoided a recession. Iceland suffered a total collapse of its banking system. Based on total gross domestic product, the United States lost over 4 percent. Europe was hit much harder with gross domestic product losses in excess of 6 percent.

*See also:* Panic of 1837; Panic of 1857; Panic of 1873; Panic of 1893; Panic of 1907; Savings and Loan Crisis; Stock Market Crash/Great Depression

**References**

Paulson, Hank. *On the Brink.* London: Headline, 2010.

Read, Colin. *Global Financial Meltdown: How to Avoid the Next Financial Crisis.* New York: Palgrave Macmillan, 2009.

Wessel, David. "Did 'Great Recession' Live Up to the Name?" *Wall Street Journal,* April 8, 2010.

# General Motors Bankruptcy (2009)

The unlikely bankruptcy of General Motors was one of the largest (and the largest of an industrial company) in American history. Officially, it ranks as number four after Lehman Brothers, Washington Mutual, and Worldcom. While many had believed it unthinkable, there had been rumors as early as 2006. The decline to bankruptcy of General Motors and Chrysler had deep roots, starting with the flood of imports in the 1970s that steadily eroded the market share of the automotive giants. The bankruptcy filing of General Motors confirmed that America's deindustrialization had reached the top of the food chain. General Motors had negotiated long-term reductions in wages with the United Auto Workers, but nothing helped immediately in their struggle with imports. General Motors had not made a profit since 2004. The Great Recession and 2008 financial crisis caught General Motors in a cash-short position, which forced its filing on June 1, 2009. In the filing, General Motors reported $172 billion in debt and $82 billion in assets. The bankruptcy would be far from a normal bankruptcy as the deal was "pre-packaged," controlled by the federal government and financed by the taxpayers. The American taxpayers ended up with about a 60 percent ownership in General Motors.

The real root of General Motors' problem was typical of the deindustrialization of American industry. Market share was lost while pension and health care costs for employees soared. In 2005, these costs were estimated at $1,600 per car. General Motors had struggled through the 1990s with some major setbacks and a few successes. The 1990s actually ended on a high note, with both General Motors and Ford gaining market share and profitability with sales of sport-utility vehicles (SUVs) and light trucks. The stock actually soared to $80 a share on huge profits. The recession of the early 2000s showed a basic weakness that had been growing for years. The rise in interest rates, stock market drop, and increasing retirees put General Motors into a pension fund crisis. The pension fund was $15 billion underfunded in 2003, which the company responded to by fully funding the pensions to keep bond creditors from downgrading its rating. Losses started to mount in the mid-2000s. General Motors had been selling units such as General Dynamics, Hughes Electronics, and Delphi for cash. Still, in 2005, General Motors was a huge company with sales of $193 billion and a payroll near $8 billion. General Motors was spending almost $5 billion a year in health care for retirees, which was part of a major structural problem below the surface. By 2006, the company was short of cash, and even the unthinkable rumors of bankruptcy began. General Motors was able to raise $14 billion in 2006 by selling 51 percent of its highly profitable financing arm, GMAC, to Cerberus Capital Management. General Motors, whose stock had hit $19 a share, managed to improve in 2006, and the company remained afloat. In 2007, General Motors sold Allison Transmission for $5.6 billion.

A fluctuating stock market changed the funding ratio of the pension funds, while market share declines continued to rack up losses for the company. General Motors continued to sell assets, close plants, and restructure. Its bond ratings declined, making it more difficult to raise cash. The 650,000 retirees continued to be a problem, as companies like Toyota and Honda had few legacy costs. Regardless, Toyota and Honda opened American nonunion plants with lower wages and minimal employee benefits. The American Japanese plants purchased capital in American political ties as well. Finally, in 2008, the rise of gas prices to four dollars a gallon caused truck sales to plummet. Chrysler was experiencing similar problems by 2007 and had been taken over by Cerberus Capital Management. In October 2008, Cerberus was proposing a merger of General Motors and Chrysler, but the deal fell through. General Motors was now losing $3 billion a month as the economy came to a standstill. The Senate refused to give General Motors a bailout loan in early December 2008, but the Bush administration managed to give them the money from the TARP bill (Troubled Assets Relief Program). It was too late, as burn rates ("burning" through of cash reserves) were now $5 billion a month.

With the Obama administration coming into office in late January 2009, the efforts to save General Motors accelerated. The financial crisis had eroded sales to the point that it was hopeless to generate the cash needed to operate. In late March, the U.S. Treasury committed a fund to provide a government guarantee of General Motors' warranty liabilities. General Motors entered bankruptcy in June 2009 with the government in full charge of the details. The bankruptcy would overturn 200 years of bankruptcy law. It devalued the bondholders, who under law would have first claim on the assets. At the same time, because of the large stock ownership position of the union, stockholders got preferred treatment. Bondholders received pennies on the dollar, and legal suits are still pending over the arrangement, most of them by government unions whose pension funds had large amounts of General Motors bonds. Both the United States and Canada infused money into the bankruptcy restructuring. The United Auto Workers held onto most of their wages and benefits in the deal. Under normal bankruptcy, the union contract would have been voided and required a new negotiated contract. The government was spared a takeover of the pension fund, which would have happened under normal bankruptcy.

Results to date have been mixed, but jobs were saved as well as most of the American auto industry. Money has been paid back, although the real amount is in question. General Motors is much leaner. The union remains a major stockholder in General Motors. In fairness, the United Auto Workers proved much more flexible than other heavy-industry unions such as the United States Steel Workers in the decades of deindustrialization. General Motors was scaled down to the core brands of Chevrolet, Cadillac, Buick, and GMC. It has once again become competitive worldwide with Toyota, which suffered from quality problems and recalls shortly after the General Motors bankruptcy. General Motors has developed a strong base in the Chinese market. General Motors has also moved aggressively into electric and hybrid cars. It also plans to move into the subcompact market.

*See also:* Deindustrialization of America—General Tire Akron Closes; General Motors Corporation Formed; Henry Ford Wins Race of the Century

### References

Taylor, Alex. *Sixty to Zero: Inside Look at the Collapse of General Motors—and the Detroit Auto Industry.* New Haven, CT: Yale University Press, 2011.

Welch, David, and Dan Beucke. "Why GM's Plan Won't Work." *Bloomberg Businessweek,* May 9, 2005.

# APPENDIX: PRIMARY DOCUMENTS

## THE PETITION TO PARLIAMENT FROM CA. 1750 ON REPEAL OF THE IRON PROHIBITION ACT OF 1750

*In 1750 the British Parliament enacted the Iron Prohibition Act of 1750 as part of a series of Navigation Acts, which would become the root of the American Revolution. The colonial parliament in Virginia responded with a petition to repeal. The restriction prohibited colonists from making iron implements. Pig iron made in colonial furnaces had to be shipped to Britain and made into implements to be shipped back. The colonists also paid a tax on these implements coming back to the colonies.*

It was never thought the Interest of England to en courage the Colonies to Manufacture any Thing that was Manufactured in England; and the Iron Manufacture is the second in the Kingdom, which maintains at least 200,000 People; and, if lost, those People must be an heavy Burthen to their Parishes, particularly in the counties of Worcester, Stafford, Warwick, Salop, Lancaster, York, great Part of Wales, and other Places, and consider ably lessen the Value of the Land and Rents in those counties.

Should Encouragement be given to the Colonies, especially to Virginia, 'twould not encourage our Navigation; for there's no Ship that comes from thence, but will bring a considerable Quantity of Iron, and her full Quantity of Tobacco also; and therefore not employ many more Ships in the Virginia Trade. And the Making of Iron in any other Parts of America, will occasion a larger Fleet to convoy the Ships from thence than from Sweden, should we have a War with any Nation whatever.

There is no Iron yet known proper for Steel made here, but the best Swedish; and the Steel Manufacture is very advantageous to England, at least Fifty per cent in Manufacturing.

There are Collieries in New England, and the Smiths there buy Coals as cheap as a Smith in London; and by that and other Advantages, the People of New England did Manufacture considerably; which being laid before the Honourable the

House of Commons, they took off the Drawback from unmanufactured Iron and Steel Exported to America in the year 1711, being the Ninth of Queen Anne.

The Encouraging the Making of Iron in America, will put them upon Manufacturing, and they will supply them selves first, and all the Colonies; so that the Manufacturers here must starve. America cannot supply England with any Iron for many Years; and the Want of Iron is already sufficiently known to all Traders, Handicrafts, Husband men, Shipwrights, Merchants, and others.

The Americans have the Advantage of 5*l*. per Tun and upwards, in Making of Iron in their Wood, and Oar, more than the English have; which will over and above pay the great Wages in America, and the Freight to England.

When there was an open Trade with Sweden, the Swedish Iron Imported into England paid annually 40,000*l*. Custom, which will be so much Loss to the Revenue if the Americans Import Iron free, and much more if a Bounty be given them, could they supply us.

---

*Source:* http://www.virginiaplaces.org/geology/iron.html

## THE PATENT ACT OF 1790

*At the request of Thomas Jefferson, Congress enacted the protection of patents and intellectual rights to foster creativity and invention. Jefferson, an inventor himself, realized this as a type of right. In Europe patents were the property of the king or assigned designate. The ability of the original inventor to own the rights to his invention created a base for national capitalism and America's rapid industrial development.*

## SEC. 1

*Be it enacted by the Senate and House of Representatives of the United States of America in Congress assembled,* That upon the petition of any person or persons to the Secretary of State, the Secretary for the department of war, and the Attorney General of the United States, setting forth, that he, she, or they, hath or have invented or discovered any useful art, manufacture, engine, machine, or device, or any improvement therein not before known or used, and praying that a patent may be granted therefor, it shall and may be lawful to and for the Secretary of State, the Secretary for the department of war, and the Attorney General, or any two of them, if they shall deem the invention or discovery sufficiently useful and important, to cause letters patent to be made out in the name of the United States, to bear teste by the President of the United States, reciting the allegations and suggestions of the said petition, and describing the said invention or discovery, clearly, truly and fully, and thereupon granting to such petitioner or petitioners, his, her or their heirs, administrators or assigns for any term not exceeding fourteen years, the sole and exclusive right and liberty of making, constructing, using and vending to others to be used, the said invention or discovery; which letters patent shall be delivered to the Attorney General of the United States to be examined, who shall, within fifteen days next after the delivery to him, if he shall find the same conformable to this act, certify it to be so at the foot thereof, and present the letters patent so certified to the President, who shall cause the seal of the United States to be thereto affixed, and the same shall be good and available to the grantee or grantees by force of this act, to all and every intent and purpose herein contained, and shall be recorded in a book to be kept for that purpose in the office of the Secretary of State, and delivered to the patentee or his agent, and the delivery thereof shall be entered on the record and endorsed on the patent by the said Secretary at the time of granting the same.

_Source:_ http://ipmall.info/hosted_resources/lipa/patents/Patent_Act_of_1790.pdf

## REPORT ON MANUFACTURING (1791)

_Secretary of the Treasury Alexander Hamilton submitted his "Report on Manufacturing" to Congress on December 5, 1791. Hamilton proposed a shift from Jefferson's agrarian vision of the nation. Hamilton believed that the United States needed to develop domestic manufacturing as a means of protecting its economic freedom. The United States remained dependent on foreign governments in economic goods, and Hamilton believed there could be no freedom without domestic manufacturing. Hamilton argued that if the United States would initiate a protective tariff, then investors would contribute to the development of industries within the country. Although Congress failed to fully implement all of Hamilton's proposals, after the War of 1812 the first protective tariff was passed. Hamilton's philosophy of protectionism became known as the American System. The American System was adopted by Henry Clay as the platform of the Whig Party in the 1820s and taken by Whig Abraham Lincoln into the Republican Party. It became the core of the Republican Party of William McKinley, leading America into a great age of industry._

The Secretary of the Treasury, in obedience to the order of the House of Representatives, of the 15th day of January 1790, has applied his attention, at as early a period as his other duties would permit, to the subject of Manufactures; and particularly to the means of promoting such as will tend to render the United States, independent of foreign nations, for military and other essential supplies. And he there (upon) respectfully submits the following Report.

The expediency of encouraging manufactures in the United States, which was not long since deemed very questionable, appears at this time to be pretty generally admitted. The embarrassments, which have obstructed the progress of our external trade, have led to serious reflections on the necessity of enlarging the sphere of our domestic commerce: the restrictive regulations, which in foreign markets abridge the vent of the increasing surplus or our Agricultural produce, serve to beget an earnest desire, that a more extensive demand for that surplus may be created at home: And the complete success, which has rewarded manufacturing enterprise, in some valuable branches, conspiring with the promising symptoms, which attend some less mature essays, in others, justify a hope, that the obstacles to the growth of this species of industry are less formidable that they were apprehended to be; and that it is not difficult to find, in its further extension: a full indemnification for any external disadvantages, which are or may be experienced, as well as an accession of resources, favorable to national independence and safety.

There still are, nevertheless, respectable patrons of opinions, unfriendly to the encouragement of manufacturers. The following are, substantially, the arguments, by which these opinions are defended.

In every country (say those who entertain them) Agriculture is the most beneficial and *productive* object of human industry. This position, generally, if not universally true, applies with peculiar emphasis to the United States, on account of their immense tracts of fertile territory, uninhabited and unimproved. Nothing can afford so advantageous an employment for capital and labour, as the conversion of this extensive wilderness into cultivated farms. Nothing equally with this, can contribute to the population, strength and real riches of the country.

To endeavor by the extraordinary patronage of Government, to accelerate the growth of manufactures, is in fact, to endeavor, by force and art, to transfer the natural current of industry, from a more, to a less beneficial channel. Whatever has such a tendency must necessarily be unwise. Indeed it can hardly ever be wise in a government, to attempt to give a direction to the industry of its citizens. This, under the quick-sighted guidance of private interest, will, if left to itself, infallibly find its own way to the most profitable employment: and 'tis by such employment, that the public prosperity will be more effectually promoted. To leave industry to itself, therefore, is, in almost every case, the soundest as well as the simplest policy.

*Source:* American Memory: Annals of Congress, 2nd Congress, pp. 971–1035, http://www.loc.gov.

## EMBARGO ACT OF 1807

*The Embargo Act of 1807 and the subsequent Nonintercourse Acts were American laws restricting American ships from engaging in foreign trade between the years of 1807 and 1812. The acts were diplomatic responses designed to protect American interests and avoid war. They failed and helped cause the War of 1812 between the United States and Britain. An unintended consequence was the rebirth of the American iron, textile, and general manufacturing industries.*

Agreeably to the notice given yesterday; Mr. SMITH, of Maryland. asked and obtained leave to bring in a bill in addition to the act, entitled "An act laying an embargo on all ships and vessels in the ports and harbors of the United States," and the several acts supplementary thereto, and for other purposes; and the bill was read; and ordered to the second reading. The bill is as follows:

Be it enacted, by the Senate and House of Representatives of the United States of America, in Congress assembled, That during the continuance of the, act laying an embargo on all ships and vessels in the ports and harbors of the United States, no vessels of any description whatever, and wherever bound, whose employment is confined to the navigation of bays, sounds, rivers, and lakes, within the jurisdiction of the United States, (packets, ferry-boats, and vessels, exempted from the obligation of giving any bond whatever, only excepted,) shall be allowed, to depart from any port of the United States without having previously obtained a clearance, nor until the master or commander shall have delivered to the collector or surveyor of the port of departure, a manifest of the whole cargo on board, including articles of domestic growth or manufacture, as well as foreign merchandise. And it shall also be the duty of the owners agents, or factors of every such vessel to produce within one month thereafter, to the collector of the district from which the vessel departed, a certificate of the landing of the whole of such cargo in a port of the United States, within the bay, sound, rivers, or lakes, to which the navigation of such vessel is confined, signed by the collector or surveyor, of the port, where the cargo shall have been landed.

_Source:_ http://www.napoleon-series.org/research/government/us/c_embargo.html

## PACIFIC RAILWAY ACT OF 1862

_The Pacific Railroad Acts were a series of congressional acts that promoted the construction of the transcontinental railroad in the United States through authorizing the issuance of government bonds and the grants of land to railroad companies. It also allowed for access for telegraph lines. It remains one of the most successful joint ventures of government and private business._

. . . Commissioners to be appointed by the Secretary of the Interior, and all persons who shall or may be associated with them, and their successors, are hereby created and erected into a body corporate and politic in deed and in law, by the name, style, and title of "The Union Pacific Railroad Company;" and by that name shall have perpetual succession, and shall be able to sue and to be sued, plead and be impleaded, defend and be defended, in all courts of law and equity within the United States, and may make and have a common seal; and the said corporation is hereby authorized and empowered to layout, locate, construct, furnish, maintain, and enjoy a continuous railroad and telegraph, with the appurtenances, from a point on the one hundredth meridian of longitude west from Greenwich, between the south margin of the valley of the Republican River and the north margin of the valley of the Platte River, in the Territory of Nebraska, to the western boundary of Nevada Territory, upon the route and terms hereinafter provided, and is hereby vested with all the powers, privileges, and immunities necessary to carry into effect the purposes of this act as herein set forth. The capital stock of said company shall consist of one hundred thousand shares of one thousand dollars each, which shall be subscribed for and held in not more than two hundred shares by anyone person, and shall be transferable in such manner as the by-laws of said corporation shall provide. The persons hereinbefore named, together with those to be appointed by the Secretary of the Interior, are hereby constituted and appointed commissioners, and such body shall be called the Board of Commissioners of the Union Pacific Railroad and Telegraph Company, and twenty-five shall constitute a quorum for the transaction of business. The first meeting of said board shall be held at Chicago at such time as the commissioners from Illinois herein named shall appoint, not more than three nor less than one month after the passage of this act, notice of which shall be given by them to the other commissioners by depositing a call thereof in the post office at Chicago, post paid, to their address at least forty days before said meeting, and also by publishing said notice in one daily newspaper in each of the cities of Chicago and Saint Louis. Said board shall organize by the choice from its number of a president, secretary, and treasurer, and they shall require from said treasurer such bonds as may be deemed proper, and may from time to time increase the amount thereof as they may deem proper. It shall be the duty of said board of commissioners to open books, or cause books to be opened, at such times and in such principal cities in the United States as they or a quorum of them shall determine, to receive subscriptions to the capital stock of said corporation, and a cash payment of ten per centum on all subscriptions, and to receipt therefor.

---

*Source:* http://www.ourdocuments.gov/doc.php?doc=32

## SHERMAN ANTI-TRUST ACT (1890)

*The Sherman Act was passed in 1890 and was named after its author, Senator John Sherman, an Ohio Republican and chairman of the Senate Finance Committee. It was part of an overall package of legislation that included the McKinley Tariff Act and the Sherman Silver Act. It was offered as a compromise to anti-business Democrats. Initially the law was not used by the Justice Department, but in the early 1900s it became a tool to address growing trusts in oil, sugar, and steel.*

Be it enacted by the Senate and the House of Representatives of the United States of America in Congress assembled,

Sec. 1. Every contract, combination in the form of trust or otherwise, or conspiracy, in restraint of trade or commerce among the United States, or with foreign nations, is hereby declared to be illegal. Every person who shall make any such contract or engage in any such combination or conspiracy, shall be deemed guilty of a misdemeanor, and, on conviction thereof, shall be punished by fine not exceeding five thousand dollars, or by imprisonment not exceeding one year, or by both said punishments, in the discretion of the court.

Sec. 2. Every person who shall monopolize, or attempt to monopolize, or combine or conspire with any other person or persons, to monopolize any part of the trade or commerce among the several States, or with foreign nations, shall be deemed guilty of a misdemeanor, and, on conviction thereof, shall be punished by fine not exceeding five thousand dollars, or by imprisonment not exceeding one year, or both said punishments, in the discretion of the court.

Sec. 3. Every contract, combination in form of trust or otherwise, or conspiracy, in restraint of trade or commerce in any Territory of the United States or of the District of Columbia, or in restraint of trade and commerce between any such Territory and another, or between any such Territory or Territories and any State or States or the District of Columbia, or with foreign nations, or between the District of Columbia and any State or States or foreign nations, is hereby declared illegal. Every person who shall make any such contract or engage in any such combination or conspiracy, shall be deemed guilty of a misdemeanor, and, on conviction thereof, shall be punished by fine not exceeding five thousand dollars, or by imprisonment not exceeding one year, or by both said punishments, in the discretion of the court.

Sec. 4. The several circuit courts of the United States are hereby invested with jurisdiction to prevent and restrain violations of this act; and it shall be the duty of the several district attorneys of the United States, in their respective districts, under the direction of the Attorney General, to institute proceedings in equity to prevent and restrain such violations. Such proceedings may be by way of petition setting forth the case and praying that such violation shall be enjoined or otherwise prohibited. When the parties complained of shall have been duly notified of such petition the court shall proceed, as soon as may be, to the hearing and determination of the case; and pending such petition and before final decree, the court may at any time make such temporary restraining order or prohibition as shall be deemed just in the premises.

Sec. 5. Whenever it shall appear to the court before which any proceeding under section four of this act may be pending, that the ends of justice require that the other parties should be brought before the court, the court may cause them to be summoned, whether they reside in the district in which the court is held or not; and subpoenas to that end may be served in any district by the marshal thereof.

Sec. 6. Any property owned under any contract or by any combination, or pursuant to any conspiracy (and being the subject thereof) mentioned in section one of this act, and being in the course of transportation from one State to another, or to a foreign country, shall be forfeited to the United States, and may be seized and condemned by like proceedings as those provided by law for the forfeiture, seizure, and condemnation of property imported into the United States contrary to law.

Sec. 7. Any person who shall be injured in his business or property by any other person or corporation by reason of anything forbidden or declared to be unlawful by this act, may sue therefor in any circuit court of the United States in the district in which the defendant resides or is found, without respect to the amount in controversy, and shall recover three fold the damages by him sustained, and the costs of suit, including a reasonable attorney's fee.

Sec. 8. That the word "person," or "persons," wherever used in this act shall be deemed to include corporations and associations existing under or authorized by the laws of either the United States, the laws of any of the Territories, or the laws of any State, or the laws of any foreign country.

Approved, July 2, 1890.

_Source:_ http://www.ourdocuments.gov/doc.php?flash=true&doc=51

## McKINLEY TARIFF ACT OF 1890

_The McKinley Tariff Act was an example of scientific and well-planned protection of key American industries such as steel, iron, and glass. The tariff rates averaged 40 percent but required congressional review to assure any profits were put into plant expansion and employment. It was a rebirth of Henry Clay's American System by the Republican Party and would usher in the golden era of American industry. Note the extreme detail of the tariff schedules developed by William McKinley. While an extremely long bill, it was very specific for the time. The following excerpt includes just one of the many schedules in the act._

An act to reduce the revenue and equalize duties on imports, and for other purposes. Be it enacted by the Senate and House of Representatives of the United States in Congress assembled, That on and after the sixth day of October, eighteen hundred and ninety, unless otherwise specially provided for in this act, there shall be levied, collected and paid upon all articles imported from foreign countries, and mentioned in the schedules herein contained, the rates of duty which are, by the schedules and paragraphs, respectively prescribed, namely:

[...]

## SCHEDULE C. METALS AND MANUFACTURES OF IRON AND STEEL—

132. Chromate of iron, or chromic ore, fifteen per centum ad valorem.

133. Iron ore, including manganiferous iron ore, also the dross or residuum from burnt pyrites, seventy-five cents per ton.

Sulphur ore, as pyrites, or sulphuret of iron in its natural state, containing not more than three and one-half per centum copper, seventy-five cents per ton: Provided, That ore containing more than two per centum of copper shall pay, in addition thereto, one-half of one cent per pound for the copper contained therein: Provided, also, That sulphur ore as pyrites or sulphuret of iron in its natural state, containing in excess of twenty-five per centum of sulphur, shall be free of duty, except on the copper contained therein, as above provided: And provided further, That in levying and collecting the duty on iron ore no deduction shall be made from the weight of the ore on account of moisture which may be chemically or physically combined therewith.

134. Iron in pigs, iron kentledge, spiegeleisen, ferro-manganese, ferro-silicon, wrought and cast scrap iron, and scrap steel, three-tenths of one cent per pound; but nothing shall be deemed scrap iron or scrap steel except waste or refuse or steel fit only to be remanufactured.

135. Bar-iron, rolled or hammered, comprising flats of not less than one inch wide, not less than three-eighths of one inch thick, eight-tenths of one cent per pound; round iron not less than three-fourths of one inch in diameter, and square iron not less than three-fourths of one inch square, nine-tenths of one cent per pound; flats less than one inch wide, or less than three-eighths of one inch thick; round iron less than three-fourths of one inch and not less than seven-sixteenths of one inch in diameter; and square iron less than three-fourths of one inch square, one cent per pound.

136. Round iron, in coils or rods, less than seven-sixteenths of one inch in diameter, and bars or shapes of rolled iron, not specially provided for in this act, one and one-tenth cents per pound: Provided, That all iron in slabs, blooms, loops, or other forms less finished than iron in bars, and more advanced than pig-iron, except castings, shall be rated as iron in bars, and be subject to a duty of eight-tenths of one cent per pound; and none of the iron above enumerated in this paragraph shall pay a less rate of duty than thirty-five per centum ad valorem: Provided further, That all iron bars, blooms, billets, or sizes or shapes of any kind, in the

manufacture of which charcoal is used as fuel, shall be subject to a duty of not less than twenty-two dollars per ton.

137. Beams, girders, joists, angles, channels, car-truck channels, TT, columns and posts or parts or sections of columns and posts, deck and bulb beams, and building forms, together with all other structural shapes of iron or steel, whether plain or punched, or fitted for use, nine-tenths of one cent per pound.

138. Boiler or other plate iron or steel, except saw-plates hereinafter provided for, not thinner than number ten wire gauge, sheared or unsheared, and skelp iron or steel sheared or rolled in grooves, valued at one cent per pound or less, five-tenths of one cent per pound; valued above one cent and not above one and four tenths cents per pound, sixty five hundredths of one cent per pound; valued above one and four tenths cents and not above two cents per pound, eight tenths of one cent per pound; valued above two cents and not above three cents per pound, one and one-tenth cents per pound; valued above three cents and not above four cents per pound, one and five-tenths cents per pound; valued above four cents and not above seven cents per pound, two cents per pound; valued above seven cents and not above ten cents per pound, two and eight-tenths cents per pound . . .

---

*Source:* Annals of 51st Congress. www.loc.gov

## PANAMA CANAL TREATY (1903)

*The Panama Canal offers another excellent example of Henry Clay's American System of government leading the economic development of the United States. The canal opened world trade for American businesses. The project itself was well managed, with government and private business cooperating. The canal would ultimately be paid off by fees and was returned to the government of Panama in the 1970s.*

Concluded November 18, 1903; ratification advised by the Senate February 23, 1904; ratified by President February 25, 1904; ratifications exchanged February 26, 1904; proclaimed February 26, 1904. (U.S. Stats., vol. 33.)

The United States of America and the Republic of Panama being desirous to insure the construction of a ship canal across the Isthmus of Panama to connect the Atlantic and Pacific oceans, and the Congress of the United States of America having passed an act approved June 28, 1902, in furtherance of that object, by which the President of the United States is authorized to acquire within a reasonable time the control of the necessary territory of the Republic of Colombia, and the sovereignty of such territory being actually vested in the Republic of Panama, the high contracting parties have resolved for that purpose to conclude a convention and have accordingly appointed as their plenipotentiaries,

The President of the United States of America, John Hay, Secretary of State, and The Government of the Republic of Panama, Philippe Bunau-Varilla, Envoy Extraordinary and Minister Plenipotentiary of the Republic of Panama, thereunto specially empowered by said government, who after communicating with each other their respective full powers, found to be in good and due form, have agreed upon and concluded the following articles:

## ARTICLE I

The United States guarantees and will maintain the independence of the Republic of Panama.

## ARTICLE II

The Republic of Panama grants to the United States in perpetuity the use, occupation and control of a zone of land and land under water for the construction, maintenance, operation, sanitation and protection of said Canal of the width of ten miles extending to the distance of five miles on each side of the center line of the route of the Canal to be constructed; the said zone beginning in the Caribbean Sea three marine miles from mean low water mark and extending to and across the Isthmus of Panama into the Pacific ocean to a distance of three marine miles from mean low water mark with the proviso that the cities of Panama and Colon and the harbors adjacent to said cities, which are included within the boundaries of the zone above described, shall not be included within this grant. The Republic of Panama further grants to the United States in perpetuity the use, occupation and control of any other lands and waters outside of the zone above described which may be necessary and convenient for the construction, maintenance, operation, sanitation and protection of the said Canal or of any auxiliary canals or other works necessary and convenient for the construction, maintenance, operation, sanitation and protection of the said enterprise.

The Republic of Panama further grants in like manner to the United States in perpetuity all islands within the limits of the zone above described and in addition thereto the group of small islands in the Bay of Panama, named, Perico, Naos, Culebra and Flamenco.

## ARTICLE III

The Republic of Panama grants to the United States all the rights, power and authority within the zone mentioned and described in Article II of this agreement and within the limits of all auxiliary lands and waters mentioned and described in said Article II which the United States would possess and exercise if it were the sovereign of the territory within which said lands and waters are located to the entire exclusion of the exercise by the Republic of Panama of any such sovereign rights, power or authority.

_Source:_ http://historymartinez.wordpress.com/2011/11/24/panama-canal-treaty-1903-primary-source-document/

## FEDERAL RESERVE ACT (1913)

_The Federal Reserve Act came after years of studying the problems created by the Panic of 1907 and the lack of a central bank to stop large runs. The plan adopted in the original Federal Reserve Act called for the creation of a system that contained both private and public entities. There were to be at least 8, and no more than 12, private regional Federal Reserve banks (12 were established), each with its own branches, board of directors, and district boundaries (Sections 2, 3, and 4), and the system was to be headed by a seven-member Federal Reserve Board made up of public officials appointed by the president and confirmed by the Senate (strengthened and renamed in 1935 as the Board of Governors of the Federal Reserve System, with the secretary of the Treasury and the comptroller of the currency dropped from the board—Section 10). Also created as part of the Federal Reserve system was a 12-member Federal Advisory Committee (Section 12) and a single new U.S. currency, the Federal Reserve Note (Section 16)._

Sec. 2. As soon as practicable, the Secretary of the Treasury, the Secretary of Agriculture and the Comptroller of the Currency, acting as "The Reserve Bank Organization Committee," shall designate not less than eight nor more than twelve cities to be known as Federal Reserve cities, and shall divide the continental United States, excluding Alaska, into districts, each district to contain only one of such Federal Reserve cities. The determination of said organization committee shall not be subject to review except by the Federal Reserve Board when organized: Provided, That the districts shall be apportioned with due regard to the convenience and customary course of business and shall not necessarily be coterminous with any State or States. The districts thus created may be readjusted and new districts may from time to time be created by the Federal Reserve Board, not to exceed twelve in all. Such districts shall be known as Federal reserve districts and may be designated by number. A majority of the organization committee shall constitute a quorum with authority to act.

Said organization committee shall be authorized to employ counsel and expert aid, to take testimony, to send for persons and papers, to administer oaths, and to make such investigation as may be deemed necessary by the said committee in determining the reserve districts and in designating the cities within such districts where such Federal reserve banks shall be severally located. The said committee shall supervise the organization in each of the cities designated of a Federal reserve bank, which shall include in its title the name of the city in which it is situated, as "Federal Reserve Bank of Chicago."

Under regulations to be prescribed by the organization committee, every national banking association in the United States is hereby required, and every eligible bank in the United States and every trust company within the District of Columbia, is hereby authorized to signify in writing, within sixty days after the passage of this Act, its acceptance of the terms and provisions hereof. When the organization committee shall have designated the cities in which the Federal reserve banks are to [be] organized, and fixed the geographical limits of the Federal reserve districts, every national banking association within that district shall be required within thirty days after notice from the organization committee, to subscribe to the capital stock of such Federal reserve bank in a sum equal to six per centum of the paid-up capital stock and surplus of such bank, one-sixth of the subscription to be payable on call of the organization committee or of the Federal Reserve Board, one-sixth within three months and one-sixth within six months thereafter, and the remainder of the subscription, or any part thereof, shall be subject to call when deemed necessary by the Federal Reserve Board, said payments to be in gold or gold certificates.

The shareholders of every Federal reserve bank shall be held individually responsible, equally and ratably, and not for one another, for all contracts, debts, and engagements of such bank to the extent of the amount of their subscription to such stock at the par value thereof in addition to the amount subscribed, whether such subscriptions have been paid up in whole or in part, under the provisions of this Act.

Any national bank failing to signify its acceptance of the terms of this Act within the sixty days aforesaid, shall cease to act as a reserve agent, upon thirty days notice, to be given within the discretion of the said organization committee or of the Federal Reserve Board.

Should any national banking association in the United States now organized fail within one year after the passage of this Act to become a member bank or fail to comply with any of the provisions of this Act applicable thereto, all of the rights, privileges, and franchises of such association granted to it under the national-bank Act, or under provisions of this Act, shall be thereby forfeited. Any noncompliance with or violation of this Act shall, however, be determined and adjudged by any court of the United States of competent jurisdiction in a suit brought for that purpose in the district or territory in which such bank is located, under direction of the Federal Reserve Board, by the Comptroller of the Currency in his own name before the association shall be declared dissolved. In cases of such noncompliance or violation, other than the failure to become a member bank under the provisions of this Act, every director who participated in or assented to the same shall be held liable in his personal or individual capacity for all the damages which said bank, its shareholders, or any other person shall have sustained in consequence of such violation.

Such dissolution shall not take away or impair any remedy against such corporation, its stockholders or officers, for any liability or penalty which shall have been previously incurred.

Should the subscriptions by banks to the stock of said Federal reserve banks or any one or more of them be, in the judgment of the organization committee, insufficient to provide the amount of capital required therefor, then and in that event the said organization committee may, under conditions and regulations to be prescribed by it, offer to public subscription at par an amount of stock in said Federal reserve banks, or any one or more of them, as said committee shall determine, subject to the same conditions as to payment and stock liability as provided for member banks.

No individual, copartnership, or corporation other than a member bank of its district shall be permitted to subscribe for or to hold at any time more than $25,000 par value of stock in any Federal reserve bank. Such stock shall be known as public stock and may be transferred on the books of the Federal reserve bank by the chairman of the board of directors at such bank.

Should the total subscriptions by banks and the public to the stock of said Federal reserve banks, or any one or more of them, be, in the judgment of the organization committee, insufficient to provide the amount of capital required therefor, then and in that event the said organization committee shall allot to the United States such an amount of said stock as said committee shall determine. Said United States stock shall be paid for at par out of any money in the Treasury not otherwise appropriated, and shall be held by the Secretary of the Treasury and disposed of for the benefit of the United States in such manner, at such times, and at such price, not less than par, as the Secretary of the Treasury shall determine.

Stock not held by member banks shall not be entitled to voting power.

The Federal Reserve Board is hereby empowered to adopt and promulgate rules and regulations governing the transfers of said stock.

No Federal reserve bank shall commence business with a subscribed capital less than $4,000,000. The organization of reserve districts and Federal reserve cities shall not be construed as changing the present status of reserve cities and central reserve cities, except in so far as this Act changes the amount of reserves that may be carried with approved reserve agents located therein. The organization committee shall have power to appoint such assistants and incur such expenses in carrying out the provisions of this Act as it shall be deemed necessary; and such expenses shall be payable by the Treasurer of the United States upon voucher approved by the Secretary of the Treasury, and the sum of $100,000, or so much thereof as may be necessary, is hereby appropriated, out of the moneys in the Treasury not otherwise appropriated, for the payment of such expenses.

_____

*Source:* Public Statutes at Large, Vol. 38, Part I, pp. 251–275.

## REVENUE ACT OF 1913

*In 1895, the Supreme Court ruled an income tax to be unconstitutional, requiring the 16th Amendment to the Constitution, which passed the states in 1913. The Revenue Act was then passed by Congress. The target was the top 1 percent of American income earners, but once on the books, the target quickly increased to include most wage earners. The top rate also increased quickly as the government phased out tariffs and became more dependent on domestic taxes.*

## SECTION II

A. Subdivision 1. That there shall be levied, assessed, collected and paid annually upon the entire net income arising or accruing from all sources in the preceding calendar year to every citizen of the United States, whether residing at home or abroad, and to every person residing in the United States, though not a citizen thereof, a tax of 1 per centum per annum upon such income, except as hereinafter provided; and a like tax shall be assessed, levied, collected, and paid annually upon the entire net income from all property owned and of every business, trade, or profession carried on in the United States by persons residing elsewhere.

Subdivision 2. In addition to the income tax provided under this section (herein referred to as the normal income tax) there shall be levied, assessed, and collected upon the net income of every individual an additional income tax (herein referred to as the additional tax) of 1 per centum per annum upon the amount by which the total net income exceeds $20,000 and does not exceed $50,000, and 2 per centum per annum upon the amount by which the total net income exceeds $50,000 and does not exceed $75,000, 3 per centum per annum upon the amount by which the total net income exceeds $75,000 and does not exceed $100,000, 4 per centum per annum upon the amount by which the total net income exceeds $100,000 and does not exceed $250,000, 5 per centum per annum upon the amount by which the total net income exceeds $250,000 and does not exceed $500,000, and 6 per centum per annum upon the amount by which the total net income exceeds $500,000. All the provisions of this section relating to individuals who are to be chargeable with the normal income tax, so far as they are applicable and are not inconsistent with this subdivision of paragraph A, shall apply to the levy, assessment, and collection of the additional tax imposed under this section. Every person subject to this additional tax shall, for the purpose of its assessment and collection, make a personal return of his total net income from all sources, corporate or otherwise, for the preceding calendar year, under rules and regulations to be prescribed by the Commissioner of Internal Revenue and approved by the Secretary of the Treasury. For the purpose of this additional tax the taxable income of any individual shall embrace the share to which he would be entitled of the gains and profits, if divided or distributed, whether divided or distributed or not, of all corporations, joint-stock companies, or associations however created or organized, formed or fraudulently availed of for the purpose of preventing the imposition of such tax through the medium of permitting such gains and profits to accumulate instead of being divided or distributed; and the fact that any such corporation, joint-stock company, or association, is a mere holding company, or that the gains and profits are permitted to accumulate beyond the reasonable needs of the business shall be prima facie evidence of a fraudulent purpose to escape such tax; but the fact that the gains and profits are in any case permitted to accumulate and become surplus shall not be construed as evidence of a purpose to escape the said tax in such case unless the Secretary of the Treasury shall certify that in his opinion such accumulation is unreasonable for the purposes of the business. When requested by the Commissioner of Internal Revenue, or any district collector of internal revenue, such corporation, joint-stock company, or association shall forward to him a correct statement of such profits and the names of the individuals who would be entitled to the same if distributed.

[. . .]

The net income from property owned and business carried on in the United States by persons residing elsewhere shall be computed upon the basis prescribed in this paragraph and that part of paragraph G of this section relating to the computation of the net income of corporations, joint-stock and insurance companies, organized, created, or existing under the laws of foreign countries, in so far as applicable.

That in computing net income under this section there shall be excluded the interest upon the obligations of a State or any political subdivision thereof, and upon the obligations of the United States or its possessions; also the compensation of the present President of the United States during the term for which he has been elected, and of the judges of the supreme and inferior courts of the United States now in office, and the compensation of all officers and employees of a State or any political subdivision thereof except when such compensation is paid by the United States Government.

C. That there shall be deducted from the amount of the net income of each of said persons, ascertained as provided herein, the sum of $3,000, plus $1,000 additional if the person making the return be a married man with a wife living with him, or plus the sum of $1,000 additional if the person making the return be a married woman with a husband living with her; but in no event shall this additional exemption of $1,000 be deducted by both a husband and a wife: Provided, That only one deduction of $4,000 shall be made from the aggregate income of both husband and wife when living together.

D. The said tax shall be computed upon the remainder of said net income of each person subject thereto, accruing during each preceding calendar year ending December thirty-first: Provided, however, That for the year ending December thirty-first, nineteen hundred and thirteen, said tax shall be computed on the net income accruing from March first to December thirty-first, nineteen hundred and thirteen, both dates inclusive, after deducting five-sixths only of the specific exemptions and deductions herein provided for. On or before the first day of March, nineteen hundred and fourteen, and the first day of March in each year thereafter, a true and accurate return, under oath or affirmation, shall be made by each person of lawful age, except as hereinafter provided, subject to the tax imposed by this section, and having a net income of $3,000 or over for the taxable year, to the collector of internal revenue for the district in which such person resides or has his principal place of business, or, in the case of a person residing in a foreign country, in the place where his principal business is carried on within the United States, in such form as the Commissioner of Internal Revenue, with the approval of the Secretary of the Treasury, shall prescribe, setting forth specifically the gross amount of income from all separate sources and from the total thereof, deducting the aggregate items or expenses and allowance herein authorized.

---

*Source:* Statutes at Large of the United States of America from March, 1913, to March, 1915.

## CLAYTON ANTI-TRUST ACT (1914)

*Passed by Congress in 1914, the Clayton Anti-Trust Act was designed to modify the Sherman Anti-Trust Act. The Clayton Anti-Trust Act was passed to strengthen the government's move on large American trusts following legal battles over Standard Oil and United States Steel. This act together with the Sherman Anti-Trust Act has been used against AT&T, Microsoft, and most recently Google.*

An Act to supplement existing laws against unlawful restraints and monopolies, and for other purposes.

Be it enacted by the Senate and the House of Representatives of the United States in Congress assembled, That "antitrust laws," as used herein, includes the Act entitled "An Act to protect trade and commerce against unlawful restraints and monopolies," approved July second, eighteen hundred and ninety; sections seventy-three to seventy-seven, inclusive, of an Act entitled "An Act to reduce taxation, to provide revenue for the Government, and for other purposes," of August twenty-seventh, eighteen hundred and ninety-four; an Act entitled "An Act to amend sections seventy-three and seventy-six of the Act of August twenty-seventh, eighteen hundred and ninety-four, entitled 'An Act to reduce taxation, to provided revenue for the Government, and for other purposes,'" approved February twelfth, nineteen hundred and thirteen; and also this Act. "Commerce," as used herein, means trade or commerce among the several States and with foreign nations, or between the District of Columbia or any Territory of the United States and any State, Territory, or foreign nation, or between any insular possessions or other places under the jurisdiction of the United States, or between any such possessions or place and any State or Territory of the United States or the District of Columbia or any foreign nation, or within the District of Columbia or any Territory or any insular possession or other place under the jurisdiction of the United States: Provided, That nothing in this Act contained shall apply to the Philippine Islands. The word "person" or "persons" whenever used in this Act shall be deemed to include corporations and associations existing under or authorized by the laws of either the United States, the laws of any of the Territories, the laws of any State, or the laws of any foreign country.

Sec. 2. That it shall be unlawful for any person engaged in commerce, in the course of such commerce, either directly or indirectly to discriminate in price between different purchasers of commodities, which commodities are sold for use, consumption, or resale within the United States or any Territory thereof or the District of Columbia or any insular possession or other place under the jurisdiction of the United States, where the effect of such discrimination may be to substantially lessen competition or tend to create a monopoly in any line of commerce: Provided, That nothing herein contained shall prevent discrimination in price between purchasers of commodities on account of differences in the grade, quality, or quantity of the commodity sold, or that makes only due allowance for difference in the cost of selling or transportation, or discrimination in price in the same or different communities made in good faith to meet competition: And provided further, That nothing herein contained shall prevent persons engaged in selling goods, wares, or merchandise in commerce from selecting their own customers in bona fide transactions and not in restraint of trade.

Sec. 3. That it shall be unlawful for any person engaged in commerce, in the course of such commerce, to lease or make a sale or contract for sale of goods, wares, or merchandise, machinery, supplies or other commodities, whether patented or unpatented, for use, consumption or resale within the United States or any Territory thereof or the District of Columbia or any insular possession or other place under the jurisdiction of the United States, or fix a price charged therefore, or discount from, or rebate upon, such price, on the condition, agreement or understanding that the lessee or purchaser thereof shall not use or deal in the goods, wares, merchandise, machinery, supplies or other commodities of a competitor or competitors of the lesser or seller, where the effect of such lease, sale, or contract for sale or such condition, agreement or understanding may be to substantially lessen competition or tend to create a monopoly in any line of commerce.

Sec. 4. That any person who shall be injured in his business or property by reason of anything forbidden in the antitrust laws may sue therefore in any district court of the United States in the district in which the defendant resides or is found or has an agent, without respect to the amount in controversy, and shall recover threefold the damages by him sustained, and the cost of suit, including a reasonable attorney's fee.

Sec. 5. That a final judgment or decree hereafter rendered in any criminal prosecution or in any suit or proceeding in equity brought by or on behalf of the United States under the antitrust laws to the effect that a defendant has violated said laws shall be prima facie evidence against such defendant in any suit or proceeding brought by any other party against such defendant under said laws as to all matters respecting which said judgment or decree would be an estoppel as between the parties thereto: Provided, This section shall not apply to consent judgments or decrees entered before any testimony has been taken: Provided further, This section shall not apply to consent judgments or decrees rendered in criminal proceedings or suits in equity, now pending, in which the taking of testimony has been commenced but has not been concluded, provided such judgments or decrees are rendered before any further testimony is taken.

Whenever any suit or proceeding in equity or criminal prosecution is instituted by the United States to prevent, restrain or punish violations of any of the antitrust laws, the running of the statute of limitations in respect of each and every private right of action arising under said laws and based in whole or in part on any matter complained of in said suit or proceeding shall be suspended during the pendency thereof.

*Source:* Public Statutes at Large, Vol. 38, Part I, pp. 730–740.

## BOULDER CANYON PROJECT ACT (HOOVER DAM) (1928)

*The Boulder Canyon Project Act was passed in 1928 and signed by President Calvin Coolidge. The bill allocated $126 million, but little happened until the onset of the Great Depression, when President Herbert Hoover pushed to start the project. In the end, Hoover Dam would be one of America's best examples of cooperation between government and private industry. It came in under budget using the best materials.*

[PUBL IC-NO. 642–70TH CONGRESS)
[H.R. 5773]

AN ACT To provide for the construction of works for the protection and development of the Colorado River Basin, for the approval of the Colorado River compact, and for other purposes.

*Be it enacted by the Senate and House of Representatives of the United States of America in Congress assembled,* That for the purpose of controlling the floods, improving navigation and regulating the flow of the Colorado River, providing for storage and for the delivery of the stored waters thereof for reclamation of public lands and other beneficial uses exclusively within the United States, and for the generation of electrical energy as a means of making the project herein authorized a self-supporting and financially solvent undertaking, the Secretary of the Interior, subject to the terms of the Colorado River compact hereinafter mentioned, is hereby authorized to construct, operate, and maintain a dam and incidental works in the main stream of the Colorado River at Black Canyon or Boulder Canyon adequate to create a storage reservoir of a capacity of not less than twenty million acrefeet of water and a main canal and appurtenant structures located entirely within the United States connecting the Laguna Dam, or other suitable diversion dam, which the Secretary of the Interior is hereby authorized to construct if deemed necessary or advisable by him upon engineering or economic considerations, with the Imperial and Coachella Valleys in California, the expenditures for said main canal and appurtenant structures to be reimbursable, as provided in the reclamation law, and shall not be paid out of revenues derived from the sale or disposal of water power or electric energy at the dam authorized to be constructed at said Black Canyon or Boulder Canyon, or for water for potable purposes outside of the Imperial and Coachella Valleys: *Provided, however,* That no charge shall be made for water or for the use, storage, or delivery of water for irrigation or water for potable purposes in the Imperial or Coachella Valleys; also to construct and equip, operate, and maintain at or near said dam, or cause to be constructed, a complete plant and incidental structures suitable for the fullest economic development of electrical energy from the water discharged from said reservoir; and to acquire by proceedings in eminent domain, or otherwise all lands, rights-of-way, and other property necessary for said purposes.

SEC. 2. (a) There is hereby established a special fund, to be known as the "Colorado River Dam fund" (hereinafter referred to as the "fund"), and to be available, as hereafter provided, only for carrying out the provisions of this Act. All revenues received in carrying out the provisions of this Act shall be paid into and expenditures shall be made out of the fund, under the direction of the Secretary of the Interior.

(b) The Secretary of the Treasury is authorized to advance to the fund, from time to time and within the appropriations therefor, such amounts as the Secretary of the Interior deems necessary for carrying out the provisions of this Act, except that the aggregate amount of such advances shall not exceed the sum of $165,000,000. Of this amount the sum of $25,000,000 shall be allocated to flood control and shall be repaid to the United States out of 62½ per centum of revenues, if any, in excess of the amount necessary to meet periodical payments during the period of amortization, as provided in section 4 of this Act. If said sum of $25,000,000 is not repaid in full during the period of amortization, then 62½ per centum of all net revenues shall be applied to payment of the remainder. Interest at the rate of 4 per centum per annum accruing during the year upon the amounts so advanced and remaining unpaid shall be paid annually out of the fund, except as herein otherwise provided.

(c) Moneys in the fund advanced under subdivision (b) shall be available only for expenditures for construction and the payment of interest, during construction, upon the amounts so advanced. No expenditures out of the fund shall be made for operation and maintenance except from appropriations therefor.

(d) The Secretary of the Treasury shall charge the fund as of June 30 in each year with such amount as may be necessary for the payment of interest on advances made under subdivision (b) at the rate of 4 per centum per annum accrued during the year upon the amounts so advanced and remaining unpaid, except that if the fund is insufficient to meet the payment of interest the Secretary of the Treasury may, in his discretion, defer any part of such payment, and the amount so deferred shall bear interest at the rate of 4 per centum per annum until paid.

(e) The Secretary of the Interior shall certify to the Secretary of the Treasury, at the close of each fiscal year, the amount of money in the fund in excess of the amount necessary for construction, operation, and maintenance, and payment of interest. Upon receipt of each such certificate the Secretary of the Treasury is authorized and directed to charge the fund with the amount so certified as repayment of the advances made under subdivision (b), which amount shall be covered into the Treasury to the credit of miscellaneous receipts.

SEC. 3. There is hereby authorized to be appropriated from time to time, out of any money in the Treasury not otherwise appropriated, such sums of money as may be necessary to carry out the purposes of this Act, not exceeding in the aggregate $165,000,000.

SEC. 4. (a) This Act shall not take effect and no authority shall be exercised hereunder and no work shall be begun and no moneys expended on or in connection with the works or structures provided for in this Act, and no water rights shall be claimed or initiated hereunder, and no steps shall be taken by the United States or by others to initiate or perfect any claims to the use of water pertinent to such works or structures unless and until (1) the States of Arizona, California, Colorado, Nevada, New Mexico, Utah, and Wyoming shall have ratified the Colorado River compact, mentioned in section 13 hereof, and the President by public proclamation shall have so declared, or (2) if said States fail to ratify the said compact within six months from the date of the passage of this Act then, until six of said States, including the State of California, shall ratify said compact and shall consent to waive the provisions of the first paragraph of Article XI of said compact, which makes the same binding and obligatory only when approved by each of the seven States signatory thereto, and shall have approved said compact without conditions, save that of such six-State approval, and the President by public proclamation shall have so declared, and, further, until the State of California, by act of its legislature, shall agree irrevocably and unconditionally with the United States and for the benefit of the States of Arizona, Colorado, Nevada, New Mexico, Utah, and Wyoming, as an express covenant and in consideration of the passage of this Act, that the aggregate annual consumptive use (diversions less returns to the river) of water of and from the Colorado River for use in the State of California, including all uses under contracts made under the provisions of this Act and all water necessary for the supply of any rights which may now exist, shall not exceed four million four hundred thousand acre-feet of the waters apportioned to the lower basin States by paragraph (a) of Article III of the Colorado River compact, plus not more than one-half of any excess or surplus waters unapportioned by said compact, such uses always to be subject to the terms of said compact. The States of Arizona, California, and Nevada are authorized to enter into an agreement which shall provide (1) that of the 7,500,000 acre-feet annually apportioned to the lower basin by paragraph (a) of Article III of the Colorado River compact, there shall be apportioned to the State of Nevada 300,000 acre-feet and to the State of Arizona 2,800,000 acre-feet for exclusive beneficial consumptive use in perpetuity, and (2) that the State of Arizona may annually use one-half of the excess or surplus waters unapportioned by the Colorado River compact, and (3) that the State of Arizona shall have the exclusive beneficial consumptive use of the Gila River and its tributaries within the boundaries of said State, and (4) that the waters of the Gila River and its tributaries, except return flow after the same enters the Colorado River, shall never be subject to any diminution whatever by any allowance of water which may be made by treaty or otherwise to the United States of Mexico but if, as provided in paragraph (c) of Article III of the Colorado River compact, it shall become necessary to supply water to the United States of Mexico from waters over and above the quantities which are surplus as defined by said compact, then the State of California shall and will mutually agree with the State of Arizona to supply, out of the main stream of the Colorado River, one-half of any deficiency which must be supplied to Mexico by the lower basin, and (5) that the State of California shall and will further mutually agree with the States of Arizona and Nevada that none of said three States shall withhold water and none shall require the delivery of water, which cannot reasonably be applied to domestic and agricultural uses, and (6) that all of the provisions of said tri-State agreement shall be subject in all particulars to the provisions of the Colorado River compact, and (7) said agreement to take effect upon the ratification of the Colorado River compact by Arizona, California, and Nevada.

(b) Before any money is appropriated for the construction of said dam or power plant, or any construction work done or contracted for, the Secretary of the Interior shall make provision for revenues by contract, in accordance with the provisions of this Act, adequate in his judgment to insure payment of all expenses of operation and maintenance of said works incurred by the United States and the repayment, within fifty years from the date of the completion of said works, of all amounts advanced to the fund under subdivision (b) of section 2 for such works, together with interest thereon made reimbursable under this Act.

Before any money is appropriated for the construction of said main canal and appurtenant structures to connect the Laguna Dam with the Imperial and Coachella Valleys in California, or any construction work is done upon said canal or contracted for, the Secretary of the Interior shall make provision for revenues, by contract or otherwise, adequate in his judgment to insure payment of all expenses of construction, operation, and maintenance of said main canal and appurtenant structures in the manner provided in the reclamation law.

If during the period of amortization the Secretary of the Interior shall receive revenues in excess of the amount necessary to meet the periodical payments to the United States as provided in the contract, or contracts, executed under this Act, then, immediately after the settlement of such periodical payments, he shall pay to the State of Arizona 18¾ per centum of such excess revenues and to the State of Nevada 18¾ per centum of such excess revenues.

SEC. 5. That the Secretary of the Interior is hereby authorized, under such general regulations as he may prescribe, to contract for the storage of water in said reservoir and for the delivery thereof at such points on the river and on said canal as may be agreed upon, for irrigation and domestic uses, and generation of electrical energy and delivery at the switchboard to States, municipal corporations, political subdivisions, and private corporations of electrical energy generated at said dam, upon charges that will provide revenue which, in addition to other revenue accruing under the reclamation law and under this Act, will in his judgment cover all expenses of operation and maintenance incurred by the United States on account of works constructed under this Act and the payments to the United States under subdivision (b) of section 4. Contracts respecting water for irrigation and domestic uses shall be for permanent service and shall conform to paragraph (a) of section 4 of this Act. No person shall have or be entitled to have the use for any purpose of the water stored as aforesaid except by contract made as herein stated. After the repayments to the United States of all money advanced with interest, charges shall be on such basis and the revenues derived therefrom shall be kept in a separate fund to be expended within the Colorado River Basin as may hereafter be prescribed by the Congress.

---

*Source:* http://www.usbr.gov/lc/region/pao/pdfiles/bcpact.pdf

## SOCIAL SECURITY ACT (1935)

*The Social Security Act was part of the New Deal safety net. It was a reaction to the crushing effects of the Great Depression on the old of the nation. It has been amended many times over the years.*

AN ACT to provide for the general welfare by establishing a system of Federal old-age benefits, and by enabling the several States to make more adequate provision for aged persons, blind persons, dependent and crippled children, maternal and child welfare, public health, and the administration of their unemployment compensation laws; to establish a Social Security Board; to raise revenue; and for other purposes.

Be it enacted by the Senate and House of Representatives of the United States of America in Congress assembled,

### TITLE I—GRANTS TO STATES FOR OLD-AGE ASSISTANCE APPROPRIATION

SECTION 1. For the purpose of enabling each State to furnish financial assistance, as far as practicable under the conditions in such State, to aged needy individuals, there is hereby authorized to be appropriated for the fiscal year ended June 30, 1936, the sum of $49,750,000, and there is hereby authorized to be appropriated for each fiscal year thereafter a sum sufficient to carry out the purposes of this title. The sums made available under this section shall be used for making payments to States which have submitted, and had approved by the Social Security Board established by Title VII (hereinafter referred to as the Board), State plans for old-age assistance.

### STATE OLD-AGE ASSISTANCE PLANS

SEC. 2. (a) A State plan for old-age assistance must

(1) provide that it shall be in effect in all political subdivisions of the State, and, if administered by them, be mandatory upon them;

(2) provide for financial participation by the State;

(3) either provide for the establishment or designation of a single State agency to administer the plan, or provide for the establishment or designation of a single State agency to supervise the administration of the plan;

(4) provide for granting to any individual, whose claim for old-age assistance is denied, an opportunity for a fair hearing before such State agency;

(5) provide such methods of administration (other than those relating to selection, tenure of office, and compensation of personnel) as are found by the Board to be necessary for the efficient operation of the plan;

(6) provide that the State agency will make such reports, in such form and containing such information, as the Board may from time to time require, and comply

with such provisions as the Board may from time to time find necessary to assure the correctness and verification of such reports; and

(7) provide that, if the State or any of its political subdivisions collects from the estate of any recipient of old-age assistance any amount with respect to old-age assistance furnished him under the plan, one-half of the net amount so collected shall be promptly paid to the United States. Any payment so made shall be deposited in the Treasury to the credit of the appropriation for the purposes of this title.

(b) The Board shall approve any plan which fulfills the conditions specified in subsection (a), except that it shall not approve any plan which imposes, as a condition of eligibility for old-age assistance under the plan—

(1) An age requirement of more than sixty-five years, except that the plan may impose, effective until January 1, 1940, an age requirement of as much as seventy years; or

(2) Any residence requirement which excludes any resident of the State who has resided therein five years during the nine years immediately preceding the application for old-age assistance and has resided therein continuously for one year immediately preceding the application; or (3) Any citizenship requirement which excludes any citizen of the United States.

## PAYMENT TO STATES

SEC. 3. (a) From the sums appropriated therefor, the Secretary of the Treasury shall pay to each State which has an approved plan for old-age assistance, for each quarter, beginning with the quarter commencing July 1, 1935,

(1) an amount, which shall be used exclusively as old-age assistance, equal to one-half of the total of the sums expended during such quarter as old-age assistance under the State plan with respect to each individual who at the time of such expenditure is sixty-five years of age or older and is not an inmate of a public institution, not counting so much of such expenditure with respect to any individual for any month as exceeds $30, and

(2) 5 per centum of such amount, which shall be used for paying the costs of administering the State plan or for old-age assistance, or both, and for no other purpose: Provided, That the State plan, in order to be approved by the Board, need not provide for financial participation before July 1, 1937, by the State, in the case of any State which the Board, upon application by the State and after reasonable notice and opportunity for hearing to the State, finds is prevented by its constitution from providing such financial participation.

(b) The method of computing and paying such amounts shall be as follows:

(1) The Board shall, prior to the beginning of each quarter, estimate the amount to be paid to the State for such quarter under the provisions of clause (1) of subsection (a), such estimate to be based on

(A) a report filed by the State containing its estimate of the total sum to be expended in such quarter in accordance with the provisions of such clause, and stating the amount appropriated or made available by the State and its political subdivisions for such expenditures in such quarter, and if such amount is less than one-half of the total sum of such estimated expenditures, the source or sources from which the difference is expected to be derived,

(B) records showing the number of aged individuals in the State, and

(C) such other investigation as the Board may find necessary.

(2) The Board shall then certify to the Secretary of the Treasury the amount so estimated by the Board, reduced or increased, as the case may be, by any sum by which it finds that its estimate for any prior quarter was greater or less than the amount which should have been paid to the State under clause (1) of subsection (a) for such quarter, except to the extent that such sum has been applied to make the amount certified for any prior quarter greater or less than the amount estimated by the Board for such prior quarter.

(3) The Secretary of the Treasury shall thereupon, through the Division of Disbursement of the Treasury Department and prior to audit or settlement by the General Accounting Office, pay to the State, at the time or times fixed by the Board, the amount so certified, increased by 5 per centum.

## OPERATION OF STATE PLANS

SEC. 4. In the case of any State plan for old-age assistance which has been approved by the Board, if the Board, after reasonable notice and opportunity for hearing to the State agency administering or supervising the administration of such plan, finds—

(1) that the plan has been so changed as to impose any age, residence, or citizenship requirement prohibited by section 2 (b), or that in the administration of the plan any such prohibited requirement is imposed, with the knowledge of such State agency, in a substantial number of cases; or

(2) that in the administration of the plan there is a failure to comply substantially with any provision required by section 2 (a) to be included in the plan; the Board shall notify such State agency that further payments will not be made to the State until the Board is satisfied that such prohibited requirement is no longer so imposed, and that there is no longer any such failure to comply. Until it is so satisfied it shall make no further certification to the Secretary of the Treasury with respect to such State.

## ADMINISTRATION

SEC. 5. There is hereby authorized to be appropriated for the fiscal year ending June 30, 1936, the sum of $250,000, for all necessary expenses of the Board in administering the provisions of this title.

## DEFINITION

SEC. 6. When used in this title the term old age assistance means money payments to aged individuals.

_____

*Source:* http://www.ourdocuments.gov/doc.php?flash=true&doc=68

## NATIONAL LABOR RELATIONS ACT OF 1935

*The National Labor Relations Act, or Wagner Act (after its sponsor, Robert Wagner), was passed in 1935. This New Deal legislation launched a wave of unionization that included the steel and rubber industries for the first time. The act does not apply to workers who are covered by Railway Act; agricultural employees; domestic employees; supervisors; federal, state or local government workers; independent contractors; and some close relatives of individual employers.*

## SECTION 7

SEC. 7. Employees shall have the right of self-organization, to form, join, or assist labor organizations, to bargain collectively through representatives of their own choosing, and to engage in concerted activities, for the purpose of collective bargaining or other mutual aid or protection.

SEC. 8. It shall be an unfair labor practice for an employer—

(1) To interfere with, restrain, or coerce employees in the exercise of the rights guaranteed in section 7.

(2) To dominate or interfere with the formation or administration of any labor organization or contribute financial or other support to it: *Provided,* That . . . an employer shall not be prohibited from permitting employees to confer with him during working hours without loss of time or pay.

(3) By discrimination in regard to hire or tenure of employment or any term or condition of employment to encourage or discourage membership in any labor organization: *Provided,* That nothing in this Act or in any other statute of the United States, shall preclude an employer from making an agreement with a labor organization (not established, maintained, or assisted by any action defined in this Act as an unfair labor practice) to require as a condition of employment membership therein, if such labor organization is the representative of the employees in the appropriate collective bargaining unit covered by such agreement when made.

(4) To discharge or otherwise discriminate against an employee because he has filed charges or given testimony under this Act.

(5) To refuse to bargain collectively with the representatives of his employees.

_____

*Source:* http://www.civics-online.org

## GENERAL AGREEMENT ON TARIFFS
## AND TRADE (GATT) (1947)

*The General Agreement on Tariffs and Trade (typically abbreviated GATT) was negotiated during the United Nations Conference on Trade and Employment and was the outcome of the failure of negotiating governments to create the International Trade Organization (ITO). GATT was signed in 1947 and lasted until 1993, when it was replaced by the World Trade Organization (WTO) in 1995. The original GATT text (GATT 1947) is still in effect under the WTO framework, subject to the modifications of GATT 1994. GATT along with the postwar dollar policy would eventually be the start of American deindustrialization.*

The Governments of the COMMONWEALTH OF AUSTRALIA, the KINGDOM OF BELGIUM, the UNITED STATES OF BRAZIL, BURMA, CANADA, CEYLON, the REPUBLIC OF CHILE, the REPUBLIC OF CHINA, the REPUBLIC OF CUBA, the CZECHOSLOVAK REPUBLIC, the FRENCH REPUBLIC, INDIA, LEBANON, the GRAND-DUCHY OF LUXEMBURG, the KINGDOM OF THE NETHERLANDS, NEW ZEALAND, the KINGDOM OF NORWAY, PAKISTAN, SOUTHERN RHODESIA, SYRIA, the UNION OF SOUTH AFRICA, the UNITED KINGDOM OF GREAT BRITAIN AND NORTHERN IRELAND, and the UNITED STATES OF AMERICA:

Recognizing that their relations in the field of trade and economic endeavour should be conducted with a view to raising standards of living, ensuring full employment and a large and steadily growing volume of real income and effective demand, developing the full use of the resources of the world and expanding the production and exchange of goods, Being desirous of contributing to these objectives by entering into reciprocal and mutually advantageous arrangements directed to the substantial reduction of tariffs and other barriers to trade and to the elimination of discriminatory treatment in international commerce, Have through their Representatives agreed as follows:

## PART I

### Article I: General Most-Favoured-Nation Treatment

1. With respect to customs duties and charges of any kind imposed on or in connection with importation or exportation or imposed on the international transfer of payments for imports or exports, and with respect to the method of levying such duties and charges, and with respect to all rules and formalities in connection with importation and exportation, and with respect to all matters referred to in paragraphs 2 and 4 of Article III,* any advantage, favour, privilege or immunity granted by any contracting party to any product originating in or destined for any other country shall be accorded immediately

and unconditionally to the like product originating in or destined for the territories of all other contracting parties.

2. The provisions of paragraph 1 of this Article shall not require the elimination of any preferences in respect of import duties or charges which do not exceed the levels provided for in paragraph 4 of this Article and which fall within the following descriptions:

---

*Source:* http://www.worldtradelaw.net/uragreements/gatt.pdf

## ATOMS FOR PEACE (1953)

*On December 8, 1953, President Dwight D. Eisenhower gave his "Atoms for Peace" speech to the United Nations. It was followed by the first American nuclear power plant at Shippingport and a major construction program for nuclear power plants around the world.*

**Address by Mr. Dwight D. Eisenhower, President of the United States of America, to the 470th Plenary Meeting of the United Nations General Assembly Madam President and Members of the General Assembly;**

When Secretary General Hammarskjold's invitation to address the General Assembly reached me in Bermuda, I was just beginning a series of conferences with the prime Ministers and Foreign Ministers of the United Kingdom and France. Our subject was some of the problems that beset our world. During the remainder of the Bermuda Conference, I had constantly in mind that ahead of me lay a great honour. That honour is mine today as I stand here, privileged to address the general Assembly of the United Nations.

At the same time that I appreciate the distinction of addressing you, I have a sense of exhilaration as I look upon this Assembly. Never before in history has so much hope for so many people been gathered together in a single organization. Your deliberations and decisions during these sombre years have already realized part of those hopes.

But the great tests and the great accomplishments still lie ahead. And in the confident expectation of those accomplishments, I would use the office which, for the time being, I hold, to assure you that the Government of the United States will remain steadfast in its support of this body. This we shall do in the conviction that you will provide a great share of the wisdom, of the courage and of the faith which can bring to this world lasting peace for all nations, and happiness and well-being for all men.

Clearly, it would not be fitting for me to take this occasion to present to you a unilateral American report on Bermuda. Nevertheless, I assure you that in our deliberations on that lovely island we sought to invoke those same great concepts of universal peace and human dignity which are so clearly etched in your Charter.

Neither would it be a measure of this great opportunity to recite, however hopefully, pious platitudes. I therefore decided that this occasion warranted my saying to you some of the things that have been on the minds and hearts of my legislative and executive associates, and on mine, for a great many months: thoughts I had originally planned to say primarily to the American people.

I know that the American people share my deep belief that if a danger exists in the world, it is a danger shared by all; and equally, that if hope exists in the mind of one nation, that hope should be shared by all. Finally, if there is to be advanced any proposal designed to ease even by the smallest measure the tensions of today's world, what more appropriate audience could there be than the members of the General Assembly of the United Nations.

I feel impelled to speak today in a language that in a sense is new, one which I, who have spent so much of my life in the military profession, would have preferred never to use. That new language is the language of atomic warfare.

The atomic age has moved forward at such a pace that every citizen of the world should have some comprehension, at least in comparative terms, of the extent of this development, of the utmost significance to every one of us. Clearly, if the peoples of the world are to conduct an intelligent search for peace, they must be armed with the significant facts of today's existence.

My recital of atomic danger and power is necessarily stated in United States terms, for these are the only incontrovertible facts that I know, I need hardly point out to this Assembly, however, that this subject is global, not merely national in character.

On 16 July 1945, the United States set off the world's biggest atomic explosion. Since that date in 1945, the United States of America has conducted forty-two test explosions. Atomic bombs are more than twenty-five times as powerful as the weapons with which the atomic age dawned, while hydrogen weapons are in the ranges of millions of tons of TNT equivalent.

Today, the United States stockpile of atomic weapons, which, of course, increases daily, exceeds by many times the total equivalent of the total of all bombs and all shells that came from every plane and every gun in every theatre of war in all the years of the Second World War. A single air group whether afloat or land based, can now deliver to any reachable target a destructive cargo exceeding in power all the bombs that fell on Britain in all the Second World War.

In size and variety, the development of atomic weapons has been no less remarkable. The development has been such that atomic weapons have virtually achieved conventional status within our armed services. In the United States, the Army, the Navy, the Air Force and the Marine Corps are all capable of putting this weapon to military use.

But the dread secret and the fearful engines of atomic might are not ours alone.

In the first place, the secret is possessed by our friends and allies, the United Kingdom and Canada, whose scientific genius made a tremendous contribution to our original discoveries and the designs of atomic bombs.

The secret is also known by the Soviet Union. The Soviet Union has informed us that, over recent years, it has devoted extensive resources to atomic weapons. During this period the Soviet Union has exploded a series of atomic devices, including at least one involving thermo-nuclear reactions.

If at one time the United States possessed what might have been called a monopoly of atomic power, that monopoly ceased to exist several years ago. Therefore, although our earlier start has permitted us to accumulate what is today a great quantitative advantage, the atomic realities of today comprehend two facts of even greater significance. First, the knowledge now possessed by several nations will eventually be shared by others, possibly all others.

Second, even a vast superiority in numbers of weapons, and a consequent capability of devastating retaliation, is no preventive, of itself, against the fearful material damage and toll of human lives that would be inflicted by surprise aggression.

The free world, at least dimly aware of these facts, has naturally embarked on a large programme of warning and defence systems. That programme will be accelerated and extended. But let no one think that the expenditure of vast sums for weapons and systems of defence can guarantee absolute safety for the cities and citizens of any nation. The awful arithmetic of the atomic bomb doesn't permit of any such easy solution. Even against the most powerful defence, an aggressor in possession of the effective minimum number of atomic bombs for a surprise attack could probably place a sufficient number of his bombs on the chosen targets to cause hideous damage.

Should such an atomic attack be launched against the United States, our reactions would be swift and resolute. But for me to say that the defence capabilities of the United States are such that they could inflict terrible losses upon an aggressor, for me to say that the retaliation capabilities of the United States are so great that such an aggressor's land would be laid waste, all this, while fact, is not the true expression of the purpose and the hopes of the United States.

To pause there would be to confirm the hopeless finality of a belief that two atomic colossi are doomed malevolently to eye each other indefinitely across a trembling world. To stop there would be to accept helplessly the probability of civilization destroyed, the annihilation of the irreplaceable heritage of mankind handed down to us from generation to generation, and the condemnation of mankind to begin all over again the age-old struggle upward from savagery towards decency, and right, and justice. Surely no sane member of the human race could discover victory in such desolation. Could anyone wish his name to be coupled by history with such human degradation and destruction? Occasional pages of history do record the faces of the "great destroyers", but the whole book of history reveals mankind's never-ending quest for peace and mankind's God-given capacity to build.

It is with the book of history, and not with isolated pages, that the United States will ever wish to be identified. My country wants to be constructive, not destructive. It wants agreements, not wars, among nations. It wants itself to live in freedom and in the confidence that the peoples of every other nation enjoy equally the right of choosing their own way of life.

So my country's purpose is to help us to move out of the dark chamber of horrors into the light, to find a way by which the minds of men, the hopes of men, the souls of men everywhere, can move forward towards peace and happiness and well-being.

In this quest, I know that we must not lack patience. I know that in a world divided, such as ours today, salvation cannot be attained by one dramatic act. I know that many steps will have to be taken over many months before the world can look at itself one day and truly realize that a new climate of mutually peaceful confidence is abroad in the world. But I know, above all else, that we must start to take these steps—now.

The United States and its allies, the United Kingdom and France, have over the past months tried to take some of these steps. Let no one say that we shun the conference table. On the record has long stood the request of the United States, the United Kingdom and France to negotiate with the Soviet Union the problems of a divided Germany. On that record has long stood the request of the same three nations to negotiate an Austrian peace treaty. On the same record still stands the request of the United Nations to negotiate the problems of Korea.

Most recently we have received from the Soviet Union what is in effect an expression of willingness to hold a four-Power meeting. Along with our allies, the United Kingdom and France, we were pleased to see that this note did not contain the unacceptable pre-conditions previously put forward. As you already know from our joint Bermuda communique, the United States, the United Kingdom and France have agreed promptly to meet with the Soviet Union.

The Government of the United States approaches this conference with hopeful sincerity. We will bend every effort of our minds to the single purpose of emerging from that conference with tangible results towards peace, the only true way of lessening international tension.

We never have, and never will, propose or suggest that the Soviet Union surrender what rightly belongs to it. We will never say that the peoples of the USSR are an enemy with whom we have no desire ever to deal or mingle in friendly and fruitful relationship.

On the contrary, we hope that this coming conference may initiate a relationship with the Soviet Union which will eventually bring about a freer mingling of the peoples of the East and of the West—the one sure, human way of developing the understanding required for confident and peaceful relations.

Instead of the discontent which is now settling upon Eastern Germany, occupied Austria and the countries of Eastern Europe, we seek a harmonious family of free European nations, with none a threat to the other, and least of all a threat to the peoples of the USSR. Beyond the turmoil and strife and misery of Asis, we seek peaceful opportunity for these peoples to develop their natural resources and to elevate their lot.

These are not idle words or shallow visions. Behind them lies a story of nations lately come to independence, not as a result of war, but through free grant or peaceful negotiation. There is a record already written of assistance gladly given by nations of the West to needy peoples and to those suffering the temporary effects of famine, drought and natural disaster. These are deeds of peace. They speak more loudly than promises or protestations of peaceful intent.

But I do not wish to rest either upon the reiteration of past proposals or the restatement of past deeds. The gravity of the time is such that every new avenue of peace, no matter how dimly discernible, should be explored.

There is at least one new avenue of peace which has not been well explored -an avenue now laid out by the General Assembly of the United Nations.

In its resolution of 28 November 1953 (resolution 715 (VIII)) this General Assembly suggested: "that the Disarmament Commission study the desirability of establishing a sub-committee consisting of representatives of the Powers principally involved, which should seek in private an acceptable solution and report . . . on such a solution to the General Assembly and to the Security Council not later than 1 September 1954.

The United States, heeding the suggestion of the General Assembly of the United Nations, is instantly prepared to meet privately with such other countries as may be "principally involved", to seek "an acceptable solution" to the atomic armaments race which overshadows not only the peace, but the very life, of the world.

We shall carry into these private or diplomatic talks a new conception. The United States would seek more than the mere reduction or elimination of atomic materials for military purposes. It is not enough to take this weapon out of the hands of the soldiers. It must be put into the hands of those who will know how to strip its military casing and adapt it to the arts of peace.

The United States knows that if the fearful trend of atomic military build-up can be reversed, this greatest of destructive forces can be developed into a great boon, for the benefit of all mankind. The United States knows that peaceful power from atomic energy is no dream of the future. The capability, already proved, is here today. Who can doubt that, if the entire body of the world's scientists and engineers had adequate amounts of fissionable material with which to test and develop their ideas, this capability would rapidly be transformed into universal, efficient and economic usage?

To hasten the day when fear of the atom will begin to disappear from the minds the people and the governments of the East and West, there are certain steps that can be taken now.

I therefore make the following proposal.

The governments principally involved, to the extent permitted by elementary prudence, should begin now and continue to make joint contributions from their stockpiles of normal uranium and fissionable materials to an international atomic energy agency. We would expect that such an agency would be set up under the aegis of the United Nations. The ratios of contributions, the procedures and other details would properly be within the scope of the "private conversations" I referred to earlier.

The United States is prepared to undertake these explorations in good faith. Any partner of the United States acting in the same good faith will find the United States a not unreasonable or ungenerous associate.

Undoubtedly, initial and early contributions to this plan would be small in quantity. However, the proposal has the great virtue that it can be undertaken without the irritations and mutual suspicions incident to any attempt to set up a completely acceptable system of world-wide inspection and control.

The atomic energy agency could be made responsible for the impounding, storage and protection of the contributed fissionable and other materials. The ingenuity of our scientists will provide special safe conditions under which such a bank of fissionable material can be made essentially immune to surprise seizure.

The more important responsibility of this atomic energy agency would be to devise methods whereby this fissionable material would be allocated to serve the peaceful pursuits of mankind. Experts would be mobilized to apply atomic energy to the needs of agriculture, medicine and other peaceful activities. A special purpose would be to provide abundant electrical energy in the power-starved areas of the world.

Thus the contributing Powers would be dedicating some of their strength to serve the needs rather than the fears of mankind.

The United States would be more than willing—it would be proud to take up with others "principally involved" the development of plans whereby such peaceful use of atomic energy would be expedited.

Of those "principally involved" the Soviet Union must, of course, be one.

I would be prepared to submit to the Congress of the United States, and with every expectation of approval, any such plan that would, first, encourage world-wide investigation into the most effective peacetime uses of fissionable material, and with the certainty that the investigators had all the material needed for the conducting of all experiments that were appropriate; second, begin to diminish the potential destructive power of the world's atomic stockpiles; third, allow all peoples of all nations to see that, in this enlightened age, the great Powers of the earth, both of the East and of the West, are interested in human aspirations first rather than in building up the armaments of war; fourth, open up a new channel for peaceful discussion and initiative at least a new approach to the many difficult problems that must be solved in both private and public conversations if the world is to shake off the inertia imposed by fear and is to make positive progress towards peace.

Against the dark background of the atomic bomb, the United States does not wish merely to present strength, but also the desire and the hope for peace. The coming months will be fraught with fateful decisions. In this Assembly, in the capitals and military headquarters of the world, in the hearts of men everywhere, be they governed or governors, may they be the decisions which will lead this world out of fear and into peace.

To the making of these fateful decisions, the United States pledges before you, and therefore before the world, its determination to help solve the fearful atomic dilemma—to devote its entire heart and mind to finding the way by which the miraculous inventiveness of man shall not be dedicated to his death, but consecrated to his life.

I again thank representatives for the great honour they have done me in inviting me to appear before them and in listening to me so graciously.

*Source:* http://www.iaea.org/About/history_speech.html

## FEDERAL AID HIGHWAY ACT OF 1956

*The Federal-Aid Highway Act of 1956, popularly known as the National Interstate and Defense Highways Act, was enacted on June 29, 1956, when President Eisenhower signed it into law. It originally authorized $25 billion for the construction of 41,000 miles (66,000 kilometers) of the interstate highway system. The money for the interstate and defense highways was handled by the Highway Trust Fund, which paid for 90 percent of highway construction costs while the states were required to pay the remaining 10 percent. It was expected that the money would be generated through new taxes on fuel, automobiles, trucks, and tires. As a matter of practice, the federal portion of the cost of the interstate highway system has been paid for by taxes on gasoline and diesel fuel.*

### AN ACT

To amend and supplement the Federal-Aid Road Act approved July 11, 1916, to authorize appropriations for continuing the construction of highways; to amend the Internal Revenue Code of 1954 to provide additional revenue from the taxes on motor fuel, tires, and trucks and buses; and for other purposes.

Be it enacted by the Senate and House of Representatives of the United States of America in Congress assembled,

## TITLE I—FEDERAL-AID HIGHWAY ACT OF 1956

SEC. 101. SHORT TITLE FOR TITLE I.

This title may be cited as the "Federal-Aid Highway Act of 1956".

SEC. 102. FEDERAL-AID HIGHWAYS.

(a) (1) AUTHORIZATION OF APPROPRIATIONS.—For the purpose of carrying out the provisions of the Federal-Aid Road Act approved July 11, 1916 (39 Stat. 355), and all Acts amendatory thereof and supplementary thereto, there is hereby authorized to be appropriated for the fiscal year ending June 30, 1957, $125,000,000 in addition to any sums heretofore authorized for such fiscal year; the sum of $850,000,000 for the fiscal year ending June 30, 1958; and the sum of $875,000,000 for the fiscal year ending June 30, 1959. The sums herein authorized for each fiscal year shall be available for expenditure as follows:

(A) 45 per centum for projects on the Federal-aid primary high-way system.

(B) 30 per centum for projects on the Federal-aid secondary high-way system.

(C) 25 per centum for projects on extensions of these systems within urban areas.

(2) APPORTIONMENTS.—The sums authorized by this section shall be apportioned among the several States in the manner now provided by law and in accordance with the formulas set forth in section 4 of the Federal-Aid Highway Act of 1944; approved December 20, 1944 (58 Stat. 838) : Provided, That the additional amount herein authorized for the fiscal year ending June 30, 1957, shall be apportioned immediately upon enactment of this Act.

(b) AVAILABILITY FOR EXPENDITURE.—Any sums apportioned to any State under this section shall be available for expenditure in that State for two years after the close of the fiscal year for which such sums are authorized, and any amounts so apportioned remaining unexpended at the end of such period shall lapse: Provided, That such funds shall be deemed to have been expended if a sum equal to the total of the sums herein and heretofore apportioned to the State is covered by formal agreements with the Secretary of Commerce for construction, reconstruction, or improvement of specific projects as provided in this title and prior Acts: Provided further, That in the case of those sums heretofore, herein, or hereafter apportioned to any State for projects on the Federal-aid secondary highway system, the Secretary of Commerce may, upon the request of any State, discharge his responsibility relative to the plans, specifications, estimates, surveys, contract awards, design, inspection, and construction of such secondary road projects by his receiving and approving a certified statement by the State highway department setting forth that the plans, design, and construction for such projects are in accord with the standards and procedures of such State applicable. . . .

. . .

SEC. 108. NATIONAL SYSTEM OF INTERSTATE AND DEFENSE HIGHWAYS.

(a) INTERSTATE SYSTEM.—It is hereby declared to be essential to the national interest to provide for the early completion of the "National System of Interstate Highways", as authorized and designated in accordance with section 7 of the Federal-Aid Highway Act of 1944 (58 Stat. 838). It is the intent of the Congress that the Interstate System be completed as nearly as practicable over a thirteen-year period and that the entire System in all the States be brought to simultaneous completion. Because of its primary importance to the national defense, the name of such system is hereby changed to the "National System of Interstate and Defense Highways". Such National System of Interstate and Defense Highways is hereinafter in this Act referred to as the "Interstate System".

(b) AUTHORIZATION OF APPROPRIATIONS.—For the purpose of expediting the construction, reconstruction, or improvement, inclusive of necessary bridges and tunnels, of the interstate System, including extensions thereof through urban areas, designated in accordance with the provisions of section 7 of the Federal-Aid Highway Act of 1944 (58 Stat. 838), there is hereby authorized to be appropriated the additional sum of $1,000,000,000.

*Source:* http://www.ourdocuments.gov/doc.php?flash=true&doc=88&page=transcript

# BIBLIOGRAPHY

Abbate, Janet. *Inventing the Internet*. Cambridge, MA: MIT Press, 1999.

Abramson, Albert. *The History of Television, 1880 to 1941*. Jefferson, NC: McFarland, 1987.

Albert, Robert. *The Good Provider*. Boston: Houghton Mifflin, 1973.

Altman, Nancy. *The Battle for Social Security: From FDR's Vision to Bush's Gamble*. New York: Wiley, 2005.

Ambrose, Stephen E. *Nothing Like It in the World*. New York: Simon & Schuster, 2000.

Andrist, Ralph. *The Erie Canal*. New York: Harper & Row, 1964.

Apelt, Brian. *The Corporation: A Centennial Biography of United States Steel Corporation*. Pittsburgh, PA: University of Pittsburgh Press, 2000.

Appelbaum, Stanley. *The Chicago World's Fair of 1893*. New York: Dover, 1980.

Arthur, Anthony. *Radical Innocent: Upton Sinclair*. New York: Random House, 2006.

Austrian, Geoffrey. *Herman Hollerith: Forgotten Giant of Information Processing*. New York: Columbia University Press, 1982.

Avrich, Paul. *The Haymarket Tragedy*. Princeton, NJ: Princeton University Press, 1984.

Badger, Reid. *The Great American Fair: The World's Columbian Exposition and American Culture*. Chicago: Nelson Hall, 1979.

Bagwell, Kyle, and Robert W. Staiger. "An Economic Theory of GATT." *American Economic Review*, 89, no. 1 (March 1999): 215–248.

Baldwin, Leland. *Whiskey Rebels: The Story of a Frontier Uprising*. Pittsburgh, PA: University of Pittsburgh Press, 1939.

Banks, Michael. *On the Way to the Web: The Secret History of the Internet and Its Founders*. New York: Apress, 2010.

Battelle, John. *The Search: How Google and Its Rivals Rewrote the Rules of Business and Transformed Our Culture*. New York: Portfolio, 2005.

Beaver, William. *Nuclear Power Goes On-Line: A History of Shippingport*. Westport, CT: Greenwood, 1990.

Beland, Daniel. *Social Security: History and Politics from the New Deal to the Privatization Debate*. Lawrence: University of Kansas, 2007.

Bellesiles, Michael. *1877: America's Year of Living Violently.* New York: New Press, 2010.

Bethell, Thomas. *The Noblest Triumph: Property and Prosperity through the Ages.* New York: St. Martin's, 2007.

Boorstin, Daniel. *The Americans: The Democratic Experience.* New York: Vintage Books, 1974.

Boorstin, Daniel. *The Americans: The National Experience.* New York: Vintage, 1965.

Bourne, Russell. *Americans on the Move: A History of Waterways, Railways, and Highways.* Golden, CO: Fulcrum, 1995.

Bradford, William. *Of Plymouth Plantation.* New York: Knopf, 2002.

Bray, John. *The Communications Miracle—The Telecommunications Pioneers.* New York: Plenum, 1995.

Breyfogle, F. W. *Implementing Six Sigma.* New York: Wiley, 1999.

Bridge, James Howard. *The Inside History of Carnegie Steel Company.* New York: Aldine, 1903.

Bringhurst, Bruce. *Antitrust and the Oil Trust: The Standard Oil Cases, 1890–1911.* New York: Greenwood, 1979.

Brinkley, Douglas. *Wheels for the World: Henry Ford, His Company, and a Century of Progress.* New York: Viking, 2003.

Bromberg, Joan Lisa. *NASA and Space Industry.* Baltimore, MD: Johns Hopkins University Press, 2000.

Brownlee, Elliot. *Federal Taxation in America: A Short History.* Cambridge: Cambridge University Press, 2004.

Bruce, Robert. *1877: Year of Violence.* Lanham, MD: Ivan R. Dee, 1989.

Bruce, Robert V. *Lincoln and the Tools of War.* Urbana: University of Illinois Press, 1989.

Bruner, Robert, and Sean Carr. *The Panic of 1907: Lessons Learned from the Market's Perfect Storm.* Hoboken, NJ: Wiley, 2009.

Buck, Solon. *The Planting of Civilization in Western Pennsylvania.* Pittsburgh, PA: University of Pittsburgh Press, 1968.

Bustillo, Miguel. "Wal-Mart Radio Tags to Track Clothing." *Wall Street Journal,* July 23, 2010.

Cain, Peter. *Free Trade and Protectionism: Key Nineteenth Century Journal Summaries.* London: Routledge, 1996.

Calamiris, Charles, and Gary Gorton. *The Origins of Banking Panics: Models, Facts, and Bank Regulation.* Chicago: University of Chicago Press, 1992.

Calamiris, Charles, and Larry Schueikart. "The Panic of 1857: Origins, Transmission, and Containment." *Journal of Economic History,* 51, no. 4 (1991): 15–21.

Cannadine, David. *Mellon: An American Life.* New York: Knopf, 2006.

Carr, Charles C. *ALCOA: An American Enterprise.* New York: Rinehart, 1952.

Carringer, Robert L. *The Jazz Singer.* Madison: University of Wisconsin Press, 1979.

Carroll, Paul. *Big Blues: The Unmaking of IBM.* New York: Crown, 1994.

Carroll, Peter N. *It Seemed Like Nothing Happened: America in the 1970s.* New Brunswick, NJ: Rutgers University Press, 1990.

Ceruzzi, Paul E. *A History of Modern Computing.* Cambridge, MA: MIT Press, 2003.

Chandler, William U. *America's Greatest Depression, 1929–1941.* New York: Harper & Row, 1970.

Chapman, Arthur. *The Pony Express: The Record of a Romantic Adventure in Business.* New York: Cooper Square, 1971.

Chernow, Ron. *Alexander Hamilton.* New York: Penguin, 2004.

Chernow, Ron. *House of Morgan: An American Banking Dynasty and the Rise of Modern Finance.* New York: Grove, 1990.

Chernow, Ron. *Titan: The Life of John D. Rockefeller, Sr.* New York: Vintage Books, 1998.

Coe, Lewis. *The Telephone and Its Several Inventors: A History.* Jefferson, NC: McFarland, 1995.

Condit, Carl. *The Chicago School of Architecture.* Chicago: University of Chicago, 1964.

Cotter, Arundel. *The Authentic History of the United States Steel Corporation.* New York: Moody, 1916.

Crafton, Donald. *The Talkies: American Cinema's Transition to Sound.* Berkeley: University of California Press, 1999.

Cravens, Gwyneth. *Power to Save the World: The Truth about Nuclear Energy.* New York: Knopf, 2007.

Curry, Timothy, and Lynn Shibut. "The Cost of the Savings and Loan Crisis: Truth and Consequences." *FDIC Banking Review,* December 2000.

Dangerfield, George. *Awakening of American Nationalism.* New York: Wineland, 1994.

David, Henry. *The History of the Haymarket Affair: A Study of the American Social-Revolutionary and Labor Movements.* New York: Collier Books, 1963.

Davidson, John. *Commercial Federation and Colonial Trade Policy.* Ithaca, NY: Cornell University Library, 2009.

Davies, R. E. *A History of the World's Airlines.* Oxford: Oxford University Press, 1964.

Deming, W. Edwards. *Out of the Crisis.* Cambridge, MA: MIT Center for Advanced Engineering Study, 1986.

Derry, T. K., and Trevor Williams. *A Short History of Technology.* New York: Oxford University Press, 1960.

DiLorenzo, Thomas J. *How Capitalism Saved America.* Boston: Three Rivers, 2004.

Dilts, James. *The Great Road: The Building of Baltimore & Ohio, the Nation's First Railroad.* Stanford, CA: Stanford University Press, 1993.

Dobelstein, Andrew. *Understanding the Social Security Act: The Foundation of Social Welfare for America in the Twenty-First Century.* Oxford: Oxford University Press, 2009.

Douglas, George. *The Early Years of Radio Broadcasting.* Jefferson, NC: McFarland, 1987.

Douglas, Susan. *Inventing American Broadcasting, 1899–1922.* Baltimore, MD: Johns Hopkins University Press, 1987.

Dunar, Andrew, and Dennis McBride. *Building Hoover Dam: An Oral History of the Great Depression.* Reno: University of Nevada Press, 2001.

Edsforth, Ronald. *The New Deal: America's Response to the Great Depression.* London: Blackwell, 2000.

Eggert, Gerald. *Steelmasters and Labor Reform, 1886–1923.* Pittsburgh, PA: University of Pittsburgh Press, 1981.

Elliot, Jay, and William L. Simon. *The Steve Jobs Way: iLeadership for a New Generation.* New York: Vanguard, 2011.

Everson, George. *The Story of Television, The Life of Philo T. Farnsworth.* New York: Norton, 1945.

Eyman, Scott. *The Speed of Sound: Hollywood and the Talkie Revolution, 1926–1930.* New York: Simon and Schuster, 1997.

Facella, Paul. *Everything I Know about Business I Learned at McDonald's: The 7 Leadership Principles That Drive and Break Success.* New York: McGraw-Hill, 2008.

Findling, John E. *Chicago's Great World's Fair.* Manchester, UK: Manchester University Press, 1994.

Finler, Joel W. *The Hollywood Story.* New York: Crown, 1988.

Fisher, Claude. *America Calling: A Social History of the Telephone to 1940.* Berkeley: University of California Press, 1994.

Fishman, Charles. *The Wal-Mart Effect: How the World's Most Powerful Company Really Works—and How It's Transforming the American Economy.* New York: Penguin, 2006.

Foner, Philip S., ed. *The Autobiographies of the Haymarket Martyrs.* New York: Pathfinder, 1969.

Foster, William Z. *The Great Steel Strike and Its Lessons.* Charleston, SC: BiblioBazaar, 2009.

Freeman, Joanne. *Affairs of Honor: National Politics in the New Republic.* New Haven, CT: Yale University Press, 2001.

Friedman, Milton, and Anna Schwartz. *A Monetary History of the United States, 1867–1960.* Princeton, NJ: Princeton University Press, 1971.

Fryman, Mark A. *Quality and Process Improvement.* Albany, NY: Delmar, 2002.

Galbraith, John Kenneth. *The Great Crash: 1929.* Boston: Houghton Mifflin, 1988.

Gali, Jordi. *Monetary Policy, Inflation, and the Business Cycle: An Introduction to the New Keynesian Framework.* Princeton, NJ: Princeton University Press, 2008.

Gates, Bill. *Business @ the Speed of Thought: Succeeding in the Digital Economy.* New York: Warner Business Books, 2000.

Gavaghan, Helen. *Something New under the Sun: Satellites and the Beginning of the Space Age.* New York: Springer, 1997.

Gillmore, Jesse. *Disastrous Financial Panics.* Charleston, SC: BiblioBazaar, 2009.

Goodrich, Carter. *Canals and American Economic Development.* New York: Columbia University Press, 1961.

Gordon, Sarah. *Passage to Union: How the Railroads Transformed American Life.* Chicago: Ivan Dee, 1996.

Gould, Lewis. *The Presidency of William McKinley.* Lawrence: University of Kansas Press, 1980.

Green, James R. *Death in the Haymarket: A Story of Chicago, the First Labor Movement and the Bombing That Divided Gilded Age America.* New York: Pantheon Books, 2006.

Greene, Julie. *Canal Builders: Making America's Empire at the Panama Canal.* New York: Penguin, 2009.

Gross, Linda, and Theresa Snyder. *Philadelphia 1876 Centennial Exhibition.* Mount Pleasant, SC: Arcadia, 2005.

Gustin, Lawrence R. *Billy Durant: Creator of General Motors.* Ann Arbor: University of Michigan Press, 1973.

Hafner, Katie. *Where Wizards Stay Up Late: Origins of the Internet.* New York: Simon & Schuster, 1998.

Hammond, J. *Men and Volts: The Story of General Electric.* New York: J. B. Lippincott, 1941.

Hanson, Jarice. *24/7 How Cell Phones and the Internet Changed How We Live, Work, and Play.* Santa Barbara, CA: Praeger, 2007.

Herzberg, Frederick, Bernard Mausner, and Barbara Snyderman. *The Motivation to Work.* New York: Wiley, 1959.

Hiltzik, Michael. *Colossus: Hoover Dam and the Making of the American Century.* New York: Free Press, 2010.

Hirsch, Susan. *After the Strike: A Century of Labor Struggle at Pullman.* Urbana: University of Illinois, 2003.

Hoerr, John P. *And the Wolf Finally Came: The Decline of the American Steel Industry.* Pittsburgh, PA: University of Pittsburgh Press, 1988.

Hoge, Cecil. *The First Hundred Years Are the Toughest.* Berkeley, CA: Ten Speed, 1988.

Hogeland, William. *The Whiskey Rebellion: George Washington, Alexander Hamilton, and the Frontier Rebels Who Challenged America's Newfound Sovereignty.* New York: Scribner, 2006.

Holland, David. *When Regulation Was Too Successful—The Sixth Decade of Deposit Insurance.* Westport, CT: Greenwood, 1998.

Hooker, Richard. *The History of Food and Drink in America.* New York: Bobbs-Merrill, 1981.

Hounshell, David. *From American System to Mass Production, 1800–1932, The Development of Manufacturing Technology in the United States.* Baltimore, MD: Johns Hopkins University Press, 1984.

Howe, Daniel Walker. *The Political Culture of the American Whigs.* Chicago: University of Chicago Press, 1979.

Hudec, Robert. *The GATT Legal System and World Trade Diplomacy.* New York: Praeger, 1990.

Jackway, Gwenyth L. *Media of War: Radio's Challenge to the Newspapers, 1924–1939.* Westport, CT: Praeger, 1995.

Jonnes, Jill. *Empires of Light.* New York: Random House, 2003.

Joseph, Richard. *Origin of the American Income Tax: The Revenue Act of 1894.* Syracuse, NY: Syracuse University Press, 2004.

Juglar, Clement, and W. DeCourcy. *A Brief History of Panics in the United States.* Old Chelsea, NY: Cosimo, 2005.

Kaempffert, Waldemar. *Modern Wonder Workers.* New York: Blue Ribbon Books, 1924.

Kanigel, Robert. *The One Best Way: Frederick Winslow Taylor and the Enigma of Efficiency.* New York: Viking, 1997.

Kaplan, Edward. *The Bank of the United States and the American Economy.* Westport, CT: Greenwood, 1999.

Kato, Hiroko, Keng T. Tan, and Douglas Chai. *Barcodes for Mobile Devices.* Cambridge: Cambridge University Press, 2010.

Kaufman, Bruce E. *The Origins and Evolution of the Field of Industrial Relations.* Ithaca, NY: ILR Press, 1993.

Kennedy, John F. *A Nation of Immigrants.* New York: Harper & Row, 1964.

Khan, Zorina. *The Democratization of Invention: Patent and Copyrights in American Economic Development.* Cambridge: Cambridge University Press, 2009.

Kindleberger, Charles P. *The World in Depression: 1929–1939.* Berkeley: University of California Press, 1986.

Kindleberger, Charles P., and Robert Aliber. *Manias, Panics, and Crashes: A History of Financial Crises.* Hobokcn, NJ: Wiley, 2005.

Klemens, Guy. *The Cellphone: History of the Gadget That Changed the World.* Jefferson, NC: McFarland, 2010.

Kranz, Gene. *Failure Is Not an Option: Mission Control from Mercury to Apollo 13 and Beyond.* New York: Simon & Schuster, 2009.

Kranzberg, Malven, and Carroll Pursell Jr. *Technology in Western Civilization.* New York: Oxford University Press, 1967.

Krass, Peter. *Carnegie.* New York: Wiley, 2002.

Krause, Paul. *Battle of Homestead.* Pittsburgh, PA: University of Pittsburgh Press, 1992.

Kroc, Ray. *Grinding It Out: Making of McDonald's.* New York: St. Martin's, 1992.

Kroll, Steven. *Robert Fulton: From Submarine to Steamboat.* New York: Holiday House, 1999.

Labrador, Virgil. *Heavens Fill with Commerce—A Brief History of Satellite Communications Industry.* Sonoma, CA: Satnews, 2005.

Lahiri, Sandip. *RFID Sourcebook.* Armonk, NY: IBM Press, 2011.

Laing, Alexander. *The Clipper Ships and Their Makers.* New York: G. P. Putman's Sons, 1966.

Land, Michael. *Hamilton's Republic: Readings in the American Democratic Nationalist Tradition.* New York: Free Press, 2004.

Lauch, Jett. *The Causes of the Panic of 1893.* Charleston, SC: Nabu, 2010.

Lee, Susan, and Peter Passell. *A New Economic View of American History.* New York: Norton, 1979.

Leupp, Francis. *George Westinghouse: His Life and Achievements.* Boston: Little, Brown, 1918.

Lewis, Thomas. *Divided Highways: Building the Interstate Highways, Transforming American Life.* New York: Penguin, 1999.

Liker, Jeffery. *The Toyota Way.* New York: McGraw-Hill, 2003.

Liker, Jeffery, Michael Hoseus, and Center for Quality, People, and Organization. *Toyota Culture: The Heart and Soul of the Toyota Way.* New York: McGraw-Hill, 2008.

Lindsay, Almont. *The Pullman Strike: The Story of a Unique Experiment and of a Great Labor Upheaval.* Chicago: University of Chicago Press, 1943.

Link, Arthur S. *Woodrow Wilson and the Progressive Era.* New York: Harper Books, 1954.

Love, John F. *McDonald's: Behind the Arches.* New York: Bantam Books, 1995.

Love, Steve, and David Giffels. *Wheels of Fortune: The Story of Rubber in Akron.* Akron, OH: University of Akron Press, 1999.

Lubbock, Basil. *The China Clippers.* Glasgow, UK: Brown, Son & Ferguson, 1946.

Lubetkin, John. *Jay Cooke's Gamble: The Northern Pacific Railroad, the Sioux, and the Panic of 1873.* Norman: University of Oklahoma Press, 2006.

MacLaren, Malcolm. *The Rise of the Electrical Industry during the Nineteenth Century.* Princeton, NJ: Princeton University Press, 1943.

Mandell, Lewis. *Credit Card Industry: A History.* New York: Macmillan, 1990.

Maney, Kevin. *The Maverick and His Machine: Thomas Watson, Sr. and the Making of IBM.* New York: Wiley, 2004.

Marcello, Patricia Cronin. *Ralph Nader: A Biography.* Westport, CT: Greenwood, 2004.

Marcus, James. *Amazonia: Five Years at the Epicenter of the Dot.Com Juggernaut.* New York: Norton, 2004.

Mashaw, Jerry. *The Struggle for Auto Safety.* Cambridge, MA: Harvard University Press, 1990.

Maslow, Abraham. *Eupsychian Management.* Homewood, IL: Richard D. Irwin, 1965.

Mayer, Martin. *The Greatest Ever Bank Robbery: The Collapse of the Savings and Loan Industry.* New York: C. Scribner's Sons, 1992.

Mayo, Elton. *The Human Problems of an Industrial Civilization.* New York: Macmillan, 1933.

McCartney, Scott. *ENIAC: The Triumphs and Tragedies of the World's First Computer.* New York: Walker, 1999.

McCreadie, Karen. *Adam Smith's The Wealth of Nations: A Modern Day Interpretation of an Economic Classic.* New York: Infinite Ideas, 2009.

McCullough, David. *The Path between Seas: The Creation of the Panama Canal, 1870–1914.* New York: Simon & Schuster, 1977.

McGrane, Reginald. *The Panic of 1837: Some Financial Problems of the Jacksonian Era.* New York: Russell & Russell, 1965.

McNichol, Dan. *The Roads That Built America: The Incredible Story of the U.S. Interstate System.* New York: Sterling, 2006.

McNichol, Tom. *AC/DC: The Savage Tale of the First Standard War.* New York: Jossey-Bass, 2006.

McPherson, James. *Abraham Lincoln*. New York: Oxford University Press, 2010.

Meltzer, Allan. *A History of the Federal Reserve*. Vol. 1, *1913–1951*. Chicago: University of Chicago Press, 2004.

Merk, Fredrick. *History of the Westward Movement*. New York: Knopf, 1978.

Merrill, Harwood. *Classics in Management*. New York: American Management Association, 1960.

Merrill, Karen. *The Oil Crisis of 1973–1974: A Brief History with Documents*. New York: St. Martin's, 2007.

Millis, Harry, and Emily Brown Clark. *From the Wagner Act to Taft-Hartley: A Study of National Labor Policy and Labor Relations*. Chicago: University of Chicago Press, 1950.

Montgomery, David. *The Fall of the House of Labor*. Cambridge: Cambridge University Press, 1987.

Moody, Ralph. *Stage Coach West*. New York: Crowell, 1967.

Morita, Akio, and Sony Corporation. *Made in Japan*. New York: HarperCollins, 1994.

Morris, Charles. *The Blue Eagle at Work: Reclaiming Democratic Rights in the American Workplace*. Ithaca, NY: Cornell University Press, 2004.

Morris, Charles R. *The Tycoons: How Andrew Carnegie, John D. Rockefeller, Jay Gould, and J. P. Morgan Invented the American Super Economy*. New York: Henry Holt, 2005.

Nader, Ralph. *Unsafe at Any Speed*. New York: Grossman, 1965.

Nathan, John. *Sony: The Private Life*. New York: Houghton Mifflin, 1999.

Nelson, Daniel. *Frederick W. Taylor and the Rise of Scientific Management*. Madison: University of Wisconsin Press, 1980.

Nelson, Daniel. *A Mental Revolution: Scientific Management since Taylor*. Columbus: Ohio State University Press, 1992.

Olsen, Byron, and Joseph Cabadas. *The American Auto Factory*. St. Paul, MN: MBI, 2002.

O'Rourke, P.J. *P.J. O'Rourke on the Wealth of Nations*. New York: Atlantic Monthly Press, 2007.

Osterwalder, Alexander. *Business Model Generation: A Handbook for Visionaries, Game Changers, and Challengers*. New York: Wiley, 2010.

Palmer, Roger C. *The Bar Code Book: Fifth Edition—A Comprehensive Guide to Reading, Printing, Specifying, Evaluating, and Using Bar Code and Other Machine-Readable Symbols*. Bloomington, IN: Trafford, 2007.

Pangborn, J. G. *The Golden Age of the Steam Locomotive*. New York: Dover, 2003.

Papke, Ray. *The Pullman Case: The Clash of Labor and Capital in Industrial America*. Lawrence: University of Kansas, 1999.

Paulson, Hank. *On the Brink*. London: Headline, 2010.

Payne, Robert. *The Canal Builders*. New York: Macmillan, 1959.

Peek, J. B., J. Bergmans, Frank Toolenaar, and S. Stan. *Origins and Successors of the Compact Disc: Contributions of Philips to Optical Storage*. New York: Springer, 2010.

Pellerin, Charles. *How NASA Builds Teams: Mission Critical Soft Skills for Scientists, Engineers and Project Teams*. New York: Wiley, 2009.

Phillips, Kevin. *William McKinley.* Boston: Houghton Mifflin, 2003.

Poage, George. *Henry Clay and the Whig Party.* Chapel Hill: University of North Carolina Press, 1936.

Pretzer, William. *Working at Inventing: Thomas Edison and the Menlo Park Experience.* Baltimore, MD: Johns Hopkins University Press, 2001.

Pugh, Emerson. *Building IBM: Shaping an Industry and Its Technology.* Cambridge, MA: MIT Press, 1995.

Pursell, Carroll. *Technology in America.* Cambridge, MA: MIT Press, 1990.

Rae, John B. *The American Automobile.* Chicago: University of Chicago Press, 1965.

Raitz, Karl. *The National Road.* Baltimore, MD: Johns Hopkins University Press, 1996.

Read, Colin. *Global Financial Meltdown: How to Avoid the Next Financial Crisis.* New York: Palgrave Macmillan, 2009.

Remini, Robert. *Andrew Jackson.* San Francisco: Harper Perennial, 1999.

Remini, Robert. *Henry Clay: Statesman for the Union.* New York: Norton, 1991.

Rockoff, Hugh. *Drastic Measures: A History of Wage and Price Controls in the United States.* Cambridge: Cambridge University Press, 2004.

Rydell, Robert. *World of Fairs.* Chicago: University of Chicago Press, 1993.

Sabbagh, Karl. *Skyscrapers: The Making of a Building.* New York: Penguin Books, 1991.

Sale, Kirkpatrick. *The Fire of Genius: Robert Fulton and the American Dream.* New York: Free Press, 2002.

Schiffer, Michael Brian. *The Portable Radio in American Life.* Tucson: University of Arizona Press, 1991.

Schlereth, Thomas. *Victorian America: Transformations in Everyday Life.* New York: Harper Perennial, 1991.

Schneider, Norris. *The National Road: Main Street of America.* Columbus: Ohio Historical Society, 1975.

Seifer, Marc. *Wizard: The Life and Times of Nikola Tesla.* New York: Citadel, 1998.

Sharp, James Roger. *The Jacksonians versus the Banks: Politics in the United States after the Panic of 1837.* New York: Columbia University Press, 1970.

Shepherd, James, and Gary Walton. *Shipping, Maritime Trade and the Economic Development of Colonial North America.* Cambridge: Cambridge University Press, 2010.

Shlaes, Amity. *The Forgotten Man: A New History of the Great Depression.* New York: Harper Perennial, 2007.

Simmons, Matty. *The Credit Card Catastrophe: The 20th Century Phenomenon That Changed the World.* Fort Lee, NJ: Barricade, 1995.

Skrabec, Quentin. *Edward Drummond Libbey: A Biography of an American Glassmaker.* Jefferson, NC: McFarland, 2010.

Skrabec, Quentin. *George Westinghouse: Gentle Genius.* New York: Algora, 2007.

Skrabec, Quentin. *Henry Clay Frick: The Life of a Perfect Capitalist.* Jefferson, NC: McFarland, 2010.

Skrabec, Quentin. *H. J. Heinz.* Jefferson, NC: McFarland, 2009.

Skrabec, Quentin. *The Metallurgic Age.* Jefferson, NC: McFarland, 2006.

Skrabec, Quentin. *Pig Iron Aristocracy.* Westminster, MD: Heritage Books, 2008.

Skrabec, Quentin R. *William McKinley: Apostle of Protectionism.* New York: Algora, 2008.

Skrabec, Quentin R. *The World's Richest Neighborhood: How Pittsburgh's East Enders Forged American Industry.* New York: Algora, 2010.

Sloan, Alfred. *My Years at General Motors.* New York: Crown Business, 1990.

Smelser, Marshall. *The Democratic Republic.* New York: Harper & Row, 1968.

Smith, Adam. *An Inquiry into the Nature and Causes of the Wealth of Nations.* New York: Random House, 1937.

Smith, Andrew. *Pure Ketchup.* Washington, DC: Smithsonian Institution, 2001.

Smulyan, Susan. *Selling Radio: The Commercialization of American Broadcasting, 1920–1934.* Washington, DC: Smithsonian Institution Press, 1994.

Sobel, Robert. *The Panic of 57, Machines and Morality: The 1850s.* New York: Crowell, 1973.

Sobel, Robert. *Panic on Wall Street: A History of America's Financial Disasters.* New York: Macmillan, 1968.

Solberg, Carl. *Conquest of the Skies: A History of Commercial Aviation in America.* Boston: Little, Brown, 1979.

Sorenson, Charles. *My Forty Years with Ford.* Detroit: Wayne State University Press, 2006.

Spector, Robert. *Amazon.com—Get Big Fast: Inside the Revolutionary Business Model That Changed the World.* San Francisco: HarperBusiness, 2000.

Spivak, Burton. *Jefferson's English Crisis: Commerce, Embargo, and the Republican Revolution.* Charlottesville: University Press of Virginia, 1979.

Stamp, Kenneth. *America in 1857: A Nation on the Brink.* New York: Oxford University Press, 1990.

Standage, Tom. *The Victorian Internet.* New York: Walker, 1998.

Steeples, Douglas, and David Whitten. *Democracy in Desperation: The Depression of 1893.* Santa Barbara, CA: Greenwood, 1998.

Stern, Nancy. *From ENIAC to UNIVAC: An Appraisal of the Echert-Mauchly Computers.* Bedford, MA: Digital Press, 1981.

Stevens, Joseph E. *Hoover Dam: An American Adventure.* Norman: University of Oklahoma Press, 1956.

Stewart, John J. *The Iron Trail to the Golden Spike.* New York: Meadow Lark, 1994.

Stockwell, Foster. *A History of Information Storage and Retrieval.* Jefferson, NC: McFarland, 2007.

Stover, John. *The History of the Baltimore and Ohio Railroad.* West Lafayette, IN: Purdue University Press, 1987.

Stowell, David. *The Great Strikes of 1877.* Urbana: University of Illinois Press, 2008.

Stowell, David. *Streets, Railroads, and the Great Strike of 1877.* Chicago: University of Chicago Press, 1999.

Stross, Randall. *Planet Google: One Company's Audacious Plan to Organize Everything We Know.* New York: Free Press, 2008.

Surhone, Lambert, Miriam Timpledon, and Susan Marseken. *Panic of 1873: Long Depression, Jay Cooke.* Saarbrucken, Germany: Betascript, 2010.

Swedin, Eric, and David Ferro. *Computers: The Life Story of a Technology.* Baltimore, MD: Johns Hopkins University Press, 2007.

Taylor, Alex. *Sixty to Zero: Inside Look at the Collapse of General Motors—and the Detroit Auto Industry.* New Haven, CT: Yale University Press, 2011.

Taylor, Frederick Winslow. *Principles of Scientific Management.* New York: Harper & Brothers, 1911.

Temin, Peter. *Iron and Steel in the Nineteenth Century.* Cambridge, MA: MIT Press, 1964.

Thompson, Robert Luther. *Technology and Society.* New York: Arno, 1972.

Tobin, James. *To Conquer the Air: The Wright Brothers and the Great Race for Flight.* New York: Free Press, 2003.

Turak, Theodore. *William Le Baron Jenney: A Pioneer in Modern Architecture.* Ann Arbor: University of Michigan Press, 1986.

Turner, Clair. *I Remember.* New York: Vantage, 1974.

Vogelstein, Fred. "The Untold Story: How the iPhone Blew Up the Wireless Industry." *Wired Magazine,* January 9, 2008, 27–28.

Walker, Samuel. *Three Mile Island: A Nuclear Crisis in Historical Perspective.* Berkeley: University of California Press, 2004.

Wall, Bennett H. *Growth in a Changing Environment: A History of Standard Oil Company (New Jersey), Exxon Corporation, 1950–1975.* New York: HarperCollins, 1989.

Wall, Joseph Frazier. *Andrew Carnegie.* Pittsburgh, PA: University of Pittsburgh Press, 1970.

Wallace, James, and Jim Erickson. *Hard Drive: Bill Gates and the Making of the Microsoft Empire.* New York: Harper Business, 1999.

Walters, Raymond. *Albert Gallatin: Jeffersonian Financier and Diplomat.* New York: Macmillan, 1959.

Walton, Sam. *Sam Walton: Made in America.* New York: Bantam, 1993.

Warren, Kenneth. *Big Steel: The First Century of the United States Steel Corporation 1901–2001.* Pittsburgh, PA: University of Pittsburgh Press, 2001.

Watts, Steven. *The People's Tycoon: Henry Ford and the American Century.* New York: Knopf, 2005.

Weil, Gordon L. *Sears, Roebuck, U.S.A.* New York: Stein and Day, 1977.

Welch, David, and Dan Beucke. "Why GM's Plan Won't Work." *Bloomberg Businessweek,* May 9, 2005, 31–33.

Wells, Donald R. *Federal Reserve System: A History.* Jefferson, NC: McFarland, 2004.

Wessel, David. "Did 'Great Recession' Live Up to the Name?" *Wall Street Journal,* April 8, 2010.

Whalen, David J. *The Origins of Satellite Communications, 1945–1965.* Washington, DC: Smithsonian Institution Press, 2002.

Whipple, A. B. *The Clipper Ships.* Alexander, VA: Time-Life Books, 1980.

Wiener, Gary. *Workers' Rights in Upton Sinclair's The Jungle.* Detroit: Greenhaven, 2008.

William, John Hoyt. *A Great and Shining Road: The Epic Story of the Transcontinental Railroad.* New York: Time Books, 1988.

Winston, Brian. *The Telegraph in Media Technology and Society, A History: From the Telegraph to Internet.* London: Routledge, 1998.

Wittke, Carl. *We Who Built America.* New York: Prentice-Hall, 1945.

Worthy, James. *Shaping an American Institution: Robert E. Woods and Sears.* Chicago: University of Illinois Press, 1984.

Wozniak, Steve. *IWoz: Computer Geek to Cult Icon.* New York: Norton, 2006.

Wren, Daniel A. *The History of Management Thought.* New York: Wiley, 2005.

Yergin, Daniel. *The Prize: The Epic Quest for Oil, Money, and Power.* New York: Simon & Schuster, 1991.

Zieger, Robert. *Republicans and Labor.* Lexington: University of Kentucky Press, 1969.

# INDEX

**About the Author**

Quentin R. Skrabec, Jr., is associate professor in the Business Department at the University of Findlay. He is the author of more than 5 articles and 18 books on business history, published by Purdue University Press, University of Michigan Press, McFarland, and Algora. He has a PhD in manufacturing management from the University of Toledo (1998) and an MBA from Robert Morris University (1983).